P9-CFI-374

The Bride of the Wind

By the same author

Lost Berlin

The Bride of the Wind

The Life and Times
of Alma Mahler-Werfel

SUSANNE KEEGAN

VIKING

VIKING
Published by the Penguin Group
Viking Penguin, a division of Penguin Books USA Inc.,
375 Hudson Street, New York, New York 10014, U.S.A.
Penguin Books Ltd, 27 Wrights Lane,
London W8 5TZ, England
Penguin Books Australia Ltd, Ringwood,
Victoria, Australia
Penguin Books Canada Ltd, 10 Alcorn Avenue, Suite 300,
Toronto, Ontario, Canada M4V 3B2
Penguin Books (N.Z.) Ltd, 182–190 Wairau Road,
Auckland 10, New Zealand

Penguin Books Ltd, Registered Offices:
Harmondsworth, Middlesex, England

First American Edition
Published in 1992 by Viking Penguin,
a division of Penguin Books USA Inc.

1   3   5   7   9   10   8   6   4   2

Copyright © Susanne Keegan, 1991
All rights reserved

Illustration credits appear on page x.

LIBRARY OF CONGRESS CATALOGING IN PUBLICATION DATA
Keegan, Susanne.
The bride of the wind : the life and times of Alma Mahler-Werfel /
Susanne Keegan.
p.   cm.
Originally published: London : Secker & Warburg, 1991.
Includes bibliographical references and index.
ISBN 0-670-80513-0
1. Mahler, Alma, 1879–1964.   2. Mahler, Gustav, 1860–1911.
3. Gropius, Walter, 1883–1969.   4. Werfel, Franz, 1890–1945.
5. Arts — Austria — History — 20th century.   I. Title.
DB844.M34E94   1992
780'.92 — dc20
[B]   92–6727

Printed in the United States of America
Set in Sabon

Without limiting the rights under copyright reserved above, no part
of this publication may be reproduced, stored in or introduced into a
retrieval system, or transmitted, in any form or by any means
(electronic, mechanical, photocopying, recording or otherwise),
without the prior written permission of both the copyright owner
and the above publisher of this book.

In memory of Anna Mahler

Contents

Illustrations

Illustrations nos. 4, 8, 12, 13, 14, 18, 19, 20, 21, 22, 23, 24 are reproduced by kind permission of the Special Collections, Van Pelt Library, University of Pennsylvania; nos. 5, 7, 9, 11 by kind permission of the Bildarchivs der Österreichischen Nationalbibliothek; nos. 15, 16 by kind permission of Oskar Kokoschka Dokumentation; and no. 17 by kind permission of the Kunstmuseum, Basel.

Acknowledgements

I owe a great deal of thanks to a number of people. First and foremost to Anna Mahler, to whom, without any posthumous strings, I dedicate this book. Without her friendship it would not have been written. She hoped and worked for its completion. I was always conscious when we met of the extraordinary pleasure and privilege of talking to Gustav Mahler's daughter. She was also, of course, her mother's daughter but, understandably, she could not, as her father had done, appreciate Alma's life-giving qualities, seeing her (again understandably) as a rather difficult mother. But I suspect that, despite their differences, Anna admired her mother enormously. Alma was, despite her faults, a *Grande Dame*. Anna's one great sorrow was the publication of Reginald Isaacs' biography of Walter Gropius. It shocked her to the core that Alma should have deceived Mahler so thoroughly. It is entirely in character for Anna to have been taken so aback.

Almost as high on the list comes Anna's husband, Albrecht Joseph. He provided me with the historical background, besides adding a much-needed element of sanity to our discussions. It was he who put me right on the subject of Viennese anti-Semitism and gently directed me away from my rather conventional views on the subject.

My thanks are also due to Lady Isolde Radzinowicz, William Melitz, Emeritus Dean, College of Fine Art, University of California, Marina Fistoulari-Mahler, Mrs Elisabeth Fistoulari and Mr Henri de la Grange for their generosity and their time; to Mrs Olda Kokoschka for being so sympathetic to the idea of the book; to Daniel Johnson for reading several chapters; to my daughter

Lucy Newmark for doing the musical analysis of Alma's songs; to Malcolm Deas, John and Victoria Jolliffe, Inka and Stewart Steven, Jean Fiddian-Green, Michael and Carilla Carter, and Gwenda David for endless conversations on the subject of Alma Mahler over the years; and to Wolfgang Fischer for giving me a great deal of amusement over lunch at the gestation of the book. I am also grateful to the staff of several libraries, particularly the Central Library, Royal Military Academy, Sandhurst; the Charles Van Pelt Library, University of Pennsylvania; the London Library and the Library of the Austrian Institute, London.

Without publishers and editors, too, the book would not be in existence. Tom Rosenthal was brave enough to commission it, Amanda Vaill at Viking Press both kept it going and has been a particularly sympathetic editor. Dan Franklin has been equally sympathetic. Stephen Cox has saved me from both grammatical and factual errors, and has been tact itself. Anthony Sheil has been not just an agent, but a true friend.

Most importantly, I have to thank my husband, my son-in-law, my children and my grandchildren. My husband, John, has had to put up with interminable dissertations on Alma Mahler and her circle, for more time than duty calls for. Rose, Thomas and Matthew, Lucy and Brooks, Benjamin and Sam have, with John, added greatly to the pleasure of the past ten years.

Susanne Keegan
Kilmington, January 1991

Introduction

Alma Mahler-Werfel arouses curiosity at various levels. During the course of her long life (born in Habsburg Austria in 1879, she died in New York in 1964, at the age of eighty-five) she saw Vienna fade from imperial glory, witnessed the aftermath of the First World War, fled from Nazi-dominated Austria to America and died a year after President Kennedy met his death in Dallas. Through her birth, marriages (to Gustav Mahler, Walter Gropius and Franz Werfel), her notorious affair with Oskar Kokoschka and her friendships with such men as Max Burckhard, Gustav Klimt, Alexander von Zemlinsky, Hanz Pfitzner, Franz Schreker, Paul Kammerer, Gerhart Hauptmann, Arthur Schnitzler, Arnold Schönberg and Alban Berg, she was intimately involved with the most prominent movements in twentieth-century music, art, architecture and literature. She was, when young, both a beautiful woman and a promising composer. She remained a gifted pianist, although she never performed in public, confining her talents to playing duets with close friends.

When considering this catalogue of achievement several questions spring to mind. What unique quality did Alma have in order to attract and hold the attention of so many outstanding men for so long? What effect, if any, did she have on their work? And why, in the light of her early promise, did she have such a slender output as a composer (she published only fourteen songs in her lifetime, none dated after 1915)?

It is the first question that is the least easy to answer, for Alma evoked extreme reactions from all who knew her. Those who did not like her remembered her as a monster of egocentricity, a devouring maenad whose only thought was to use others for her own ends. Those who loved her and admired her remembered her generosity, her idiosyncratic ways of expressing herself and her selfless devotion to her third husband, Franz Werfel, during his last illness in 1945.

To Werfel Alma was always a source of wonderment. 'She gets her insight from a sibylline core,' he wrote of her in 1918. 'She is one of the very few magical women there are. She lives in a light *blond* magic that contains much will to destroy, much urge to subjugate, but it is all cloudy and moist – while the poetess Else Lasker Schuler, another strong personality, practises a *black* magic that is incredibly helpful, comforting, brotherly and loving, but arid and lacklustre for all its romantic enthusiasm.'[1]

The playwright Franz Theodor Csokor also believed Alma to be a force for good. To him she represented a female type categorized by the poet Peter Altenberg: 'an energizer of heroes; that is to say a women whose companionship stimulates her chosen man to the ultimate heights of his creative ability.' She was a 'pure light, the flame of an Olympic fire'.[2]

Even those who were fond of Alma, however, hinted that she was not without fault. 'Alma was a woman of great stature,' William W. Melitz wrote to me in 1981. 'Many people will emphasize the flaws in her character, but they were amply compensated by her humaneness and her rich creative talents.'

The strengths and weaknesses in Alma's character were picked up by a graphologist, Margarete Bardach, to whom Alma, always fascinated by the science, gave some of her handwriting for analysis at the end of 1918. 'The handwriting of a very generous, spirited, impressionable person,' the report, dated 18 December 1918, began. 'The writer possesses great intelligence and mental alertness, in harmony with a well developed imagination; an extremely lively emotional and nervous life; an extraordinarily strong but fluctuating expression of will, and has predominantly aesthetic interests. She is capable of passion and is excessively ambitious, vain and single-minded in her ideas and dealings, and possesses a strong sense of purpose. She sets great store by outward appearances, which makes itself felt in her bearing and her whole way of life. She has little ability to conform. She is very proud, candid, and extremely reticent in matters close to her heart.' At the end of a lengthy analysis, the graphologist came to the conclusion that her subject had 'always found satisfaction in dominating. She could never be in complete harmony with one man and continually needed a chorus of people who envied and marvelled at her. She needed jealous women, otherwise life seemed insipid.'[3]

In pursuit of my own conclusions I consulted a number of sources. In many ways the most valuable were the conversations I had, until her death in 1989, with Anna Mahler, the only surviving child of Alma and Gustav Mahler, and with Anna's fifth husband, Albrecht Joseph. Although Anna's relationship with her mother had never been an easy one and – partly through loyalty to Anna and partly due to his own mixed first impressions – Albrecht Joseph had never succumbed to Alma's charms, they nevertheless remembered her without rancour. Both admitted that Alma had a fineness that rose above her many blind spots. It shocked Anna deeply when Professor Reginald Isaacs' biography of Walter Gropius (published in 1983) revealed that her mother had, in 1910, been physically unfaithful to her father at a time when they seemed to have drawn closer together; she felt that Alma had not only betrayed Mahler, but that she had betrayed herself by such perfidy.

The second most important source of information has been the forty-seven manuscript boxes housed in the Van Pelt Library at the University of Pennsylvania, Philadelphia. These contain letters to Alma, some from her to Gropius, Alma's handwritten diaries from the age of eighteen to twenty-two, part of a draft manuscript of her autobiography, and fragments of a later diary, typed up for her own use when preparing her life-story.

The third source was Alma's published work. The first, *Gustav Mahler, Memories and Letters*, written during the Twenties but not published in German until 1940, is Alma's contribution to literature and, if not to great musical scholarship, to a wider understanding of her husband as a man. Her autobiography, begun in the immediate aftermath of Franz Werfel's death in 1945, when she was sixty-six, went through a number of transmogrifications. The original draft was not thought printable as it stood, mainly due to Alma's illogically offensive attitude towards the Jews. Her views on the subject were well known to her Jewish friends, who chose either to take them or leave them, but remarks (taken at random from the draft) such as 'Jews have no place in politics', 'A new messiah will come but not from the Jews' and 'At one and the same time the Jews are the greatest threat to mankind and the greatest force for good', were not likely to endear her to those who had never met her.

A heavily edited version of her life-story was eventually published in English by Hutchinson & Co. in 1959, under the title *And the Bridge is Love*, and in German by Fischer Bücherei in 1960, under the title *Mein Leben*. They are, to all intents and purposes, the same book, differing only in the sensitivity of the editing: *Mein Leben* is the better of the two, and has the advantage of a perceptive introduction by Willy Haas, in which he mentions that Alma was 'not free of racial prejudice' but that she lived her life on an altogether superior artistic plane.

To a large extent Alma was her own worst enemy, and it has been my task to present her in a way that does justice to her many virtues and her considerable artistic gifts. For, in the words of the critic and poet Friedrich Torberg, whom Alma had known well in Vienna, and who became a fellow exile in 1938: 'She was a woman of colossal artistic understanding and intuitiveness. Success bewitched her, but lack of it did not worry her. Her enthusiasm, her dedication and her ability for self-sacrifice had no limits. She was a catalyst of incredible intensity.'[4] There have been worse epitaphs.

1 *The Heroic Model*

In old age Alma Mahler-Werfel had a recurring daydream. She was a child again in the old manor-house of Plankenberg, beyond the Vienna Woods. Her father, the landscape painter Emil Jacob Schindler, whose grave she visited every year after his death in 1892 and whom she had loved better than anyone in the world, was still living. Echoes of his light tenor voice singing Schumann or reading from Goethe's *Faust*, visions of lakes and grottoes, memories of a childhood filled with mystery and fantasy haunted her mind. The lost domain of Plankenberg, where the wind sighed in the linden trees and the bell pealed the hour from the onion-tip clock-tower, floated before her eyes. Once more she wandered among its woods and meadows, once more she felt ghostly presences in the room where she slept, and once again she sat in her father's studio, watching him paint and marvelling at the 'revelations of the hand that led the brush'.

The romantic image of a child of nature untutored and alone, with a prince for a father, was one of which Alma Mahler was particularly fond. She was *la princesse lointaine*, her father a knight in shining armour, unfettered by bourgeois convention. Life as art was a concept familiar to them both, but the elusiveness of happiness and the ceaseless yearning for total fulfilment (with the melancholy realization that such things were rarely possible) were ideas that troubled Emil Schindler all his life. Unlike his daughter, whose childhood dreams were apparently both altruistic and prophetic – 'I dreamed of wealth merely in order to smooth the paths of creative personalities. I wished for a great Italian garden filled by many white studios; I wished to invite many outstanding men there – to live for their art alone, without mundane worries – and never to show myself'[1] – he yielded to frequent bouts of depression. Neither the beauties of Plankenberg nor the pleasures of family life were adequate compensation for the worries induced by mounting debts, pictures unsold or unfinished and persistent ill-health. The only thing that mattered was to have enough money in the house and, as he wrote in his diary in 1879, 'there is not even enough . . . to bury me'.[2]

To Alma his pessimism was a source of mournful pleasure. He was, after all, the living embodiment of the romantic ideal. Mysteriously set apart by birth and circumstance, handsome, gifted, misunderstood, other-worldly and quixotic, he was the quintessence of the artist of popular legend, 'wild-eyed, wild-haired, poor, solitary, mocked-at; but independent, free, spiritually superior to his Philistine tormentors'. He even managed to die comparatively young, of appendicitis.

If she had one criticism of this giant among men it was that he had made an unsuitable marriage. (One suspects that she would have preferred to have been the love-child of a Hungarian princess, rather than the legitimate offspring of the daughter of a bankrupt Hamburg brewery owner.) 'Marriage', she wrote in *And the Bridge Is Love*, 'brought a narrowness into my father's life. True, he lived in a castle and called a park with baroque statuary his own, but in the depths of his soul he harboured unfulfilled longings for the beauty he sought to infuse into this crude, workaday world. My mother, a product of the middle class of Hamburg, had to catch up rationally with all that was in my father's blood. Not until after his death would she grasp his importance.' That her father's antecedents were not aristocratic, and that their fortunes were dogged by much the same calamities as had beset her mother's family, was for Alma a half-truth to be brushed aside in the interests of the broad view.

Emil J. Schindler's paternal great-grandfather made scythes and lived in Steyral in Upper Austria. His grandfather became the owner of a wool factory in Fischamend, which was inherited by his two sons, Alexander and Julius. Alexander studied law, became a member of parliament and published a number of novels and legal treatises under the pseudonym Julius von der Traun. His brother Julius, Emil's father, ran the factory and married a beautiful wife, whose picture by Ameling hangs in the Gallery of Beauties in the Vienna Hofburg. Julius's life, like his son Emil's, born on 27 April 1842, was full of worry. A fire destroyed his factory, the basis of the family's livelihood, he went bankrupt and died 'in the full flower of his manhood' of tuberculosis. His widow married an officer in the Austrian army and in 1859 she and Emil, then aged seventeen, went with him to Italy on a military campaign which ended with his death and Austria's defeat at the hands of the French and the Italians at the battle of Solferino. During this brief excursion to Lombardy Schindler met the painter Albert Zimmerman, who was then teaching in Mailand, and later became his pupil at the Imperial Academy in Vienna. In 1863 Zimmerman took him and one or two others on a walking tour in the Bavarian Alps and there, engulfed by the elements and surrounded by mountain peaks, they contemplated nature in the raw.

It was an awe-inspiring experience for a group of artists steeped in early nineteenth-century concepts of romantic wanderlust. The exhilaration of the climb and the emotions aroused by the grandeur of the scenery produced enjoyably unsettling reflections on the mysteries of creation, the senselessness of man's existence and the uncertainty of life after death, whilst satisfying unexpressed yearnings to be part of the mystic union between man and the spirit of the universe. 'Everything beautiful and poetic is to be found in nature,' wrote Schindler in his diary. 'Among men every atom of poetry is lost. But when I am surrounded by nature I feel as no man has ever felt before. In this world so full of misery it is nature, most beautiful and most cruel of all women, who bewitches us with her charms . . .'[3]

Few people are to be found in Schindler's paintings. His woods, lakes, hills and waterfalls have mills and cottages dotted among them, but apart from the fanciful *Waldfräuleins Geburt* (*Birth of the Wood Maiden*) and the *Küss im Wald* (*Woodland Kiss*), both painted in 1868, there is little sign of human life. There is one exception. In 1884 he painted a blond child in a kitchen garden. She is holding a bunch of flowers and, although she is dwarfed by giant sunflowers, foxgloves, red cabbages and melons, they are all leaning towards her in respectful homage. Even at that age nature was no match for Alma.

In 1873 Schindler struck up a friendship with Hans Makart, who lent him a small studio in his house on the Gubhausstrasse in Vienna. A professor at the Imperial Academy, Makart spent much of his time covering vast canvases with ornate versions of mythological subjects in the neo-classical style, richly decorated with voluptuous nudes, or painting portraits of fashionable women. In general his work inspired lavish praise and admiration, its robust theatricality and formal outline appealing both to those students who still believed in formalism in art and to patrons who believed strongly that paintings should uplift, titillate and flatter rather than disturb, upset or shock. It also brought him fame and enough money to indulge his insatiable appetite for elaborate parties, to which, according to Alma Mahler, he invited 'the loveliest women . . . dressing them in his genuine Renaissance costumes. Rose garlands trailed from the ballroom ceiling, Liszt played through the nights, the choicest wines flowed, behind each chair stood a page clad in velvet, and so forth to the limits of splendour and imagination.'4

On the face of it, Schindler and Makart were ill-assorted companions. Each, however, had an admiration for the other's romantic fantasies – Makart for Schindler's love-affair with Nature, and Schindler for Makart's passion for spectacle and show. (They also liked the same jokes. When Schindler imported a large pet sheep into the studio and christened it Hans, Makart's response was to ask him to call any pig he might want to own Emil.) It was during this uninhibited and comparatively carefree period that Schindler met his wife, Anna Bergen.

Alma Mahler persistently denied her mother. It was not only her burgher background, or the fact that she considered her incapable of scaling the Olympian heights to which her father soared so effortlessly; rather was it her failure to give her daughter the exclusive love, attention and admiration which she demanded from all those around her and without which she felt cheated and insecure. Her diaries written between 1898 and 1902 (the only ones currently available in manuscript) were studded with accusations of such emotional bias and lack of understanding. Variations of 'I know Mama doesn't love me as much as Grete' (her younger sister) and 'It's impossible for Mama to know what I feel' cropped up frequently and were obviously well tried sentiments that had bitten deep in childhood. Fortunately for Anna Schindler, her granddaughter had kinder memories. Anna Mahler remembered her as 'a most charming person, always smiling, always full of life, never cross', and in the only photograph that exists of her as a young married woman she appears warm-hearted and serene, her arm round her daughter, her cheek against her hair. Alma, on the other hand, looks sultry and discontented.

Both as a girl and whilst married to Emil Schindler, Anna Bergen needed all her reserves of charm and good nature. In 1871, when she was fourteen, her father went bankrupt, forcing Anna and her brother to turn for support to their talents and the financial help of friends. Anna, who had a good soprano voice, was sent to Vienna to study music – an investment which reaped early dividends. She made her début in 1877 at the Ringtheater in *Etna*, an early opera by the Czech composer Josef Bohuslav Förster, under the direction of the Austrian conductor and composer Felix Mottl. This led to an engagement at the Leipzig Stadttheater, but before she could fulfil this obligation she was invited to appear as a guest singer in an amateur production of the operetta *Leonardo and Blondine*. It was whilst singing Blondine that she fell in love with Emil Schindler, who had taken the tenor part of Leonardo.

In the autumn of 1878 they were married, and Anna almost immediately became pregnant. Apart from youth, talent and good looks they had little of material value with which to start married life. Schindler's contribution was a case of Rhine wine (from Hans Makart), a small rented flat in the Mayerhofgasse, a pile of unpaid bills and a pair of newly soled shoes. His wife provided her own modest wardrobe and a torn-up contract for Leipzig. Unlike Hans Makart, who had a keen head for business and was able to command prices of 50,000 gulden (about £5,000) a picture, Schindler had to do with rather less. While he was living with Makart he sold a painting to his doctor, Joseph Scholz, for ten gulden. Later, Dr Scholz spotted a particularly large canvas in Schindler's studio and bet him one hundred gulden that he couldn't cover it in twelve hours. Schindler won the bet but lost the picture, which the doctor somehow managed to convince him was part of the deal.

Muddles of this kind happened all too often. Alma Mahler, in *And the Bridge Is Love*, cites an episode in which her father's shoes had cracks in the soles, but 'because they were unpaid for, he could not order new ones. What to do? He hired a cab for a month, to save wear, and "stretch" the shoes over the weeks it would take him to complete a picture. Thus he floundered through the world of affairs, getting along somehow, for every now and then he did manage a sale. If only his debts had not kept mounting in the meantime!'

The difficulties of making ends meet, and doubts about his ability to support a wife, filled Schindler's diary to the exclusion of everything else. Anna had given up singing professionally on her marriage in order to look after him and, as he gloomily observed, there was no money to buy canvases or to pay the rent. 'What I wouldn't do for forty gulden,' he wrote on 14 March 1879, and, later that month: 'This evening received notice for the flat. Went out. Two gulden to spare. Anna went shopping. I lost the remains of the two gulden . . . I tremble each time the bell rings . . . Unlucky man! . . . I won't think of it . . . I must live among men, however much I despise them. Oh! to have enough to live on, so I need see nobody, speak to nobody. Then I would write a book . . .'[5]

The burdens of everyday living became more and more oppressive. Mentally and physically at a low ebb – in 1880 he suffered an attack of diphtheria and blood-poisoning from which it took him six months to recover – Schindler comforted himself by indulging in orgies of self-examination. 'The life of the spirit exists no more for me,' he wrote in February 1880. 'I have no more artistic ideas. I make myself a laughing stock in front of others. I should have abandoned this bourgeois existence long ago, but I became ill, so ill that I was already near the end. Why couldn't I have died two years ago? Then I should have made nobody into a victim. My poor Anna will be saddled with an invalid . . .'[6]

These morbid reflections were not only the result of ill-health and feelings of inadequacy, nor were they merely expressions of the spiritually nihilistic longing for death recommended by Wagner and counselled by Schopenhauer as an antidote to despair. By that time his domestic problems had multiplied twice over. On 31 August 1879, Anna had given birth to their first child, Alma Maria, and within six months their second child, Grete, had been conceived.

There is no record of Anna's feelings about these events. Her husband, on the other hand, regarded them with unmitigated gloom. 'On 31st August I became a father, a natural consequence of my marriage,' he wrote in his diary in October 1879. 'Why I married I have no idea, but when I say that, I love my Anna, so I have no reason even to think of such a thing . . .'[7] As for the confinement itself, he was horrified. 'It is the most shameful and despicable act of nature. My Anna was a martyr, and I felt only indifference towards the child. Even now I can't say I like it much. But for a father a child means nothing. To me it just means a partial separation from my wife. I tell Anna, so as not to hurt her, that I love it, but really I feel nothing.' Later he relented so far as to admit that there was a possibility he might feel differently if his financial position improved. 'When I think about it, this lack of love has something to do with circumstance. After all, my child looks magnificent, and my home becomes more and more pleasant.'[8]

Early in 1881 things did, at last, take a turn for the better: Schindler acquired a patron, the Viennese banker, Moritz Mayer.

No penniless, debilitated artist could have had a more understanding champion. Realizing that his protégé was too ground
down by his affairs to paint the pictures that he needed for his
new flat at once, Mayer came up with an alternative plan. 'Just
take what you need to live on every month,' he wrote to him,
'and I will wait for the pictures until you are ready.'[9] Absolved
from the pressure of painting to order and released from the fear
of debt and eviction, Schindler fulfilled his obligations in his own
time and in return received a monthly sum of two hundred gulden,
the amount Anna calculated would cover their immediate needs.
Not only that – in the spring an old college friend invited the
whole family to stay with him in Carlsbad, where Schindler met
another Austrian financier, who was taking the cure with his
wife. Both were very taken with Schindler and would not rest
until they, too, had one of his pictures. He sold them *Moonrise
in the Prater*, the work for which he had received the Carl Ludwig
Medal in 1878.

These commissions did more for Schindler than ease his financial path. They restored his shattered nerves and brought an
element of fun and relaxation into the household. As Heinrich
Fuchs put it in his irresistibly pompous study of the artist: 'With
the return to health of the painter there came a long-absent
harmony. In his house there was once more work, laughter,
singing. In the evening friends gathered, groups of sympathetic
beings whose personalities were delightfully agreeable . . .'[10] They
also made it possible for the family to move from the cramped
Viennese flat to an old mill house in the valley of Salzkammergut,
near Goisern. Here they lived until the winter of 1884 and here,
in close communion with nature and with the music of the mill-
wheel in his ears, Schindler's pulse quickened, his spirits rose and
he worked with a will, producing a stream of Corot-inspired
landscapes.

Attracted by the force of his creative energy a small circle of
admirers began to form around him, among them Carl Moll,
Marie Baga-Parmentier, Tina Blau, Maria Egner and Olga Wisin-
ger-Florian. All studied with him for a time, but by far the most

tenacious of these acolytes was Carl Moll. Originally drawn to Schindler through admiration for his picture *Altwasser an der Traun*, he became an ardent and lifelong disciple. Indeed, so devoted was he to his master that he rarely strayed from his side, becoming an almost permanent fixture in the Schindler household. (Moll's devotion, however, was not entirely altruistic. He fell in love with Anna, whom he married five years after Schindler's death.)

The impression he made on Alma was less favourable. Resentment at his eternal presence, irritation with his sycophancy and dismissal of what she considered to be his small-scale talents as an artist produced a number of unflattering remarks in *And the Bridge Is Love*: 'That everlasting pupil of my father . . . goes from one master to another . . . to the detriment of his minor talent . . .'

Despite Alma's private strictures Moll remained, and when, after three pleasant and fruitful summers at Goisern interspersed by painting trips with his pupils to Thaya bei Lundenburg on the North Sea, Schindler decided to move his family and his by now considerable number of finished canvases nearer Vienna, Moll followed them. In the course of his search for something suitable Schindler had come across a small manor-house on the edge of the Vienna Woods, which seemed to offer 'a welcome opportunity for the development of a comfortable family life'. Moll wrote of it:

> Beyond the Vienna Woods, between Neulengbach and Tulln, in an old park, stood an old castle, part of the estate of Prince Karl Lichtenstein . . . A rectangular fifteenth-century building, two stories high, crowned by a gabled roof. An onion-tower with a clock in the baroque style furnished the only ornament to the façade. The two-acre grounds bore traces of their former grandeur, in particular a magnificent baroque gate, flanked by linden trees more than a hundred years old. Still more mighty lindens and plane trees flank an avenue of old walnut trees. Behind the castle vineyards climb up the hills, and in front, lower down, enclosed by the park, lies a tiny village of just a few houses. Schloss Plankenberg's natural surroundings are charming, rich in variety – hills, wide clear views, woods and fields, poplar-lined lanes and a peaceful running brook. To live in the castle is to be lord of the countryside.[11]

Freud believed the essential foundations of character were laid down by the age of three. When analysing himself he was able to revive memories of his sense of antagonism towards his younger brother and his mixed feelings when he died (at eight months); of falling and cutting himself badly on the lower jaw at the age of two; and, also at two, of seeing his mother naked and of the passionate turmoil this aroused in his infant breast. If the importance of these self-discoveries is to be upheld, then it is only fair to point out that as far as the well-spring of Alma Mahler's nature is concerned, the reader will search in vain among her memoirs for references to her early childhood, for recollections of her sensations at the birth of her sister, for revelations of jealousies, suppressed or expressed, or, indeed, for descriptions of any of the violent infantile emotions so necessary to the Freudian explanation of adult behaviour. With a sweeping disregard for armchair analysts she began her life without more ado at the age of five – for the perfectly good reason that the play had only just begun. The prologue was of no particular interest, and it was not until the Schindlers moved into Plankenberg that the proper setting had been provided for the first act of the melodrama which, with Alma as the central character, was to run uninterrupted for the next seventy-nine years.

The house itself, steeped in legend and full of ghostly corners, was likely to foment the imagination of the dullest child and excite delightful fears and fancies in the breasts of the susceptible. The children believed the house was haunted and 'lay trembling through many a night'. Halfway up the stairs on their way to bed they had to pass a flower-decked effigy of the Virgin Mary, dimly lit by gilded baroque candelabra, which far from warding off the evil eye sent shudders of ecstatic dread through their hearts.

Upstairs, too, was their father's studio: not as hedonistic as Makart's, whose palate was titillated by negroid statues, marble ladies in various states of undress, stuffed animals, bowls of wax fruit, zebra and tiger skins on the floor and enormous sofas covered in plush, but quite interesting enough for a young child.

There were a number of palm trees growing up to the ceiling, an assortment of curious natural objects, and oriental rugs on the walls and on the floor.

Alma wrote that she spent hours in this studio, watching her father paint and listening to his 'fascinating and never commonplace' conversation. What he actually said is not recorded by either of them. (Nor does Alma refer to the private language she told Anna Mahler they sometimes spoke together, in which A's became E's.) However, if his diary is anything to go by, as it records Schindler's Schopenhauerian craving for the essence of things, his dedication to the cause of Nature as a cure for *Weltschmerz* and his belief (shared by the moral philosopher Johann Gottlieb Fichte) that the struggle to achieve artistic integrity was an end in itself, it seems likely that these themes cropped up in one form or another.

Another favourite subject for reflection was man: his imperfections, his perpetual susceptibility to temptation, and his tendency to destroy and plunder the natural world. 'Doubtless', Schindler wrote in his diary, 'the demon of destruction created man, endowing him with brilliant gifts, but leaving him unclear as to his mission on earth, all done with such consummate skill that he was led to believe that he could outshine God himself. For the earth, as he found it, seemed on the one hand to have more than enough man-made catastrophes, and on the other to be lurching towards the year two thousand without a thought. All in all, the Demons could be proud of their handiwork.'[12]

With such thoughts as these frequently in his mind, it was not surprising that Schindler should want to give his daughters an illustration of the pitfalls in store for those who fell victim to the desire for earthly powers at the expense of their immortal souls. 'My father always took me seriously,' wrote Alma. 'One day he called me and my sister into his studio to tell us the story of Goethe's *Faust*. We were seven and eight years old and wept, not knowing why. When we were all enraptured, he gave us the book. "This is the most beautiful book in the world," he said. "Read it. Keep it." '[13]

Anna Schindler, on the other hand, thought it unsuitable reading for children of that age and confiscated it – no doubt feeling that her daughters would have more difficulty grasping the complexities of Faust's redemptive odyssey than understanding the plain language used to describe his seduction and desertion of a devout fourteen-year-old girl. This act of prudence went unappreciated by her elder daughter. 'We went and read until my mother came and had a fit,' she wrote. 'There followed violent arguments between our parents . . . and we children listened behind closed doors, with bated breath. In the end the so-called sensible side won, as usual.'

Although she deplored her mother's blinkered attitude, considering that her own 'hop-skip-and-jump brains of precocity' were more likely to be attuned to the beauty and mystery of *Faust* than to works written specifically for young children, Alma felt her education had lacked method. 'Our whole upbringing', she wrote, 'was . . . all experiment and no system.' By her own admission, however, systematic learning did not come easily: 'I was a nervous child, fairly bright . . . But I could not think anything through, and was never able to keep a date in mind, and took no interest in anything but music.' Certainly, the attempts of various tutors to hold her attention met with little response – all were dismissed as either 'nasty' or 'nice but ineffectual', and only the more sadistic appeared to have made the slightest impression.

Even less successful were her mother's teaching efforts. In the winter of 1887 she took charge of her daughter's lessons, an arrangement which suited none of them. Alma complained that she was 'so inept that she gave us the entire multiplication table to learn by heart in a day', and as for Anna, the struggle to make her daughters memorize unwelcome facts by rote took its toll, for, after a few months, she became ill. 'The end of the winter', wrote Alma unsympathetically, 'saw her under medical care for a throat ailment, contracted as a result of yelling at us.'[14]

During the winter in question Anna Schindler had more to cope with than a sore throat. The previous year her husband's work had come to the attention of Crown Prince Rudolf, and as a result he had been commissioned to illustrate the text for the Prince's book, *The Austro-Hungarian Monarchy in Words and Pictures*. Schindler had already completed a number of pen and ink drawings for this ambitious project whilst travelling alone on foot in the Alps and, with another new friend, Rudolf's cousin, Archduke Johann Salvater, exploring the islands off the Istrian peninsula.* When, therefore, in the autumn of 1887, the banker Hermann Herwitz gave him *carte blanche* and a handsome advance payment to paint a 'large picture of the south', Schindler took the opportunity of travelling further afield in search of suitable subjects for both his patrons.

The Archduke was accustomed to travel in style and the expedition to Istria had been no exception. His imperial rank and considerable entourage created flutters of excitement wherever they went, and their progress took on some of the aspects of a royal tour. In the absence of such an illustrious companion Schindler and his family had to make do with more primitive arrangements. They travelled by freighter from Trieste and sailed down the Dalmatian coast to Ragusa (now Dubrovnik), where they took clifftop lodgings with a view of the Adriatic. From there Schindler visited the neighbouring villages of Lacroma and Canosa in pursuit of material for the Crown Prince. From there, too, he made the first studies for Herwitz of *Brandung bei Scirocco (Breakers in the Scirocco)*, inspired by the sight of waves crashing over the rocks beneath his window.

By January he felt he had done enough. The party, which included Carl Moll and a maid, moved south to Spizza (now Petrovac) and then to Corfu, where they spent the rest of the winter. 'Ragusa, Lacroma – it all remains in my memory like a dream Paradise,' wrote Alma in *And the Bridge Is Love*. 'On Corfu, where my father no longer had to work to order, we soon left the town for a small stone villa at San Teodoro, on a lonely

---

*Salvater later renounced his title after a quarrel with the Emperor and took the name Johann Orth. He suffered from depression and eventually died at sea, apparently by his own hand, when he drove his ship onto rocks off Cape Horn.

mountain top.' There her father was able to paint 'beautiful pictures for his own enjoyment' and she was able to satisfy her need for musical expression by playing a small upright piano sent up from the town, on which she began to compose and on which 'as the only musician in the house' she could 'find my way . . . without being pushed'.[15]

Meanwhile her mother (whose musical gifts she chose to ignore) was left with the job of dealing with a surly Greek landlord, fending off malevolent Greek children intent on stoning the intruders, and attempting to put right some of the villa's more glaring deficiencies. At last she earned a few kind of words from her daughter: 'My mother, too, came into her own then, for without her foresight we would not have been able to stay. There was no lighting in the house, but our piles of luggage (carried because Mother always set up house-keeping everywhere) contained some oil lamps that were promptly put into use . . .'

Despite these shortcomings the trip could be counted a success. Undertaken in a spirit of optimism and completed with comparative ease under the protective umbrella of the Crown Prince's patronage, it marked the end of Schindler's hand-to-mouth existence. From then on he could rely on his pictures being exhibited not only in Vienna but also in Berlin and Munich. He won a number of prizes and was elected in 1887 to the Academy of Pictorial Art in Vienna, and in 1888 to the Royal Academy of Munich.

This pleasant state of affairs was marred by the suicide of Crown Prince Rudolf in 1889, an event both shocking and unexpected. True, Rudolf had been given to excesses of various kinds. He drank too much, was never without a number of sexual entanglements, and took drugs to deaden the clamouring of his hyper-active mind. These weaknesses, however, although worrying, did not prepare those around him for the suddenness and violence of his death. What was not generally known was that Rudolf had a strongly melancholic streak, which frequently took the form of trying to persuade some of the girls with whom he made love to die with him in a self-immolating suicide pact.

Most of them sensibly declined but in one, the seventeen-year-old Baroness Marie Vetsera, he found a willing accomplice.

Any attempt at an explanation of Rudolf's state of mind must remain inconclusive. The most likely theory, put forward by Edward Crankshaw in *The Fall of the House of Habsburg*, is that he felt himself to be a failure by his own exacting standards. Equipped with the intellectual means to perceive ways of securing the future of the Habsburg Empire, he lacked the ability to transform his visions into practical politics. Even if he had had the capacity to do so, he was not given the opportunity. Out of touch with his father, who gave him little chance to take part in affairs of state, and with his mother, who had long ago drifted away from the oppressive atmosphere of the Hofburg into a mentally unstable world of her own on Corfu, there seemed no alternative to Rudolf but to put himself to the ultimate test. When he pulled the trigger at his hunting lodge at Mayerling in January 1889, the game of Russian roulette in reverse was over – in this case the gamble had paid off.

Marie Vetsera died for a different reason, known only to herself. She was undoubtedly in love, and undoubtedly slightly overwhelmed by the grandeur of the object of her passion. She was seventeen, an age when the idea of death seems remote and dying with the one you love a romantic part to play. She also realized that although Rudolf was trying to get his marriage annulled, it was extremely unlikely that he would substitute Marie, the offspring of a minor diplomat and his socially ambitious wife, for the daughter of Leopold of Belgium. Far better, therefore, to submit to Rudolf's blandishments. To be with him, united in life and death, was a prospect of awesome significance.

Just before Rudolf died, Crown Princess Stephanie went to see her father-in-law, the Emperor Franz Josef. She had become worried about her husband's health and hoped to obtain imperial sanction for him to go on a 'long voyage to recover his health and his balance'. The Emperor was evasive. (He told her that what Rudolf really needed was to spend more time with her.) Nevertheless, a journey to the East was planned and Schindler was asked to accompany the party. Anna was packing for the trip when news of the Crown Prince's death was announced. 'My mother was just packing his trunks when somebody burst in,' wrote Alma. ' "There's been an accident – the Crown Prince is dead!" The dream was over before it had begun.'[16] In Alma's view the Crown Prince's death deprived the Habsburg monarchy of a man of stature and promise and marked the beginning of its decline.

Three years later the Schindler family was struck by its own catastrophe. On 8 August 1892, on the North Sea island of Sylt, after a prolonged battle with recurring bouts of indigestion and abdominal pain, Emil Schindler died.

Several weeks before, troubled by pains in his stomach, he had consulted a doctor in Vienna. Partially reassured by the diagnosis of 'nerves', he decided to recoup his strength by going to Sylt for fresh air and a complete rest. Anna, Carl Moll and the children went on ahead to stay with Anna's mother in Hamburg, while Schindler went to visit his old friend Prince Regent Luitpold of Bavaria, in order to supervise the hanging of seven of his paintings at an exhibition in Munich. On the first evening Schindler and Luitpold took the waters at Nymphenburg, returning to the Prince's castle for supper on the terrace. Normally this would have left Schindler refreshed and relaxed. This time, however, the Prince, an inveterate practical joker, decided to disrupt the evening peace by spraying his guests with water from a hidden cascade. As a result Schindler caught a bad chill and his abdominal pains flared up. Nevertheless, he managed to join his family in Hamburg and they went on together to Sylt. Within a few days he felt so ill he could not go with them to the beach, and the local doctor could do nothing to relieve his pain. By this time extremely alarmed, Anna sent a telegram to Professor Esmarch in Kiel, a specialist in disorders of the stomach. He could not come himself but promised to send his assistant. All to no avail – Schindler was dead before he arrived.

His death not only deprived Alma of a male prototype, it left her emotionally rootless and marked the beginning of her determination to find a heroic model to replace him. By virtue of their sex, neither her sister (in any case never a close companion) nor her mother, who in fact provided Alma with consistent emotional and practical support during the course of her long life, was able to fill the void. No woman ever could. Although she maintained several long friendships with members of her own sex, Alma did not rate their creative potential very highly – even those of her two most ardent admirers, the distinguished art critic Bertha Zuckerkandl and Alban Berg's wife Helene. With women, as with men, Alma expected (and for the most part got) uncritical devotion, which she accepted as fitting tribute to her beauty and talent. She regarded herself in a different light. Convinced of her creative gifts as a composer and burning with unharnessed artistic and imaginative fires, Alma, at thirteen, was desperately in need of a male mentor. Only a man such as Emil Schindler, whose life had been consumed by art, and whose genius had raised him, in her eyes, above the mundane considerations of everyday life, could help Alma lead the creative life she considered her due. Without him, she was bereft.

Alma recorded her impressions of events in *And the Bridge Is Love*:

> One day we were called out of the restaurant. I knew instinctively that Papa was dead. In a howling wind we ran across the dunes, I sobbing loudly all the way. Moll met us at the cottage. 'Children, you've no father any more.'
> We were locked in a room. But somebody forgot one of the doors so we sneaked out and found Papa lying in a wooden box on the floor of the next room. He was beautiful. He looked like a fine wax image, noble as a Greek statue. We felt no horror. I was astonished only by the smallness of this man who had been my father, now that I saw him in his coffin.
> We travelled home and took him with us, for burial in Vienna. Hamburg was under a cholera quarantine, so the coffin was concealed inside a piano box and thus crossed the border unnoticed. What followed has slipped my memory. I was not fully aware of all that happened. I was proud of Papa's fine, gold-embroidered pall, and at the cemetery I was bothered by my mother's crying. But I grew more and more conscious of having lost my guide. He had been my cynosure – and no one had known. All I did had

been to please him. All my ambition and vanity had been satisfied
by a twinkle of his understanding eyes.

2 The Old Order

Inside Schloss Plankenberg, Alma's world had been turned upside-down. Outside, the parts of the world that constituted Austria-Hungary appeared to be on an even enough keel. There were a few tremors – mainly taking the form of minor outbreaks of discontent among some of the empire's subject peoples – but none violent enough to shake the sprawling edifice of the Dual Monarchy to its foundations. The hordes of administrators who were scattered over the disparate and far-flung Habsburg lands might grumble occasionally at the routine boredom of their daily lives, but the majority were satisfied with the rank and status imperial service offered. The army, perhaps the single most important element in the stability of the empire – not least because it managed to avoid most of the conflicts of nationality that beset civilian society – was united in loyalty to the Emperor. And at the centre, the focal point for all political, social and cultural life in central and eastern Europe, was Vienna.

In the opening chapter of volume I of Robert Musil's novel, *The Man Without Qualities*, a man and a woman are strolling along a city street. Exactly where they are is not particularly important, according to their creator. But although there are no descriptions of buildings, street layouts, or the distinctive flavour of individual areas, Musil does allow that cities can be recognized by their pace, 'just as people can by their walk', and that this city is made up of a multitude of unmistakeable sounds. So unmistakeable, indeed, that 'even though the peculiar nature of this noise could not be defined, a man returning after years of absence would have known, with his eyes shut, that he was in that ancient capital and imperial city, Vienna.' And, he continues, when the same man opened his eyes, he would 'recognize it all again by the way the general movement pulsed through the streets, far sooner than he would discover it from any characteristic detail.'[1]

By 1913, the year in which *The Man Without Qualities* is set, both the pulse-beat and the physical characteristics of the capital in which Alma spent most of her life had undergone a considerable change. Vienna's transformation from a walled city, sheltering a mandarin court, to an open city, proclaiming by the magnificence of its public buildings and its richly ornamented apartment blocks that there had been a triumphal marriage between imperial confidence and bourgeois aspiration, had long since been completed. The sounds of the city reflected the change: the noise of horses' hoofs clattering on the cobbled streets of the inner city had given way to the roar of motor traffic flowing through the wide boulevards of the Ringstrasse; private cars hooted as they overtook horse-drawn cabs; steam trams and doubledecker buses had replaced horse-drawn streetcars, and the rattle of wheels on steel tracks announced the existence of the metropolitan railway.

Unlike Berlin, which, until German unification in 1871, remained, despite its royal status, the provincial capital of a sovereign state, Vienna had been the nerve centre of an imperial system since the middle of the eighteenth century. What before had merely been a collection of lands acquired by the Habsburgs through marriage became in 1723 a unified empire, after the Emperor Charles VI, worried that his lack of a male heir would lead to their dissipation, secured their indivisibility by legal charter. His daughter, Maria Theresa, consolidated her inheritance by reducing the self-governing powers of individual provinces and creating a centralized German-speaking bureaucracy at the Imperial Chancellery in Vienna.

Maria Theresa's capabilities were inherited by her son Josef II, whose stamp on the empire was even more forceful. His mother had introduced German as a language of diplomacy more as a convenient means of oiling the wheels of the Austrian imperial system than as an expression of national characteristic. Josef pushed this a stage further. As far as he was concerned the empire *was* German – an attitude that clung on for the next hundred and fifty years and one which the Habsburgs would have cause to regret.

For one thing, this insistence on an Austria divided between German-speakers and the rest, with German as the first language of the court, the army and the Chancellery, was a constant thorn in the flesh of other member states, made up as they were of such diverse peoples as Ruthenians, Serbs, Croats, Hungarians, Slovenes, Poles, Czechs, Magyars, Slovaks, Transylvanians, Romanians and Italians. It annoyed and confused those who merely wished to preserve their identity whilst remaining loyal to the crown, and gave fresh impetus to those with overt desires for national freedom. The revolutions of 1848, therefore, although mirrored to some extent by uprisings in other parts of Europe, maintained a character of their own. They were expressions of frustration that went beyond the struggle to weaken the power of the aristocracy or ritual cries for liberalization of the regime. Side by side with demands for radical change came appeals for individual autonomy, respect for minority national interests and an inchoate desire for a democratic brotherhood of all Austrians unfettered by the taint of Germanism. The radical leader Adolf Fischhof addressed a crowd of students in Vienna on 13 March 1848, and said: 'Let the ambitious Germans, possessed as they are by ideas, the tenacious, hard-working, patient Slavs, the chivalrous and spirited Magyars, the clever and clear-sighted Italians – let them all concentrate on the common problem of the state. . . . Hail to Austria and its glorious future! Hail to the united peoples of Austria! Hail to freedom!'

Needless to say, these admirable sentiments were easier to formulate than to put into practice. During the halcyon days between July and October 1848 – part of the period described by A. J. P. Taylor as the 'only liberal episode in Habsburg history' – a host of outspoken words of variable quality poured from the pens of journalists, dramatists and poets intent on awakening their contemporaries from their deep, censored, sleep. One of the most fertile, Johann Nestroy, an actor/playwright whose cat-and-mouse games with the censor began before the revolution and continued long after it had been suppressed, allowed his satirical pen free rein in *Freiheit in Krähwinkel* (*Freedom in Krähwinkel*). Audiences accustomed to a high level of theatrical allegory flocked to the Carl Theater nightly to stretch their eyes at the sight of Nestroy's radical journalist hero openly lampooning Metternich, and to gape at the spectacle of young women impersonating students manning barricades.

The last performance of *Freedom in Krähwinkel* was on 4 October 1848; by the time Nestroy's next play opened, in February 1849, Vienna was under martial law. The death-knell of effective liberalism sounded when the dynasty, having rallied its wits, decided that the time had come to restore the status quo.

The result was something of a pyrrhic victory. The ruthless military force with which this was done – in Prague and Vienna, in June and October 1848, Field Marshal Prince Windischgrätz stamped out all signs of dissidence by the simple expedient of ordering his troops to fire on anyone foolhardy enough to incite it – succeeded in re-establishing the old order but left a legacy of ill-will from which the Habsburgs never completely recovered.

Six weeks after Vienna had capitulated to the field marshal, the Emperor Franz Ferdinand, old, epileptic and never entirely in his right mind, was finally persuaded to abdicate in favour of his eighteen-year-old nephew, Franz Josef. On 2 December 1848 the new Emperor assumed the mantle of the Holy Roman Empire inherited from his ancester, Charlemagne, sustaining himself with the thought that despite his youth he held the Mandate of Heaven and thus had an absolute right to rule.

He exercised this right for the next sixty-eight years, presiding over the creaking bureaucratic machinery of empire with punctilious attention to detail. To begin with, fear of further disturbances brought a rash of repressive measures. Aided and abetted by his prime minister, Prince Schwarzenberg, he reintroduced censorship, gradually transferred ultimate political power from the elected constituent assembly to the Emperor alone, and brought Hungary to heel with the help of Russian troops willingly supplied by the Tsar in the interests of imperial solidarity.

Eventually, in 1867, Franz Josef had to bow to some extent to liberalism and the pressures of nationalism and permitted the creation of a separate sovereign state to be known as Austria-Hungary. Under the Dual Monarchy, as the Habsburg lands came to be called, Franz Josef ruled as King of Hungary and Emperor of Austria. Each state had its own parliament, but shared an army, a legislature and a foreign policy, a state of affairs fraught with possibilities for bureaucratic muddle. The morass of official documents shuttling between Vienna and Budapest were stamped with the initials 'k. u. k.' (imperial and royal) if they dealt with matters relating to common institutions, 'k' (royal) if they touched on purely Hungarian affairs, and 'k. k.' (imperial royal) if they had to do solely with the Austrian half of the monarchy. Even Austria itself was not officially referred to as 'Austria' but as 'The Kingdom and Lands Represented in Austria' (it was not called Austria until 1915). Unofficially, of course, it was always called Austria.

The creation of the new Dual Monarchy also revived old confusions as to the exact definition of 'Austrian' culture. Was it, as Robert Musil's character Diotima thought, a distillation of 'our old Austrian culture', essentially Viennese and rooted in the aristocratic pleasures of a vanished baroque age, or was it a synthesis of the cultures of all the Habsburg lands?

Musil himself seemed to feel there was no precise answer, since neither the Slav, Romance nor Magyar peoples of the Monarchy acknowledged any culture but their own, and the Austro-Germans were torn between their dislike of being thought culturally inseparable from Germany and their belief, echoed by the writer Karl Kraus, that 'in the Viennese confusion of values there was only one incorruptible, unassailable, totally reliable authority: the authority of the German language.'[2] In the end Musil came to the conclusion that to attempt any such categorization was fruitless, for ' "Austrian" culture was an error of perspective on the part of the Viennese; it was an abundant collection of local cultures, to be familar with them was an enriching experience, but that should not have deceived anyone into thinking that they constituted a synthesis.'

Stefan Zweig, on the other hand, whose Jewish parents emigrated from Moravia in the 1880s, was convinced that Vienna was the guardian of a unique multi-national cultural tradition. Only there, exposed to the city's urbane charms and united by a common passion for the theatre, conversation, food, drink and, above all, music, were all races able to fuse into the imperial melting pot, shed their national and lingual skins and emerge transformed into that most agreeable of all human beings, a Viennese. 'For the genius of Vienna – a specifically musical one – ' he wrote in *The World of Yesterday*, 'was always that it harmonized all the national and lingual contrasts. Its culture was a synthesis of all Western cultures.'

The Viennese, however, like the imperial Chinese, were past masters at appropriating anything from foreign sources that attracted them, and squeezing out everything they either disliked or did not understand. There could be no common ground, cultural or otherwise, unless German, and its curious, hybrid, almost untranslatable colloquial form peculiar to the Viennese – a dialect containing snippets of Czech, Turkish, Croat, Yiddish and French, but primarily Bavarian and Alemannic in origin – was the means of communication. The Viennese might sprinkle paprika on their food, drink Hungarian wine and Moravian beer, shed sentimental tears over melancholy Bohemian songs or thrill to the sound of gypsy violins, but few (apart from the Emperor, who was said to be able to make himself understood in nineteen languages) bothered to learn the language of their countries of origin.

This linguistic insularity spilled over into indifference towards writers working in languages other than German and composers who drew their inspiration from local themes: it was one thing for Haydn to allude to Turkish music, quite another for Smetana or Janáček to create operas entirely peopled by Czechs singing in their native tongue (Janáček even went so far as to base the melodic lines of his opera *Jenufa* on the rhythmic patterns of the Lachian dialect), or for Kodály to resurrect forgotten Hungarian music. None of this was likely to appeal to German-speaking audiences reared in the German musical tradition. All these composers had difficulty in getting their work performed outside Prague or Budapest and if they did – as when Smetana's *Bartered Bride* was performed at the Vienna Exhibition in 1892 – they had to be translated into German. Dvořák had more success, but only, it has been pointed out, because he had a German publisher.[3]

Writers came up against the same problem. Contact between the German literary community in Prague and their Czech counterparts was minimal until just before the First World War, when a number of young German-speaking intellectuals, including Franz Kafka, the playwright Max Brod and the Expressionist poet Franz Werfel, took an interest in Czech language and literature, reading Czech classics in the original and translating the work of their contemporaries into German. But even these attempts at mutual understanding were not entirely free from the taint of Germanism. Franz Werfel wrote in 1914: 'For it cannot be denied that Czech culture can only exist as a ward of the German culture in the midst of which it dwells. Prague is only seven hours away from Vienna and Berlin by express train. And, if in a sudden fit of arrogance this nation, oblivious of historical necessity, begins to vaunt its independence, it will have lost its unique and remarkable cultural opportunity and, for all its fashionable European elegance, succumbed to barbarism.'[4] Adolf Fischhof's dreams of unity and brotherhood had still not come to fruition.

Troublesome thoughts about political and cultural hegemony were, in the main, confined to the intellectual bourgeoisie. The landowning classes had no such crises of identity. Long accustomed to intermarriage within a catholic mixture of nationalities, it mattered little to them whether their estates were in Bohemia,

Dalmatia or Galicia, so long as they could turn to Vienna for social and professional sustenance. Neither did such matters preoccupy the speculators and bankers who jostled for prime positions on the Ringstrasse. Between 1857, when the Emperor Franz Josef announced his plans for scrapping and redeveloping the fortified walls of the old city, and 1873, when the crash on the Vienna Stock Exchange caused a slump in private building, flagrantly opulent neo-Renaissance palaces sprang up, their grandiose façades and voluptuously decorated interiors designed to demonstrate to the aristocratic owners of the baroque town houses inside the inner city and the palatial villas outside the walls that there was a new class vying for status and power. It was for clients such as these, among them the industrialist Nikolaus Dumba, that Hans Makart allowed his theatrical streak full reign. Commissioned to decorate the dining-room of Dumba's *Palast* on the Parkring, Makart covered the walls with an allegorical frieze in the Venetian style. Art, Science, Labour, Industry, Agriculture, Astronomy, Chemistry, glowed, shimmered and glittered in every colour: 'the chiaroscuro of the painting', one admirer wrote approvingly, 'encompasses the entire room, which has come to be a monument to the Viennese style of grand display.'[5]

Dumba was one of the few speculators unaffected by the slump of 1873. Another was Makart – demand for his luxuriant canvases remained insatiable, and in 1879, whilst his friend Emil Schindler was gloomily contemplating the birth of his elder daughter, he was busy arranging his most spectacular display, a procession to celebrate the silver wedding of the Emperor and Empress. Allowed a free hand by the City Council, Makart spared no effort or expense to give Vienna its money's-worth. Casting himself in the lead, dressed as Rubens and mounted on a heavily caparisoned white charger, he rode slowly through the streets followed by a long line of floats carrying tableaux depicting scenes from Renaissance life.

Six years later he died of cerebral palsy, but, long after it became subjected to ridicule by artists interested only in simplicity and purity of line, his decorative influence lingered on. Only a handful of enlightened enthusiasts responded to the call for minimal adornment – the majority of Viennese clung to the Makart principle that there could never be too much of a good thing, and continued to crowd their living rooms with stuffed animals, Japanese vases filled with peacock feathers and bulrushes, occasional tables covered with velvet draperies and sofas smothered in fringed, plush-covered cushions.

Alma Mahler's early urges to 'be rowed in gondolas with velvet draperies floating astern'[6] and to wear trailing velvet gowns were fantasies that only Makart could have inspired. And after her father died it was only natural that she should withdraw into herself and brood on ways and means of realizing the mordant hankerings of her early youth.

She began with a library. All her old children's books 'I used to lug to a second-hand bookshop to exchange for modern literature.' She did not specify their titles, merely alluding to the fact that she managed to build up 'a nice collection, of which no one was allowed to know'.[7] It is tempting to make up a reading list: did she, for instance, like the sixteen-year-old Stefan Zweig, read Rilke, Nietzsche, Strindberg and Hauptmann rather than Schiller, Eduard von Hartmann and Gottfried Keller? Did she smuggle copies of Flaubert's *Madame Bovary* or Zola's *Thérèse Raquin* into the house to read under the bedclothes?

Certainly she was out of sympathy with both her mother and Carl Moll, who had become 'the dominating influence' at home. Nor did she seem to find any companionship with her sister Grete, who is scarcely mentioned in her memoirs. Carl Moll she found particularly irritating. Although not yet her stepfather, he took it upon himself to fill her father's role as educator and guide – a task he must have undertaken with a certain amount of apprehension – and his pupil reacted with predictable asperity. 'He used me to test his skill as an educator,' she complained, 'but all he reaped was hatred. It was not in him to be my guide. He looked like a medieval wood carving of St Joseph, doted on old paintings, and most obnoxiously disturbed the tenor of my ways.' Poor Moll did not have much of a chance. Unfavourable compari-

sons with Schindler were not all that he was up against. Like
others throughout her life with whom Alma felt ill at ease, he
failed to summon up the necessary energy to respond to her
highly charged demands for complete personal attention. All he
was capable of was to attempt to fulfil the obligations imposed
on him by the death of his friend and his love for his widow.
None of this was good enough for Alma, who sought a mentor
with eyes for her alone.

Two years later she found him. After a time when she 'grew
completely away from [her] surroundings' and 'became indifferent to them, engrossed in music',[8] she came under the influence
of Max Burckhard.

In 1896 Max Burckhard was forty-two and had been director
of the Burgtheater for six years. A lawyer by training, he had
become a civil servant in 1886, after having written a treatise on
Austrian civil law. He was described by Bertha Zuckerkandl, wife
of the anatomist Emil Zuckerkandl, as 'of medium height, well
set up, carelessly elegant; a fine-drawn face, clear, bold eyes;
friendly, although inclined to be abrupt, very susceptible to
humour. Much loved by women, women swarm round him. Very
fond, also of his library, his sailing boat and his precise divorce
laws. Not for nothing had he breathed in the atmosphere of
bureaucracy from his youth. He was capable of appearing calm
and unruffled . . .'[9] He was already known to Alma, as one of
the 'older, knowledgeable men of our artists' circle'. He therefore
possessed a number of qualifications likely to endear him to his
future protégée, among them age, familiarity and intellect, but,
most appealing of all, he occupied a public position of the highest
importance and glamour.

There is little to compare with the Burgtheater among the cities
of Western Europe. The Comédie Française, with its history of
royal patronage and its resident company, comes nearest to it.
But Parisians did not wake up every morning and, ignoring the
banalities of politicians or the movement of money markets, turn
in unison to the pages of their newspaper that reported theatre
news. They did not have the face and figure of every member of

the company indelibly printed on their minds, neither did they follow their every move with an avidity not even accorded to British royalty. Only the Viennese had this obsession, 'For', as Stefan Zweig wrote in *The World of Yesterday*, 'the Imperial theatre, the Burgtheater, was for the Viennese and for the Austrian more than a stage upon which actors enacted parts; it was the microcosm that mirrored the macrocosm, the brightly coloured reflection in which the city saw itself, the only true cortigliano of good taste.'

Another reason for the Burgtheater's special place in Viennese affections was that it brought them into physical proximity with the Emperor and Empress. The original theatre, built by Josef II in 1776, adjoined the Hofburg, and members of the court had direct access from the palace to their boxes. Ticket prices were comparatively cheap: 1 gulden for the stalls, 20 kreuzer for the first floor, going down to 7 kreuzer for the fourth floor, 3 gulden for boxes on the ground floor, compared to 20 kreuzer for a simple but substantial meal with wine.

By the time Max Burckhard took over as director, the old theatre had been abandoned for larger, grander premises on the Franzens ring. Many people found the new building with its pillared façade and imposing staircases a poor substitute for the intimate atmosphere of the old court theatre, where everybody could rub shoulders with everyone else, conversations could be overheard and gossip exchanged, and behind the closed doors of the boxes amorous affairs could be conducted in comparative privacy. The repertoire, however, had remained much the same – predominantly classical, interspersed with light comedy. Although technically given a free hand, director, actors and authors were under some pressure to satisfy the Emperor, whose whims occasionally determined not only the choice of play, but its content. (Josef II, for instance, disliked sad endings and, in 1777, announced that 'His Majesty the Emperor will have no play performed in which funerals, churchyards, gravediggers and other unhappy occurrences appear' – thus causing considerable alterations to be made to *Hamlet* and *Romeo and Juliet*.)

Burckhard, however, was cast in a different mould. A progressive man of catholic tastes, whose appointment had come as a
complete surprise even to his friends, he immediately set about
engaging new actors with an eye to enlarging and improving the
Burgtheater's repertoire. Deaf to malicious tongues putting it
about that he had set foot in a theatre only seven times in his
life, unperturbed by complaints from the critic Karl Goldmann
that he was undermining the theatre's role as arbiter of high
moral standards, and impervious to digs from Karl Kraus, who
proclaimed him 'profaner of the sacred cliché', Burckhard injected
new blood into the repertoire. Viennese audiences were introduced to Ibsen, Hauptmann and Schnitzler and, in keeping with
the spirit of their work, he persuaded the actors to abandon the
formal declamatory style of delivery to which they were accustomed in favour of a more natural approach. He also insisted
that the stage designers strip their sets of Makartian dross.

Alma therefore had good reason to be satisfied with her choice
of mentor. But why such an illustrious figure should have devoted
so much time to the further education of a self-obsessed seventeen-year-old is worth a moment's reflection.

When she first met Burckhard, at Carl Moll's house on the
Hohe Warte, Alma was, by her own account, 'seventeen and
very innocent; people called me beautiful; I read a great deal; I
composed . . .'[10] A photograph of her at this age bears out the
second claim and reveals the physical temptations to which Burckhard must have been subject. Long, flowing hair, piercing eyes,
a determined mouth, a black bear cub sitting on her knee, Alma
leans towards her photographer with a calculating air. The bear
is not to be allowed to steal all the limelight. Tantalizing, independent, provocative, musically talented, she must have appeared a
strange, alluring figure. Unlike her convent-bred contemporaries,
fed on bowdlerized versions of the classics and sheltered from
the outside world in preparation for the serious business of capturing a husband, Alma had been stimulating her imagination
among her stockpile of Nietzsche, Schopenhauer and Plato,
immersing herself in music and (encouraged by the despised Carl

Moll) cutting her conversational teeth amongst his fellow artists in the Café Imperial.

Whilst subscribing to the moral conventions of the time, Frau Schindler had therefore allowed her daughter freedoms of thought and movement not given to many of her social background. Frau Schindler did not wish Alma to live, as Stefan Zweig claimed young girls of the time were expected to live, 'in a completely sterilized atmosphere, from the day of her birth until the day when she left the altar on her husband's arm'. It was she who recognized Alma's unusual musical gifts, teaching her the piano, giving her singing lessons and furthering her compositional ability by sending her to study counterpoint with the blind Viennese organist, Josef Labor. In contrast to the majority of Viennese matrons, eager to see their fledgeling daughters bound in holy matrimony as soon as they had left the schoolroom, Frau Schindler put the quest for artistic self-fulfilment before the pursuit of a suitable husband.

Thus mentally stimulated, but by her own account living in a musical and mystical world of her own making, reading voraciously, fascinated by words such as 'humans at play in the locks of the deity' (a phrase coined by her father whilst watching bathers in the surf at Sylt), Alma was ripe for intellectual impregnation. And when Burckhard, at first merely interested in her mercurial mind, sent her as a Christmas present two laundry baskets of books, 'all the classics, in the finest editions' (among them some of the works of Nietzsche), he was not only reinforcing his protégée's own estimate of her intellectual abilities but tapping a hitherto unplumbed source – that of reconciling self-worship with the wider implications of music as a substitute for religion: 'the last mystery of faith, the fully revealed religion', the spiritual contradictions of which were to haunt her to the end of her life.

These excursions into the life of the mind led, inevitably, to a more emotional state of affairs. Burckhard, long accustomed to charming his way through rehearsals, became himself susceptible to the charms of his young friend. Her challenging gaze, her mental agility, her disquieting ability to alert him to her physical possibilities whilst preserving a maddeningly proper front, all disarmed and intrigued him, and he became hopelessly infatuated.

Alma, however, having succeeded in drawing him into her web, found his amorous attentions ridiculous. She wrote callously: 'Burckhard was forty-two, and his ardour sickened me. On my side, our relationship lacked any erotic tinge. We had some odd scenes when I was first intrigued by his strong masculinity, only to turn it aside with a heartless joke. This maddened him; he used to call me coquettish and disappear for a while. But he always came back, and the game would start all over again.'[11]

Nevertheless, despite distaste for his lusts of the flesh, Alma allowed Burckhard to remain. They went cycling together, chaperoned by Alma's mother, who brought up the rear in a landau. There were frequent stops, partly to consume the champagne, partridge and pineapple which Burckhard considered essential to keep them going, and partly to escape from Frau Schindler. Not that she had anything much to worry about. His physical overtures having been repulsed, Burckhard confined himself to conversation. Alma recorded two of his more memorable aphorisms in her memoirs. 'Death', he told her, 'does not exist. It's a human invention.' And, 'I'd rather be with enemies than with friends. An enemy, at least, won't dare spout malice to your face, as friends are so fond of doing.' It was all, as Alma said, 'perfectly innocent, for . . . he was not my type'.[12]

Even if he had been her type, Burckhard's fleshly desires would have had little outlet. The moral code of the time would have prevented it. Alma herself observed it rigorously, not merely, she hastened to point out, because it was expected of her, but because it was inherent in her nature to do so. 'I believed in a virginal purity in need of preservation,' she observed. 'It was not merely a trait of the period, it was a trait of mine. My old-fashioned upbringing and my mother's daily sermons had strapped me into a mental chastity belt.'

Frau Schindler's sermons on the desirability of modest behaviour in the company of the opposite sex were preached with the practical aim of curbing her daughter's wayward impulses.

She did not, apparently, do much about teaching her the rudiments of the Christian faith. Alma complained that between her mother's Protestantism and her father's Catholicism she and her sister were left completely ignorant of Church practice: had it not been for a Catholic servant who introduced them to 'a few primitive prayers' they would have had a totally agnostic upbringing. As it was, she said, it was as 'good as irreligious'. But, later, she admitted having been taught the catechism, and throughout her life she maintained a strong, if occasionally unorthodox, link with the Catholic Church.

Although she practised sexual restraint, Alma's upbringing had spared her the worst excesses of middle-class prudishness. She had, in consequence, broken free of the stifling mould remembered by Stefan Zweig, in which 'the young of the last century . . . . fought their way through life', battling against a 'sticky, perfumed, sultry, unhealthy atmosphere' polluted by a 'dishonest and unpsychological morality of secrecy and hiding'. Her every book had not been 'discreetly vetted' and her every outing chaperoned, and her clothes had a softer outline than the formidably encased ladies of Zweig's acquaintance, whose 'careful and complicated attire' violated Nature in every single detail: the middle of their bodies 'laced into a wasp's shape in corsets of stiff whalebone, blown out like a huge bell from the waist down, the neck closed in up to the chin, legs shrouded to the toes, the hair towering with countless curls, locks and braids under a majestically swaying monstrosity of a hat, the hands encased in gloves, even on the warmest day . . .', all designed to distort and conceal the female form, lest a glimpse of bare flesh should 'open the way for some impropriety'.[13]

Karl Kraus, Stefan Zweig and Arthur Schnitzler were among those who condemned the duplicity of a society that buried what Freud referred to as 'the misunderstood and much-maligned erotic' so deep in its subconscious that its very existence was denied. As most men, and a larger number of women than would have been considered proper, knew, Vienna, like any other capital, catered handsomely for anyone in search of illicit sexual gratification. Tucked away in well-defined areas of the old city were bars, erotic cabarets and seedy hotels where any young man eager to uncover the secrets of sex could find enlightenment.

Ibsen's play *Ghosts* painted a ghastly portrait of the penalties likely to be suffered by those that succumbed to such temptations; Karl Kraus's sympathies, on the other hand, lay with the prostitutes, many of whom did not comply with the law of 1873, requiring them to register with the police and submit to a medical examination by a police doctor. He considered them 'more heroic than soldiers', for although the latter risked injury and death in the service of their country, the former risked arrest and imprisonment as well as disease and death in the service of the social order. 'A trial involving sexual morality', he wrote, 'is a deliberate step from individual to general immorality.[14] It was, therefore, in Kraus's opinion, the height of hypocrisy for society on the one hand to attempt to preserve the sanctity of the daughters of the prosperous bourgeoisie by denying them all knowledge of their capacity for carnal enjoyment, and on the other hand to condemn those who put their erotic skills at the disposal of ignorant or disenchanted men.

Kraus saw women as fecund, the fount of the eternal feminine, the well-spring of all fantasy, the source of all masculine reason and thus, despite their irrationality, the linchpin of civilization. Alma appealed to a more egalitarian brand of German Romantic. Her striking looks, her musical gifts, her independence of mind and her strong will transformed her into a heroine of another kind, in whom lay latent the ultimate fulfilment of the Romantic ideal, wherein spiritual stimulation, sexual love and intellectual compatibility were united in perfect harmony. In her they saw the embodiment of all their hopes that the 'quest for the absolute, so characteristic of the Romantics',[15] which united 'complete satisfaction of the senses, the lofty emotion of spiritual love, a fruitful interchange of ideas coupled with a comrade-like bond of friendship', was not in vain. So potent, indeed, was Alma's appeal to this type of romantic that, long after her youth and beauty had faded and her figure had lost all its curvaceous charms, she continued to arouse powerful emotions in susceptible male breasts. Neither age nor her many maddening vanities and inconsistencies could detract from this, her most enduring quality. Whatever Alma looked like, said or did, she was surrounded, in the eyes of all who were drawn into her circle, by an aura of enchantment.

In 1897, when Alma was eighteen, Anna Schindler and Carl Moll were married, and shortly afterwards the family moved from Plankenberg to Carl Moll's house on the Hohe Warte, a fashionable district on the edge of the Vienna Woods.* Of the marriage, Alma wrote disparagingly: 'The poor woman . . . There she went and married a pendulum, and my father had been the whole clock.'[16] Of the move there is no mention. Plankenberg vanished as mysteriously as it had appeared, unremarked until old age brought it once again to life.

As for the Hohe Warte, it was there that Alma's budding charms once again came to the attention of a middle-aged romantic. This time, however, her mother had legitimate grounds for alarm: the painter Gustav Klimt, although unmarried and, at thirty-five, younger than his friend Burckhard, had serious drawbacks as an object of her daughter's affections. His mother and one of his sisters suffered from delusions, and he himself had the dreadful horror trickling in his own blood that had poisoned the life of so many powerful people – that most feared of nineteenth-century diseases, syphilis.

Wien XIX, Hohe Warte, Steinfeldgasse 8. The house had been designed by Joseph Olbrich as part of a new estate whose other occupants included the designer Koloman Moser and the art photographer Dr Friedrich Spitzer. Olbrich left for the artists' colony at Darmstadt before the scheme was realized and it was left to Josef Hoffmann to carry it through. The whole project was completed in 1901.

3 Liebestod

Early in June 1898, Alma Schindler went to the Stadtspark in Vienna for the unveiling of a memorial to Hans Makart. With her were Carl Moll, his mother and the painters Josef Engelhart and Ernst Nowak. By the time they arrived 'there was already a mass of people,' she wrote in her diary. 'Makart's mother, her son – the daughter did not arrive until the end – and people from the Künstlerhaus and the Secession. Klimt was extremely charming. He came up to me at once and we had a good gossip. Then the moment came for Felix* and Klimt to stand together and lay their wreaths . . . Afterwards I talked to Klimt for a while. He asked when we could meet . . . [1]

These attentions did not go unnoticed by Frau Lammer, a friend of the Molls. 'You have very good taste, Alma,' she said, 'but, you know, more often than not, people who look so alike end up marrying each other!' – a lighthearted remark that stirred Alma to write: 'I must say it never occurred to me that Klimt and I looked alike. Everything tormented me . . .'

Despite the discrepancy between their ages, Frau Lammer's observations contained a grain of truth. Contemporary photographs show similarities around the eyes and mouth and in the set of the cheekbones. Only the noses differ – Alma Schindler's long and sloping, Gustav Klimt's small with a tendency to turn up. They could well have been, as Klimt later suggested to Alma they should try to be, brother and sister.

In its early stages, however, their friendship had little to do

---

*Eugene Felix had been president of the Künstlerhaus since 1895.

with sibling harmony. They were, as Alma put it in *Mein Leben*, drawn together by a mutual recognition of each other's talents: 'His looks and my young charm, his genius and my talent, our common, deeply vital musicality, all helped to attune us to each other.' Their first meetings took place in the Molls' house on the Hohe Warte, in the conspiratorial and highly charged atmosphere of the Secession.

The handful of painters, sculptors and architects who initiated defection from the two most powerful and conservative temples of Viennese art, the Akademie der Künstler Wiens and the Künstlerhaus, which owned the city's only exhibition building, were only part of what Carl Schorske referred to as the 'widespread, collective, oedipal revolt'[2] which swept through the Austrian middle class in the Seventies, after the financial crash of 1873 obliged the liberal middle class to put aside their old liberal-minded principles in the interests of economic practice. The crisis of identity that resulted lay hidden behind Vienna's official mask. Few politicans or civil servants were able to rouse themselves from profound apathy, induced by paying lip-service to high moral standards in public life in the knowledge that they harboured within their ranks seeds of decay and corruption the like of which (if the writers of the breakaway literary movement Jung-Wien were to be believed) had not been seen since the decline of the Roman Empire.

It was in rebellion against the suffocating tentacles of the official institutions of the Dual Monarchy, and to cheat what the Viennese writer Hermann Bahr referred to as 'the ghostly hand of death strangling the growth of the human intellect and spirit', that the founder members of the 'Vereinigung bildender Künstler Wiens – Secession' – Gustav Klimt, Carl Moll, Ernst Stohr, Johann Victor Krämer, Rudolf Bacher, Julius Mayreder, Joseph Olbrich and Josef Hoffmann – formed their association. They too felt, with Walter, the young musician and artist in Musil's *The Man Without Qualities*, that the century going to its grave had not exactly distinguished itself in its second half: 'It had painted like the Old Masters, written like Goethe and Schiller, and built its houses in the Gothic and Renaissance style.' And they too responded to the kindling fever that rose out of 'the oil-smooth spirit of the last two decades of the nineteenth century' when 'nobody knew exactly what was on the way, nobody was able to say whether it was to be a new art, a New Man, a new morality, or perhaps a reshuffling of society.'[3] In common with the English pre-Raphaelites, the Belgian Naturalists, the French Impressionists and the German Jugendstilisten they sought liber-ation from the artistic straitjacket of the past.

The first general meeting of the Secession was held on the Hohe Warte on 21 June 1897, with Klimt as the elected president. 'The first meetings of the insurgents took place in the house of my new stepfather,' wrote Alma, 'and their first president was Gustav Klimt, a painter of Byzantine delicacy who sharpened and deep-ened the "eyesight" I had learned from Papa. I was still quite childish when I met him at those secret sessions; he was the most gifted of them all, already famous at thirty-five, and strikingly good-looking.'[4]

In 1897 Klimt was, indeed, famous. The precociously talented son of an engraver, he had entered the School of Arts and Crafts in 1876 at the age of fourteen. Seven years later, his studies completed, he went into partnership with two fellow students, his brother Ernst and Franz von Matsch, and in 1886 they landed their first large Viennese commission – a series of ceiling decor-ations above the staircase of the newly completed Burgtheater. Like Makart before them the three young men rose, as Carl Schorske put it in an essay on Klimt,[5] 'to fame in the service of the bourgeois culture of the Ringstrasse'. Also like Makart, into whose shoes they had stepped following his death in 1886, they set out to please the city fathers, adorning the ceilings with a colourful assortment of ancient and modern theatrical scenes in the neo-classical style.

The following year Klimt and Matsch further enhanced their reputation by responding to an invitation from the city council to paint a picture commemorating the old Burgtheater and its past patrons. Such was the social distinction accorded anyone associated with the theatre that the two artists found their studio in the Josefstädterstrasse besieged by financiers, army officers, aristocrats, government officials and ladies of fashion, all offering their credentials in a desperate attempt to have their social standing immortalized on canvas.

From the two hundred hopeful applicants just over half were selected for inclusion in the vast group portrait. Klimt, however, having dutifully paid tribute to the Emperor, the Emperor's friend, the actress Katherina Schratt, the surgeon Professor Theodor Billroth, the future mayor of the city, Karl Lueger, and other prominent members of Viennese society, allowed himself the luxury of adding a few less illustrious but more physically attractive models. Dotted about amongst the corsets, beards and watchchains were portraits of his sisters, Hermine and Klara, as well as numerous nameless young women. 'Klimt', observed his biographer, Christian Nebehay, 'livened up the picture with studies of elegant young ladies of his acquaintance. [It was] his first attempt at depicting Viennese beauties.'

Later on, much of Klimt's creative energy went into exploring the feminine ideal, and attempting to translate this elusive concept from philosophical into visual terms. Like Schopenhauer, Kraus and Weininger he found its distillation a minefield of complexity. Unlike Schopenhauer, his female images exuded a voluptuous, androgynous life-force that had little in common with the philosopher's gloomy estimate of the human condition.

In *Fin-de-Siècle Vienna* Carl Schorske suggested that Klimt's vision of the universe was Schopenhauer's – 'The World as Will, as blind energy in an endless round of meaningless parturience, love and death.' But although, together with his contemporaries, unable to escape the influence of Schopenhauer, it was Goya, rather than Klimt, whose paintings realized the pessimistic view that man's essential role was to endure the sufferings of a senseless existence, with only the prospect of empty nothingness ('das leere Nichts') at the end of it. 'The fact', wrote H. G. Schenk, 'that man, deprived of his belief in God, must be in danger of losing all sense of spiritual orientation was clearly realized by Goya. In

the *Desastres de la Guerra* . . . a number of human beings, roped
to each other and obviously full of anguish, aimlessly [wander]
up and down the globe . . . the caption leaves no margin for
doubt. It reads "No saben el camino" (They don't know the
way).'[6]

Far from not knowing their way, Klimt's seductive maidens,
snakes entwined in their hair or around their arms, embraced life
with unholy abandon. (Curiously, although Alma was voluptuous
enough to have modelled for Klimt, she does not appear to have
done so.) Not since the daemonic goddesses of pre-Hellenic times,
or the lyrical murals of Rajput paintings, had so many erotic and
sensually decorative females flaunted themselves so flagrantly in
the name of art. Even when, as in the final panel of the Beethoven
frieze exhibited at the Secession in 1902, Klimt alluded to Richard
Wagner's essay on Beethoven, in which Wagner extolled the Schopenhauerian vision of music as the only art capable of expressing
the essence of human longings, the passionate embrace of two
figures, surrounded by a heavenly chorus of hermaphrodites,
brought the theme of the work (Desire and Fulfilment) to a
conclusion unlikely to have appealed to Schopenhauer, for whom
the fulfilment of human love was anathema.*

Preparations for the Secession's first exhibition, and the drawing up of a manifesto outlining its aims, dominated the Molls'
life during 1897 and 1898. Max Burckhard, who had just lost
his job at the Burgtheater, became co-editor of the movement's
magazine, *Ver Sacrum*, a journal that owed much to the English
arts magazine, *The Studio*. The first issue, published on 1 January
1898, proclaimed the Secessionists' intention to open the eyes of
all people, rich or poor, to the universality of an artistic world
in which all the decorative arts played an equal part; and on 26
March, when the first exhibition opened in the premises of the
Vienna Horticultural Society on the Parkring, the Viennese public
were able to judge for themselves whether the association could

---

*Although Wagner undoubtedly looked to Schopenhauer for philosophical
guidance, Schopenhauer had a poor opinion of Wagner's musical ability:
he once remarked that Wagner 'did not know what music was'.

live up to its promises. The design and arrangements for the entrance and main exhibition rooms were executed by Joseph Olbrich and Josef Hoffmann; Klimt provided a poster, taking as his theme slaying the Minotaur, watched by the goddess Athena, symbol of the Austrian parliament. Alongside works by other members of the Secession were contributions from Rodin, Puvis de Chavannes, Klinger, Whistler, Sergantini, Fernand Khnopff and Walter Crane, who sent book illustrations, wallpaper, stained glass and watercolours.

The exhibition was a great success. Franz Josef was among the early visitors and by the time it ended in June nearly 57,000 people had seen it and 218 items had been sold. It was a triumph for the Secessionists and an encouragement to their supporters on the city council to speed up the construction of a permanent exhibition building on the Friedrichstrasse, the design for which had already been drawn up by Joseph Olbrich.

'With what joy did I give birth to this building,' Olbrich wrote in *Der Arkitekt* in 1899. '. . . There were to be walls, white and shining, sacred and chaste. Solemn dignity should pervade . . .', and, true to his dream, but to the astonishment of passers-by, a pagan temple arose, white and simple, crowned by an openwork golden dome of laurel leaves, its entrance emblazoned with the Secessionists' motto: '*Der Zeit Ihre Kunst/Der Kunst Ihre Freiheit*' (To the Age its Art/To Art its Freedom). The Viennese were, on the whole, unimpressed with their new acquisition. The art critic Ludwig Hevesi overheard it being called 'The Mahdi's Tomb', 'a cross between a glasshouse and a blast furnace' and 'The Assyrian Convenience'. Eventually, when the dome was in position, it became known as 'The Golden Cabbage'. No amount of high-flown rhetoric could convince them that it was anything other than a monstrous joke.

Alma judged both the architect and his work more kindly. 'One has only to look at Olbrich to see that he is a delightful fellow – instantly everyone judges him sympathetically, just as I did,' she wrote in her diary on 30 July 1898, after visiting the site of the new Secession building with her stepfather. Together they had 'climbed up ladders and over planks' to the top of the unfinished building where, she recorded, 'there were wonderful large rooms lit from above. Further up one had a breathtaking view of the Carlskirche [sic] and of Vienna's future boulevards.'[7]

Throughout 1898 Alma recorded faithfully every visit made to the Secession with her mother or stepfather, every outing to the theatre and every drive in the Prater, covering notebook after notebook in a huge, sprawling, decisive hand.

'To the town before lunch,' began a typical entry, dated 17 April.

> In the afternoon, Dr Pollack, Settel and Knopff [sic] – we all drove in the Prater. Knopff spent the whole time in the Prater with me and Gretl, and was charming. He called me Alma Viva, then Alma Tadema – eventually he managed to bring out the words Fräulein Alma. He is a very fine man and an outstanding artist. In the evening Fischel and Mayreder came round . . . Fischel and Mayreder discussed the Secession, Fischel pro, Mayreder contra, in particular against Olbrich. 'Yes it is very easy to criticize, but you try and do better, my dear Mayreder.' It was the fourth time that Mayreder had been to our house, and we were very pleased to see him go. None of us missed him, I least of all.

'But what', she added, 'if he had a soft spot for me?'[8] Possibly he did – or possibly Alma was unable to resist challenging Mayreder to an emotional duel and he was equally unable to resist picking up the gauntlet – for on 28 April, the day on which the foundation stone for the Secession building was laid, her grandmother Moll came to the house with the news that a rumour was going round the city that she had become engaged to be married. 'I had never heard of such an idiotic idea,' she wrote in her diary – 'it was supposed to be with Herr Mayreder – that was the absolute limit . . .' The idea of Emil J. Schindler's daughter throwing herself away on an architect of modest repute, even if he did have a brother prominently placed on the city council, was, quite simply, laughable. Laughable, too, to have her name linked with Julius Mayreder when Gustav Klimt was making no secret of his predilection for her company.

On 18 June Klimt spent the evening with the Molls on the

Hohe Warte. 'I was very pleased that Klimt came . . .' wrote Alma in her diary, 'and I eavesdropped as he talked about his work, etc. He is an attractive fellow – one can have no idea what a free spirit he is . . . I said to him that his character had little to do with his outward appearance; I understand him very well. . . . I can only repeat, what I have always said, that he is a very, very nice man, and I am very fond of him.'[9]

Klimt's exact intentions towards Alma were, however, not clear. Later in the month, on holiday in Goisern, Alma occupied much of her time reliving the unveiling of the Makart memorial and wondering if Frau Lammer's prophecy could come true. '[I] tormented myself once more over Klimt. . . . it's been the same ever since the Makart memorial . . . he stared at me intently, but he didn't seem aware of it, even though he stood so close to me.'[10]

Speculation along these lines cropped up at intervals in her diary throughout 1898. A visit from Klimt was liable to give rise to anguished questionings as to his intent, and lead to sleepless nights. In July Klimt came to stay in Goisern for a few days, and she met him at the station. He suggested lunch but, she said, she 'couldn't bring herself to eat alone with him', adding that she was 'far too honest for this world'. A couple of days later, after he had been 'particularly charming' to her the previous evening, she wrote that she was so worked up that her 'eyes refused to shut all night'.

At the beginning of August, Frau Moll, aware of the effect Klimt was having on her daughter, decided to tackle her on the subject. 'Listen, Alma,' she said, 'I can only repeat what I have said to you before: it is not at all proper of Klimt to flatter you so much. He can twist you round his little finger with his flirtations, and if (which is the impression I get) you have shown him how much pleasure this gives you, he is bound to go on with it. It is thoroughly unscrupulous and abominable of him.' Alma's reply – 'Well? What has that got to do with anything?' – could have done little to reassure her, but she persevered. 'You like him very much, I can see that. But you are all too convincing as a plaything, which is why I am saying these things to you.'[11]

Frau Moll's strictures fell on deaf ears. In May Carl Moll had announced that, in March the following year, he planned to take the whole family on a trip to Italy, and that he was hoping to persuade Klimt to go with them. 'I hardly dare think about it,' Alma wrote. Nothing her mother could say could detract from the excitement of the prospect of visiting Italy in such stimulating company. Neither, under the circumstances, was there much Frau Moll could do to prevent her daughter's feelings being intensified during the intervening months, but, given Alma's proclivity for the emotional chase and Klimt's well-known susceptibility to the opposite sex, Frau Moll's fears were understandable. Alma's capacity to attract admirers was not at the root of her worries – any mother with a beautiful nineteen-year-old daughter would expect her to bask in her new-found ability to excite love and attention from the opposite sex – but, as Frau Moll had become increasingly aware, what distinguished Alma from other pretty young women playing flirtatious games with grown-up men for the first time was her budding penchant for playing them with men twice her age.

Had Emil Schindler been alive, Alma might well have contented herself with testing the emotional waters amongst her contemporaries whilst looking to her father's friends for additional creative stimulation. As it was, fate cast Alma in the role of seductive pupil, a part, it turned out, for which she was admirably suited. Once sure of being able to intrigue her mentors with her quick mind and musical gifts, Alma tantalized them with all the callousness of the young and sexually immature. It was her daughter's näivety in seeking to attract men of the world such as Burckhard and Klimt, seemingly oblivious of the possible consequences, that so preyed on Frau Moll's mind. As for Klimt, the very fact that he was considering accompanying the Molls to Italy at all indicated that he was in the grip of something other than the desire for a companionable holiday; he had a horror of foreign travel, he spoke no Italian, and had, since the establishment of the

Secession, been in the midst of a period of intense artistic experimentation and change. Furthermore, in 1898, whilst flirting with Alma, he had already formed what was to become a lifelong bond with his sister-in-law, Emilie Flöge, and had, since his father's loss of his job in 1874, shared the responsibility of supporting his mother and two sisters with his brother Ernst.

Klimt's domestic ties carried little weight with Alma. 'He had nothing round him but worthless women,' she observed. 'That was why he sought me out – he felt that I could help him.'[12] There was more than a grain of truth in this. Klimt later admitted that his outings to the Hohe Warte provided a welcome escape from his own troubled life, and that they had become more frequent with the prospect of feasting his eyes on Alma's 'childlike' beauty. But he did so, he assured Carl Moll, in a spirit of harmless fun, and it was not until after the invitation to Italy had been proffered and accepted that he began to suspect that Alma was nurturing feelings for him that had crossed the boundary from flirtation to love. Torn between the dictates of his conscience, which told him that he would be betraying his friendship to Moll by throwing himself into conditions of dangerous proximity with Alma, and a longing to be in new surroundings, Klimt decided to leave things as they were. As arranged, he would meet the Molls in Florence and accompany them on the last third of their Italian trip.

The Molls left Vienna for Venice on 22 March 1899, en route for Naples. Alma admired the bay – '*herrlich*', the frescoes at Pompeii – 'rather faded, but with some good colour', and Mount Vesuvius. After a week they went to Capri, where they took walks and explored the grottoes, and Alma danced the tarantella in a café. From there they moved to Rome, travelling via Sorrento and Amalfi and arriving in time for Easter.

Rome was an intoxicating experience for them all. Round every corner they came upon vistas that reminded them of the regenerative aims of the Secession: amongst the ruins of ancient Rome lay the heart of modern man, whose beat they had worked so hard to revive, and buried in the Vatican lay countless heroic effigies to stir their imagination and raise their spirits. The Apollo Belvedere, the Laocoön, the torso of Hercules, statues of Hermes and Mercury – 'one cannot take it all in', wrote Alma Schindler in her diary, ' – everything is so noble and sublime – one should not utter a word, only throw oneself at the feet of these master-pieces in awe and wonder.'

At intervals notes and postcards from Vienna leavened the rich cultural fare. An Easter card came from Klimt, in the form of a drawing of Alma striking a coquettish pose in the middle of a circle of admiring toy sheep, who, when the hyphenated initials on their backs were deciphered, revealed themselves to be Fischel, Mayreder, Lammer, Zierer, Schmedes, Tannsig, Klimt, Pollak, Tellner and Dorian Krassny, all frequent visitors to the Hohe Warte. On 8 April an anonymous poem (possibly from Krassny) arrived, the first of whose four verses ran:

> Einem Gruss aus der Heimat!
> Einem Gruss von dem Ort
> aus dem Alma die reiche
> log so ungerne fort!*[13]

After ten days in Rome the Molls moved on to Florence, staying at the Hotel Galactia on the Via de Pescioni, and on Monday, 22 April, they were joined by Klimt. The next day Alma Mahler wrote in her diary: 'Yesterday evening Klimt came. Is there any need to write more..?'[14]

She was very nearly denied his company. In an article for the *Neue Wiener Tagblatt*, dated 24 January 1943, Carl Moll wrote his own account of his friend's visit:

> During the years of our work together in the Secession Klimt developed a most convivial relationship with my family, who always greeted him with the utmost friendliness. When I, together with my own ones, was planning my first Italian journey, we suggested to Klimt that he should go with us, so that, at last, he would see something of the world. He was sorely tempted, but he could not leave his work for months on end. When else however, would he be offered such an opportunity to go to Italy, without having to speak Italian, and without having to worry about the

*A greeting from home! A greeting from the place whence the divine Alma has so unkindly run away!

thousand practical details? He decided to follow us to Florence and accompany us on the last third of our trip.

After an unpromising start, when Klimt and Moll nearly missed each other at the station, Moll found the unhappy Klimt sitting in a waiting room, complaining that he had been feeling so exposed to the mercies of foreigners that he had been on the point of catching the next train home. Later on, however, he brightened up.

> At the hotel, the family welcomed him with jubilation, promising Klimt risotto and Asti Spumante. The next day, in the highest spirits, we were ready to savour all the wonderful things the city had to offer. After a week we moved on, travelling via Pisa, Genoa, Milan, Verona to Venice. With this fairy-tale ending Klimt's visit came to an end; we put him into a through compartment and provided him with everything that he most liked.[15]

For the purposes of the *Neues Wiener Tagblatt* Moll chose to ignore the turbulent emotions seething beneath the surface of this congenial occasion. His stepdaughter, on the other hand, poured every inflection of her impressionable mind into her diary.

'Yesterday evening in Genoa,' she wrote on Saturday, 27 April 1899, 'I stood alone in the room – "Are you alone?" – Yes! – and without my knowing it he took me in his arms and kissed me. It was only for a tenth of a second, because a noise came from next door and we fell apart, but I will always remember that moment. . . . for the first time in my life I had been kissed, and by a man whom I love more than anything on earth.'

Whilst a wary eye had to be kept on Frau Moll, who had read Alma's diary and thus knew the worst, this state of affairs continued unchecked. In Venice in early May Klimt asked her to give him the 'picture with the bear', and she did so, with the word 'Genoa' inscribed on it. The following day a slight coldness developed between them, after Alma had apparently devoted more time than Klimt felt necessary to entertaining two male dinner guests. He attempted to make amends for his hasty behaviour over coffee and cakes in the café Florian, but Alma was not mollified and asked for her picture back. 'Not for anything in

the world,' cried Klimt. 'You only brought it to me yesterday. I
will never give it up.' At that Alma left the café in high dudgeon,
pursued 'continually' by Klimt, who beseeched her to calm down.

Back at the hotel, Alma was confronted by her stepfather. 'I
know everything. I know how things stand between you. . . .
tomorrow morning I will have a word with him. I think it's
scandalous, Alma. We will talk to each other about this again
tomorrow.'[16]

When the interview took place the next day, Moll questioned
his stepdaughter closely as to the state of her feelings, and asked
whether Klimt had spoken to her about the future. He told her
that if he felt Klimt would make her happy he would be only too
glad for them to continue to see each other, but that under
the circumstances it was impossible: Klimt would never separate
himself from his sister-in-law. He must, therefore, ask Alma to
refrain from speaking to Klimt alone again.[17]

This ultimatum produced an orgy of self-examination and
recrimination – the unfairness of life and the blindness of those
who 'presumed to play Providence' filled many embittered pages
of her diary. But, in fact, the next day they managed to defy the
embargo. After a concert in the Piazza San Marco they mingled
with the crowd, and, unobserved, were able to exchange promises
of undying love. When they parted Alma told Klimt to keep
her picture, 'as a reminder of me, and of our beautiful time
together'.[18]

On 4 May Klimt was, as Carl Moll wrote, 'put in a through
compartment' to Vienna, leaving Alma, by her own account,
prostrate with grief. Four days later she too was back in Vienna
but, in spite of her proximity to Klimt, she was miserable; not
even a visit from him two days after their homecoming revived
her spirits, for he brought flowers that reminded her of her loss:
'I trembled – they were lilies of the valley, the same kind as he
had given me in Florence . . .'.[19]

Frau Moll was another thorn in Alma's side. She made it her
business to keep an eye on her daughter and, if possible, to go
everywhere with her. 'She never let me go out alone,' wrote Alma

on 11 May, 'because she was afraid Klimt would find some way of meeting me' – restrictions to her freedom that led to tears of frustration: 'Today . . . I became so worked up over Mama, – that I cried.'[20]

Worse was to come, however. On 14 May Carl Moll extracted a promise from Klimt that he would have no further amorous dealings with Alma. On 19 May Klimt wrote a long and repentant reply:*

Dear Moll,
  Your letter hurt me to the quick. It pains me all the more when I think that I am causing one of my *dearest* friends to worry and suffer. Dear Moll, are you not painting too black a picture of things? I believe various other things to be the cause of your anxiety. The same goes for your dear wife and, because of your fatherly concern, you're seeing things in a more gloomy light than they are in reality. As a true friend, I write to boldly outline the whole proceedings to you – we ought to wipe the slate clean.
  I visited your house in all innocence. I knew Alma already, that is to say I had caught a fleeting glimpse of her at the unveiling of the Schindler monument. She appealed to me in just the way that a beautiful child does appeal to us artists. I saw her again at the home of the Molls, found her more lovely than ever, and was amazed that neither you nor anyone else had ever painted her. She paid no attention to me. In your kind way you often invited me when you had company. I am no great friend of large gatherings but to that house I came gladly.
  Everyone believed I was happy to come along. For years I have been a terribly unhappy person – no one sees this – in fact they believe me to be the opposite – yes, people envy me. Whichever path I have decided to follow in the past 7 or 8 years – misery and despair have been my constant companions. I yearn for happy moments, for pure pleasure, and I snatch at these like a stray dog desperate for a bite of solid food. Being in such a state of inner turmoil, I felt myself invigorated by your rational nature and I felt myself drawn to you in sincere friendship, in a way I have seldom felt with anyone. I felt at home within your family circle – your way of life seemed to me to be perfect and I am envious of people

*According to Christian M. Nebehay, who compiled a detailed set of biographical notes on Klimt, Alma's account of her frustrated passion in *And the Bridge Is Love* provides the sole written reference to the artist's penchant for romantic, but necessarily platonic friendships with women. For obvious reasons, therefore, not least that it refutes the claim that Klimt confined himself to communicating with others on postcards, the letter is reproduced, except for repetitions, in full.

who have a clear vision of what they should do and what they want to do in life. I don't believe that I shall ever achieve this.

Alma was often my partner and we talked of harmless topics – she spoke of her adoration for Wagner, *Tristan*, music – the pleasures of dancing. I considered her to be one of the happy people in this world, and I delighted in her. I never courted her, in the true sense of the word, and even if I had, I would never have held out any hope – many men visited that house, and all paid their addresses to her. I falsely raised her expectations as regards many of them – and drew false conclusions.

But this winter the young lady and I were no longer put next to each other at the table when we were with the neighbours whom we frequently visited. This had been pre-arranged by a written seating plan. I noticed this and was puzzled. I began to think things over. I thought to myself, it must be the young lady's wish, I have become too dull for her. I also found it natural that I shouldn't always be her partner because of the dictates of society – people would start talking. I didn't then pay so many visits to your house. I had previously come only when you invited me or if there was something of importance to be discussed. There were social gatherings at Spitzer's, at the Henneberg exhibition, etc., but always with a pre-arranged seating plan, so we were separated. I was hurt, as this seemed to me to be a sign of mistrust . . .

Only very recently – the trip to Florence had already been decided upon – did it occur to me that the young lady must have heard of my liaisons, some of this talk being true, much of it false. I myself am not absolutely clear about my liaisons, neither do I want to be. I can only be sure of one thing – that I am a poor fool. In short, as a result of certain revealing questions and remarks, I began to think that the young lady was not as completely indifferent to these matters as I had originally thought. I became somewhat afraid – for I am in awe of and respect genuine love. I became somewhat at odds with myself and with my true feelings of friendship towards you. But I comforted myself with the thought that it was only a lighthearted game on her part – a passing mood – Alma is beautiful, clever and witty. She had all those things in abundance which a discerning man could ever wish for in a woman. I believe that wherever she goes, and whenever she sets foot in the world of men she is mistress. Perhaps she became tired of this and perhaps she wished for a minor romance. Perhaps I behaved differently from the way I would have done under other circumstances, or differently from other admirers, and perhaps it was just this which interested her. This state of affairs seemed too dangerous even if it was only a game and now it was up to me to behave rationally as I was experienced in such matters.

And here is the beginning of my weakness. I had all sorts of muddled and clear thoughts – everything seemed confused. All at once – it became clear – it *cannot* be. Everything had been based on inferences and guesses – I had no certain proof. It also seemed to me too stupid and too vain that such an old fool as I felt myself to be should believe that I could arouse the pangs of first love in this beautiful young blossoming child. . . . I expected to be heartily laughed at . . .

My dear friend, this is the kind of thing I was afraid of. Yet, on the other hand, is it really so easy to remain indifferent towards her – doesn't everyone admire her? Doesn't everyone love her? Don't you realize that there are times when she throws one into confusion? Then came your Italian trip. I was working fairly hard. The date of my Florentine trip was getting closer. I was anxious. Something was holding me back – I'm not sure what – perhaps it was my conscience – saying to me 'You must not.' I wavered. This should have been the moment for me to prove how real my friendship was – I sensed I was not being totally honest – I wanted to write immediately to say I was not coming – I cannot come. But . . . the longing to escape from everyday routine – to be in new surroundings and to see fresh works of art, the prospect of undertaking a lovely trip in the most pleasant of company – all this helped to make me feel unsure once more. Then your telegram arrived – I set off – uncertain – even of myself. All went well initially, although I was not totally at ease. In strange surroundings one is forced to become more intimate – and I became closer to your family now than I had been in the past two years. I was aware of the completely understandable and natural efforts of your dear wife to prevent my being together with Fräulein Alma – our relationship demanded an explanation. I had many serious talks with the young lady, sometimes of a general nature and sometimes more specific. These talks were conducted in a friendly manner – but never did they border on what coujld be described as the talk of courtship. It was completely clear to us both how the matter stood – 'Just so far and no further.' And that meant taking a step back so that one could not be guilty of behaving wrongly. There was no other way.

Then came that evening in Vienna. There is a bitterness in my nature and this bitterness sometimes manifests itself in a malicious guise that is not completely harmless – and is something I always deeply regret afterwards. Such was the case in this instance. I had drunk too much too quickly – I don't want to use that as an excuse – I was less than usually cautious in what I said – and it is this which you have probably heard about and from which you made your judgement – a judgement which is certainly too severe. Your intervention made us both fully aware that one cannot live life as a dream, but that one must lead one's life with one's eyes open. The situation was clear – there could be no doubt. I am now more ready to accept that the embarrassing interview, as well as the

letter, which would have caused you and me so much pain, was
no longer necessary. Forgive me, dear Moll, if I caused you anxiety
– I beg your dear wife for forgiveness and Fräulein Alma; I don't
think it will be hard for her to forget. We must hope for the quick
passing of time – the great healer.

As I think things over, I fear for myself as I have always done.
My father died from a disorder of the brain, my elder sister has
been deranged for years, perhaps the first signs are visible in me . . .
dear Moll my madness won't be a happy one. Hopefully, it hasn't
come to this yet. I now want to avoid company as I did in the
past. I don't wish to go into society as I cannot trust myself to
behave as I should.

I beg you for friendship. Your punishment is severe – I don't
know if it is necessary – but I am resigned to your judgement –
for you are cleverer than I. I have now made my full confession –
because I value you as a friend, because I want to keep you as a
friend. I have said certain things to you which must remain a secret
between us – and I trust you to keep it. I have written exhaustively
– and would have written more – not to justify my behaviour, or
to clear myself, but only in order to put your mind at rest for the
future. For my part I have shaken hands on and given you my
word on certain assurances and you can count on me. I hope that
the time will come when I will be able to return to your house in
the innocence of former days. It causes me everlasting pain to
think that things have come to this. You needn't worry about my
relation's country seat – I shall try, as far as possible, to avoid
being in the vicinity of Goisern – I myself am going to the country
only for one month at the end of July – I shall let you know where.

With best wishes, Your unhappy friend, Gustav Klimt.[21]

There is no knowing whether Moll showed the whole of this
letter to Alma, but he obviously told her the gist of it, for she
was thrown into a state of despair by Klimt's perfidy. 'Now I
know what life means . . . Betrayal!' she wrote the next day,
underneath a drawing of a black cross. 'Klimt betrayed me – he
indicated that he had acted hastily and by so doing has proved
himself a weakling. Now I know what unhappiness is – he is a
traitor. I cannot write for weeping.'[22]

It was indeed a bitter pill to swallow. Rage at Klimt's duplicity
mingled with humiliation at having her subterfuges uncovered
and discussed behind her back. Her diary was the repository for
much melodramatic breast-beating. 'God in Heaven,' she complained on the same day, 'I went behind my family's back for

him . . . I can't believe it – Klimt, Klimt, what have you done . . . you could never have done it if you'd had any feelings – or if you had remembered the kiss in Genoa!'

In *And the Bridge Is Love* Alma wrote that parental interference in this matter left her 'on the verge of suicide'. Her diary, however, is full of indications to the contrary. Almost immediately after the burning passage quoted above she recorded that Carl Moll came to see her. 'Alma,' he pleaded, 'are you really so upset? It was just a game for you, wasn't it?' She hung her head, and he went on: 'You can still find happiness.' Alma, for her part, maintained that she had been forced to 'think on this matter', and came to the conclusion that Klimt had rendered her powerless – 'he, who had betrayed me.'[23]

Despite these depressing thoughts life went on. Later in the month there was the annual trip to Goisern, where Alma took comfort from the view from her window: 'Had my window open,' she wrote on 30 May, 'and gazed out – how beautiful is nature! The sun shines through the leaves – the little boats bob along on the crest of the waves . . . God in Heaven, there is still happiness . . . nature can still speak to me, in nature there are no lies, as there are in some men's eyes!'[24]

And so, uplifted by the scenery and to some degree purged of self-pity by reliving every moment of her encounters with Klimt in her diary, Alma eventually relented and accorded him the ultimate accolade. 'He reminds me often of Papa,' she wrote on 31 May, 'in his being, in his way of thinking, in his way of speaking and in his noble, genuine artistry.' It was the first step towards resuming her old life. 'Embittered,' she wrote in *And the Bridge Is Love*, 'I took up the threads of life again . . . I began to compose . . . to seek some creative outlet for my grief . . . I lived only for my work, and withdrew from all social activities, though I could have been the queen of every ball I chose.'

This self-imposed dedication to duty had fruitful results. On 3 June she wrote in her diary: 'Composed non-stop. It is a song, that I began yesterday, and which I worked on today. It is not cheerful!'[25] She did not record which, if any, of her published songs this might have turned into. But her 'frenzied tune-smithing' came to the attention of Alexander von Zemlinsky, and his acceptance of her as one of his pupils ensured her a place, at least, in the list of promising musicians who came under his tutelage during the last years of the old century.

4 Music's Command

Zemlinsky first came under scrutiny from his future pupil on the afternoon of Sunday, 11 February 1900, at a Gesellschaft concert, during the last part of which he conducted his choral work *Frühlingsbegräbnis* (*Spring Burial*). The first part of the programme, Bruckner's Mass in D Minor, made little impact on her. 'He is rich in beautiful things, but also rich in distractions . . . and, from a formal point of view, his conclusions irritated me.' The final item evoked a more favourable response – although she found the composer's physical appearance somewhat eccentric. 'Zemlinsky truly original – instrumentation magnificent,' she wrote in her diary, 'but the man himself is as odd as can be – a character, chinless, small, and one of the most *complete* originals.[1]

A fortnight later she was able to observe him at closer quarters. On 26 February she went out to dinner 'with the utmost reluctance' with the art critic Daniel Spitzer, to be rewarded by Zemlinsky's presence among the guests. As a result she enjoyed herself tremendously: 'Spent most of the evening with Alexander von Zemlinsky – the twenty-eight-year-old composer. He was quite something. He is dreadfully ugly. He really has no chin at all – but he still made a delightful impression on me . . .' The impression she made on Zemlinsky is not recorded, but was probably coloured as much by her opening sally as by her looks. 'Do you think', she challenged him, 'that someone as extraordinarily creative as I am could still not have heard your opera?'*

Es war einmal (*Once Upon a Time*), based on a comedy of the same name by H. Drachmanns, had its first performance at the Hofoper on 22 January 1900.

To which he retorted: 'Aha! cool down! – as long as it's in the repertoire you'll have a chance of catching it!'

Banter of this kind, laced with gossip, continued during dinner. Eventually Zemlinsky decided to put his companion to a more serious test. 'Quite calmly,' Alma wrote, 'he asked what stand I took over Wagner. "He was the greatest genius of all time." "And what", he said, "in your view is his best work?" "Tristan" was my answer. He was so delighted with this that he no longer felt the need to test me, and from then on behaved perfectly. So – we understood one another!'[2]

For once Alma was not referring to an emotional but to a musical understanding. Until agreement had been reached over the hotly contested matter of whether Wagner was the greatest genius of all time or merely a musical charlatan to be resisted at all costs, there could be no real harmony between them. Alma herself had long believed the former. 'I love no one so much as Wagner,' she wrote rapturously in her diary in June 1899. 'He is to me the dearest person on earth . . . yesterday I paid homage to my God – I laid white cut roses in front of Wagner's picture . . .' Entry after entry found her playing her hero's works on the piano. He was a particularly potent source of solace after Gustav Klimt's duplicity. 'Evening, 11 o'clock,' she wrote in June 1899, 'played *Tristan* until now – it is the most heavenly work I know,' and, two days later: '*Meistersinger* – Wonderful,' *Parsifal*, too, gave her an opportunity to escape and was, also, a 'heavenly work'.[3]

In July she had an experience of such overpowering magnitude that even her diary could not do it justice. Carl Moll, in Munich for an exhibition of the Secession, sent tickets for his family to join him. They arrived in Munich on 29 July, settled into the Hotel Rheinischer, and at dawn the next day set out for Bayreuth. 'I can still hardly take it in', Alma wrote, 'that I am in Bayreuth . . . Ah, how I long to hear the first note.' She did not have long to wait. 'Today I realized my heart's desire,' she wrote on 1 August, 'to hear the Meistersinger in Bayreuth for the first time. It was utterly fulfilling – so full of the joys of life, so extraordinarily lovely . . . The Meistersinger themselves are so mortally perfect that they became almost divine . . . Life', she added, 'is once more beautiful!'⁴

The beauties of life in Bayreuth were by no means confined to visits to the Villa Wahnfried (where she chastised herself on not feeling enough grief at the sight of Wagner's grave) or to operatic ecstasies. There were brief encounters with Cosima Wagner and her son Siegfried in the hotel restaurant: 'everyone introduced themselves – that was for me the greatest joy . . .' and a satisfactory flirtation with another member of the party, Ernst Kraus. 'I began at once to flirt with Ernst Kraus', Alma recorded, '. . . we entwined ourselves rather furtively – but enthusiasm allows for everything! With continual pauses, he devoured me with his glances . . .' When they all arrived at Goisern on 4 August, to be met by Grandmother Moll, it was an anticlimax: 'the dream disappeared, dreary reality was before us.'

Unlike his volatile neighbour, Zemlinsky had approached Wagner more circumspectly. During his last two years at the Vienna Conservatoire he studied composition technique under the Court Director of Music, Johann Nepomuk Fuchs, whose musical roots were embedded in the classical tradition upheld by Brahms, and who harboured a deep distrust of Wagnerian deviations from the harmonic norm. In consequence, his pupil's early work reflected his master's bias: his first songs were written in the strophic mode (i.e. several verses set to the same music – the form used by Brahms), and the finale of his First Symphony, written in 1892 as a journeyman's piece to mark the culmination of his studies, owed much to Brahms's Fourth Symphony.

Johann Fuchs was not alone in his suspicion of Wagner's musical sleights of hand. The influential music critic Eduard Hanslick, a professor at the University of Vienna, whilst admitting Wagner's stature as a composer, was repelled not only by his heretical disregard for harmonic law but also by the naked assault on all the senses made by his use of plot and spectacle as a means of realizing his conception of a total work of art. He sinned, as far as Hanslick was concerned, in every direction. His harmonies were suspect, his themes dramatic rather than musical, and his musical subject often subordinated to his own libretto.

It was not long, however, before Zemlinsky took a few steps of his own towards harmonic unorthodoxy. His first opera, *Sarema*, written in 1895, contained an unconventional nine-bar cadenza designed to span an harmonic suspension bridge between two opposing musical ideas – Neapolitan and oriental – and in *Es war einmal* his Wagnerian leanings were allowed an even fuller rein (much to Hanslick's disapproval: in a review of the opera he 'deplored the influence of Wagner on young composers who "elaborate modest themes to excess" '[5]).

Zemlinsky was unrepentant. As he wrote in an undated letter to Alma soon after she had become his pupil:

> Wagner's time was nearly always pure allegro or alla breve . . . purely from a musical standpoint, the distribution of tempi, rhythm and motif count above all else . . . To delineate so exactly the deepest motives for mankind's actions! That, in outline, would be my basis for a thorough study of opera, and from my own experience, plus a little bit of talent, I think I have achieved it![6]

The importance of establishing a dominant theme with a distinctive mood had already been pointed out to Alma by her first composition teacher, the blind organist and composer, Joseph Labor. 'In the morning, Labor,' she wrote in her diary on 20 December 1898. 'I played him my piano piece, "Vom Küssen" – he was really pleased – but said that I had loaded too many themes on top of one another. "You would do better to have one theme and bring out more mood." ' And, she added, 'He was right. I'd already had the feeling that something was wrong with the piece, I just didn't know where it lay.'[7]

Labor's lack of sight prohibited any attempts by his pupil to lay siege to his emotions. As a result, their lessons were conducted on strictly professional lines. References to them throughout her diary reflect this matter-of-fact state of affairs, recording Labor's reactions to her work, her pleasure at his praise and her low spirits when he felt she could have done better. 'I played him my new song,' she wrote in December 1898, 'but told him I thought it bad. When I'd finished he said "That isn't as bad as you think – let me have it . . ." He corrected my mistakes and told me to write another one before next time. "Finish them more often." he said, and I was walking on air, I was so pleased.'[8] At her next lesson she found her teacher in an unaccountably bad mood, and she refused to play him her new song. A few days later she was inspired to write another song, 'Are you within?' 'The text', she wrote, 'is sorrowful – as the song is intended for Labor!'

On 7 January 1899 Alma composed 'a little song' ('Ich wandle unter Blumen'), set to a poem by Heinrich Heine: "I wander among flowers/And bloom with them/I wander in a dream/Trembling with every step./Oh, hold me fast, beloved!/Lest drunk with love/I fall at your feet/And the garden is full of people!' 'I've no idea whether it's good,' she wrote. 'I only know that love's passion went into it. That, at least, is in character! It would be most peculiar if Labor did not have a low opinion of it.' Labor, however, when she played it to him three days later, was encouraging. 'There is talent here,' he told her, '. . . it is quite as good as some of the things that will be sung in the Brandt production . . .' Alma was overjoyed: 'He asked me to bring all my songs next time and play them to him . . . my happiness was complete.'[9]

But when a week later Alma returned with the rest of her *Lieder*, he commented: 'That is all very praiseworthy, for a young girl. Yes, it is a young girl's work – we cannot avoid that limitation.' If she felt any pique at these remarks, Alma kept it to herself. The next day she played them through again, with her mother singing, in front of an old family friend, Dr Pollak, and Carl Moll. 'Carl liked them,' she wrote, 'but he would keep suggesting little alterations to each song.' Dr Pollak's reaction was more flattering – he was full of plans for their performance and possible publication. 'It would be nice,' observed Alma of the first idea, 'however, the publication of my songs is of absolutely no concern to me at all.'

In the event, Dr Pollak's schemes to publish these youthful works came to nothing, but 'Ich wandle unter Blumen' survived to appear as the last of five songs selected by Gustav Mahler from his wife's folder and printed by Universal Edition in December 1910. All have hitherto remained undated, but if Alma Mahler's own date for 'Ich wandle unter Blumen' is correct, it seems likely that both this and its predecessor, 'Bei dir ist es traut' ('It's Comfortable with You'), were written before Alexander von Zemlinsky's influence encouraged her to break new musical ground, for their strict tonality, simple melodies and straightforward rhythms provide a complete contrast to the experimental nature of the first three.

Mahler apparently chose the songs partly for their development of a different aspect of a common theme – emotion – and partly for their exploration and exploitation of different compositional techniques. The first, 'Die stille Stadt' (The Silent City'), set to a poem by Richard Dehmel, attempted to create an atmosphere of uncertainty and fear by the use of shifting chromaticisms and play on diminished sevenths within major and minor moods; the second, 'In mein Vaters Garten' ('In My Father's Garden'), a hymn to chivalry and innocent love by Otto Hartleben, concentrated on the juxtaposition of two very different keys, E major and A major, with much play on enharmonic changes; and the third, set to Gustav Falke's exploration of the boundaries of sensual love, 'Laue Sommernacht' ('Mild Summer Night'), introduced a daringly atonal vocal line.

Zemlinsky constantly stressed the need for musical order, something he felt his pupil lacked. In a long letter, he wrote to her:

> Above all, you must have a clear layout, i.e. a proper tonal plan – how far to go with the first theme, how far with the second, etc. Then: we have laid the foundations! . . . Once a scene has been planned, one must be absolutely clear about its dominant musical theme . . . Only then can the real mood – tone, tempo, rhythm, melody, be altered. Mistakes can be made, i.e. by seeming to change the mood with dialogue. But a musician has the ability to approach this dialogue from the most profound level, to extract from the poet's total concept a mood, which can then, regardless of dialogue and with only minor modifications, control the whole scene. Another very important thing: the mood . . . should be instantly recognizable. Then it must be transposed into purely musical terms . . . [10]

Only in 'Laue Sommernacht', however, does Alma Schindler pay real heed to Zemlinsky's advice on the importance of transposing mood into instantly recognizable musical terms. Slow-moving and intense, harmonic movement is kept to a minimum. The accompaniment, built up from regular four-bar phrases stemming from the first four chords, allows the atonal line of the voice to take the dominant role. As the song moves towards its climax, piano and voice alternate in taking the melodic role and the musical texture becomes more complex, resolving itself on an inconclusive, disturbing, dominant seventh.

The first two are less satisfactory. The passionate ramblings of 'Die stille Stadt', redolent of Spanish guitar music, Schumann and Brahms, rely on chromatic shifts for dramatic effect, but have little harmonic value. 'In mein Vaters Garten', the giant of the collection both in size and structure (134 bars spread over nine printed pages), contains one or two descriptive moments – the sound of drums illustrated by staccato chords throbbing over a persistent C natural in the bass; the sun rising on 'my beloved marching into battle' accompanied by ascending thirds over a pedal-sustained bass E – but all too often the musical styles of not only Schumann and Brahms but Debussy, Wagner and Hugo Wolf battle for supremacy amongst a wilderness of carefully contrived harmonic progressions.

The simplicity of the final songs comes, therefore, as a chronological surprise. 'Bei dir ist es traut' rarely strays more than a fourth up or down and its rhythm is based on the beat of a clock. 'Ich wandle unter Blumen' follows an even more straightforward line. Step by step, above a swaying Schubertian accompaniment, the voice climbs to its peak, drops an octave and stays on the same note until the final chord. Not for nothing had Joseph Labor instilled the need for contrapuntal rules in his capricious pupil. If one could not deal comprehensibly with two musical ideas at once, then it was better to stick to one thing at a time.

The day after her first meeting with Zemlinsky, Alma had another session with Labor. Little music was played, but there was much discussion about her evening out. 'I told him everything that the cunning old devil had said,' she wrote in her diary. 'He roared with laughter . . . "Ha, Ha, that really pleases me – to see how the little vixen squirmed!" ' This jibe goaded Alma into action. Sensible of the challenge, she set out to capture Zemlinsky as her teacher. 'I think day and night about one thing . . .' she wrote. 'I would like to learn from Zemlinsky. If only Mama would allow it . . .'[11]

Frau Moll or no, Alma devoted the next few months to stalking her prey. Bumping into Zemlinsky after a concert in March 1900 she told him that he was becoming 'far too attractive to her'. Zemlinsky was sceptical: 'He didn't believe this,' she remarked, and told her that she was only 'playing games'. The game continued apace. She bombarded him with her songs and he admitted that she had talent. He took to calling at the Hohe Warte at all hours and they played duets. They went through the whole of *Tristan and Isolde* together (he at the piano, she singing). One day he failed to turn up as promised. 'Tristan, TRISTAN,' she wrote. 'At the moment I hate Zemlinsky. He didn't come yesterday evening . . . he had spent the whole evening drinking . . . it was not to be borne.'[12]

The year crept on. Commenting on the latest batch of songs, Zemlinsky continued to find 'much talent' but complained about her lack of seriousness. 'I have ideas, and everything else,' she wrote in April, 'but not the seriousness to get down to the foundations.'[13] In an undated but formally addressed letter (indicating that he wrote it before succumbing completely), Zemlinsky pursued his theme:

> Dear and most honoured Fräulein: You take improper liberties! You wish to embarrass me with unprecedented friendship! But I – I refuse to be embarrassed! . . . You are altogether extraordinary – particularly in the way you write – one minute enchantingly polite, the next cold and indifferent; it makes for a few complications, don't you think? Pretty obvious for interested observers. Have you any idea how trivial it can look! The first part of your composition – warm, feminine, sympathetic, and – then the racing, stylized passages! You ought to get Herr Olbrich to sing it at the Gesellschaft, dressed up in a tailcoat with a clown's cap on his

head – put it to him! But please don't let me have anything to do with it!

Also, Lobestanz: Please don't ask my opinion; but I congratulate you on the idea . . . But, enough of old songs . . . I have dealt with all this very clumsily. You must forgive me. Heartfelt greetings from, your obedient Zemlinsky.[14]

Undaunted by these caustic observations (which were in any case soon supplanted by praise and pleasantries), Alma continued her assault. Victory came in June, after she had sent him her photograph. In his letter of thanks Zemlinsky began: 'Your picture is standing on the writing table in front of me – exactly as you knew it would,' and ended by setting her mind at rest. 'By the way, at this point let me reassure you – it will give me great pleasure to come on Wednesday to give you a lesson.' From then on, although she kept up her lessons with Labor, it was Zemlinsky who exerted the main influence over her musical development.

Labor and Zemlinsky had shared a pupil before. During the winter of 1895 Zemlinsky was in charge of an amateur orchestra, 'founded by music-mad students and taking the proud name "Polyhymnia" '. It was small – 'a couple of violins, a viola, a cello and a double bass'. The cellist was a young man distinguished by his energy and his haphazard technique. 'Despite his maltreatment of his instrument,' Zemlinsky wrote, 'which in any case deserved no better, having been bought at a considerable saving for three gulden in a Viennese flea-market,' he was 'on fire with enthusiasm . . . This player was none other than Arnold Schönberg.'[15]

Both Schönberg and Alma wrote warmly of their mentor in later life. Schönberg had already acknowledged his musical debt by dedicating some of his early songs to his 'teacher and friend, Alexander von Zemlinsky', but in his memoirs[16] he went further, thanking him for all his 'knowledge of technique and of the problems of composition'. Alma too wrote warmly of her teacher in her memoirs: 'Zemlinsky was one of the finest musicians. He was a magnificent teacher. He could take a simple little theme, squeeze it dry, and then transform it into countless variations – the fact that he is not a master of our times had to do with his rickety constitution,' she added. 'From such a lowly twig no tall tree can grow . . .'[17] Alma blamed Zemlinsky's physical defects on what she referred to as his 'complicated racial mixture of a Christian father and a Turkish/Jewish mother' – one of her many tasteless anti-Semitic asides.

However, Zemlinsky's unprepossessing gnome-like appearance did nothing to hinder the progress of Alma's Wednesday lessons, which rapidly took a more intimate turn. Week after week of close proximity at the piano stool became too much for both of them and early in July Alma's diary began to reflect the by now familiar palpitations of her ever-susceptible heart. 'I yearn for the touch of his hands, and for his kiss,' she wrote, and 'for his greatness of spirit – dear Alex!'[18]

As for Zemlinsky, he soon became as infatuated as his two predecessors – although, to begin with at least, his passion was mitigated by a desire to improve her work. 'The whole thing lacks a characteristic theme,'[19] he wrote on the subject of a sonata movement she had submitted:

> Both the main subjects as well as the secondary subjects are song themes: they should be strongly contrasting! With what rhythmical motif should one challenge the exposition? Something more powerful! More energetic! Not always murmuring: not always chocolate, candied fruit, white dress at dinner, Queen of Society: that sort of thing produces at best a second subject and a rich bride! A little failure, some ugliness, possibly also sadness in love, everyday worries and strict attention to kindness to others, plus a separate soft-heartedness: now that would be a life-enhancing subject!!

The content of Alma's letters has, unfortunately, to be gleaned from references to them by their recipients. In Zemlinsky's case they provide evidence of her ability to maintain her balance on an emotional tightrope strung between frivolity and seriousness. 'You asked whether I was really so idiotic as to kiss your letter!' he wrote. 'But that very morning, before your enchanting letter came, I kissed another one that I had left lying about, and I asked myself the same question! Now you can laugh! . . . but I thank you from the bottom of my heart for writing back so promptly . . . certainly you can study Bach's Italian Concerto . . .'[20]

Neither was he too besotted to puncture some of her more excessive flights of fancy. 'My Sweet,' began another undated letter:

> you are a sentimentalist! If, without knowing your temperament, I listened to all your gushing critiques of the members of your circle and those with whom you have just become acquainted, i.e. if I didn't deduct 50% from the qualities of those praised, I would be under the impression that you only associated with demi-gods. Siegfrieds are at a premium at the moment! You talk of 'free, great human beings'. Truly great men are solitary creators, and have little time for Society . . . great men, heroes and intellectual giants are sadly lacking in our time, and anyone who thinks otherwise is in danger of creating sham heroes . . . [21]

Nor, indeed, was he prepared to suffer her jibes in silence:

> My dear, you have so often emphasized . . . how laughably small I am and how little I have and how unselfish I have to make myself in order to listen to you! Again and again I hear from you what people are saying: I am horribly ugly, I don't have any money, perhaps not even any talent, and at the very least I am pretty stupid. The result is to stir up my pride. Don't be cross – it is inevitable. It is, I know, extraordinarily unnatural – against all nature – that you should listen to me at all!!! But why? . . . your mother, whom I honour . . . takes my ugliness as it comes . . . I really cannot allow myself to be dragged down to such a level. My pride depends on it . . . [22]

Frau Moll, however, although by now presumably accustomed to her daughter's taste for master-pupil relationships, was, despite her own fondness for him, not keen to see her current dalliance turn into anything more serious. 'Tell me what you think about the coming winter,' wrote Zemlinsky to Alma at St Gilgen in the summer of 1901. 'Will you be able to go on studying with me? Do you think it will work out? I know your mother is dead against it. But in any case you must go on learning. Just at the moment I have no ideas on the subject. Shall I come to St Gilgen for a few days and we can talk it over? Have your mother and Herr Moll any idea that we write to each other? Has no one asked about it? It would be too odd if they had not . . .'[23]

In the event there was no need for Zemlinsky to leave Vienna. Alma's reply, referred to in an undated letter, gave him 'the answer to his question'[24] and Frau Moll also wrote to him, assuring him that, provided he remained 'sensible', the lessons could continue.

Her decision might have been reversed had she been able to dip into the pages of her daughter's diary, which revealed that she was arousing earthier temptations than those she had stirred up in Genoa. Zemlinsky's letters implored her to come and see him alone. 'Tell me why you will not give me more proof of your love,' he wrote, 'you could if you wanted to, if you would come to me alone, all alone. Don't you trust me? . . . are you never able to spend an afternoon in the town, and be with me for an hour, without attracting attention? Surely you can visit people, buy things, etc., or is it prudery? With me in particular?'[25]

Thrust into a turmoil of conflicting emotions that threatened to burst Frau Moll's moral straitjacket open at the seams, Alma wrestled with her conscience. The 'ghastly Turkish parlour', belonging to some friends with whom she was staying, was nearly the scene of her downfall but, as she observed in *And the Bridge Is Love*, she was 'too much of a coward to take the ultimate step'. But on Sunday, 5 October, after Zemlinsky had snatched a fleeting kiss during a moment alone with her, she wrote that she felt 'like a devil', and vowed that she would give him 'everything . . . everything'. Two weeks later, however, the situation was still unresolved, with Alma lying sleepless at night, brooding on its outcome. 'I don't know how it will turn out,' she wrote in her diary on 26 October, 'I lay awake with my eyes open . . . thinking . . . yearning . . . If he were suddenly to appear in front of me at this moment, I know I would not be able to resist him . . .'[26]

This unsatisfactory state of affairs was unwittingly resolved by two friends. Early in November 1901 Alma was asked to dinner by Bertha and Emil Zuckerkandl to meet another musician. In spite of her dislike of his First Symphony, which she had heard him conducting the previous year, she accepted, and on 3 November in the company of two old friends, Max Burckhard and Gustav Klimt, Alma Schindler was introduced to Gustav Mahler.

Recording the events of the evening in her diary, she merely wrote: 'Evening with the Zuckerkandls. Met Mahler. Present: Frau Clemenceau, Burckhard, Spitzer, Mahler, Klimt. I spoke a couple of words to Klimt. I was quite calm. With Mahler, to begin with, nothing.'[27]

Curiously, for his appearance was quite as remarkable as Zemlinsky's, Alma made no reference to Mahler's looks or distinctive mannerisms in any of her subsequent accounts of their first meeting, apart from noting his 'flashing teeth' and abundance of nervous energy. Yet Mahler – at forty-one eleven years older than Zemlinsky – made a strong physical impression on all who met him; not only because his below-average height (he was about 5' 5") and slight frame concealed athletic strengths a more powerful person might envy (he was, according to his adoring friend, the viola player Natalie Bauer-Lechner, an outstanding cyclist, swimmer and mountaineer), or because his high-browed, ascetic, beardless features could become aged or boyish according to his mood, but also because of his habit, when excited in conversation, of grabbing his listener by the lapels and stamping the ground with his feet 'like a wild boar'. And since, as Bertha Zuckerkandl recorded, her dinner party put him in excellent spirits, and he engaged in a more than usually excitable conversation with Alma, both Mahler's youthful appearance and his reactions to lively repartee must have been somewhere in evidence.

An element of the apocryphal, however, surrounds this encounter. Bertha Zuckerkandl apparently hoped it would lead to 'the marriage of two minds' and sent a detailed account of every word the two principal characters addressed to each other throughout the evening in a puzzling letter to her sister Sophie Clemenceau, dated 30 November 1900:*

Dearest, It is three weeks since I have written to you, and first of

*Puzzling because Sophie was the main reason for having the dinner party. Mahler had met her at the Austrian Embassy in Paris the year before, when he was conducting the Philharmonic Orchestra, and they had agreed to meet when she was next in Vienna. One can only conclude, therefore, since the episode took place early in November 1901, that the date in Bertha Zuckerkandl's book was a publisher's mistake.

all I must tell you about Gustav Mahler. Just imagine, he telephoned me himself a few days ago to give me greetings from you.
He also reminded me of an evening he spent with us. The Third
of November. Choosing equally hyper-sensitive guests was no easy
matter – and one most people would have shied away from . . .
well, I arrived at my choice: Hermann Bahr, Max Burckhard and
Gustav Klimt.

No women, only a young girl . . . Alma Schindler, the daughter
of the great painter, Emil Schindler . . . Naturally the menu was
chosen for Mahler, as he only liked light food. He came punctually
at eight o'clock. Much nicer than we had thought! Lively talk then
got under way, with everyone except Alma speculating on the
corrupting effect of patronage in the arts. Eventually she spoke.
'Why', she demanded, 'has the public allowed this to happen?'
Mahler, who so far had not noticed her, answered: 'Such a question
can only be asked by someone young, who knows nothing of
cowardice and compromise.'

Mahler then became distracted by the dessert, and it was not
until coffee in the next room that Alma regained her combative
powers. The subject in question was the score of Zemlinsky's
ballet, *Das Gläserne Herz*, which, Bertha Zuckerkandl reported,
had thrown them both into a rage.

'You have no right', Alma accused Mahler, 'to leave a score
that has been submitted to you lying around for a year – particularly when it comes from a true musician like Zemlinsky. You
could have said "no", but you should have answered.' Mahler
(who forbore to remind Alma of his role in bringing *Es war
einmal* to the stage – something of which his fiery companion
was well aware) defended himself on the grounds that Zemlinsky's ballet was a miserable one, adding: 'I don't understand –
you study music, how on earth can you stand up for that rubbish?'
Hotly denying that it was any such thing, Alma went on to accuse
him of not having gone through it, adding: 'One can be courteous
even if one is dealing with poor music.'[28]

Peace was restored when Mahler, without committing himself,
promised to ask Zemlinsky to come and see him. Alma, Bertha
continued, 'visibly shaken by her temperamental outburst', sought
refuge with Klimt and Burckhard. Mahler, on the other hand,
had enjoyed himself. It was the first time, he told his hostess, that

he had felt comfortable in society. On his way out, he invited her to the dress rehearsal of *The Tales of Hoffmann* at the Opera in two days' time. And, he added, 'if Fräulein Schindler would be interested, it would give me great pleasure if she would come as well.' Well satisfied with the outcome of the evening, Bertha turned to her friend. Pointing to Klimt and Burckhard she said: 'Alma, you can't complain. I have invited your history – the past, the present and the future!'[29]

Alma's discomfiture at her erratic behaviour was probably the reason for her short diary entry that night. With hindsight she remembered things rather differently. In her *Gustav Mahler: Memories and Letters*, begun after the First World War, she wrote:

> Mahler observed me closely, not simply because of my face, which might have been called beautiful in those days, but also because of my piquant air. He studied me long and searchingly through his spectacles. The last guest arrived and we went in to dinner. I was between Klimt and Burckhard, and we three made a merry trio and laughed a lot. Mahler, at the other end of the table, looked on and listened, covertly at first and then without disguise. At last he called out enviously: 'Mayn't we be allowed to share the joke?' His unfortunate neighbour [Sophie Clemenceau] was ignored that evening.[30]

After dinner, she went on, 'there was a discussion on the relativity of beauty. "Beauty," Mahler said, "the head of Socrates is beautiful." I agreed and added that in my eyes Alexander von Zemlinsky . . . was a beauty . . . Mahler shrugged his shoulders. That was going a bit too far, he thought.'

Undeterred, Alma returned to the vexed subject of *Das Gläserne Herz*. Why, she demanded, would Mahler not stage the ballet? Because, he replied, he could not understand it. Alma then offered to explain it to him – but first he would have to unravel the plot of a notoriously incomprehensible ballet by Josef Bayer, *The Bride of Korea*. 'Mahler laughed loudly,' she continued, 'showing all his flashing white teeth. He went on to ask me about my musical studies and I told him I studied composition with

Zemlinsky. He begged me to bring some of my work to the Opera
for him to see.'

Already they had 'drawn apart from the rest . . . There was
that magic circle round us which quickly encloses those who have
found each other.' After she had promised to visit him when she
had 'something good to show him' he 'smiled ironically, as though
to say that he would have a long time to wait, and then invited
me to the dress-rehearsal next morning of *The Tales of Hoffmann*.
Madame Clemenceau and Frau Zuckerkandl came up at that
moment and he invited them also. I hesitated at first: my composition for Zemlinsky was not done yet . . .' She only hesitated for
a moment. 'Then', she wrote, 'my feelings carried me away and
I accepted.'

Before he left Mahler asked her where she lived, and offered
to walk her to the Hohe Warte. She refused, but after he had
gone felt vaguely dissatisfied. 'I had the distinct feeling', she wrote,
'of having put myself in a false light. Owing to my wretched,
inborn shyness I could never be my real self in company and
when I met people for the first time. Either my obstinate silence
was broken by distracted replies, or else, as tonight, I was as bold
as brass and kept nothing back.'[31]

This self-examination was not included in her diary. After
promising to take Mahler some of her work when she had 'something good', she observed that she 'liked him very much –
although [he's] terribly nervous. He moved round the room like
a wild animal. The fellow exists purely on oxygen. One burns
when one comes near him.'[32] As an afterthought she added: 'I
should like to tell Alex about all this.'

But before a fortnight was out, Alma was once more in the
throes of an emotional upheaval, and the business of alerting
Zemlinsky to her condition preyed increasingly on her mind. 'It
is simply dreadful,' she wrote on 20 November, 'I ought to be
ashamed of myself – but *Mahler's* image is alive in me. I will
root out this poisonous weed . . . my poor, poor Alex . . . I could
hate myself!'[33]

Hate herself she might, but none of these enjoyably dramatic protestations could alter the fact that nothing was going to induce her to interfere with the growth of a plant of such luxuriant promise, and none of the rhetorical questions with which she filled her diary was going to divert her from the alluring prospect of captivating the jewel in Vienna's musical crown.

5 The Pleasures of Heaven

At the time of his meeting with Alma, Gustav Mahler was forty-one. It was, however, almost impossible to judge Mahler's age by his face for, as his friend, Natalie Bauer-Lechner, has described, it could seem as 'youthful as a boy's' or 'furrowed and aged far beyond his years', according to mood. When in a rage the two blue veins that ran over his temples bulged alarmingly, his small brown eyes would flash and all his black hair appeared to stand on end. When in a good humour, his hawk-like features were transformed: his skin softened, and the severity of his thin, turned-down mouth, with its habitually scornful expression, vanished completely. Equally deceptive were his less than average height and slight build, which gave an impression of physical frailty when, in fact, the reverse was true. 'Many a more powerfully built person might envy him his extraordinary strength and suppleness,' Natalie wrote, '. . . he shows great skill and stamina in athletics; he's an outstanding swimmer, cyclist and mountaineer . . . and no giant could compare with him in his effortless control of the mightiest pianos.'[1]

In pursuit of his cherished goal to become director of the Court Opera in Vienna, Mahler had also proved himself to be an able politician. His appointment, on 15 April 1897, as second conductor to the ailing incumbent, Wilhelm Jahn, cheated the Viennese public of one of their most cherished pastimes – the opportunity to indulge their appetite for intrigue. So carefully did Mahler plot his move from Germany (where he had been first Kapellmeister at the Hamburg Opera since March 1891) that even the director himself was under the impression that he had consented to the engagement of an assistant for a year, rather than an heir-apparent. The imperial management, however, having been bombarded with favourable recommendations from all sides, took the unprecedented step of ratifying his contract on the same day and, in a matter of months, on 12 October, announced his appointment as artistic director.

The press, too, had little to get their teeth into. The only journalist to be told of the impending overthrow was Ludwig Karpath, music critic of the *Neue Freie Presse*, and according to Mahler's biographer, Kurt Blaukopf, he had been sworn to secrecy: 'No one in Vienna's editorial offices had any idea that the chief conductor at Hamburg was preparing his *coup d'état* against the Vienna Opera. Rational speculation might settle on Felix Mottl at Munich, or Ernst von Schuch at Dresden, or any other man of Court Theatre standing. It simply did not make sense to consider a mere Stadttheater conductor, let alone a Jew.'[2]

At thirty-seven, and with a curriculum vitae that included a year as second conductor at the German Theatre in Prague, two years as second conductor, next to Arthur Nikisch, at the Neues Stadttheater in Leipzig, and two and a half years as director of the Royal Hungarian Opera in Budapest, where his First Symphony was completed and given its first performance, the fact that Mahler was merely a Stadttheater conductor was of secondary importance. Even more extraordinary was the choice of a prominent public servant, over whom even the Emperor had no absolute control, whose origins were not only humble but thoroughly Jewish. For, although Mahler had anticipated and overcome the obstacle of his Jewish faith by converting to Catholicism (his baptism took place in the Kleine Michaelis Kirche, Hamburg, on 23 February 1897), it was not enough to insulate him from sporadic eruptions of anti-Semitic prejudice – outbursts that sprang from a peculiarly Viennese mixture of parochial jealousy, monetary envy and dislike of the unfamiliar.

This form of social assimilation was one way of attempting to resolve the quandary Jews found themselves in after emancipation. In 1867 the constitution technically abolished all disabilit-

ies on the ground of religious differences. In practice, these liberal
sentiments foundered on the rocks of Czech nationalism, Pan-
Germanism, Christian Socialism, Social Democracy and Zionism,
each in their way anti-liberal, separatist movements that left those
Jews who identified with German culture open to attack from
nationalists seeking to delineate the frontiers of their own particular creed. 'As late as the turn of the century,' wrote Kurt Blaukopf,
'a representative of the Young Czechs in the Vienna Parliament
maintained that antisemitic excesses in Moravia were entirely due
to the Jews' identifying with German culture. If the Jews would
change their attitude, the Czechs would leave them in peace.'[3]

Jewish adherence to all things German was also a thorn in the
side of the fanatical German nationalist leader, Georg Ritter von
Schönerer. A second-generation knight (his father had been
ennobled for building the Empress Elizabeth Railway, much of
the money for which had been provided by the House of Rothschild), he had no intention of leaving the Jews in peace, however
much they might modify their attitude. Described by Carl Schorske as 'a curious compound of gangster, philistine, and aristocrat',
Schönerer believed himself to be 'the militant knight-redeemer of
the German Volk', and his determination to re-implant notions
of chivalry amongst those of German blood within the empire
left no room for those whose birth, he considered, barred them
from all knightly virtues. An addendum to the Linz programme
(a policy document drafted in 1882 in conjunction with the Social
Democrats) proclaimed the nationalist faction of the Liberal
party's intention to work 'for the removal of Jewish influence
from all sections of public life'.

Fortunately for the many Jews who were prospering in Vienna
at the time,* Schönerer's extreme views were regarded with a
certain amount of suspicion even within his own party. His efforts
to purge the empire of elements he felt to be alien to its ideals

---

*Although the empire's Jewish population amounted, in 1880, to only 4.33%
of the total, a large proportion gravitated to the capital city. Between 1869
and 1910 the Jewish population of Vienna rose from 40,227 to 175,294 (or
8% of the total inhabitants).

never provided enough inspiration to spark off a mass movement on the scale of Adolf Hitler's (later an ardent admirer), or to a lesser degree of his contemporary Karl Lueger's. In the end, his rantings in the Reichsrat against Jews in general and Jews associated with finance and the press in particular led to his downfall: on 8 March 1888 Schönerer and his band of sympathizers entered the offices of the *Neue Wiener Tagblatt*, where they broke up the printing presses and assaulted the staff – a lapse that cost him his political rights for five years and for which he served a short prison sentence.

Whereas Schönerer's teutomania led to his downfall, Karl Lueger, leader of the Christian Socialist Party and mayor of the city at the time of Mahler's return to Vienna, was a politician of a subtler kind. No less anti-Semitic, he used his striking good looks and acute legal mind (he graduated as a Doctor of Roman and Canon Law before he was twenty-five) as effective weapons in his crusade against what he felt, in the wake of the building of the Ringstrasse, to be a rising tide of Jewish capitalism.

Viennese to his fingertips, Lueger never made the mistake of allowing rhetoric to obscure reason. By combining a spirit of Roman Catholic renewal with a holy war against 'corruption, mismanagement and profiteering in municipal affairs' and against the 'corrupting influence of big business', he managed to enlist the support both of the old Catholic aristocracy – long without a positive political role – and of the many small businessmen and artisans who had felt swamped and aggrieved by the fresh competition threatening their livelihoods.

Unlike Schönerer, too, whose very knighthood had a whiff of the spurious about it, Lueger led a blameless life. His enemies among the press tried in vain to dredge up evidence of moral laxity, private wealth or shady dealings, but found nothing. Personally abstemious, one of his first acts after becoming mayor was to halve his own salary, and any attempts at bribery were scotched by publicly naming those concerned. He dealt equally deftly with his political opponents. To any of his violently anti-Semitic henchmen who might venture to comment on his habit of dining frequently with prominent Jews, his reply was '*Wer ein Jude ist, bestimme ich*' (I decide who is a Jew), and any complaints from his hosts were likely to be met with: 'I am no enemy of our Viennese Jews; they are not so bad and we cannot do without them. My Viennese always want to have a good rest; the Jews are the only ones who always want to be active.'

Lueger's jovial brand of anti-Semitism had, however, much to answer for. By attempting to rationalize the irrational face of racial prejudice he betrayed his Jewish friends and corrupted his Christian followers. Alma herself, catholic in every sense of her upbringing, frequently gave way in her diaries to anti-Semitic outpourings as irrational as any to be found in *Mein Kampf*, but when taken to task in conversation would answer, in effect, that it was she who decided who was Jewish. Zemlinsky, Schönberg and Mahler fell into Alma's highest category of human being – the creative artist – and were thus (despite her mockery of Zemlinsky's wizened looks) allowed to be honorary Gentiles.

In this Alma differed from her musical hero, Wagner, for whom celebration of the spirit of Aryanism was a vital ingredient of the total work of art, and whose persistent antipathy towards all non-Aryans later moved Nietzsche to prophesy that the effects of Wagner's art would 'ultimately pour into that torrent which takes its rise on the other side of the mountains, and which knows how to flow even over the mountains'.

Such was Wagner's stature as a composer that many Jews were prepared to turn a blind eye to his offensive views on their musical abilities (in a polemic written under a pseudonym and published in the *Neue Zeitschrift für Musik* in 1850 he explored the Hebrew taste in aesthetic matters and came to the conclusion that 'Jewish composers debased Western music by contaminating it with the musical traditions of the ghetto'), putting them down to the eccentricities of genius.'Whenever my spirits are low,' Mahler said to Natalie Bauer-Lechner, 'I have only to think of Wagner and my mood improves. How amazing that a light like his ever penetrated the world! What a firebrand! Those who are born after such great spirits as Beethoven and Wagner, have no easy task. For the harvest is already gathered in, and there remain only a few solitary ears of corn to glean!'[4]

Never a regular attender at the synagogue (his father was a freethinker), Mahler appeared to suffer few of the crises of identity that beset so many of his Jewish contemporaries: not for him the self-hatred of Karl Kraus, or Sigmund Freud's renunciation of Germanism. He did, however, share some of the sense of exile common to all Jews born on the other side of the mountain. 'I am thrice without a country,' he once said, 'a Bohemian among Austrians, an Austrian among Germans, and a Jew among all the peoples of the world.'

Soon after his birth, Mahler's parents moved just over the Bohemian border into the German-speaking enclave of Iglau, in Moravia, and it was there that he spent his childhood. His father, Bernhard Mahler, the son of a pedlar, has been variously described as an 'innkeeper', a 'licensed victualler', a 'distiller and baker' and a 'distiller and liquor dealer'.*The Mahler family, understandably wishing to lay a patina of respectability over their famous son's background, always called the business 'the factory'. Mahler himself told his first biographer, Richard Specht, that he thought 'licensed victualler' sounded 'somewhat trivial'. 'Businessman', he felt, put his origins in a more reputable light.

Whatever the exact nature of his occupation, Bernhard Mahler kept up an outwardly respectable front. None of the intoxicating products sold in his tavern were allowed into the family home and, despite the precariousness of his finances, his living-room was well stocked with German books. Relations with his wife, Marie, a girl from 'a good Jewish family' of soap-boilers, whom he had married when she was under twenty, were less harmonious. Lame from birth and with a weak heart, her qualities of gentleness and endurance were not enough to endear her to her husband, who bullied her mercilessly.

Luckily much of this unpleasantness washed over her second

*Kurt Blaukopf refers to his 'small-time brandy distillery' and Henry de la Grange says that 'there was no doubt there was also a liquor store and a tavern'.

son, who, according to Alma Mahler, 'Indoors and out . . . lived in a dream: he dreamed his way through family life and childhood. He saw nothing of the unending tortures his mother had to endure from the brutality of his father, who ran after every servant, domineered over his delicate wife and flogged the children.'[5]

He was also spared much of the latter. Early discovery of his pianistic gifts – at four years old he was found strumming on an old piano in his maternal grandparents' attic – insulated him from the worst of his father's rages. His son's aptitude for the piano was balm to Bernhard Mahler's wounded social sensibilities: at last he could be on a cultural, if not a financial, par with his prosperous in-laws. He decided to buy a piano, engage a teacher and turn Gustav into a professional musician.

'From my fourth year I have always made music,' Mahler said. 'I was composing long before I could play scales.'[6] Nothing survives of his youthful compositions, but there is ample evidence of his startling prowess on the piano. He quickly outgrew his first teacher, a double bass player in the local band, and progressed to another, a violinist called Bosch. At ten he made his début as a recitalist in the Iglau theatre, moving a local paper to comment respectfully on the achievements of 'the future piano virtuoso'.

Except for an unhappy interlude in Prague in the autumn of 1871, where he had been sent to lodge with the Grunfeld family, Gustav stayed in Iglau until 1875. Then, through the intervention of another music-lover, Gustav Schwarz, the manager of a neighbouring estate, his father was persuaded to allow him to go to Vienna, and on 20 September, at the age of fifteen, he enrolled at the Conservatoire.

Images of his childhood stayed with Mahler throughout his life. Memories of his quiet, submissive mother, his violent father and the death from pericarditis, in the spring of 1874, of his thirteen-year-old brother Ernst, never left him: the fact that these aberrations could occur in the midst of the idyllic Bohemian countryside seemed particularly shocking, and did much to heighten his sense of the transitory nature of beauty and the ultimate frailty of human emotions. 'How dark is the foundation upon which our life rests?' he once reflected. 'Whence do we come? Whither does our road take us? . . . What is the object of our toil and sorrow? How am I to understand the cruelty and malice in the creations of a kind God? Will the meaning of life finally be revealed by death?'[7]

To help him find answers to these melancholy questions Mahler turned to Schopenhauer and Nietzsche. Neither offered a satisfactory explanation: the former's pessimistic view of mankind's inability to prise itself free from the grip of circumstances beyond its control and the latter's denial of the existence of God offered little consolation to those in search of spiritual sustenance.

Musical sustenance at the Conservatoire was provided by Mahler's piano teacher, Julius Epstein, Robert Fuchs, who taught him harmony, and Franz Krenn, under whose direction he perfected his composition and counterpoint. Earthly sustenance was catered for by various sympathetic landladies, prepared, as Kurt Blaukopf observed, to put up with the loud music played by their youthful lodgers: 'When [Rudolf] Krzyzanowski, [Hugo] Wolf and Mahler got hold of a Wagner vocal score and roared out the parts of Gunther, Brünnhilde and Hagen at the tops of their voices, a furious landlady was only too likely to throw the whole Götterdämmerung crew out, bag and baggage, without benefit of notice.'[8]

In 1878 Mahler justified Gustav Schwarz's faith in him by winning first prize in the Conservatoire composition contest with a piano quintet, written at the last minute as a substitute for his original entry, a symphony which was spurned by the principal on the grounds that it contained copying errors. 'Since he could not pay a copyist,' wrote Natalie Bauer-Lechner, who witnessed the scene, 'he had worked for days and nights copying the parts for all the instruments and, here and there, some mistakes had crept in. Hellmesberger became furious, flung down the score at Mahler's feet, and cried out in his peevish way: "Your parts are full of mistakes; do you think that I'll conduct something like that?" ' As Mahler said to his friend later, it was an ill wind. 'Since it was a much weaker and more superficial work, it won a prize, while my good things were all rejected by the worthy judges.'[9]

Had Alma Schindler been able to fully comprehend her future husband's compositions at the time of their courtship, she might have found less difficulty in adjusting to her early married life. For among these deeply subjective works lay clues to the nature of their creator. 'My whole life is contained in them,' Mahler wrote of his first two symphonies. 'I have set down in them my experience and suffering . . . to anyone who knows how to listen, my whole life will become clear, for my creative works and my existence are so closely interwoven that, if my life flowed as peacefully as a stream through a meadow, I believe I would no longer be able to compose anything.'

Leonard Bernstein dwelt heavily on the Jewish element in Mahler's music. Within it he claimed to have spotted evidence of Jewish symbolism, Jewish tensions and rabbinical themes; references to the Jewish Cross and to the Day of Atonement (he described the final movement of the Third Symphony as 'one long day of atonement'); signs of shame at being Jewish and (after Mahler's conversion to Catholicism) signs of guilt at his defection from the faith of his forefathers.

It would have been strange, as Kurt Blaukopf has pointed out, if there had been no trace of the Jewish musical tradition in Mahler's music: as odd as if there had been no trace of any of the other multiple national influences brought to bear on late nineteenth-century Austrian composers. But to pigeonhole Mahler as a 'Jewish' composer not only isolates him from his Austrian musical heritage but misunderstands both Mahler himself and the well-spring of his creative life. The conflicts that beset him were ones familiar to all currently wrestling with the nature of man and his place in the universe. Mahler's religious impulses sprang from German Romantic soil, nourished by a diet of Catholic mysticism, metaphysical speculation and panpsychism, overshadowed by a cloud of *Weltschmerz*.

'The greatest intensity of the most joyful vitality and the most consuming yearning for death dominate my heart in turn,' he wrote to the Austrian lawyer Josef Steiner in June 1879, and went on:

> One thing I know: I can't go on like this much longer ... Wildly I wrench at the bonds that chain me to the loathsome, insipid swamp of this life, and with all the strength of despair I cling to sorrow, my only consolation. – Then all at once the sun smiles upon me – and gone is the ice that encased my heart, again I see the blue sky and the flowers swaying in the wind, and my mocking laughter dissolves in tears of love.... Oh, would that some god might tear the veil from my eyes, that my clear gaze might penetrate to the marrow of the earth! Oh, that I might behold this earth in its nakedness, lying there without adornment or embellishment before its Creator; then I would step forth and face its genius ...
> 10

Translated into musical terms, these inspirational feelings were transformed into themes of awesome magnitude, demanding nothing less from those prepared to listen than that they should face up to their own mortality in the sight of an unpredictable and fearsome God. 'We are confronted once more with terrifying questions,' Mahler wrote of the fifth movement of his Second Symphony. 'A voice is heard crying aloud: "The end of all living things is come – the Last Judgement is at hand" ... The earth quakes, the graves burst open, the dead arise and stream on in endless procession. The great and little ones of the earth – kings and beggars, righteous and godless – all press on; the cry for mercy and forgiveness strikes fearfully in our ears ...'[11]

Mahler disliked programmatic explanations of his works, feeling that they should stand on their own as pure music. But by inserting allusions to the external world – birdsong, military marches (from a neighbouring barracks at Iglau), bugle fanfares, bells tolling, extracts from popular music – into themes that explored an interior world he forced his listeners to confront the relationship between the two. For one who before his marriage had little interest in the visual arts – on a trip to Florence, Bologna and Milan with his sister Justine in 1890, he wrote to the archaeologist Friedrich Löhr that 'the weather and things in general have turned out very well', but made no mention of visiting a single art collection – Mahler's approach to creating music representative of the whole of life was surprisingly pictorial. Without degenerating into a genre he detested, the tone-poem, he built up structures of musical sound that often contained impressionistic elements more in tune with Debussy than with Wagner or with his mentor at the Conservatoire, Anton Bruckner.

Neither Debussy nor Mahler would have been pleased by this analogy: at a performance of Mahler's Second Symphony in Paris in 1910, Debussy, Dukas and Pierné left in the middle of the second movement, saying afterwards 'that it was too Schubertian for them, and even Schubert they found too foreign, too Viennese, too Slav'. And, in a radio interview with Berndt W. Wessling in 1962, Alma Mahler claimed that it was Bruckner's 'immense religiousness' that fascinated her husband. 'That was exactly what lay behind Gustav Mahler's motivation – unbounded spirituality. And it was that that separated him from his contemporaries, from Richard Strauss, from the French . . . Sentimentality can never be a substitute for real feelings. Mahler's music has a spiritual self-discipline never seen before. Musical forms were destroyed, not merely from destructive pleasure, but to find a new sense of direction, and to build up something fresh . . . within the bounds of legitimate aesthetics – something hitherto unknown to nineteenth-century composers.'

At the time of their first meeting, however, Alma Schindler was more interested in her future husband's public role as a conductor and in the speculation surrounding his private life than in his music. 'I knew him well by sight', she wrote in her *Gustav Mahler: Memories and Letters*; 'he was a small fidgety man with a fine head. I was acquainted, also, with the scandals about him and every young woman who aspired to sing in opera. I had been to the concert when he conducted his First Symphony [18 November 1900], a work I had thoroughly disliked and even angrily rejected. At the same time, he was of importance to me as a conductor and I was conscious of his mysterious and powerful fascination . . .'[12]

Mahler's gifts as a conductor had been recognized from the outset. Neither the oddity of his unkempt appearance, the idiosyncrasies of his eating habits (he became both vegetarian and teetotal for a time in 1879), nor his habit of stamping his right foot when walking along, blinded his first employers in Laibach and subsequently in Olmutz* to the prodigious energy and talent of their young conductor. Soloists, choruses and orchestral players alike might groan under the weight of what they considered to be endless, unreasonable demands made on them by a fanatical zealot whose aims were nothing less than to take on the mantle of each and every composer in the repertoire, but there was no doubt that he produced results. 'Between 11 January and 17 March 1883', wrote Kurt Blaukopf, 'Mahler directed twelve opera performances – among them Bizet's *Carmen* – and two repeats . . . This artistic achievement on the part of a man not yet twenty-two [*sic*] cannot . . . be dismissed as one of the many legends that have sprung up about Mahler.'[13]

A year later he was in Kassel, followed by periods in Prague and Leipzig. His friend, the musicologist Guido Adler, then a Professor at the German University in Prague, wrote that he directed:

> operas by Weber, Marschner, Meyerbeer, Cherubini, Mozart, Beethoven, Wagner, Gluck . . . and even Mozart and Wagner cycles. . . . He prepared fresh productions of the most difficult works and as a concert conductor even undertook the Ninth Symphony of Beethoven . . . He created such a deep impression with this performance in Prague . . . that at the instigation of the pathologist Philipp Knoll, a political leader of the Germans in Bohemia, an address was presented to him by the academic community, with the participation of other circles of society . . . [14]

Adler also recorded the highlights of his friend's time as director of the Hungarian Opera in Budapest. Although he only served three years of a ten-year contract, at the end of which he was paid a 25,000 gulden indemnity, Mahler managed to achieve the near-impossible feat of pruning the deadwood common to most German and Austro-Hungarian opera houses: i.e. cutting down to ensemble size conceited guest soloists accustomed in the past to quelling musical directors with a single imperious glance. To

*Now respectively Ljubljana, in Yugoslavia, and Olomouc, in Czechoslovakia.

their chagrin many stars found they had been replaced by singers from within the company, and, even more startling, saw libretti of established favourites translated into Hungarian. The first Brünnhilde to sing in Hungarian was Mme Arabella Szilágyi, 'a member of the ensemble who had received scant attention until now'.[15]

As he himself spoke only a smattering of Hungarian, Mahler began to regret these concessions to nationalist culture. 'No one appreciated the sacrifice Mahler was making,' wrote Kurt Blaukopf, 'or that the "Magyarization" he pursued with such moral conviction was in fact a torture to him. "If only I could hear a word sung in German again!" His longing for this was "almost unbearable".'[16]

He had his reward on 16 December 1890, when Brahms, visiting Budapest, attended, much against his will, a performance of *Don Giovanni*. 'In front of the theatre,' recorded Guido Adler, 'Brahms said: "No one does *Don Giovanni* the way I like it. If I wish to enjoy it, I lie down on the sofa and read the score." ' Mahler's interpretation apparently converted him. Adler continued: 'During the performance: "Excellent! Splendid! Magnificent! Yes, that's it, finally. What a devil of a fellow!" . . . How often during Mahler's subsequent activity in Hamburg and Vienna were artists and friends of art, with an appreciation similar to, or the same as, that of Brahms, able to experience such efficacy! But the avowal of such enthusiasm is to be expected only from those who are unprejudiced and devoid of hate or envy!'[17]

Envy, prejudice and gossip were familiar bedfellows to any new incumbent of an opera house, but in Vienna, where the rewards were higher than anywhere else in the German-speaking world, they were not adversaries to be taken lightly. Toppling the two most powerful figures in Viennese artistic life, the director of the Opera and the director of the Burgtheater, was a national sport engaged in with gusto by all those to whom creative originality was a threat, and interfering with tradition tantamount to a crime against the state.

During his first four years as director of the Opera and his three years as conductor of the Vienna Philharmonic (1898–1901) Mahler's quest for artistic purity attracted more opprobrium than praise. His replacement of older singers by a succession of new young faces, his insistence on singers curbing any histrionic tendencies to dwell on top notes a moment longer than indicated in the score, his 're-interpretation' of some of Beethoven's works in the interests of 'authentic' sound, his restoration of Wagner's operas to their full length, his prohibition of latecomers to performances – all these changes unsettled musicians, critics and audiences alike.

Bruno Walter, arriving in Vienna in 1901 to take up a post as assistant conductor, found himself thrown in at the deep end of these currents of hostility. 'At that time,' he wrote in his autobiography, *Theme and Variations*, 'the fourth year of Mahler's directorial activity, his relentless opponents had closed their ranks firmly. It must be admitted that Mahler's violent actions, his peremptory manner in questions of art, his engagements and dismissals, and his fight against tradition and time-honoured customs had helped to swell the ranks of his enemies among the artistic personnel, especially among members of the orchestra, but also among the theatre's officials, the public and the press. But', he added, 'even if he had been innocent of any tangible offence, the very fact of his positive creative existence would have been an insult to the Philistines and a challenge to the *internationale* of the negatively inclined, abundantly represented in Austria. For the rich flowering of culture had its counterpart in a violent oppositional current.'[18]

Others were more appreciative. Habitués of what Bruno Walter referred to as the Fourth Gallery – equivalent to the Gods at Covent Garden – were 'attracted by the fiery impetuosity of [Mahler's] character, by his courage, and even by his extravagances'. And the 'old aristocratic public, the patrician middle classes, and, generally, all those to whom Austria owed her fame as a land of music . . . saw in Mahler the musician destined to continue and revitalize the exalted tradition of Viennese cultivation of music.' As Bertha Zuckerkandl wrote later:

> For ten years Gustav Mahler had stood against routine . . . nepotism, laxity, intrigue and stupidity. In ten years he revitalized the opera. Not merely the Viennese opera, but opera as an art form. His operatic style was the answer to decades of empty aria-singing. In Vienna bel canto ruled unrestrained. . . . Mahler's dynamism, and his daemonic nature put one in mind of a character from E.T.A. Hoffmann. The impression he made was of having a deep-down longing to revive artistic integrity, and to shake up singers, orchestra leaders and public alike . . .
>
> Vienna was split into two camps. It is impossible to imagine nowadays, when artistic issues are no longer capable of arousing passionate controversy, with what fanaticism pro and anti Mahler factions fought one another. The intellectual minority that stuck to Mahler through thick and thin tried to drag down the solid majority of 'Niggerltums'* . . .
>
> But this extraordinary man, who along his hard road to aestheticism had lost his feeling for god-given pleasures, found, like so many other musicians, deliverance in Vienna. He was captivated by the landscape, the city, and the beauties of Beethoven and Schubert.

And, Frau Zuckerkandl concluded with some satisfaction, 'a wonderful Viennese girl brought this about'.[19]

Alma, however, was soon on the horns of a dilemma. The visit to the Opera arranged at their first meeting took place as planned on 10 November 1901. But whereas Madame Clemenceau and Frau Zuckerkandl remained oblivious to the undercurrents of emotion ebbing and flowing all around them, Alma's sharply attuned antennae picked them up at once. 'My two companions began a conversation, apparently unaware of the tensely emotional atmosphere of the room,' she wrote. 'I went to the piano and turned the pages of the music I found there. I was not in a state to join in the commonplaces of conversation. Mahler stole glances at me, but I was in a malicious mood and would not help him out. I was in all the glory of untrammelled youth

---

* ' "Niggerl" ', Bertha Zuckerkandl explained, 'is an untranslatable word. It describes a type of reactionary, determined, malicious, pseudo-genial, treacherous Viennese.' 'Niggerltums', equally untranslatable, appears to refer to the whole class of such people.

and not to be imposed upon by fame or position. The one thing that might have humbled me, his inner significance, was at that time almost hidden from me.'[20]

After the dress rehearsal, which impressed her deeply, Alma went home 'overawed', but feeling that her work for Zemlinsky still came first. The next day she received an anonymous poem. Frau Moll (whose antennae were equally sharp) asked her who she thought it was from. 'I said it could only be from Mahler, but she replied that I need not imagine that a man like Mahler would write verses to a raw girl and laughed at me. Somebody must have been playing a joke on me, she said.'[21]

Nevertheless, instinct told her that the poem had been written by Mahler. This sign of admiration posed something of a problem. Although 'loving him not yet', even as accomplished an amatory illusionist as Alma was aware that it obliged her to choose between a man whose creative abilities were, as far as she was concerned, as yet an unknown quantity but whose worldly achievements were proven, and a man whose creative abilities were, in her opinion, enormous but whose worldly achievements were, by comparison, few. Even she could not have both at the same time.

A fortnight later Alma and her mother went to a performance of Gluck's *Orpheus and Eurydice*. During the interval Mahler appeared in the foyer 'as though conjured up from the floor' and asked to be introduced to Frau Moll, with whom he struck up an instant rapport. They all went up to his private room to continue their conversation, and before they left Mahler agreed to visit them at the Hohe Warte the following Saturday. On their way out Alma, who had remained silent, countered with a characteristic display of verbal pyrotechnics. 'I said I should like to be engaged as a conductor at the Opera and he promised in all seriousness to let me try my hand: it would give him at least great pleasure. I replied that that was not enough: his verdict would not, I thought, be impartial. To which he replied: "No verdict is ever impartial." ' With this mutually satisfactory exchange they parted, 'feeling that something great and beautiful' had come into their lives.

This agreeable atmosphere was punctured by Carl Moll and Max Burckhard, with whom they went on to have supper. Moll (possibly with memories of Klimt fresh in his mind) was 'furious' with his wife for taking 'an innocent girl, your own daughter, into the private room of a roué like him'; and Burckhard, who had apparently been quizzed about Alma by Mahler after the Zuckerkandls' party and had rebuffed him, took it upon himself to cure his former protégée 'of what he clearly saw to be a rising fever'. In words that would have done justice to Georg von Schönerer he implored her, a girl of 'good pedigree', not to throw herself away on a 'dirty Jew', adding: 'Think of your children – it'd be a sin! Besides, fire and water, that's all right. But fire and fire, that's all wrong. It would be for you to give way, not him. And you're too good for that.'[22]

Needless to say, their exhortations fell on deaf ears. Later in life Alma Mahler maintained the right to be as outspokenly anti-Semitic as the mood took her, on the grounds that she had had two Jewish husbands. As for Mahler's reputation as a rake, it was unlikely to deter someone as compelling as Alma.

In fact, despite rumours to the contrary, Mahler, at forty-one, had had comparatively few serious liaisons. His deepest emotions were probably contained in the protective love he felt for his delicate mother – feelings that spilled over after her death in 1889 onto his two younger sisters, Justine and Emma, and his sixteen-year-old brother Otto, for all of whom he made himself financially responsible. Justine, the elder, had nursed her mother throughout her last illness, and Mahler felt a particular bond with her on this account. Although, until he met his future wife, the intensity of these private feelings exceeded those aroused by other women, Mahler was far from having been immune to romantic love: at nineteen he fell in love with Josephine Poisl, the daughter of an Iglau postmaster, an attachment that bore creative fruit – he dedicated three songs to her and wrote the first version of *Das klagende Lied* (*The Song of Lament*), described by the composer as a 'fairy-tale for chorus, soloists and orchestra'. At twenty-three, in Kassel, he developed a passion for a young actress, Johanna Richter, a relationship that ended when he went to Prague, but which again influenced his musical life. He wrote to his friend Friedrich Löhr on 1 January 1885:

> Yesterday evening I was alone with her, both of us awaiting the new year's arrival almost without exchanging a word. Her thoughts were not bent on the present, and when the bell chimed and tears gushed from her eyes, it overwhelmed me. . . . Ah, dear Fritz – it was all as though the great director of the universe had meant to stage manage it perfectly. I wept all through the night in my dreams.
>
> . . . I have written a cycle of songs,* six of them so far, all dedicated to her. She does not know them. What can they tell her but what she knows. I shall send with this the concluding song, although the inadequate words cannot render even a small part. The idea of the songs as a whole is that a wayfaring man, who has been stricken by fate, now sets forth into the world, travelling wherever his road may lead him.[23]

Mahler's road led to Leipzig, and there he fell in love again – this time with Frau von Weber, wife of the composer's grandson, in whose house he was editing Carl Maria von Weber's unfinished opera, *Die drei Pintos*. Once again, his romantic feelings found a musical outlet: 'I must write you a few lines,' he wrote to Friedrich Löhr on 4 January 1888. 'It is all I can manage now in this trilogy of the passions and whirlwind of life! Everything in me and around me is in a state of becoming! Nothing is! Let me have just a little longer to see it through! Then you shall hear all!'[24] 'The reader may surmise a love story behind these words,' Kurt Blaukopf remarked. 'But it was more than that, it was a very epic of love. Mahler had succumbed to the symphony.'[25]

Frau von Weber remained with her husband (possibly, as Henri Louis de la Grange has suggested, to Mahler's slight relief). He was therefore able to devote himself to the completion of his First Symphony – which, as he said later, 'had been inspired by a passionate love' – and to begin work on the first movement of

---

*Lieder eines fahrenden Gessellen (Songs of a Wayfarer).

the Second, which he finished six years later in the summer of 1894.

The completion of the Third Symphony in August 1896 again coincided with an affair of the heart. The object of his affections was Anna von Mildenburg, a gifted soprano who had joined the Hamburg Stadttheater in 1895, at the age of twenty-three. 'From the moment Anna von Mildenburg entered Mahler's life,' wrote Kurt Blaukopf, 'his struggle for recognition as a composer gained a new impetus. She was, so far as we can tell, the first woman he considered his intellectual equal. . . . At last he could tell all that he had expressed in conversations with Foerster and Behn . . . to a sympathetic woman whom he doubtless loved with his whole heart. . . . By December 1895 the formal *sie* had given way to the familiar *du*.'[26]

But, as Alma was soon to find out, Mahler's creative birthpangs detached him body and soul from any human being craving his undivided attention. 'I have written to you that I am engaged on a great work,' he wrote to Anna von Mildenburg from Steinbach am Attersee in July 1896. 'Don't you see how that claims one completely, and how one is often so engrossed in it that one is virtually dead to anything else? . . . if you have any understanding of me, you must accept it. You see, everyone who was going to live with me has had to learn this. At such moments I do not belong to myself . . .'[27]

Unlike Alma, Anna von Mildenburg was not prepared to abnegate her artistic life in order that Mahler should have untroubled summers writing music, and a smooth-running household for the rest of the year whilst he devoted himself to his career as a conductor. That role, so far, had been filled by Justine, and it was to Justine that Mahler thankfully turned when Anna's demands for attention became too exigent. Equally devoted, his sister jealously guarded her brother's creative interests. For him, she and Emma immersed themselves first in the writings of Nietzsche and then the novels of Dostoevsky, of whom Mahler was a devoted disciple. For him she created a congenial atmosphere for his friends from the days of the Conservatoire: Guido Adler,

Hugo Wolf, Friedrich Löhr, Siegfried Lipiner and Albert and Nina Spiegler. It was she who was the buffer between Mahler and the outside world. She was a formidable ally, and, for those who sought to encroach on her territory, a formidable obstacle.

By 1901 passions on both sides had long since cooled. Mahler, as he had done in the past, made his move to Vienna an excuse for distancing himself from the affair and, after Anna's engagement by the Court Opera in February 1898, countered any hints of favouritism by treating her as the 'dear old friend' she eventually became.

It was all the more extraordinary that, having escaped a mismatch with one prima donna, Mahler should have plunged headlong into a match with another, and having done so should throw all caution to the winds. For this time, although he felt it necessary to warn Alma of the implications of a union with a man of his artistic temperament, there was no question of a long-standing liaison in deference to Justine's feelings: at their fourth meeting on Thursday, 27 November 1901, Mahler made up his mind that they would be married.

Alma remembered the day clearly. 'On Thursday afternoon, just as I was working out figured basses under Robert Gounod's eye . . . the servant burst into the room. "Gustav Mahler is here!" He was a celebrity even in the servants' hall. And that was the end of counterpoint for ever and a day.'[28]

To begin with Mahler inspected her books. 'We had just moved into a new house and my books were still waiting to be installed. . . . Mahler walked to and fro, inspecting them. My taste appeared to please him, except for a complete edition of Nietzsche, at which his eyebrows went up in horror . . .' Demands that they should be thrown there and then on the fire (by then Mahler had fallen out with the philosophical idol of his youth) met with spirited resistance. 'I refused and said that if his abhorrence had any justification it would be easy enough to convince me; and it would be more to his glory if Nietzsche stayed where he was and I refrained from reading him than if I consigned him to the flames and yet yearned for him ever after.'[29]

To calm themselves they went for a walk. On their way out they met Frau Moll, who persuaded Mahler to stay to dinner. He accepted, and whilst they were out took the unprecedented step of telephoning Justine to tell her, without explanation, that he would be away all evening. On the way back to the Hohe Warte he said suddenly: 'It's not so simple to marry a person like me. I am free and must be free. I cannot be bound, or tied to one spot. My job at the Opera is simply from one day to the next.' Alma, for once overtaken by events over which she had little control, could only counter: 'Of course. Don't forget that I am the child of artists and have always lived among artists and, also, I'm one myself. What you say seems to be obvious.' Oblivious to the tartness in this reply, Mahler seemed reassured. 'We went by tacit agreement straight up to my room. There he kissed me and went on to talk of a speedy marriage. . . . Those few words on the way up seemed to him to have settled everything.'[30]

The rest of the evening was full of enchantment and elemental undercurrents. By the end of it Alma, at first put out by Mahler's assumption that she would agree to his proposal, had been completely won over. After a lively discussion about Schiller (of whom Mahler was fond and Alma, then, was not), she concluded that 'he knew him almost by heart and there was such a fascination in the way he rose up in his defence that I, after letting him kiss me without really wishing it, and speed on the wedding before I had even thought of it myself, knew now that in both he was right and that I could no longer live without him. I felt that he alone could give my life meaning and that he was far and way above any man I had ever known.'[31]

Unknown to Mahler, however, the spectre of Zemlinsky continued to haunt his future bride, who could not bring herself to tell either of her suitors of the existence of the other. '*Mahler* came,' she wrote in her diary on 27 November, ' – he told me how much he likes me . . . we talked of many things – but not everything . . . a hand lay over us – Alex . . . he knows nothing.'[32]

The unsuspecting Zemlinsky was left in ignorance of his fate for a few weeks. In the meantime Alma chronicled the progress of her emotional ups and downs in her diary. 'Alex was slightly annoyed with me,' she remarked on 28 November after they had played through some songs Mahler had sent round, 'otherwise as dear as ever. I felt – *there* I belong'; and 'Mahler, Mahler,' she began on 2 December, ' – he told me that he loved me – we kissed, he played me his things . . . by degrees I must escape from Alex – I am so terribly sorry – if only all this had never happened – I would have been engaged today – as it is I couldn't respond to his caresses – someone stood between us – I told him so without mentioning any names – I *had* to tell him.'[33]

Things built up to a crescendo the following day when Alma unleashed a torrent of doubts:

> I am in a dreadful dilemma. When I'm alone I say to myself – my beloved – and afterwards I always say Alex – *Can* I love Mahler as he deserves and as much as I should? Will I ever understand his art, and he mine? With Alex these things are taken for granted. . . . Mahler only said: That is something to take into account – and I hadn't expected that! . . . How on earth can I tell Alex about all this? . . . He [Mahler] told me how much he loves me – and I could not answer him. Do I really love him? I have no idea. Sometimes, I think, simply, no. So *many things* annoy me – his *smell* – *his way of singing – something in the way he speaks!* . . . He is a stranger to me – we have different tastes – he said: Alma, think things over very carefully. If at any time you feel disappointed, tell me. Today I could face up to it – even though it would be difficult – in four months' time, possibly not.
>
> And I don't know . . . whether I love him or not – whether it's the Director – the great conductor – or the man . . . And his art, that is so far out of my reach – so terribly far. I don't believe in him as a composer . . . he is closer to me from afar than when he's with me. And what if I say no? All my lifelong dreams will vanish! . . . *What shall I do?*

On a practical note, she concluded: 'And what if Alex becomes great. . . . I have written to him – I have no idea what is going on inside me – one thing torments me – will Mahler encourage me in my work, and will he take an interest in my art – will he love it, like Alex . . .'[34]

Some of these doubts were dispelled within the next few days. On 4 December Mahler enclosed tickets for *Les Contes d'Hoffmann* in a letter reminding her that he would be leaving for a ten-day trip to Berlin on the following Monday. 'So I can neither conduct *Tristan* on Tuesday nor pay you the now so dearly loved visit on Monday . . .' he wrote. 'I feel very sad and fear that the battle I fought yesterday against the clay idols of the house was fought quite in vain . . .' Between acts Mahler threw loving glances at Alma – gestures which sent her to her diary that evening bent on seeing him before his departure: 'God! If he doesn't come to us again before he leaves I will go to him'.[35]

This, as it turned out, was unnecessary. 'Gustav came,' Alma wrote on Saturday, 7 December. 'We kissed over and over again – I have a warm feeling in my breast – if only he will go on loving me – but he is moody – terribly moody – he wants to convert me to his ways . . . I don't know what else to write – but my heart is *for him* and *against Alex*. . . . He told me all his faults today and I some of mine. He guessed Alexeus's name and was *appalled* – he couldn't grasp it . . .'[36]

The following day Mahler sent her *Das klagende Lied*. 'Dearest Almschi,' he wrote. 'Here is a fairy-tale belonging to my youthful days. You were a true joy to me yesterday. You listened as charmingly and answered so charmingly too. What a pity that such an afternoon should be so short – and the coda at night almost sad. – Today brings me the evening when we shall be in the deepest sense at one – I shall think of you in every beat, and conduct for you. It shall be as it was yesterday at the piano when I spoke to you so gladly and from my heart . . .'[37]

By the time she had read the score of *Das klagende Lied* and heard the performance of *The Magic Flute* which Mahler had privately dedicated to her, Alma was sure both of Mahler's creative talents and of her feelings for him: 'This afternoon *he* sent me *Das klagende Lied* – form excellent – melodies a little poor, but the theme good and effective. . . . In the evening, the Opera! *Zauberflöte* – divinely performed. For the very first time I saw the stature and beauty of this work – then I looked at Gustav and smiled blissfully at him . . . my dearest Gustav, think, think of me!!'[38]

All that was left was to sweep away the last remaining obstacles to the public announcement of their engagement. Justine proved to be less of an impediment than Mahler feared. It turned out that she had been in love with the leader of the Vienna Philharmonic, Arnold Rosé, for some time, and had kept it a secret from her brother for much the same reasons that had deterred him from confiding in her. When, on the evening of Sunday, 8 December, he finally confronted her with his plans, she was sympathetic. Only later, when rumours of her future sister-in-law's boundless capacity for conquest came to her ears, did she hesitate.

Understandably, Zemlinsky took a less sanguine view. Alma's letter, which she wrote on 12 December, begged him to forgive her, to answer her, and to come and see her:

> These last weeks have been martyrdom for me. You know how much I loved you – you fulfilled me completely – but this love is now over as suddenly as it came. It has been replaced – with renewed strength -! I beg you on my knees to forgive me for the misery I've caused you. There are some things that lie beyond our control – perhaps you can explain. You – you, who know me better than I know myself! I shall never forget the blissful hours I had because of you – don't you forget them either! Just one more thing: Don't desert me completely! If you're the man I think you are, come on Monday – give me your hand and the first kiss of friendship. Be kind, Alex, – we can be so much to each other, if you want . . . but above all, answer me at once . . . Mama won't read the letter. Once again, forgive me – I don't know myself any more, Your Alma.[38]

For a day or two these pleadings fell on deaf ears, leaving Alma on tenterhooks. 'I have heard nothing from him today,' she wrote on the 13th. '. . . I am in a state of misery – in case he still thinks of me violently . . . he will write me a harsh letter . . . I reproach myself endlessly – I have lost a dear teacher . . .' But on the afternoon of 16 December a 'pale and subdued' Zemlinsky came to the Hohe Warte. Alma, her senses numb and her eyes full of tears, was much struck by his dignified manner. 'He was a bit sarcastic, as usual, but kind – wonderfully kind. . . . Although it was I who told him that I no longer loved him – so any embarrassment should really have been his – it was I who felt ashamed – he seemed so great; so pure, so infinitely far above me . . .'[40]

In the meantime she received two letters from Mahler, the first, dated 9 December, imploring her to 'write down whatever comes into your head. Imagine that I'm sitting beside you and that you're talking about everything. I always want to know about your life day by day – every detail.' Her reply was obviously satisfactory: 'My precious, dear girl!' he wrote from the Palast Hotel, Berlin, on 12 December.

> Just a cry from the heart, in the tearing hurry between arrival and first rehearsal! Your dear letter of Sunday was my travelling companion. I studied it as if it had been the New Testament. It taught me the present and the future. . . . What will it be like when you share everything with me and I with you, and when this vehement and consuming longing, which is mixed with such dread and anxiety, is assuaged, and when even in separation we know everything about each other, and can love each other and be inter-penetrated without a care?[41]

Before this ecstatic union could finally be achieved there were one or two things that needed straightening out. Their exchange of letters had alerted Mahler to some tendencies in his fiancée that gave rise to concern. How could they be everything to each other when Alma persisted in thinking of herself as an individual being with a mind of her own? And what of her wilful habit of imagining that her thoughts and opinions were anything other than recitations from her literary and philosophical heroes? And what, indeed, of her apparent heartlessness to her rejected suitors – heartlessness that came from the knowledge that her beauty would always attract attention? Could she, in short, learn humility, curb her flirtatious instincts and renounce superficiality? Furthermore, could she give herself wholly to him as her husband, sublimating herself entirely to his needs and allowing him to be the sole arbiter of her desires? And, most important of all, could she renounce all claims to be considered a composer in the interests of the absolute comfort and quiet of the greater of the two talents?

All of these thoughts and questions Mahler poured out in a

long letter written just before he returned to Vienna. 'My dearest Almschi!' he began.

It's with a somewhat heavy heart that I'm writing to you today, my beloved Alma, for I know I must hurt you and yet I can't do otherwise. I've got to tell you the feelings that your letter of yesterday aroused in me, for they're so basic to our relationship that they must be clarified and thoroughly discussed once and for all if we're to be happy together . . . Again I wonder what this obsession is that has fixed itself in that little head I love so indescribably dearly, that you must be and remain yourself – and what will become of this obsession when once our passion is sated (and that will be very soon) and we have to begin, not merely residing, but living together and loving one another in companionship? This brings me to the point that is the real heart and core of all my anxieties, fears and misgivings, the real reason why every detail that points to it has acquired such significance: you write '*you and my music*' – *Forgive me, but this has to be discussed too!* In this matter, my Alma, it's absolutely imperative that we understand one another clearly at *once*, before we see each other again! . . . You won't think me vain, Alma? Believe me, this is the first time in my life that I'm talking about it to someone who doesn't have the right approach to it. Would it be possible for you, from now on, to regard *my* music as *yours*? I prefer not to discuss 'your' music in detail just now – I'll revert to it later. In general, however, – how do you picture the married life of a husband and wife who are both composers? Have you any idea how ridiculous and, in time, how degrading for both of us such a peculiarly competitive relationship would inevitably become? What will happen if, just when you're 'in the mood', you're obliged to attend to the house or to something I might happen to need, since, as you wrote, you ought to relieve me of the menial details of life? Don't misunderstand me and start imagining that I hold the bourgeois view of the relationship between husband and wife, which regards the latter as a sort of plaything for her husband and, at the same time, as his housekeeper. Surely you would never suspect me of feeling and thinking that way, would you? But one thing is certain and that is that you must become 'what I need' if we are to be happy together, i.e., my wife, not my colleague. Would it mean the destruction of your life and would you feel you were having to forgo an indispensable highlight of your existence if you were to give up *your* music entirely in order to possess and also to be mine instead? . . . What a terrible moment I'm causing you – I do realize it, Alma – but you will appreciate that I myself am suffering just as much, even though this is poor consolation. Although I'm aware that you don't yet know Him, I pray God that He may guide your hand, my beloved, so that it may write the truth and not be moved by infatuation – for this is a crucial moment that will decide the fate of two lives for eternity! God bless you, my dearest, my love, whatever you may have to tell me. I won't write tomorrow but will wait for your letter on Saturday and, as I've said, I'll send a servant to get it, so have it ready. A thousand loving kisses, my Alma, and I beg you: be truthful! Your Gustav.[42]

This highly charged letter appeared at the Hohe Warte on Friday, 20 December. 'Early in the town – visiting with my parents,' wrote Alma in her diary the same day, ' – and on our return, *this letter*. My heart stood still ... give up my music – this until now has been my life? My first thought was to give up the whole idea – to part from him. . . . Mama and I talked about him far into the night – she read the letter. . . . I was completely at a loss – I found it so heavy-handed and clumsy of him . . .'[43]

After a good night's sleep Alma was prepared to reconsider the ultimatum. 'I forced myself to sleep soundly,' she wrote on 21 December, 'and when I reread his letter a warm feeling came over me. How would it be, if I gave up everything for him! I must say that scarcely any music interests me now but his. Yes, he is right. I must live only for him, so that he can be happy. . . . I long for him more than I can say.'[44]

The same morning she went out on an errand in the neighbourhood and met a messenger from Mahler on his way to collect her answer. He brought another letter from him. 'Never have I more ardently desired or more fearfully awaited a letter from anyone than that which my servant will shortly bring me. What will you say to me?'[45] Alma, half in love with self-sacrifice, determined to immolate herself in her future husband's work for the greater good, put an end to these exhausting fervours by acceding to his demands.

'He came,' she wrote in her diary that evening, 'loving and kind as always ... I will give him everything . . .'[46]

Perfect harmony having apparently been reached, there was nothing to stand in the way of the official announcement of their engagement, and on 27 December all Vienna was buzzing with the news that its controversial musical director had betrothed himself to a girl half his age. ' "DIE VERLOBUNG DES DIREK-

TOR MAHLER," etc. etc. etc.,' wrote Alma in her diary, and the next day, overwhelmed by flowers, telegrams and letters, she reiterated: 'My only desire is to make him happy – He deserves it!'[47] At long last it seemed Alma had a heroic model worthy of her: temporarily at least, there was not a cloud on the emotional horizon.

6 *The Wound of Sorrow*

On the face of it, things did not augur well for their prospective union. Love rarely conquers all, and the likelihood of Alma regretting her decision to sublimate her own gifts in the interests of her future husband's creative stability was, to others, if not to herself, considerable. As for Mahler, whilst undoubtedly in the grip of an overwhelming passion, telling her 'with supreme tenderness and bliss' that he was 'in love for the very first time', would he not come to regret an alliance with a girl of undeniable beauty and talent, but one of a notoriously flirtatious disposition?

As a result, their engagement was eyed with considerable dismay by interested parties on both sides. Frau Moll was so horrified by Mahler's pre-marital ultimatum that, fond of him as she was, she urged Alma to give him up at once – thereby ensuring that she did no such thing. Carl Moll, too, pleaded with his stepdaughter to think carefully before committing herself. 'It isn't exactly what I would have wished for you,' he told her. 'He's not young. To my certain knowledge he's in debt. He's not strong. And then, it's all up with his job at the Opera. He's certainly no beauty. Composes, too, and they say it's no go.'[1]

Some of Mahler's old friends were equally dubious, and an introductory dinner at his apartment on the Auenbruggergasse on 5 January 1902, did little to assuage their doubts. The most influential of them, the writer Siegfried Lipiner (mainly remembered for his translations of the Polish poet Adam Mickiewicz), had already incensed Alma by calling her 'my dear girl', expecting her to agree that Guido Reni was a great painter when he 'meant nothing' to her, and (particularly insulting) telling her that Plato's

Symposium was far above her head. This, together with the feeling that under their influence Mahler was beginning to think her looks and her manner too frivolous and outspoken, put Alma in a far from complaisant mood. Confronted by Lipiner, Anna von Mildenburg, Arnold Rosé, Justine, Nina and Albert Spiegler and Koloman Moser, with only the Molls and her fiancé as allies, she lived up to their worst expectations. By turns antagonistic and sullen, her behaviour reached a peak of outrage when Anna von Mildenburg asked her what she thought of Mahler's music. 'I know very little of it,' she replied, 'and what I do I don't like.'[2]

Frau Moll blushed for her daughter's bad manners, but Mahler, wrote Alma, laughed out loud. 'The others let their heads hang lower than before . . . The atmosphere became unendurable. Then Mahler took me by the arm and we went into Justine's little room. "It was frightful in there," he said. "We'll do better on our own for a bit." '

This public declaration of his intentions alienated him irrevocably, according to Alma, from the friends of his youth. Lipiner apparently wrote to his friend the next day voicing the party's dismay at his misalliance, and was not reassured by Mahler's reply, which excused Alma on the grounds of her 'youth and inexperience'.[3]

'From that evening onwards,' Alma wrote, 'his friends launched a regular campaign against me, which ended only with Mahler's retirement from the Opera in Vienna, although during the latter years their smouldering hatred emitted only an occasional spark. Mahler, however, was from the first so firmly attached to me that all their plots miscarried. All they achieved was his final severance from themselves . . .'[4]

Lipiner, deprived of unlimited access to his old friend, did indeed distance himself. The Spieglers, too, played little part in the Mahlers' married life. Anna von Mildenburg was to be more persistent. All attempts to persuade Mahler to relapse into the informal '*du*' having failed, she took a house near his summer retreat at Maiernigg, from which she did her best to disrupt the early months of her successful rival's married life. 'Envious as ever,' wrote Alma, she:

> settled down in our immediate neighbourhood. In the evenings she paid us visits uninvited, accompanied by a mangy dog she had bought from a loafer out of pure kindness of heart, as she carefully pointed out, and from other less elevated motives.... [Mahler] escorted her home for the first few times, and this was the object of her manoeuvres, but finally her manoeuvring annoyed him. He sent the servant home with her and at once her regular visits ceased ... She was vulgar as well as voluble about Mahler and about his sister, giving me intimate details, which if I had not known his whole life from his own lips, would have suffocated me ... [5]

For his part, Mahler had begun to have pre-marital worries of his own. 'If only you had had a love affair,' he apparently burst out soon after returning from a performance of his Second Symphony in Dresden on 20 December 1901, 'or were a widow, it would be alright.'[6] Beneath this enigmatic pronouncement lay the root of the 'anxiety and torment' Alma recorded her fiancé suffering during their engagement. Would he, or would he not, be able to consummate their marriage? Alma, convinced that her future husband was a complete innocent, did her best to reassure him that all would be well, but Mahler continued to let the matter prey on his mind. To put him out of his misery, Alma agreed that things should be resolved one way or another before their wedding night.

It was a momentous decision. Even though, on her own admission, Alma had come close to losing her virginity to Zemlinsky, she had not become immune to the moral code of the times. Fear of pregnancy or possible rejection by their lovers, mixed with a horror of being publicly shamed, prevented all but a handful of brides from anticipating their wedding night. Mahler could have had no stronger proof that Alma both loved and trusted him completely.

Their first efforts were not a success. 'What I have to write today makes me so unhappy,' Alma wrote in her diary on 1 January 1902. 'I was quite alone all afternoon with Gustav in his room – he gave me his love . . . but at the very moment . . . he lost all his strength. He cried from shame. But I managed – even though in the depth of misery, to calm him down . . . My poor, poor man! I can't say how much the whole episode upset me – first the mental torment, then, the end so near, and no satisfaction . . .' Three days later all seems to have gone well. For once Alma restrained herself to one brief line: 'Joy above all joy!'[7]

The nervous strain of adjusting to one another and of concealing the by now wholly intimate nature of their relationship from the outside world began to tell on them both. Alma brooded on the stupidity of a convention that sought to deny them the fulfilment of their love before their wedding night, but wondered afterwards if the consequences had been for the best. Within six weeks she realized that she was pregnant, and by her own account the psychological side-effects of becoming so before her marriage spilled over into the early years of their married life, undermining her self-assurance and making her less certain of herself in relation to Mahler than she would otherwise have been.[8] Alma does not elaborate on the root of these particular insecurities, but no bride, even today, would want to be nauseously pregnant on her honeymoon, or to be denied a few self-engrossed months alone with her new husband. And, deep down, Alma must have wondered whether, by giving herself so completely in body and mind before marriage, she had engendered any loss of respect for herself as a person in her own right, and from the outset submerged herself too completely in Mahler's being.

Mahler, too, was affected by these events. Just over a month before the wedding, after the première of Richard Strauss's opera *Feuersnot* – a work he apparently abhorred – he went up to the Semmering mountains to calm his nerves and restore his health. (He was suffering from a dilated vein, due to a congestion of a blood vessel – similar to a haemorrhage condition he had had in the winter of 1901.) The evening of the performance had been an uncomfortable one: Strauss's wife, Pauline, who shared the director's box with Alma, held a low opinion of her husband's work, which she announced was not only shoddy but unoriginal

– 'there wasn't an original note in it, all stolen from Wagner and many others.' She did not relent even when her husband, flushed with success after several curtain calls, came into the box, bombarding him with a barrage of noisy abuse: 'You thief, how dare you show yourself in my presence . . . you make me sick . . .'[9]

This curious ménage apparently suited both the parties concerned – at supper Strauss told Alma: 'My wife's a bit rough sometimes, but that's what I need, you know' – but placed considerable strain on those around them. Alma and Mahler obviously shared the same distaste for Strauss's complaisant attitude to his virago of a wife and for his musical sleights of hand which, it seemed to them, secured him instant popularity at the expense of genuine depth of feeling. 'Beloved,' Mahler wrote from Semmering in reply to a letter from Alma:

> I, too, have been painfully awaiting the first word from you. It was not the parting only – I found the whole evening uncomfortable. Strauss sheds such a blight – you feel estranged from your very self. If these are the fruits, how is one to love the tree? Your comment on him hits the nail on the head.* And I am very proud of your penetration. Better by far, to eat the bread of poverty and follow one's star than sell one's soul like that. The time will come when the chaff shall be winnowed from the grain – and my day will be when his is ended. If only I might live to see it, with you at my side!![10]

It was a relief to both of them when, on the morning of 9 March, in the pouring rain and with only the Molls, Justine and Arnold Rosé to witness the ceremony, they were married in the Karlskirche. The next day Justine married Arnold Rosé and the Mahlers left Vienna for St Petersburg, where Mahler had been invited to conduct three concerts. At long last all clandestine meetings were at an end. 'Once in the train for St Petersburg we breathed again,' Alma wrote. 'Mahler rebounded out of his gloom; alone with him, I no longer had to conceal my condition, either. We resolved to make this concert tour a real honeymoon.'[11]

*Alma burned all her letters to Mahler after his death, so her exact words can only be guessed at.

Although they both caught a feverish cold – Mahler went down with it on the train, arriving in St Petersburg with a temperature and a cough, 'so hoarse that he could hardly speak, and afflicted further by chilblains' – it did not mar their first three weeks together. The concerts, during which Mahler conducted works by Haydn, Schubert, Wagner and Beethoven, were a success both with their Russian audiences and with Alma, who, because of her condition, was allowed to sit behind the orchestra in case she had to leave in the middle. From there she was able to observe every nuance of her husband's expressions. 'The sight of his face on these occasions,' she wrote, 'uplifted and open-mouthed, was so inexpressibly moving that I felt a thrill of utter conviction: I knew once and for all that it was my mission in life to move every stone from his path and live for him alone.'[12]

In the deep snow and ice of St Petersburg the newly married couple, escorted by a cousin of Mahler's 'high up in the public service', visited the Hermitage, watched skaters on the frozen Nevs and drove about in an open troika. They spoke French to Russian archdukes – 'easier and more amiable in manner than our nobility at home' – went to a charity performance of *Eugene Onegin* ('it was Advent and all the theatres were closed') and were surprised that no one, when they broached the subject, appeared to know anything at all about Dostoevsky.

At the end of the month they returned to Vienna. The flat in the Auenbruggergasse had been enlarged, and by May 1902 consisted of three large rooms and three smaller rooms. Instead, however, of finding herself mistress of a comparatively opulent household, Alma discovered that her husband's generosity to his family had considerably depleted his income. The education of his sister Emma and his two profligate brothers Alois and Otto had eaten into Mahler's purse to such an extent that, according to Alma, by the time he was conducting in Hamburg not only had the whole of his 25,000 gulden indemnity from Budapest been swallowed up but his salary was so oversubscribed that he had to borrow from friends to make ends meet.

Neither was Justine apparently much help. Alma accused her

sister-in-law of 'wild extravagance', claiming that her lax house-keeping had done nothing to alleviate Mahler's financial prob-lems. Indeed, it had reduced him to a state of penury uncannily similar to her own father's plight. 'Do for heaven's sake, be more careful,' Mahler once wrote to his sister. 'I have been waiting for months to get a pair of shoes soled and never have the money.' And to Alma he said: 'Justine, unfortunately did not understand housekeeping. I resigned myself long ago to being perpetually in debt. But now, see what you can do.'[13] In 1902 according to Alma, Mahler 'owed 50,000 gold crowns', and on top of that had not finished paying for the summer house at Maiernigg which he had begun to build in the autumn of 1899. There was nothing for it but to make strict economies. The director's salary of 12,000 florins (which included lodging and expense allowances and a 2,000 florin conducting supplement) would have to be more carefully managed than had at first been thought.

There were only a few weeks to put this new regime into practice before the Mahlers set off again, this time to Krefeld, near Cologne, where, on 12 June, Mahler was going to conduct the first full performance of the Third Symphony which he had completed in August 1896, a work of such gigantic stature that only he could fully grasp it. 'Only I will be able to conduct it,' he told Natalie Bauer-Lechner, when he was in the midst of the final movement in the summer of 1896, 'I can't imagine anyone else ever being able to do it. If only a few people can hear me conduct it, and understand it. I am almost afraid that even the faithful and initiated few will find it too much for them. . . . Whoever fails to comprehend it in terms of the Grand Manner will be like a dwarf faced with a mountain giant; at best, he will see details, but never grasp the whole . . .'[14]

Whether or not the audience in Krefeld understood the work in its entirety – its internal dimensions explored nothing less than the power of the creative life force – its external dimensions were rapturously received. The immense first movement, scored for five trumpets, ten horns and six clarinets and lasting over half an hour, received a 'tremendous ovation', as did the next four, which included a setting of part of Nietzsche's *Also sprach Zarathustra* for alto voice, and a choir of boys' and women's voices singing to words from the German folk-song collection, *Des Knaben Wunderhorn*, 'Three Angels were singing a sweet song'. 'The enthusiasm rose higher with each movement,' wrote Alma, and after the Adagio finale 'the whole audience got up from their seats in a frenzy and surged to the front in a body.' Alma too was carried away by emotion. Whatever her initial reservations about her husband's music might have been she was moved to the heights of ecstasy at this celebration of life and love. 'I was in an indescribable state of excitement,' she recorded. 'I cried and laughed softly to myself and suddenly felt the stirrings of my first child. The hearing of this work finally convinced me of Mahler's greatness, and . . . I saw what hitherto I had only surmised.'[15]

As there were no hotels in Krefeld the Mahlers had been housed with a local silk manufacturer and his wife who, anxious to make a good impression on the director and his bride, had given them an enormous bedroom with an equally enormous bed surrounded by black curtains. Just before they left Krefeld for Vienna, they had a visitor. Alma, whom Mahler had asked to retire behind the curtains, heard a 'thin high voice', which she instantly judged to belong to an 'artist', begging Mahler to produce his opera *Die Rose vom Liebesgarten* (*The Rose in the Garden of Love*) and heard her husband refuse outright. Horrified at the effect this rejection might have on the unknown composer, Alma leaped out from her hiding place and squeezed their guest's hand, 'to show how deeply I sympathized'.[16]

Hans Pfitzner had reason to be grateful for this intercession, but the picture of a quivering supplicant painted by this benefactor was less than accurate. In 1902 Pfitzner already occupied a prominent place in the musical life of Berlin, where he taught composition and conducting at the Stern Conservatory. His first operatic work, *Der arme Heinrich*, based on a medieval verse play of that name, had been brought to Mahler's attention in Hamburg in 1895 by Bruno Walter (who produced it himself at the Berlin Opera in 1899), and it was through Pfitzner's wife, the daughter of the Cologne composer and conductor, Ferdinand Hiller, that he was in Krefeld in 1902.

For the moment, though, Pfitzner was unable to persuade Mahler to take the risk of putting on his opera in Vienna. Alma, however, was by no means dissatisfied with the encounter: she had made a new friend and Mahler had not been angry at her intervention. So it was in a cheerful frame of mind that the Mahlers returned to Vienna, going straight on to Maiernigg for the summer, where the pattern of their married life began to take shape.

As far as Mahler was concerned, this merely meant the continuation of an already well established routine. Since 1893 he had spent his summers by lakes in the hills of Salzkammergut – first at Steinbach am Attersee a few miles north of Bad Ischl, and, from 1900, further south at Maiernigg on the Wörthersee. In both places he had had small huts built some way away from his living quarters, so that he could compose in peace. Even in the depths of the countryside, however, absolute quiet was difficult to achieve. Almost everything that moved or breathed – birdsong, children's voices, the sound of farm workers whistling – was liable to upset his concentration. 'Anything that moved or made the slightest sound was chased away from the vicinity of the little house,' wrote Natalie Bauer-Lechner in 1896.

> We had thought out a whole system intended to keep the village children at a distance and quiet. They were not only forbidden to set foot on Mahler's meadow, or play and bathe in the lake, but they dared not so much as whisper in their houses or on the streets. We achieved this end with pleas, promises, sweets and presents of toys. If an organ-grinder or any other wandering musician came that way, we would rush out so promptly with money to move him on, that he would stop playing in the middle of a note . . . even the animals . . . couldn't enjoy life in our neighbourhood. They were driven away and penned in, or, if they refused to be quiet, they were bought and eaten. Anything to get rid of their voices![17]

But by the time the villa at Maiernigg was under way Mahler's attitude towards the noises of the natural world had mellowed considerably. During the summer of 1900, whilst he completed his Fourth Symphony, the windows of his hut in the woods were often left open. 'This time,' he told Natalie Bauer-Lechner, '. . . it's the forest with its marvels and its terrors that dominates me and steals into my world of sound. I see it more and more: one does not compose, one *is* composed!'[18]

The house itself was completed in the summer of 1901. Described by Alma as having been built 'in a somewhat philistine style', and by Henri de la Grange as 'a rather graceless mass of wood and masonry of a style popular around 1900', the four-storey building stood on the edge of the lake with the woods rising steeply behind it. On the top floor Mahler had a bedroom with a balcony, a studio-bedroom 'with an enormous desk' and a small dressing-room. Immediately below was Alma's bedroom and the sitting-room, both of which opened onto a large stone terrace and behind which was a spare room. On the first floor, behind a closed verandah, were the dining-room and the main spare bedroom. Outside, at the back, was a garden and a piece of woodland full of 'all kinds of winding and climbing paths and charming clearings',[19] and, in front a shore path, a broad walk that had been 'banked and levelled between the house and the lake'.[20] A steep and slippery path through the wood led to the composing hut which lay two hundred and fifty feet above the villa.

In these idyllic surroundings Alma inherited the daily routine faithfully adhered to by Justine, Emma and, during the summers she spent with them, Natalie Bauer-Lechner. It had varied little over the years and was not to change in the time to come. Mahler got up at six and rang for the cook, who had to take his breakfast (coffee, milk, bread and butter and jam) to the hut by a separate, even more precarious route, in case her employer (who had a horror of seeing anyone first thing in the morning) should meet her on his way up.

Once there, Mahler heated up the milk on a spirit stove (he was, according to Alma, clumsy about this and often burned his fingers), then ate his breakfast at a table outside and settled down to work until midday, when he returned to the villa to change from the 'rags' he wore in the wood into something more respectable. Before lunch he either, as in Steinbach, went for a walk, or, in Maiernigg, went down to the lake, where he had built a boathouse for two boats, and a bathing hut with a platform of planks in front for sun-bathing. After swimming some way out he whistled for Alma to join him, and they talked whilst he dried himself in the sun. Several dips in the water later (sometimes four or five) they went into the house for lunch, which consisted mainly of soup, eggs or fish, plainly cooked and 'without a trace of fat or seasoning'. Afterwards there was half an hour's conversation, followed by a walk – often lasting three or four hours – whatever the weather, or else a trip in one of the rowing boats.

Mahler took a notebook with him on these expeditions and, if the mood took him, stopped to jot down his ideas whilst Alma 'sat on the grass or a tree-trunk without venturing to look at him'. On their return Mahler went back to his hut until dinner at seven. 'His life during the summer months was stripped of all dross, almost inhuman in its purity,' observed his wife. 'No thoughts of fame or worldly glory entered his head. We lived on peacefully from day to day undisturbed in mind, except for the occasional letter from the Opera, which was sure to bring trouble.'[21]

During the first summer, Alma was pregnant and found the strenuous afternoon programme tiring. 'Sometimes I was too exhausted to go on. We invented a hypnotic cure for my collapse: he used to put his arm round me and say, "I love You." Instantly I was filled with fresh energy and on we tore.'[22] She also found the transition from promising musician to dedicated housekeeper and companion a difficult bridge to cross. She wrote in her diary on 10 July:

> I don't know how to begin, there is such a silent struggle going on inside me! And such a dreadful longing for someone – who thinks about ME – that helps me to find MYSELF! I am drowning beneath the altar of family life! I went into Gustav's room. On his desk lay

a difficult philosophical book* – and I thought to myself – why couldn't he pass some of it on to me – let me have a share in it – instead of gobbling it up by himself! I sat in front of the piano – and it came over me – that I had crossed that bridge once and for all – someone had taken me roughly by the arm and led me far away – from my own self . . . [23]

Not one to keep these grievances to herself, Alma tackled her husband. 'I think quite differently today,' she wrote two days later.

Yesterday afternoon things were brought out into the open. I told him everything that was on my mind. And he – always so loving and kind, thought only of how he could help me. But I understand that at the moment he was simply not able to do so – he lives only for his work. I must make use of this summer to develop in all sorts of ways. I must learn to strive not to begrudge my own fulfilment![24]

To this end Alma gave up any attempts at piano playing during the day in case the sound filtered up to the hut and, instead, began work copying the completed parts of the Fifth Symphony. 'I copied all he had ready of the Fifth straight away,' she wrote, 'so that my manuscript was ready only a few days behind him. He got more and more into the way of not writing out the instrumental parts in the score – only the first bars; and I learnt at this time to read his score and to hear it as I wrote and was and more of a real help to him.'[25]

This in itself brought its own reward. 'Yesterday my Gustav was so happy,' she recorded later the same month, 'as a result of the peace of mind I have given him. He thanked me over and over again, and said that I shall never regret it – that made me feel so much better . . .' And, on another occasion, he told her that 'he had never before been able to work so easily and so continuously – and that he had me to thank for it. And if I know that through my own sorrows I can give him bliss – how can I hesitate for one moment!'[26]

It must not be forgotten when reading of Alma's disaffection

---

*Probably by Kant, as Alma mentions Mahler having a complete set of Goethe and Kant on his shelves.

with some aspects of her early married life, that in 1902 she was only twenty-three years old, or that she had willingly accepted the conditions laid down by her husband before their marriage. Most of her frustrations would probably have been shared by any young woman, pregnant and unused to housekeeping, who had been obliged to adapt herself totally to the well established routine of a successful creative artist twice her age. What should be remembered is that Alma's compositional abilities were by no means fully fledged before she vowed to renounce them. She still needed a critical eye to be cast over her work, and an encouraging teacher to give her the confidence she often lacked. By transferring her affections from Zemlinsky to Mahler, therefore, she had deprived herself of an essential part of her musical growth: for even had he not imposed an embargo on her as a composer, Mahler would not have been willing to devote even part of himself to her musical development. Had Alma been as confident of herself as a composer as she was as a pianist she might have continued to work – albeit against her husband's wishes – in secret. But she needed his approval and direction, and without them she was incapable of doing so. Copying his scores was one way of becoming part of Mahler's compositions: if nothing else it brought her into physical contact with the written note.

Back in Vienna the regime was much as before, except that the Opera substituted for the composing hut, and after lunch a turn four times round the Belvedere or once round the Ringstrasse took the place of country walks. After tea at five o'clock Mahler went to the Opera where, if he was not conducting, he stayed for part of the performance and was later picked up by Alma in time for dinner. In the evenings they talked, or Alma read aloud.

The birth of their first child, Maria, on 3 November 1902, affected them both deeply in different ways. It was a difficult breech birth: put down by the doctor, according to Alma, to the 'fatigues I had undergone' during pregnancy. The pain and shock of the delivery left her exhausted and depressed. 'I have been up and about a week,' she wrote on 25 November, 'on the 3rd my first child came into the world. I paid for this with the most atrocious pain. I still do not have the right amount of love for her. Everything, everything in me belongs to Gustav.'[27]

Mahler was horrified at the agonies endured by his wife – Alma wrote that she could hear him 'raging up and down in the next room, waiting in a frenzy of anxiety for the end of this frightful delivery', and when it was over he cried: 'How can people take the responsibility of such suffering and keep on begetting children!' Nevertheless, he loved his elder daughter from the moment he saw her. He picked her up, carried her about, talked to her and played with her, and, when away, repeatedly asked Alma for news of her. 'I implore you,' he wrote from Vienna to Maiernigg in September 1903, 'stay on as long as you can and enjoy this lovely weather, so as to get as strong as possible, and think of our Putzerl. Why no word of her in your letter?'[28]

Alma described the first few years of their married life as having been led in 'splendid isolation'. Her coolness towards some of her husband's old friends, his immersion in his work and his natural antipathy towards social gatherings of all kinds inevitably threw them on their own resources, or into the company of mutually compatible family, friends and colleagues, such as the Molls, the Zuckerkandls, the Rosés (although Alma had her suspicions about Justine, accusing her of malicious behaviour and jealousy), Max Burckhard, Zemlinsky and Mahler's assistant, Bruno Walter.

On the whole Alma was content with this state of affairs. She was, after all, the director's wife, and her appearances at the Opera produced a satisfactory amount of attention and respect without reducing her to the paroxysms of shyness she claimed she felt with Mahler in public at other times, when it seemed to her she was 'nothing but his shadow'. This, however, had more to do with Mahler's celebrated status than with regrets for her lost song-writing. Not even in her wildest dreams could Alma have imagined that she would have been able to compose symphonies on a par with her husband, nor would she have thought herself capable (in the unlikely event of a woman being appointed to the post) of carrying out his duties as director of the Opera.

Amongst her peers she was noteworthy both as a young musician and as a personality in her own right. It was only among strangers that she became nervous a: d tongue-tied, feeling herself to be judged dismissively.

Their first two years were, therefore, comparatively happy ones for them both. In the summer of 1903 Mahler began the first sketches for his Sixth Symphony, and later that year he composed 'Liebst du um Schönheit' – the only love song he ever wrote – for his wife, who was 'overwhelmed with joy . . . we played it that day twenty times at least'.[29]

The early part of the year, too, had brought musical manna for Alma, in the form of meetings with two other composers, Gustave Charpentier and Hans Pfitzner. Charpentier came to Vienna in February for the Austrian première of his opera *Louise*.* According to Alma, he was a 'complete bohemian' and she found the Frenchman a great tonic: his mixture of indifference to etiquette (he apparently spat under the table during meals and bit his nails in public), combined with compliments (he told Mahler he had *'un gamin, la clarté, la gaieté, le printemps'* – a child, brightness, gaiety, springtime – for a wife, and sent flowers to *'Madame Mahler, gracieuse muse de Vienne, la muse de Montmartre reconnaissante'* – Madame Mahler, gracious muse of Vienna, from the grateful muse of Montmartre –[30] entertained her enormously. Even though his gallantries were not to be taken too seriously, they reminded Alma that the burdens of her daily round had not lessened her ability to arouse interest in men with 'the mark of genius on their brows'. They also assuaged her perpetual cravings for regular professions of love and admiration from all those with whom she came into contact.†

---

*A pupil of Massenet, Charpentier had won the Prix de Rome at the Paris Conservatoire. *Louise*, first performed in Paris in 1900 and in Vienna on 24 March 1903, was his only success as an opera. The second, *Julien*, written in 1913, was a failure.
†Alma's need for reassurance on these points sometimes went to absurd lengths. Anna Mahler remembered a postman who her mother felt was behaving in an inexplicably cold manner to her one day, and how this imagined slight apparently reduced her to tears for hours on end.

Mahler, she confided to her diary, did not always come up to these expectations. Although when away he wrote daily letters protesting his love, in the flesh she felt he did not pay enough attention to the sacrifices she had made on his behalf. It was not just a problem of money and its unequal distribution between them – although in 1904 she claimed that whereas Mahler could then afford 'clothes from the best tailor' and shoes from the 'best English shoemaker' she wore the same dress 'for five or six years on end' and had to refuse an invitation from Baron Albert Rothschild because she had no hat to wear. It was also the fact that he showed no interest in anything in her life that did not touch directly on himself.

'Yesterday I told my Gustav that I was sad he took so little interest in what went on inside me,' she wrote in her diary in December 1903, 'and that he never asked me to play any of my work, and that my knowledge of music was only acceptable when it was of use to him ... He didn't take me seriously. He said: Just because your budding dreams have not been fulfilled ... that's entirely up to you ... ! Oh God, how can anyone be so merciless. How could anyone make such a mockery of someone else's deepest feelings! ... My bitterness is great ...'[31]

It was only towards the end of their married life that Mahler paid any real attention to Alma's cries for musical recognition. The bargain they had struck before their engagement seemed to him a reasonable one – the only one, in fact, that could ensure a peaceful and fulfilled married life for them both. But the frustration it engendered in Alma rankled: accustomed from adolescence to devoted mentors prepared to further her musical talent, it seemed ironic that Mahler, so generous in his encouragement of Zemlinsky and Schönberg, should be so dismissive of her own work.

A letter from Hans Pfitzner on 12 March 1903 did much to restore her sense of worth. In it he asked to be allowed to dedicate a string quartet to her (his first), his only stipulation being that she should take care of the manuscript, as he had no copy. 'I look forward to the moment ... when I shall be allowed to say:

Your Quartet,' he wrote. 'Please send warmest greetings to your husband and also, if you see him, my dear friend, Walter. You three are the first to welcome the appearance of my four-handed child into the world . . . I shall not forget this loving reception in a distant land.'[32]

They met again in June, in Basle, where Mahler was conducting his Second Symphony in the Cathedral, and Alma invited Pfitzner to visit them at Maiernigg. Regretfully, he refused. 'Dear Frau Mahler,' he wrote later that month, 'you can have no idea how much I should like to accept your kind invitation! . . . but alas the time for foolishness – for youth – is over for me; now I must put down roots, be practical, serious . . . hardworking . . .'[33]

When it arrived the quartet found favour with Mahler, who pronounced it to be the 'work of a master'. *Die Rose vom Liebesgarten*, the opera that Pfitzner had pleaded with Mahler to put on in Vienna when they were all in Krefeld a year before, had to wait for Mahler's seal of approval until the autumn. For this he had Alma to thank: determined to promote her new friend's interests, she left the piano score open on her piano-rest in Vienna and Mahler found himself playing it over and over again until, in spite of himself, he finally began to share his wife's enthusiasm – 'so fully that he decided to produce it in spite of all his previous objections. It was the one and only time,' Alma added, 'during all the six years I lived with him while he was Director of the Vienna Opera that I purposely and openly influenced him; and I certainly had no cause to regret it.'[34]

Years later Alma modified this view, conceding that there might have been some grounds for her husband's initial antipathy to the opera. 'I now think that this work is no longer performable' she told Berndt W. Wessling in a radio interview in March 1962. 'Too much pseudo-romanticism, too much inconsequentiality. Possibly Mahler saw it would not stand up to the test of time, and he put the opera on just to please me.'[35]

Mahler died six years before the first performance in Munich of *Palestrina*, the only one of Pfitzner's operatic works still in the repertory, and the only one to bring him recognition both inside and outside the German-speaking world. A strong believer in the mystical nature of the creative impulse, Pfitzner lived in a musical ivory tower, separated from his contemporaries by a wall of self-imposed prejudice. Berg, Webern, Schönberg, Hindemith, Busoni, even Mahler, stirred feelings of acute antipathy. To Pfitzner their music was simply not music at all but symbols emphasizing their isolation from 'the mainstream of God-given greatness'. His own operatic music was Wagnerian in flavour, but bled of all sensual overtones: it was the philosopher and mystic in Wagner that he admired, rather than the unsettling Romantic.

It was not surprising, therefore, that Pfitzner, like Wagner, remained persona grata during the Nazi interregnum, and no accident, either, that, despite her subsequent remarks about *Die Rose vom Liebesgarten*, Alma was more influenced by him than by any other contemporary composer. In Pfitzner she found the structural unity preached (but not always practised) by Zemlinsky, untainted by the more primitive aspects of some of her husband's work, or the dissonances of Schönberg, Berg and Webern.

1904 began on a Wagnerian note with a visit to *Tristan and Isolde* at the Opera House, where Alma, four months pregnant with their second child, was joined by the painter Ferdinand Hodler, then exhibiting at the Secession. Hodler, who was seeing the opera for the first time, did not share Alma's enthusiasm for the work and left during the third act, remarking: 'That kissing match in the second act was all very well, but they can get on with their dying without me.'[36] The year continued in a more sociable vein, Max Burckhard having apparently decided that Alma was not seeing enough of her old friends, or meeting new ones – a view shared by Alma herself: as she confessed in the fragments of her diary that survive for this period, she was beginning to find their self-imposed isolation frustrating. 'It is a terrible shame I've no friends any more,' she wrote in February 1904, 'but Gustav simply won't see anyone. What a mass of experience I had in the past – and how smoothly and quietly my life runs now. I must have some excitement. If only Pfitzner lived in

Vienna! If only I was *able* to associate with Zemlinsky. Also, Schönberg interests me. I have thought about this such a lot . . . there must be something else!'[37]

Something else was provided by a dinner invitation from Max Burckhard to meet the playwright Gerhart Hauptmann, his friend (later his wife) Margarethe Marschalk, sister of the German critic and composer, Max Marschalk, and the actor Josef Kainz. The evening was a success. Much to Alma's relief Hauptmann and Mahler became engrossed in a conversation which continued until the small hours of the morning, and spilled over into the following day, when the Mahlers visited their new friends at the Hotel Sacher.

On 14 June, together with Justine and Arnold Rosé, they went to the Burgtheater to hear Hauptmann's verse-play, *Der arme Heinrich* (based on the same medieval source as Pfitzner's opera). Alma, to whom it was 'like wine', went to bed with Hauptmann's musical verse in her ears, and awoke at five o'clock in the morning with labour pains. Mahler, when roused, went to fetch the mid-wife and when he got back attempted to take his wife's mind off her discomfort by reading aloud from Kant. Fortunately for Alma, who was beginning to find the monotonous tone of her husband's voice irritating and Kant unintelligible, their second daughter, Anna, was born by lunchtime without any of the traumas of the first confinement. 'The birth, at midday,' wrote Alma, 'in the middle of the week [Wednesday], in the middle of the month, in the middle of the year, might have been an allegory. From the first moment the child was a great joy to us and was nicknamed Guckerl, from her wide-open blue eyes.'[38]

A week later Mahler set off for Maiernigg, leaving Alma to be looked after by Frau Moll. 'I cannot spare a single day of my summer,' he wrote to Arnold Berliner before he left. 'On Wednesday I am off to Maiernigg. My wife gave birth to a daughter on the 15th, and will have to stay here for at least three weeks. I am leaving her in the care of her mother, going to the lake all on my lonesome. You know why. It is simply a duty . . .'[39]

Once there he wrote at once to Alma:

My dearest Almschili! I went to bed yesterday dog-tired at half-past nine and slept without a break till eight. Then had my first breakfast in the hut. – But it's odd – I always find the air here extremely relaxing. As soon as I reach Maiernigg all life and energy come to a stop, and it takes two or three weeks before I can rouse myself at all. You know that from the last two summers here. It's just the same this time, except that I miss you as well and have to crawl round alone all day – God knows when I shall be able to pull myself together a bit. I haven't felt so muted for years . . . [40]

To help himself unwind, Mahler read – Tolstoy's *Confessions* ('terrifyingly sad and savagely flagellant') and the recently published correspondence between Wagner and Mathilde Wesendonck – played Brahms's chamber music on the piano (which apart from 'a charming sextet in B flat major he found 'barren'), and planned a playground for Putzi. He wrote to Alma:

I've given mature consideration to the playground. The place we chose from memory is much too small. Putzi would scarcely be able to turn round. But there's a place down below which might have been designed for the purpose. I've inspected it carefully and discussed it with Theuer. I'm getting him to fence it in completely and put down 10 florins' worth of fine sand. There the children will have a playground to last them for years. I'll have it down if you agree. It's the place where we have the bench and table and the two seats. [41]

He also allayed Alma's fears about the possibility of snakes crawling into the pen. 'There can be snakes just as well higher up as lower down,' he wrote in the same letter, 'and the children will need watching wherever they are (besides, water-snakes are *never* poisonous, and the poisonous ones are only found in particularly warm and dry spots – ask any doctor) . . .' And, a few days later: 'You'll be delighted when the little one tumbles about in the sand in the best of good air. If only the time had come! Tomorrow I'll see about a bed for her in Klagenfurt. I'm not quite sure about the snakes – they are *water-snakes* and are NOT poisonous. Poisonous snakes need dryness and heat and shun the neighbourhood of water. You can ask any zoologist! So there's no cause for alarm.' [42]

By the middle of July 1904, a few days before the arrival of his family, Mahler was able to report that everything was in readiness. 'My darling Almschili,' he wrote. 'The job is done, and you'll open your eyes wide when you see what a fine playground we've made for our Putzerl. . . . There's still room for a number of improvements, but they shall wait until you come. I have just been tinkering at it a bit myself. – I can hardly wait for the moment when we inspect it together for the first time and put out Putzi inside. She will have her heart's desire before her very eyes . . .'[43]

Before they arrived Mahler gave himself a break from the lakes, where the weather had been more than usually hot, with frequent thunderstorms and pouring rain, and went walking in the Dolomites. On the eve of his departure he found time to reply to a letter from Alma, who had also been reading the Wagner-Wesendonck correspondences. Like herself, Mathilde Wesendonck was prepared to spend long hours copying drafts of her lover's operas – *Das Rheingold, Die Walküre*, the first two acts of *Siegfried* and most of *Tristan and Isolde* (for whom she was the inspiration), but unlike herself Mathilde continued to write poetry, with the added satisfaction of seeing Wagner set five of her poems to music whilst composing *Tristan and Isolde*.

Alma must have confined her observations to the satisfactions of sharing a common creative goal, for Mahler replied affectionately that he was 'rejoiced to the heart by your absorption in those wonderful pages and your comments on them. The analogies with one's own life . . . give it a peculiar fascination.' And, he continued:

> there is the supreme gratification of finding oneself related in destiny and sufferings with those whose habitat is on the heights. It will always be so for you, Alma, into whosoever life you look. Outside space and time there is a select company of solitary persons who are drawn to share an all the more intense life together. And though you find merely a poor counterfeit, still you search those effaced features for the look you understand so well, a look which only the elect can have. Your having this sympathetic insight I consider to be the most precious of blessings on your earthly course and mine.[44]

At the end of what Alma described as a 'beautiful, serene and happy' summer Mahler had finished his Sixth Symphony and added three more to the two *Kindertotenlieder* – five orchestral songs set to poems by Friedrich Rückert – that he had written in 1901. He played the symphony through to Alma on the piano in his hut, where for the first time she heard the musical portrait of herself contained in the second subject of the first movement, and his description of their children playing expressed in the episodic rhythms of the F major trio in the scherzo.

But, despite the compliment of 'the great soaring theme' that was herself, Alma found the subject matter of both the symphony and the *Kindertotenlieder* incomprehensibly depressing. Both were filled with a pessimism at odds with the circumstances of their life: the mournful ending to the scherzo, where 'ominously, the childish voices became more and more tragic, and at the end died out in a whimper', the doom-laden finale, during which 'the hero on whom fall three blows of fate' was felled to the accompaniment of blows on a sledge-hammer, reduced them both to tears as they went through it together. 'Not one of his works came so directly from his inmost heart as this,' Alma wrote. 'We both wept that day. The music and what it foretold touched us deeply.'[45]

The *Kindertotenlieder* were even more despairing. Friedrich Rückert wrote the poems after two of his children had died, and each one was a reflection on the pain of bereavement. The last two were particularly harrowing. 'How often I think they're just out walking;' began the fourth:

> They won't be much longer, they'll soon be returning.
> The day is fine, O never fear!
> They're only taking the long way back.

And 'In this grim weather, this raging storm', began the fifth:

> I'd never have dared send the children outside!
> But out of the house they've borne them.
> I had no say in the matter.
>
> In this grim weather, this howling gale,
> I'd never have dared let the children outside,

I'd fear they might catch an illness;
Now these are but idle reflections.

In this grim weather, this dreadful blast,
I'd never have dared let the children outside,
I'd fear they might die tomorrow;
Now this is no cause for worry . . . [46]

No wonder such words sent shivers down Alma's spine: the discrepancy between the terrible theme of the songs and the reality of their two healthy babies seemed to her to tempt providence to an unnecessary degree. 'I can understand setting such frightful words to music if one had no children, or had lost those one had,' she wrote. '. . . What I cannot understand is bewailing the deaths of children, who were in the best of health and spirits, hardly an hour after having kissed and fondled them.'[47]

In the early autumn the whole family returned to Vienna, where Mahler was immediately plunged into rehearsals for a performance of *Fidelio*, the second opera under his direction to have its sets designed by Alfred Roller. The first, *Tristan and Isolde* premièred on 21 February 1903, was the result of a meeting at the Hohe Warte in 1902 when Carl Moll introduced Mahler to Roller, a founder member of the Secession and a professor at the School of Arts and Crafts. It transpired that Roller had long been dissatisfied with the over-decorated sets of previous *Tristans* and had made some sketches for a sparser scenic interpretation of the opera. As soon as he saw them Mahler recognized the contribution they could make to the *Gesamtkunstwerk*, the Total Work of Art. 'That's the man for me,' Alma reported him saying on their way home. 'I'll engage him.'[48]

Although commissioned to design the sets for *Tristan* in the summer of 1902, Roller did not sign a permanent contract with the Vienna Opera until the following year. The new scenery pleased almost everyone except Anna von Mildenburg, who burst into tears at the absence of familiar landmarks on sets which, as Roller saw them, should only be constructed out of 'essentials, which do not represent the setting, but which must above all be conditioned by the purpose, like the words or the tempo'.[49]

To this end he made full use of lighting effects. 'The stage glowed with amazingly powerful colours: the first act yellow-red, orange and red, with the billowing canopy of the sun-soaked sail, the steps on the right leading to the deck hung with red,' wrote Max Mell. In the centre was Isolde's couch, 'its posts decorated with heathen ornament and carvings, black and gold, the casket containing the deadly potions gleaming with gold . . . set with semi-precious stones and decorated, like the curtains and the couch, with Celtic ornament'.[50]

The collaboration between Mahler and Roller lasted until Mahler's departure for America in 1907. During those five years they re-interpreted *Fidelio* (1904), *Don Giovanni* (1905) and in 1906, to mark the anniversary of Mozart's birth, *The Abduction from the Seraglio*, *The Magic Flute*, *Cosi fan tutte* and *The Marriage of Figaro*. Only two parts of Roller's most ambitious project – a complete new production of the Ring cycle – were performed: *Das Rheingold* in 1905 and *Die Walküre* in 1907. Finally there was *Lohengrin* on 11 March 1907 and, on 18 March (in Bruno Walter's opinion the culminating point of Mahler's activity as head of the Opera), Gluck's *Iphigenia in Aulis*.

In between feeding Anna, Alma sat in a box and watched the final rehearsals for *Fidelio*. Between them Roller and Mahler had transformed all static elements from past productions, in particular the wooden staging of the prisoner's scene where, as Kurt Blaukopf put it, 'the whole chorus stepped into the prison yard from their cells to left and right, formed a semicircle on the brightly lit stage, and away they went'. Instead, the prisoners came up from below 'in groups of twos and threes, staggering into the light, unused to walking, dazzled by the daylight, dizzy with fresh air'.[51] Gone, too, was the placing of the *Leonora* No. 3 Overture at the beginning of the performance. Because Roller needed a scene change before the finale, Mahler decided to play the *Leonora* No. 3 at that point to allow the stagehands time to build the set. 'The effect', wrote Alma, 'was indescribably beautiful. The music led away from the sombre prison, through darkness to light; the curtain rose and the Bastille towered up in a flood of brilliant sunshine. It was a stroke of genius on Mahler's part.'[52]

About a week after *Fidelio* opened on 7 October 1904, Mahler went to Cologne for the first performance of his Fifth Symphony. Alma, in the process of weaning Anna, was hoping to join him in a few days. Immediately after the first rehearsal Mahler reported back:

> It all went off tolerably well. The Scherzo is the very devil of a movement. I see it is in for a peck of troubles! Conductors for the next fifty years will all take it too fast and make nonsense of it; and the public – Oh, heavens, what are they to say to this primeval music, this foaming, roaring, raging sea of sound, to these dancing stars, to these breathtaking, iridescent and flashing breakers! . . . Oh that I might give my symphony its first performance fifty years after my death! . . . I expect you without fail on Sunday, I must have one person anyway to whom my symphony will be a pleasure. If you were here now we should take a taxi and drive along the Rhine; as it is, I must go on foot in case you should be envious. The weather is glorious. A thousand kisses from your Oh so blessed Gustl.

Much to the disappointment of them both, Alma caught a fever and had to stay at home. 'But this is horrible', Mahler wrote after hearing the news. '. . . I still can't give up all hope. Leave nothing undone – sweat it out – swallow brandy – gobble aspirin – you can get over a chill in two days and still travel on Monday night and be here for the concert on Tuesday! Almschili, please, do all you can. It would be too, too, ghastly – to be alone at this – the first – performance . . .'[53]

Despite Alma's absence, which, Mahler wrote, 'spoils everything. Turns it to dust and ashes I can almost say', the performance on 18 October was well received. Ten days later he returned home, after staying with the Mengelbergs in Amsterdam, where on 26 and 27 October he had conducted the Second Symphony and on 23 October had been paid the compliment of having the Fourth Symphony played twice running at the same concert (Mahler conducted before the interval, Willem Mengelberg after it).

Before he left he dashed off a final letter enclosing a translated copy of a review and complaining, as he had done before, about Alma's deficiencies as a letter-writer:

> With this, thank God, our very *one-sided* correspondence comes to an end: tomorrow evening I conduct for the last time and the day after I leave. I'm heartily sick of being on the racket, though very well in health, and will be thankful to have my legs under my own table once more. And I miss you three rogues more than a little, although I must say I'm not at all pleased with the eldest of them. Such a lazy correspondent, Almschi! The real curtain-lecture follows early on Saturday morning while I'm having my bath . . .
> 54

Two months later, on 14 and 22 December, the Third Symphony was performed in Vienna. After it, Mahler received a letter from Arnold Schönberg:

> I must not speak as a musician if I am to give any idea of the incredible impression your symphony made on me: I can only speak as one human being to another. For I saw your very soul naked, stark naked. It was revealed to me as a stretch of wild and secret country, with eerie chasms and abysses neighboured by sunlit, smiling meadows, haunts of idyllic repose . . . I saw the forces of good and evil wrestling with each other; I saw a man in torment struggling towards inward harmony . . . Forgive me. I cannot feel by halves. With me it is one thing or the other! In all devotion . . . 55

This adulatory letter contrasted oddly with Schönberg's views on some of Mahler's earlier work – he had already expressed himself dissatisfied with the First Symphony, and his initial reactions to the Second had been a mixture of 'rapture and scepticism'. On the whole, he had, in the past, thought Mahler's themes 'banal'. His conversion marked the beginning of a friendly association. Mahler agreed to become honorary president of the Vereinigung Schaffender Tonkünstler, a society founded at the beginning of the year by a group that included Alexander von Zemlinsky, Schönberg and Bruno Walter to provide a forum for contemporary music in Vienna. Schönberg, who had become Zemlinsky's brother-in-law in 1901, became a regular visitor at the Auenbruggergasse.

Before the association's untimely demise (it only lasted for one season) Mahler had introduced ungrateful audiences to Richard Strauss's *Sinfonia Domestica* and, in January 1905, to Schönberg's symphonic poem, *Pelleas und Melisande*, but not even Mahler's backing could induce Viennese concert-goers to sit through performances of works as alien as Schönberg's without hissing, booing, shouting and, in a few cases, applauding, as the mood took them.* Bruno Walter recorded of one such episode: 'Mahler told me later that he had spoken to one man who had been hissing right in his face. When Mahler suggested that since he himself was applauding, the man might exercise some restraint, he received the blunt answer: "Why, I hissed your symphony too." Mahler had given the man a keen look and then turned away with the words: "I might have guessed it." '[56] More successful was a concert on 25 January at which the *Kindertotenlieder* were first performed. The songs which had so distressed Alma were warmly received. Most satisfying of all, 'more welcome. . . . than the acclamation of a mass audience . . .' Bruno Walter recorded, 'was the realization of the devotion of the young musicians around him. . . . [57] That evening Mahler felt really happy.'

That year and the next were, in the light of things to come, ominously trouble-free. By the end of 1905, both at the Opera and in his creative life, Mahler was at his peak. He was widely admired as a conductor at home and abroad, six of his symphonies had been published and five of them performed in Vienna. The Seventh, mapped out the year before, had been written 'in one burst' during the summer, and in December the new production of *Don Giovanni*, with Roller's two great turrets flanking a stage hung with black and coloured velvet in place of painted backdrops, had confirmed his gifts as an operatic interpreter.

---

*Despite the violent public antipathy to Schönberg's work and some reservations of his own, Mahler continued to champion his music until his death. In the last days of his life he worried constantly about what might happen to the younger man without his patronage. To soothe him Alma promised she would do all she could, as did Carl Moll. After his death they fulfilled their obligation – a fund was set up from friends' money for the benefit of young musicians, with Strauss, Busoni and Bruno Walter as trustees. At Alma's request, the proceeds 'frequently went to Schönberg'.

Alma, too, was reasonably content. Frequent visits from Zemlinsky and Schönberg went some way towards filling the gap dividing her past musical life from her present domesticated circumstances, and although she could not rid herself of feelings of inferiority – feelings she still believed would not have existed had she been able to compose – she found solace in the company of those who continued to love and admire her.

Particularly welcome was the return of Hans Pfitzner to Vienna in March for rehearsals of *Die Rose vom Liebesgarten*. In between and after rehearsals he came to the flat, where he and Alma 'spent hours making music together and talking' – an arrangement not entirely to Mahler's taste, although, as Alma was at pains to stress, 'Mahler was always there for me whether he was in the room or not.' But Mahler would not do for Alma what Pfitzner could do without hesitation; provide a sympathetic ear for her neglected work. 'Yesterday Pfitzner asked me to play some old songs of mine,' Alma wrote in her diary in March 1905. 'He said they were good and that he was very glad to find I had a real talent for composition and a sound feeling for melody. "I wish we could work together for a time. It's such a pity about you." What melancholy joy coursed through my veins! A moment's bliss . . .'[58]

Apart from this balm to her soul, Alma had other sources of pleasure. The Hauptmanns returned to Vienna in March for the first night of *Rose Bernd* at the Burgtheater, and in May Alma left the children in Vienna and joined Mahler in Strasbourg, where he was to conduct a performance of the Fifth Symphony. Also in Strasbourg were Richard Strauss, to conduct his *Sinfonia Domestica*, and some French admirers of Mahler, including General Picquart, whose intervention in the Dreyfus affair had forced him into retirement, the mathematician Paul Painlevé (later French prime minister) and Sophie and Paul Clemenceau.

There without his nagging wife, Pauline, Strauss was in a particularly good humour. He had recently finished an opera, based on Oscar Wilde's *Salome*, and insisted that Mahler should listen to it. Despite strong misgivings about the subject matter, which he considered too immoral ever to be acceptable to Catholic countries, Mahler agreed to hear it out, and Strauss took them to the showroom of a piano shop, where he played and sang 'to perfection.'*

In June Alma went to Maiernigg as usual with the children. Mahler joined her a fortnight later, together with a bicycle, bought for 150 florins. 'Hurrah!' he wrote on 13 June. 'I'm coming the day after tomorrow, early on Thursday, about half-past seven, wobbling along on the bike. Please, a fine breakfast . . .'[59] Apart from a nerve-racking incident when a par-affin lamp overturned whilst Alma was making a fair copy of the Sixth Symphony, setting fire to the carpet and a sofa before she eventually managed to smother it with cushions and rugs, the summer was an unclouded one. 'I would so love it,' wrote the art critic Erica Conrat-Tietze to her mother Ilsa Conrat whilst staying at the villa, 'if you could have some idea how beautiful the evenings are here. A large stone terrace on the edge of the water, the mountains with their shadows on the horizon. We do not say much, because we always have the feeling that GM might want to work. If he does, he rises politely and speaks about some book that he has just read, Lichtenberg or Goethe in his old age – and I often have an almost biblical feeling that the scales are falling from my eyes . . .'[60]

The atmosphere at Maiernigg obviously had a mesmeric effect on Frau Conrat-Tietze. 'It was a beautiful night,' she recorded. 'I sat alone on the terrace. . . . at 11.30 Gustav came out . . . he told me about the astonishing wonder when a musician hears his work for the first time . . . and then he went inside and played some little Bach pieces, so clearly and simply one could almost dream one was in Greece. And I sat outside and saw the sky full of stars . . .' On another occasion, after an expedition across the lake, she wrote: 'This afternoon we rowed to Krumpendorf, Alma in the stern. GM and I finally at the oars. GM beat time and I

---

*All of it except the Dance of the Seven Veils, which Strauss left out because he had not yet written it. Mahler tried to get the opera performed in Vienna, without success – it was first performed in Dresden later that year.

felt like a whole orchestra and positively quaked in my attempts to keep time. The arrival on the other side for some refreshment was like a state visit – the beautiful woman and the famous man whom everyone knew. . . . On the way back I sat opposite Alma. Through the setting sun her hair shone flaming red, and she looked like a beautiful beast of prey. There is something tremendous about the marriage of these two people. It is the most wonderful luck in the world that these two highly talented human beings should be entwined together . . .' As for Alma's individual talents, her views were not far from Mahler's own. 'When I watched Alma, this beautiful, blond woman, whilst she calmed her children, I had to laugh over the fact that there is still a congress for the emancipation of women; it is so clear to me that all that can only ever be a substitute. I speak,' she added in her own defence, 'of the professions, not of other things one might have learned.'[61]

The following summer was equally tranquil. 'After we arrived at Maiernigg, there was the usual fortnight during which, nearly every year, he was haunted by the spectre of failing inspiration', wrote Alma. 'Then one morning just as he crossed the threshold of his studio up in the wood, it came to him – "Veni creator spiritus". He composed and wrote down the whole opening chorus to the half-forgotten words . . .'[62]

From then on Mahler worked continuously on the monumental Eighth Symphony (scored for three sopranos, two contraltos, tenor, baritone, bass, double boys' choir, orchestra and organ), only breaking off for a few days during August to go to Salzburg to conduct *The Marriage of Figaro*. Whilst he was away Alma sent him a harmonized version, done from memory, of one of the choruses ('Alles vergänglich ist nur ein Gleichnis') he had played and sung to her. Mahler was suitably impressed. 'My Almschili!' he wrote on 17 August. 'What a dear letter today. Your notation was perfectly right in feeling. I have corrected only a few trifling details. (The texture is at present not quite "clean".) It is astonishing what a memory for music you have . . .' In a postscript he added: 'Once again – your musicality really surprised me.'[63]

On his return, Alma records that Mahler worked feverishly on the symphony, whose conclusion he set to the last lines of Part Two of Goethe's *Faust*:

> All that was lost in us
> Here is corrected;
> All indescribables
> Here we descry.
> Eternal Womanhead
> Leads us on high.[64]

It was, Alma wrote, their 'last summer of peace and beauty and content. There followed years of horror, years which swept away the very foundations on which we had built.'[65]

The first intimations of unwelcome change took place in the middle of January 1907, when Mahler was summoned by the Opera management to return to Vienna from Frankfurt-am-Main, where he had gone to conduct his Fourth Symphony, in response to a newspaper rumour that their director was anxious to leave, 'in order to devote himself to composition'.

As has already been pointed out, toppling the directors of the Burgtheater and the Opera was a national sport, and Mahler had not escaped the ritual spates of criticism and backbiting meted out to all incumbents by press, public and management alike. As his friend, the music historian Guido Adler, remarked, both directors had to be prepared to brace themselves against blanket resistance to change of any kind. Alterations to the repertoire, attempts to raise the artistic standards of the cast, acceptance of new works, and, in the case of the Opera, appointment of alternative conductors, were all strenuously resisted by the management, backed up by a conservative public and a prurient press intent on making a mountain out of every molehill for the benefit of its readers. In Adler's words:

> Every insubordination of a member of the company was exaggerated into an 'affair' in which the 'tyranny', 'whim', and 'despotism' of the Director were blamed . . . Mahler was denied the ability to judge artistic personalities; he was accused of exclusively pursuing

personal goals . . . The accusations rose to monstrous proportions. When he abolished the claque as unworthy of a serious artistic institution, the clapping palms were sorely missed. When he forbade entrance during the performance in order to avoid disturbances, long-standing holders of reserved seats rebelled. Gradually his iron discipline won the upper hand among the personnel, his energy among the public. But all of the 'affairs', all the attacks, were only fractions of the opposition, which on artistic grounds was neither explainable nor justifiable.[66]

Mahler did, however, have one ally among the management. In theory at least the administration of the Court Opera, like the Burgtheater, came under the auspices of the Lord Chamberlain, Prince Rudolf Liechtenstein. In practice it was administered by his assistant, Prince Alfred Montenuovo – a grandson of the Empress Marie Louise and her second husband (after Napoleon), Baron Neipperg – who succeeded him in 1908. It was to Prince Montenuovo, therefore, that Mahler was accountable for all matters concerning the running of the opera house; and it was fortunate that beneath the Prince's somewhat chilly exterior lay a strong vein of artistic sensibility, enabling him to appreciate Mahler's gifts as a composer, and to sympathize with his innovations to the repertoire.

Another reason for the Prince's support was that between 1897 and 1907 the Opera became extremely profitable. Figures quoted by Kurt Blaukopf show that receipts for 1903 'were assessed in advance at 1,485,000 kronen. In the event, the Opera had a surplus of 58,765 kronen'; and in 1904 the Opera made a surplus of 48,909 in the first four and a half months of the year. Mahler, so indifferent to his domestic finances, approached the Court Opera's budget with the utmost caution. New or unfamiliar works were expected, if not to make a profit, at least to break even.

Amongst the few exceptions to this rule were Strauss's *Feuersnot*, given its first performance in 1902, which went down badly with press and public alike, and *Der Corregidor*, written by his friend from Conservatoire days, Hugo Wolf. Wolf had an unstable temperament, and soon after Mahler's appointment as

director he appeared in his office demanding an instant production of his opera. Mahler demurred, 'knowing the work and
its defects', Alma wrote.[67] His reluctance was enough to push
Wolf, already on the edge of insanity, over the brink. He began
to have delusions that he was director of the Opera, and shortly
afterwards was committed to a lunatic asylum, where he died in
1903.

Had he lived to see his opera performed (on 18 February 1904)
Wolf would have suffered another blow to his self-esteem. In
memory of his friend, Mahler did the best he could with material
described by one commentator as a 'song book with orchestral
accompaniment', but it was not enough to secure it a place in
the repertoire. It was a labour of love, and Der Corregidor had
a very short run in Vienna.

As long as the Opera was making a profit Mahler's enemies
could be kept at bay. Once the revenue started declining, however,
discontents from all sides bubbled to the surface. In 1907 profits
were down, a state of affairs seized upon by his enemies to
highlight the disproportionate amount of time they considered
Mahler devoted to his own work – in particular to conducting
abroad. It was also a peg on which to hang all the other grievances
harboured by his opponents over the years: the complaints about
casting, choice of repertoire, musical and scenic interpretation
and, above all, his woeful lack of reverence towards those on
whom he depended most for support – the establishment, the
press and the public.

Eventually even Prince Montenuovo conceded that he could no
longer hold back the rising tide of anti-Mahler opinion. After an
episode with the ballet master, who had registered a complaint
that Roller had arranged some rehearsals without consulting him,
the Lord Chamberlain expressed his displeasure for the first time.
And, after it had come to his attention that Mahler planned to
conduct three concerts in Rome over Easter, the Prince felt obliged
to speak to him, reminding him that his absences invariably
lowered receipts at the box office. 'Mahler', wrote Alma, 'was
able to contradict this on the spot, but the upshot was that his

resignation was regarded on both sides as a matter for consideration.'

Despite Prince Montenuovo's warnings, Mahler and Alma went to Rome on 19 March 1907. According to Alma her husband was in an unpredictable frame of mind, brought on partly by the inconvenience of temporarily losing their luggage on the way there, and partly by the prospect of his resignation. Try as she would to scale down borrowed dress-suits, or buy him substitute shirts, he remained distracted. 'Everyone we met was astonished at my patience and reproached him to his face with his caprices,' she recorded. 'For example I had to unpack our large trunk three times before we left. His rough drafts for the Seventh Symphony were packed, at his wish, at the very bottom. Then, when the hotel porters were waiting to carry our luggage down, he decided he must have the manuscript at the top . . . I had to unpack the whole trunk. . . . However understandable such behaviour was, it often made him very difficult to live with.'[68]

The general state of uncertainty intensified during the next few weeks. Many of Mahler's friends were convinced that the campaigns against him were the work of German nationalists demanding 'German' programmes from a 'German' director, requests that had little to do with the amount of Tchaikovsky, Smetana, Puccini, Leoncavallo or Charpentier in the repertoire, and more to do with those who had attempted to stop his appointment on anti-Jewish grounds and who were now campaigning for his removal.

To combat them, petitions were signed on his behalf by Arthur Schnitzler, Stefan Zweig, Hermann Bahr, Sigmund Freud, Klimt, Schönberg, Zemlinsky and others. Guido Adler worked strenuously to enable his friend to stay in Vienna, acting as intermediary in order to persuade Mahler and the government ministers concerned that he would be the right man to revitalize the Vienna Conservatoire – an institution once of the highest artistic standing, but currently, in Adler's words, 'financially pressed and . . . experiencing changes in organization and staffing that in no way benefited [it]'.

According to Adler, Mahler was not averse to this scheme, which 'conformed all the more to certain of his inclinations, since in his youth he had already intended to teach music'. A memorandum was worked out, suggesting various organizational changes and proposing that Mahler should have the title of general director, with, at Mahler's request, no honorarium whilst he remained director of the Court Opera. After his resignation he would receive 'a suitable previously agreed-upon stipend'.[69]

Protracted discussions ensued, but no firm conclusions had been reached when, in May, Mahler received another overture, this time from Heinrich Conried, manager of the Metropolitan Opera in New York. They met in Berlin at the beginning of June, and on 5 June Mahler wrote excitedly to Alma:

> ... Bath ... breakfast and straight to Conried, who is staying in the hotel. He was full of projects, all fire and fervour. First and foremost, wanted me on exactly the same terms as Caruso. Then 8 months (180,000 crowns) – then 6. Finally we got to this: 3 months (15th January to 15th April) for which 75,000 crowns net, journey and all expenses paid (first-class hotel)! We have not yet come to an agreement about the length of the contract. He wants four years, I want one only. – As soon as I have spoken to you, I am going up to him again ...

Below his signature he added:

> Kiss   Kiss
> 4 years and 6 months @ 125,000 crowns
> making ½ a million crowns
> or an annual guest visit of 6–8 weeks,
> 50,000 crowns fee
> making 200,000 crowns in four years.
> Kiss   Kiss
>   Auf Wiedersehen![70]

After this there was little hope that Mahler would decide to renounce the Metropolitan in favour of the Conservatoire. The final arrangements with Conried were completed by the beginning of July, Mahler agreeing to go to New York for three months a year for four years – a contract which would, he told Arnold Berliner, bring him '300,000 crowns clear'. Although not officially released by the Emperor until the autumn, Mahler's dealings with Prince Montenuovo over what was euphemistically referred to as his 'premature retirement' were well under way by the early summer.

Before they were concluded Mahler had the satisfaction of rebuffing the Prince who, having run into considerable difficulties over the appointment of a successor (Nikisch, Schuch and Weingartner had all dragged their feet), decided that it would be easier to back down and accede to Mahler's requests for conducting leave. But by that time Mahler was thoroughly sick of the whole business. He told the Prince that 'he, too, had altered his opinion. He saw now that a director of opera should confine himself strictly to his official duties and be always on the spot.'[71] On 17 June he wrote to Arnold Berliner that he was going because he could 'no longer endure the rabble'. And to Bruno Walter, with whom he was walking home from the Opera through the Stadtpark, he said 'that the die was cast and that he would leave'. Walter wrote in his memoirs: 'When I spoke of the Opera's terrible loss, and of the void the renunciation of his work would leave within him, he answered with the words: "In the ten years at the Opera I have completed my circle." I was deeply moved and walked silently at his side as far as his house.'[72]

At the end of June the Mahlers went to Maiernigg for their annual holiday, and a week later, on 4 July, Mahler wrote to Arnold Berliner about his contract for the Metropolitan, adding: 'We have had frightful bad luck! I shall tell you when we meet. Now my elder daughter has scarlet fever – diphtheria! Shall we see you in the summer – in August? . . .'[73] A week later, on 12 July, after an unsuccessful tracheotomy, Mahler's adored Putzi, the only one ever allowed into his studio every day, whose 'beauty and waywardness and her unapproachability, her black curls and large blue eyes' had given him so much pleasure, died at the age of five. 'Mahler, weeping and sobbing, went again and again to the door of my bedroom, where she was,' wrote Alma, 'then fled away to be out of earshot of any sound. It was more than he could bear. We telegraphed to my mother, who came at once. We all three slept in his room. We could not bear being parted for an hour. We dreaded what might happen if any one of us left the room. We were like birds in a storm and feared what each moment might bring – and how right we were!'[74]

There were more horrors to come. Within two days Frau Moll collapsed from the strain (Alma said she had a heart attack). Alma, who had borne the brunt of the nursing, was ordered to rest completely by the local doctor, who diagnosed 'extreme exhaustion of the heart'. Finally, Mahler, examined by the same doctor, was found to have a 'double-sided congenital, though compensated, valve defect' in his own heart.[75] The verdict was confirmed by Professor Kovacs in Vienna, who told him to rest and to abstain completely from climbing, cycling and swimming.

Maiernigg was tainted for ever. 'I packed the barest necessities', Alma wrote, 'and we fled from Maiernigg, which was haunted now by painful memories, to Schluderbach in the Tyrol. We revived to some extent in new and beautiful surroundings and tried to imagine our life in the future . . .'[76]

7 The Farewell

For the time being, the future was stalked by death. The terrible presentiments of the *Kindertotenlieder* had come to pass and the loss for them both was irreparable. But, if women can be divided into those who put their children before their husbands and lovers and those who do not, then Alma fell into the latter category. Terrible though Putzi's death was for her, it was Mahler's fragile health that was uppermost in her mind; and Mahler, all his life half in love with easeful Death, was finding him in practice an uneasy bedfellow. To try and cheat his coming, he took up a volume of Chinese poetry, *The Chinese Flute*, translated by Hans Bethge, sent to him earlier in the year by an old friend of Alma's father, Dr Pollak, and, finding that 'their infinite melancholy answered to his own', began to set them to music. 'Before we left Schluderbach', wrote Alma, 'he had sketched out, on our long, lonely walks, those songs for orchestra which took final shape as *Das Lied von der Erde* [*The Song of the Earth*] a year later.'[1]

Back in Vienna in the early autumn, the round of farewell concerts began. A successor had at last been found (Felix von Weingartner had been persuaded to take over as Opera director), and Mahler was formally released from his post on 5 October by imperial decree, under which he was granted an indemnity of 20,000 kronen and an annual pension of 14,000 kronen. Nothing now stood in the way of a new life in the New World, where both Alma and Mahler could submerge their grief and find solace amongst sympathizers and admirers of a different hue.

They wasted no time. The last opera having been conducted (*Fidelio* on 15 October), the last concert given (a performance of

Mahler's Second Symphony at the Vienna Conservatoire on 24 November 1907), and the final farewell party staged in their honour by Zemlinsky, Schönberg and other friends, the Mahlers were seen off by two hundred well-wishers at the Western Railway station on 9 December.

On the same day a letter from the outgoing director was pinned up at the Opera House, in the course of which he said:

> The time of our working together has come to an end. I leave a working community that has become dear to me, and bid you all farewell . . . It is not for me to pass judgement on what my work has come to mean to those to whom it was dedicated. But at a moment like this I may say of myself: I meant well and aimed high. Not always could my efforts be crowned with success . . . But I have always given my all, have subordinated my person to the cause, my inclinations to my duty. I did not spare myself and was therefore justified in demanding that others, too, should exert their strength to the utmost.
>
> In the crush of the struggle, in the heat of the moment, wounds were sustained, errors committed, by you as well as by me. But when a work had turned out right, a problem had been solved, we forgot all our care and trouble and felt richly rewarded – even without any outward sign of success. We have all progressed on our way – and with us the institute which was the object of our endeavours.[2]

With this, as Bruno Walter, one of the friends waving goodbye, remarked: 'An important chapter in Europe's cultural history had come to an end. A brilliance that had shone forth from Vienna had faded, had vanished, and the lamp of life that had shed it was flickering alarmingly.'[3]

They had not been gone for more than twenty-four hours before Alma found herself confronted by reassuring signs that she was not, as she had come to believe, 'old and ugly', but yet again capable of 'arousing love'. In Paris they stayed in the same hotel as their friend, the Russian-born pianist and conductor, Ossip Gabrilowitsch. In the evening Mahler unwisely left them alone together, dusk fell, nobody turned on the lights, and an emboldened Gabrilowitsch, according to Alma, felt for her hand in the dark and blurted out that he was on the verge of falling in love with her. This short idyll was interrupted by Mahler's return – he tactfully switched on the lights and was 'affectionate and kindly' – but it was enough to recharge Alma's batteries: 'this episode was my standby for some time in many an onset of self-deprecation.'[4]

Fortified by this boost to her morale, Alma boarded the SS *Augusta Victoria* at Cherbourg in high spirits. Mahler, too, was in an optimistic mood. A band was playing the 'Marseillaise', the state cabins were satisfactorily luxurious, the food served in the saloon exceeded all expectations, and there was a telegram from Gerhart Hauptmann: 'Dear Friend, with all my heart wish you happy voyage on the fine ship in which I myself made the return voyage some years ago. Come happily back to the Europe we love, which needs men like you as it does its daily bread. Your Gerhart Hauptmann.'[5]

Once the ship began to move, however, Mahler's spirits sank. All his forebodings about rough seas and seasickness were realized. He lay in his cabin, 'rigidly on his bunk like a cardinal on his tomb, neither eating nor speaking until the dread sensation passed', to be momentarily restored by the sight of the New York skyline, which, recorded Alma, 'so took our breath away that we forgot our troubles. But not for long.'[6]

Their troubles, when they overtook them, hung heavier over Alma than over her husband. After the initial excitement of settling in to the Majestic Hotel, in an eleventh-floor suite containing two pianos, combined with the exhilaration of discovering how easy it was to find one's way about in 'this divine city' and pleasure at the hospitable nature of its inhabitants, loneliness set in: the misery of Putzi's loss could not be expunged by a simple change of environment. As soon as he arrived Mahler was plunged into preparations for *Tristan and Isolde*, at whose première, on 1 January 1908, he made his Metropolitan début. This was immediately followed, on 7 February, by *Die Walküre* and on 19 February by *Siegfried*. A month later, on 20 March, he conducted *Fidelio*, before a replica of Alfred Roller's Viennese set.

All this activity could not mask the deep individual suffering borne by them both – a suffering that only served, according to Alma, to estrange and separate them. Alma's hyper-sensitive antennae picked up vibrations of blame. 'Mahler . . . was a different man in New York . . . What had changed was his whole attitude toward the world, and toward life. Ours could have been beautiful if we had not been undone by our child's death. Unconsciously he blamed me for it, and for a time we became strangers to one another, estranged by grief. Besides, he knew now that he was a sick man, which made everything else appear much less important.'[7]

Perhaps Alma also felt that she was being held responsible for another gap in their life: Gucki had been left behind in Vienna with Frau Moll, to allow Alma to adjust to New York unencumbered by too many domestic responsibilities, and her absence was an added source of misery for them both. Mahler could not bear to have Putzi's name mentioned in his hearing and, denied any opportunity to talk about her lost daughter or to take comfort from the presence of her other child, and with the added unhappiness of being unable to communicate fully with her husband, Alma fell ever lower in spirit.

In the end, after a wretched and lonely Christmas, the realization that the excitement and promise of their new life could, in reality, do nothing to heal the wounds inflicted on them in the recent past drove Alma to the point of nervous and physical collapse. Without the panacea of work, left for long hours alone in her hotel suite, speaking no English (more than twenty years after arriving in California with Franz Werfel in 1940 she never spoke anything other than German), disorientated, bereft, and without the prop and mainstay of her Viennese coterie, she disintegrated into despair. 'One morning,' she recorded mournfully, 'I could not rise from my bed. Mahler telephoned for a doctor, who in turn summoned another, and the two diagnosed weakness of the heart and nervous collapse, and ordered a four weeks' rest cure. I was given strychnine and forbidden to move. At long last I was able to give way to my grief and my physical exhaustion. Mahler at once felt his sorrow less and gave all his thoughts to speeding my recovery.'[8]

Mahler did, indeed, notice his wife's ailments. 'My wife has been confined to bed for the last week, poor thing,' he wrote to Alfred Roller on 20 January, and on 17 February he told the banker Paul Hammerschlag: 'my wife was indisposed most of last month and confined to her room. But she is pretty well now, and I hope she will be able to catch up with what she has missed.'[9]

By the end of the New York season Alma had recovered enough to accompany the opera company to Philadelphia, but the sight of her husband's strained face during a performance of *Tristan* induced such feelings of mortality that she fainted. Amongst the audience was Professor Leon Corning, the discoverer of spinal anaesthesia and a keen amateur flautist, who carried her to a dressing-room and then went out to a chemist for some sal volatile. This encounter led to an invitation to dinner – a doubtful privilege, as although his researches had made him immensely rich the professor spent very little of his money on food and drink. 'On each minute plate there was deposited something equally minute and of questionable edibility,' Alma recorded. 'A half-bottle of champagne was opened in our honour and yielded an egg-cupful apiece. There were seven of us.'[10]

A month before they returned to Vienna in April Mahler was able to report to his mother-in-law that Alma was 'on top of the world again, thank goodness, – fit as a fiddle'.[11] Mahler himself was in good spirits, even though the resignation of Heinrich Conried early in 1908 had led to management upheavals that threatened to throw his own contract into jeopardy. Asked by the new controlling consortium – headed by Otto F. Kahn, a philanthropic millionaire more interested in artistic integrity than financial gain – to take Conried's place as director, Mahler refused, albeit with some regret. He wrote to Paul Hammerschlag:

> If I were young and had the energy I squandered during ten years in Vienna, something might perhaps be brought about here that we groped for as an ideal in Vienna: the exclusion of any commercial consideration whatsoever. For the decisive bodies here are *so* fair and the means at their disposal are so unlimited. You will already have heard that the stockholders . . . offered me the directorship with absolute authority, and that I firmly rejected it . . . Five years

ago, however, I should not have been able to resist such an alluring
offer. The climate, the people and the extremely generous conditions suit me extraordinarily well . . . [12]

Mahler was, however, persuaded to renew his original contract,
which he had ended during the unsettled period after the change
of management. It said much for the pleasant atmosphere of New
York that he not only changed his mind, but was prepared to
work with a new general director – Giulio Gatti-Casazza, formerly director of La Scala, Milan – and to agree to share the
conducting and artistic direction with Arturo Toscanini – one of
Gatti-Casazza's conditions for leaving Milan.

There was another reason for staying in America. The performance of *Fidelio* on 20 March had attracted the attention of Mrs
George R. Sheldon, the wife of a banker and Republican politician, and her equally wealthy New York socialite friend, Mrs
Minnie Untermeyer. Together they decided to raise the money to
found an orchestra to be exclusively at Mahler's disposal, a project that had been close to Mahler's heart ever since leaving the
Vienna Philharmonic in 1901.

'Dearest Mama,' he wrote to Frau Moll at the end of March:

> Here I am sending you a 'newspaper'. Not only because it really
> lays itself out (and you enjoy that, I know), but because it gives a
> very clear picture of the present situation. *Fidelio* was a complete
> success, wholly changing my prospects from one day to the next.
> I am moving, or rather 'things' are moving, towards the formation
> of a Mahler orchestra entirely at my own disposal, which would
> not only earn me a good deal of money, but also give me some
> satisfaction. Everything now depends on the New Yorkers' attitude
> to my work. Since they are completely unprejudiced I hope I shall
> here find fertile ground for my works and thus a spiritual home,
> something that, for all the sensationalism, I should never be able
> to have in Europe. [13]

A year was to elapse before this dream was realized. In the
meantime a summer home had to be found in Austria as a substitute for Maiernigg. In May Alma and her mother found a suitable
retreat – a large farmhouse outside the village of Toblach, in
the South Tyrol, with eleven rooms, two verandahs and two
bathrooms, 'all somewhat primitive but in a lovely situation'. It

was there, between 1908 and 1910, at an upright piano in a studio in the garden, that Mahler wrote his last works: *Das Lied von der Erde*, the Ninth Symphony and the sketches for the Tenth Symphony. But all the pleasures that had been so much a part of the pattern of his summer life were now a thing of the past. For the first time the physical limitations imposed by his heart condition came home to him. 'I have been trying to settle in here,' he wrote in an undated letter to Bruno Walter:

> This time it is not only a change of pace but a change of my whole way of life. You can imagine how hard the latter comes to me. For many years I have been used to constant and vigorous exercise . . . I used to go to my desk only as a peasant goes into his barn, to work up sketches. Even spiritual indisposition used to disappear after a good trudge . . . Now I am told to avoid any exertion, keep a constant eye on myself, and not walk much . . . since I have been in the country I have been feeling worse than I did in town, where all the distractions helped to take my mind off things.[14]

In an effort to cheer themselves up, and to avoid the steady flow of visitors who both entertained and exhausted them, Mahler and Alma took the unprecedented step of taking a holiday. It was not an unqualified success. They went to Salzburg, where they stayed in the Hotel Nelböck, and to begin with it seemed that the miseries and anxieties of the past year could be put aside, and they could recapture something of the carefree atmosphere of their wedding trip. But there was no escape from the fear they both felt on Mahler's behalf. Every expedition was overshadowed by the presence of the pedometer Mahler kept in his pocket to record his steps. His pulse rate had also to be constantly monitored. 'This summer was the saddest we had ever spent or were to spend together,' Alma wrote. 'Every excursion, every attempt at distraction was a failure. Grief and anxiety pursued us wherever we went.'[15]

Work was her husband's only solace, as Alma pointed out. *Das Lied von der Erde*, completed that year, was, he wrote to Bruno Walter in September 1908, the most personal thing he had done so far. Once again he returned to the twin obsessions of his youth – death and nature – but this time death was a reality staring him in the face and eternity an unknown quantity. Only the earth, which would remain after he had left it, held the promise of everlasting beauty:

> The dear earth everywhere
> Blossoms in spring and grows green again!
> Everywhere and eternally the distance shines bright and blue
> Eternally . . . eternally . . . [16]

Reconciling himself to the prospect of dying did not come easily. In July Mahler wrote to Bruno Walter that if he was to:

> find the way back to myself again I must surrender to the horrors of loneliness . . . you do not know what has been and still is going on within me; but it is certainly not that hypochondriac fear of death, as you suppose. I had already realized that I shall have to die. – But without trying to explain or describe to you something for which there are perhaps no words at all, I'll just tell you that at a blow I have simply lost all the clarity and quietude I ever achieved; and that I stood vis-à-vis de rien, and now at the end of life am again a beginner who must find his feet . . . [17]

A superstitious desire not to follow in the footsteps of Beethoven and Bruckner, both of whom died after completing their ninth symphonies, prevented Mahler from giving *Das Lied von der Erde* its rightful title of Symphony No. 9. Strengthened by the illusion that he had outwitted fate he conducted at a series of concerts – in Prague on 19 September (where his Seventh Symphony was performed for the first time) and in Munich (its second performance), followed by appearances in Berlin, Hamburg and, just before his return to New York, in Paris.

Alma joined him in Prague, where she found many of Mahler's youthful admirers, including Ossip Gabrilowitsch, Alban Berg, Bruno Walter and Otto Klemperer (in his second year as chorusmaster), all eager to relieve him of the strain of last-minute revisions to the orchestration, but Mahler refused their offers of help. 'We younger musicians . . . would gladly have helped,' wrote Klemperer in his reminiscences of Mahler, 'but he would not hear of it . . .'[18] The Seventh Symphony was, according to Alma, the end of a phase – one that began with the Fifth Symphony – of constant retouching and polishing of orchestral

1. Emil Jacob Schindler
and his wife Anna

2. Schindler in the garden
of Plankenberg

3. Alma, her mother and her sister Grete

4. Alma Maria Schindler, 1899

5. Bertha Zuckerkandl

6. Alexander von Zemlinsky,
by Emil Orlik

7. Gustav Klimt

8. Hans Pfitzner

9. Gustav Mahler,
1899

above right
10. Gustav Mahler,
1907

11. Alma Mahler,
1909

above
12. Alma on Semmering,
1917

above right
13. Franz Werfel,
Alma and Manon
in Venice

14. Alma and her
daughter Anna

15. Drawing of Alma
by Oskar Kokoschka, 1912

16. Oskar Kokoschka, 1909

17. 'The Tempest' by Oskar Kokoschka, 1914, also known as 'The Bride of
the Wind'

above left
18. Alma and Franz Werfel,
c.1918

above
19. Franz Werfel,
c.1927

below left
20. Walter Gropius

21. Alma and Franz Werfel
on Semmering

22. Alma in New York, 1962,
with the photograph of Mahler
she kept on her piano

23. Bruno Walter,
Alma and Eugene Ormandy

24. Alma's living-room in New York,
known as 'The Power of Words' room

material before performances. The Fifth, she said, 'was differently orchestrated for practically every performance' and the Sixth and Seventh were 'constantly in process of revision'. The Eighth, possibly due to its gigantic scale, was left alone. *Das Lied von der Erde* was performed posthumously, but Alma was probably right when she remarked that she could not 'imagine him altering a note in a work so economical in its means of expression'.[19]

After Prague Alma went back to Vienna to prepare for their departure; this time Anna and an English nurse were travelling with them. Mahler wrote cheerfully from Munich, where he had asked his 'Dearest little Mama', Frau Moll, to join him (an arrangement Alma was obliged to swallow with good grace), that everything was to his satisfaction: the orchestra willing, the climate superb and the living cheap. So cheap that he became enthusiastic about the idea of settling in Munich. 'What do you think?' he asked. 'You can buy a castle in a park here for 3,000 marks, and life is actually twice as cheap as in Vienna. With our income we could live here like princes . . .'[20]

His spirits remained undimmed throughout the rest of his tour. With Frau Moll to look after him everything was splendid – the journey to Berlin, the hotel there, and the arrangements made for him in Hamburg. His only regret was that Alma was not with him: 'Everyone asks for you and laments your absence.'

Back in New York things continued to go well. Alma reported her husband to be in the best of health, and even the inevitable teething troubles between himself and Toscanini, who had arrived before him and who wanted to conduct Wagner – *Tristan* in particular – during his first season, were resolved amicably. Toscanini bowed to Mahler's defence of his own right to conduct *Tristan*, which in its current New York form, as Mahler pointed out in a letter to the management, was his brainchild, and contented himself with *Götterdämmerung*. And at the end of the 1908–9 season, during which Mahler conducted new productions of *The Marriage of Figaro* (on 13 January 1909) and *The Bartered Bride* (19 February), Mahler presided over a triumphant *Tristan* that satisfied even his stringent standards and drove the critics to their dictionaries for superlatives.

But perhaps the greatest source of pleasure for them both was the succcessful efforts of Mrs Sheldon and Mrs Untermeyer to raise money for a Mahler orchestra, which in fact became a revamped version of the New York Philharmonic, rescued by the ladies' fund-raising from a debilitating financial deficit. In return for an injection of $90,000 its members were asked to forgo their democratic habit of choosing their own conductors, to 'place themselves under the control of a governing body and to accept Mahler as their supreme commander, who would decide on the dismissal of inferior players or the admission of new instrumentalists'.[21] This, after some deliberation, they agreed to do. When, therefore, he took the rostrum at the Carnegie Hall on 31 March 1909 to conduct Schumann's *Manfred* Overture and Beethoven's Seventh Symphony, Mahler faced the human embodiment of all his dreams. From then on he worked ceaselessly to improve his orchestra's standards, for despite his satisfaction at being given absolute control over them, he found its members 'untalented and phlegmatic' and complained to Bruno Walter that he found it 'very dispiriting to have to start all over again as a conductor'. Nevertheless he admitted that he got some pleasure from rehearsing new works and that making music was 'still tremendous fun' for him.[22]

Total charge of the New York Philharmonic also gave Mahler the opportunity to prise himself loose from his Metropolitan contract. During the season of 1909–10 he conducted operas by invitation only, for a specially negotiated fee: the directorship of the Metropolitan was taken on by Toscanini. On the face of it, it seemed that at long last Mahler could divide his time in the way he liked best, without undue pressure from administrative sources, and still have some over for his wife.

Alma, too, was in a happier frame of mind, due largely to Mahler's contentment and to the presence of Gucki, but also to their change of hotel and to their blossoming social life. In the winter of 1908–9, in preference to the Majestic, they lodged at the Savoy Hotel on Fifth Avenue, where Caruso and the Polish soprano Marcella Sembrich also had rooms. From this sympathetic base, Alma began to spread her social wings. Although not averse to the novelty of lunching with Mrs Sheldon at a Ladies' Club filled with women of 'that incredible elegance to be seen only in America', or to visiting Theodore Roosevelt's sister-in-law, Mrs West Roosevelt, in her spectacular timbered farmhouse overlooking Oyster Bay, Alma preferred, as she did until the end of her life, the company of German-speakers.

Dr Joseph Fraenkel, the sculptor Karl Bitter, the sinologist Friedrich Hirth, Marcella Sembrich, Maria Uchetius, an art student and Alma's first friend in New York, Franz Kneisal, leader of the 'best quartet in New York', the painter Carl Hassmann, the composer and pupil of Paderewski, Ernst Schelling and his wife, Kurt Schindler, 'a really gifted musician', the pianist Joseph Weiss (whom Alma described as having a 'square, bald skull, with the merest tuft in the middle, and brown eyes wedged in slits, which could only mean either insanity or genius') and Albert Groll – 'a necessitous artist who lived among Indians, spoke their language and told us a lot about them' – all fitted into the European mould and made up to some extent for the absence of Burckhard, Zemlinsky, Klimt, Bruno Walter and Arnold Rosé. 'Thus,' wrote Alma, 'in a foreign land we built up a world of our own which was more European than Europe itself.'[23] Even their excursions into grander society – to Mrs Havemayer's 'fairy-tale palace' built by her friend Louis Tiffany, to Otto H. Kahn, or to the music publisher E. C. Schirmer, who had a taste for low life and took them in his chauffeur-driven car to an opium den in Chinatown, were reassuringly Germanic.

The spring, though, brought fresh troubles. When Frau Moll came to visit them at the beginning of March 1909 she went down with a mysterious illness, diagnosed by Dr Fraenkel as kidney trouble, and during her stay Alma suffered a miscarriage. Curiously, Alma mentions neither of these traumatic events in her memoirs, and referred only once[24] to what Anna's husband, Albrecht Joseph, described in his portrait of Alma written after the Second World War as her 'astounding' number of abortions. It is only through a letter Mahler wrote to Carl Moll on 10 March, setting out Dr Fraenkel's dietary plans for 'dear little Mama', that we learn that she had this and at least one other previous miscarriage, for Mahler concluded: 'Alma is very well. (About her *present state* she has doubtless written to you herself. She has been relieved of her *burden*. But this time she actually regrets it.)'[25]

Without Alma's side of the story, one can only guess at the depth of her feelings on this particular bereavement, but Putzi's death must have made it especially poignant. Although Mahler's remarks indicate that pregnancy was never very high on Alma's list of satisfying experiences, the chance to have another child to replace her first-born probably explains her unprecedented sadness at its loss.

The extent of her sorrow became apparent a couple of months later, when they arrived back in Vienna. On the face of it, there was no other immediate reason for the critical state of her nerves. Mahler, she recorded, was 'younger and less oppressed, his grief was dying down'; en route they had a 'blissful' stay in Paris, where Mahler had sat for Rodin and where they had been entertained by a number of old friends, including the Clemenceaus and General Picquart. Nevertheless her state of mind was disturbed enough for her to be ordered a rest-cure at Levico. She arrived, with Anna, feeling 'profoundly melancholy' and spent night after night sitting on her balcony weeping and brooding on the absence of love or life that had brought her to such a lamentable pass.

Mahler, whom she had settled in Toblach, was not much of a comfort. Although he obviously suspected that it was his love and attention for which Alma craved, he was immersed in the final stages of *Das Lied von der Erde* and the Ninth Symphony, and more concerned with the business of getting these to work, the abysmal state of the weather and the annoyance of being without several small necessities, than attending to his wife's emotional needs. 'Dearest Mama,' he wrote to Frau Moll on an undated postcard, 'if I am to burden you with a list of wants, I would ask for the following: 1. A small jar of *real* honey (not that disgusting liquorice syrup that Agnes has served up to me today). 2. A small bottle of fountain-pen ink. 3. Two key chains. 4. A little peppermint-oil for a mouthwash after meals.' He added that: 'Almschi has been sending me thoroughgoing letters of lamentation, from which I deduce that she is finding the cure very strenuous. Besides, I know being alone isn't the right thing for her at present. It is lucky she at least has Gucki with her . . .'[26]

They did, however, exchange letters, which to Alma lacked intimacy. In them they discussed Goethe – Alma contributed an analysis of the final stanza of *Faust* that Mahler found 'good; better, I am sure, than those offered by the learned commentators' – as well as man's restless search for fulfilment and the growth, or otherwise, of his soul along the way. 'This is the meaning, my dear Almschi,' Mahler explained, in a letter written on 27 June, 'of all that has happened to you, of all that has been laid on you, as a necessity of the growth of the soul and the forging of the personality.'[27] With this homily, and a brief, unsatisfactory visit, Alma had to be content.

The summer ended on an equally unsatisfactory note. The flat in the Auenbruggergasse had come to the end of its useful life, and early in October Alma arranged for their furniture, books and china to be put in store. From then on their base in Vienna would be with the Molls on the Hohe Warte. Whilst all this was going on, Mahler went to Moravia to put the final touches to *Das Lied von der Erde*, only returning to Vienna after both Alma and Anna had endured a painful cauterization of their tonsils, apparently undergone without anaesthetic. Alma showed a stoical disregard for the pain, discomfort and worry this must have caused her, merely noting that Mahler did not return from Moravia 'until my child and I had recovered from an operation on our tonsils'.[28] Before his return, Mahler wrote to her at the Sanatorium Luithlen, complimenting his wife on her powers of endurance: 'You have behaved splendidly. I have heard all about it: 24 incisions and without an anaesthetic. I'm delighted for you both; and convinced that it will be of life-long *benefit*. But I was very anxious. Particularly as I had to wait from four to half-past five for the news by telephone . . .'[29]

Back in New York for the winter season, life resumed its American pattern. Mahler conducted only once at the Metropolitan Opera – Smetana's *Bartered Bride* – and was therefore able to give his undivided attention to his own concerts. Once again they stayed at the Savoy Hotel, from where, every other morning when the orchestra was rehearsing, Alma went to pick Mahler up so that they could walk home together. She also resumed her social life, visiting Mrs Roosevelt at Oyster Bay and attending (with Mahler and Dr Fraenkel) a seance conducted by the medium Eusapia Palladino, at which they all felt themselves being touched by phosphorescent bodies, Mahler was hit by a flying mandolin, and the table around which the party was sitting shot up to the ceiling. Other, less dramatic, evenings were spent dining with friends at the unfamiliar hour of 7.15 p.m. (nearly two hours earlier than in Vienna), or going to the theatre or the opera, where their box became a centre for their German-speaking friends.

On 1 February 1910 the Mahlers went to the première of Strauss's opera *Elektra* at the Manhattan Opera House, but found it disappointing and boring; Mahler disliked it so much that he wanted to leave in the middle, and they both regretted their decision to see it through until the end.

April saw them in Paris for a performance of Mahler's Second Symphony, arranged by the composer Gabriel Pierné, who according to Alma had not seen the music – an oversight that led to some embarrassment. During rehearsals Pierné gave a party in their honour, and invited Debussy, Gabriel Fauré and Paul Dukas. Mahler, Alma noted, was 'not happy or at ease that evening, and he had good reason'.[30] At the performance Debussy, Dukas and Pierné left in the middle of the second movement – explaining afterwards that they had found the music too 'Schubertian . . . too Viennese – too Slav'. Mahler, Alma reported, was mortified. Despite the symphony's success with the public it was 'no consolation for the bitterness of being so misunderstood and indeed condemned by the foremost French composers'.[31]

From Paris they went to Rome, where Mahler was to give a concert, but once again, though for a different reason, the trip was not a success. Willem Mengelberg, who had been conducting a series of concerts in Rome, told Mahler to stand no nonsense from the orchestra, who were 'a job lot and quite undisciplined'. Nothing loath, Alma recorded, Mahler harangued them, dictionary in hand, for their 'stupidity and indolence' – and got a mutinous response. The resultant bad feeling spilled over into the concert itself, which received mediocre notices, and Mahler and Alma arrived back in Vienna 'in very bad humour to find a garbled version of the story in all the papers and everybody talking about it'.[32]

Possibly due to the frustrations of the last two trips, on top of four months of strenuous social life – although Alma ate almost as sparingly as Mahler she drank increasingly large quantities of alcohol – the summer found her again in a debilitated condition. Once more she was advised to take a cure: this time she and Anna went to Tobelbad, a spa in a mountain-ringed valley not far from Toblach. There, worn out by the strain of being 'driven on by a spirit so intense' and by her own account on the verge of a complete breakdown, she led a life of solitary aestheticism, adhering conscientiously to the spartan regime. Barefoot and 'clothed in a horrible nightgown',[33] she went for walks in all weathers, bathed in the hot springs – even though she fainted at the first attempt – and submitted to a diet of lettuce and buttermilk.

None of these worthy efforts to cleanse her system, however, did much to improve Alma's morale. To take her out of herself the doctor in charge prescribed dancing, and he introduced her to a young man who could, she noted with some satisfaction, 'have been well cast as Walther von Stolzing in *Die Meistersinger*'. Nothing could have been guaranteed to have a more revitalizing effect. Like a starving Frenchman scenting the promise of pot-au-feu, Alma succumbed to the sensation she liked best, and which she had been denied for so long. Soon she was basking in the healing rays of masculine admiration. No matter that she knew little about her new companion other than that he was an architect and had studied with one of her father's 'well-known friends'. The main thing was that he was twenty-seven years old, good-looking and comparatively straightforward. As dancing had made a change from penitential boiling baths, so Walter Gropius provided an antidote to years of emotional frustration. If Mahler could not, or would not, give her the love she needed, why should she deny herself such a simple cure for all the ills that had beset her in the past?

Had Alma been more curious about her inamorato's antecedents, she would have approved of them. Walter Gropius came from a long line of handsome, artistically gifted and public-spirited stock: Church, military and government service were interwoven with artists and architects in his family tree. One of his great-uncles was Martin Gropius, designer of the Museum of Arts and Crafts in Berlin and, from 1867, principal of the School of Arts and Crafts in that city. His father, Walther Gropius, was an architect, his mother came from a Huguenot family who fled to Germany in the seventeenth century. Gropius had studied architecture in Berlin and Munich and had been working since the spring of 1908 in the Berlin office of Peter Behrens, formerly head of the Düsseldorf School of Art and newly appointed artistic consultant to AEG. Stimulating though this practical training had been, Gropius had begun to want to push his own architectural ideas further than Behrens was prepared to go. To this end, encouraged by members of his family, he put plans in motion to set up in practice on his own and, by the spring of 1910, had finally made the break, taking with him as his assistant another of the Behrens team, Adolf Meyer.

By the summer, therefore, Gropius was ready for a much-needed holiday. A photograph of him, dated 1910,[34] although underexposed, gives some indication of what must have been his attraction for Alma. Tall, with dark hair, bushy eyebrows and a flourishing moustache, he lies on the grass, young, strong, genial and outwardly uncomplicated. Most important of all, he was able to give Alma his undivided attention.

By the time she left Tobelbad the cure was almost complete.

Their daily encounters had left Gropius as emotionally wrought up as his dancing partner and he told Alma that he had fallen in love with her and hoped that she could love him in return. Alma, well pleased at having kindled such an ardent flame, nevertheless did not commit herself entirely. 'I would have treasured his friendship,' she wrote. 'I felt that it could have been a more beautiful friendship than any I had known – but now I left Tobelbad.'[35]

Meanwhile, in Toblach, Mahler was deep in the final arrangements for a performance of his Eighth Symphony, to be heard for the first time in Munich on 12 September 1910. Preparations had begun at the beginning of the year and by June the chorus, 858 strong, made up of 250 members of the Choral Society of the Gesellschaft der Musikfreunde, an equal number from the Reidel-Verein of Leipzig and 350 children from the Munich Zentral-Singschule, the eight solo singers, chosen and prepared by Bruno Walter, and the 171 instrumentalists, including 84 strings, 6 harps, 22 woodwinds and 17 brass from the enlarged orchestra of the Munich Concert Society, were nearly ready for their colossal task.

Towards the middle of the month he went to Munich to rehearse the orchestra. In the midst of problems with the copyist – who had 'simply written tacit in all the parts where a number of pauses occur, instead of writing the pauses out in full'[36] – he worried about Alma. 'My Almschi,' he wrote. 'It worries me today to have no letter from you after your so sad one of yesterday. Are you hiding something?'[37] He also expressed his fears to Frau Moll, to whom he wrote from the Regina-Palast Hotel that he was 'perturbed by Almschi's letters, which have such a peculiar tone. What on earth is going on?'[38]

Before Mahler left Munich their letters had returned to safer subjects – his last delving deep into the misunderstood conception of Platonic love – and when he met Alma on Toblach station in July, her health and spirits restored by, he imagined, several weeks' rest and sensible diet, his pleasure manifested itself in an upsurge of luxurious attention. 'Mahler . . . seemed suddenly more amorous than ever,' wrote Alma. 'Whether or not the young stranger's infatuation had restored the equilibrium of my self-confidence, in any case I was happier, looking forward to the future and not eager for any change.'[39]

Walter Gropius, left behind in Tobelbad to reflect on the implications of his declarations of passion, was not so content to let matters rest. Nevertheless he had agreed to Alma's strict instructions to keep their liaison a secret, and only to correspond poste-restante, and it was as much a shock to him as to anyone else when within a fortnight he committed a solecism worthy of Spooner. On the same day two letters arrived for Alma – one correctly addressed, the other to Herr G. Mahler.

According to Alma, 'What came next defied description.' Her husband opened the letter at his piano. 'What is this?' she quotes him as saying. 'Here is a young man who asks for your hand.'[40] Completely wrong-footed, Alma tried desperately to retrieve the situation. All the pent-up grievances, all the longings 'for his love year after year . . . that he, in his fanatical concentration on his own life, had simply overlooked',[41] were poured out. Together they wept over the things they both felt they had lost and Mahler, 'for the first time in his life, felt that there was such a thing as an inner obligation toward the person with whom one has, after all, been joined together. He suddenly felt guilty.'[42] To help them heal these past and present wounds they sent for Frau Moll, and until she arrived walked about 'tearfully' together for days on end.

As soon as she could, Alma managed to send an urgent message to Tobelbad, asking Gropius for an explanation of his word-blind behaviour: '. . . the only way I could think of to convince myself that you had addressed the letter unintentionally was the bit in today's letter where you wrote, "Has your husband noticed anything? Write and tell me quite sincerely . . ." Otherwise I'd have to think you'd taken leave of your senses, and I would rather think that his loss of all confidence and belief in me was due to an accident, than to any confessions on my side . . .'[43] Once more she urged him to abide by their rules and send his reply, which she awaited with 'feverish longings', poste-restante. When it came it was brief: 'Your letter made me terribly anxious about you both . . . I shall go mad if you don't call me, I shall come to you both myself and put things right, and help to unravel the mystery.'[44]

He was not called. Frau Moll's sympathetic presence, Alma's agitation and Mahler's desperate and, to Alma, touching efforts to make things up to her created a highly charged atmosphere of confession and absolution. Alma had the 'elemental' feeling that she could never leave her husband, and when she told hm so, 'his face became transfigured and he clung to me every second of the day and night, ecstatic with love'.[45]

So terrified, indeed, was he of losing her, that Mahler insisted that his wife call for him in his hut before every meal – a duty Alma undertook with caution, for she often found him prostrate on the floor in tears. 'For thus, he said, he was nearer to the Earth.' At night he could not rest unless the door between their bedrooms was left open and even then, wrote Alma, she 'often woke up with a start, seeing him standing before me in the darkness like a departed spirit'.[46]

None of the painful raking over the past nor the protestation of love and companionship for the future could paper over the fact that, as far as Alma was concerned, some vital ingredient had vanished from her married life. 'All of a sudden I knew that my marriage was no marriage, that my own life was utterly unfulfilled,' she wrote. 'Yet I denied this truth to Mahler even though he knew it as well as I. To spare him, we both played the comedy to the end.'[47]

Had Mahler known all there was to know about the true state of his marriage during the last year of his life, his belief that his efforts to understand himself and Alma had brought them closer together would have been shattered. The comedy as narrated by Professor Isaacs in his recent biography of Walter Gropius differed considerably from the one suggested by Alma in *And the Bridge Is Love*, a difference explained by Alma's reluctance to admit her undoubtedly discreditable role in the affair.

Unable to bear the situation a moment longer, Gropius went

to Toblach, hoping to see Alma and persuade her to come away
with him. There he was spotted by Alma hiding under a bridge;
she told Mahler, who went down to fetch him and brought him
back to the house. An uneasy confrontation ensued, after which
Mahler called Alma, who had stayed in her room, and then
went back to his own room to await developments. Alma, who
professed herself in *And the Bridge Is Love* 'reluctant' to talk
to Gropius at all, decided not to leave home ('But', she wrote
mournfully, 'I had no choice') and the following morning saw
Gropius off at the station.[48]

No sooner had Gropius left Toblach than Alma began to have
second thoughts. It was inconceivable, she wrote to him, that
they should have no future together when she had such a boundless love for him. Had she, she implored her departed admirer,
made the right decision? And what, if anything, should she do
about it? Gropius could offer nothing much in reply to these
pleas, except to urge Alma to change her mind. Before leaving
Toblach he had written to Mahler, expressing regret that they
had 'had so little to say to each other' and that he had been the
cause of so much pain.[49] These genuine protestations did not,
however, prevent Gropius from continuing to try and re-open the
wound. Neither did they deter Alma who, if not an unadulterated
exponent of George Sand's doctrine of the sacred rights of love,
was nevertheless only too ready to convince herself that, in certain
circumstances, the end justified the means. With this in mind she
had no compunction about agreeing to see Walter Gropius in
Vienna before she joined Mahler in September in Munich, where
he was to conduct the first performance of the Eighth Symphony.

As for Mahler, Gropius's departure from Toblach seemed to
him to be the end of the affair. Although 'shaken to his depths'
by the episode and although he still had to endure the spate of
letters, telegrams and telephone calls Gropius sent daily to try
and get Alma to change her mind, Mahler came to believe that
her choice was irrevocable.[50] Nevertheless, there was enough
flickering of doubt in his mind to convince him that he should
consult Sigmund Freud, then in Leiden, in the hope that the great

analyst could throw some light on the terrible confusions of the past weeks.

Freud was reassuring. 'I analysed Mahler for an afternoon in Leiden,' Freud later told a colleague. 'If I may believe reports, I achieved much with him at that time . . . [During] a highly interesting expedition through his life history, we discovered his personal conditions for love, especially his Holy Mary complex (mother fixation). I had much opportunity to admire the capability for psychological understanding of this man of genius.'[51]

At the end of the consultation the subject turned to Alma and, amongst other things, Freud calmed Mahler's fears about the discrepancy in their ages. 'I know your wife,' Alma reported him as saying. 'She loved her father and can seek and love only his type. Your age, which you are afraid of, is just what attracts your wife. Don't worry about it . . .' And, added Alma, 'How right he was! I really was always searching for the short, stocky, wise, superior man I had known and loved in my father.'[52]

Greatly comforted, Mahler returned to Toblach. The misery and sense of loss that he had expressed in a series of telegrams en route to Leiden were exchanged for lyrical affirmations of love and devotion, which Alma found in her room first thing in the morning or before she went to bed at night. 'I believe there can never now be a moment when I do not feel the happiness of knowing: she loves me!' went one such letter. 'That is the whole meaning of my life! When I cannot say that, I am dead!'

Before he left for Munich at the beginning of September Mahler had broken down two more obstacles to their new-found harmony. Returning from an afternoon walk with Anna, Alma heard her songs being played and sung. 'I stopped – I was petrified. My poor forgotten songs, I had dragged them to and fro to the country and back again for ten years. I was overwhelmed with shame and also I was angry; but Mahler came to meet me with such joy in his face that I could not say a word . . .'[53] Eventually she capitulated to Mahler's demands that she should polish them up for publication, so allowing him to remove the incubus that had lain for so long between them. 'He played them over and over again,' she wrote. '. . . And that was not all; but since he was over-estimating my talent, I suppress all he went on to say in extravagant praise of it.' And one night he appeared by her bedside to ask if it would give her pleasure to have the Eighth Symphony dedicated to her, but – although overwhelmed by this greatest of all gestures of love and respect – Alma urged him not to do it. 'Don't,' she remembered saying. 'You have never dedicated anything to anybody. You might regret it.' Mahler, however, was adamant. From now on nothing was too great an honour to heap on the wife who was, as he wrote from Munich, 'the light of my life', without whom, if she had left him, he would 'have gone out like a torch deprived of air'.[54]

Alma, however, was both 'happy – and yet not happy'. She had 'been through too much' and not all the past wounds she felt had been inflicted on her had healed. As a symbol of unity Mahler had taken her wedding ring to wear in Munich until she joined him a week later, unaware that the bond it represented was more fragile than it seemed. Whilst he was pouring out all the intensity of his feelings in letters written from the Hotel Continental, Alma – as she had never ceased to do – was hankering after the continuation of her summer idyll at Tobelbad.

To this end, she met Gropius fleetingly at the Hohe Warte when she was en route to Munich. Frau Moll had once more become embroiled in her daughter's affairs, having been a comfort to both Alma and Mahler in the aftermath of Gropius's ill-judged letter, and during his appearance and disappearance from Toblach. She did not, apparently, look unkindly on the architect – no doubt Alma had confided in her mother about her marital dissatisfactions and Frau Moll felt some sympathy with their predicament. At any rate, Gropius wrote to her affectionately after his visit that he was 'much calmer and could now breathe again – my own mother could not have shown me more kindness.'[55] Whether Frau Moll's sympathy would have extended to her daughter's future arrangements is a matter for conjecture; after Gropius left Vienna for Berlin, Alma wrote begging him to follow her to Munich, so that they could snatch a few moments together, and Gropius, by then sure that his love was reciprocated, agreed.

Meanwhile, innocent of these goings-on behind his back, Mahler waited impatiently in Munich for Alma and Frau Moll to arrive. On 4 September he wrote that he had 'a sore throat and slight inflammation, but will be careful, so as to be in good health to receive my saint,' adding that he had 'made a strange discovery . . . Freud is quite right – you were always for me the light and the central point . . . and the blissful consciousness of this – now unshadowed and unconfined – raises all my feelings to the infinite. But,' he continued sadly, 'what torment and what pain that you no longer respond. But as surely as love must wake to love, and faith find faith again . . . so surely will I make a fresh conquest of all, of the heart which once was mine and can only in unison with mine find its way to God and blessedness . . .'[56]

A day or two later, having obviously been reassured as to his wife's feelings for him, Mahler wrote ecstatically: 'Is it true? Are you mine once more? Can I grasp it? At last, at last! If I only knew when you were coming! Tomorrow is Thursday, isn't that when you meant to come?'[57]

When Alma and her mother eventually arrived on 9 September they found every room in their suite at the Hotel Continental full of roses. In their own rooms they each found copies of the Eighth Symphony – for Frau Moll a piano edition, dedicated to 'Our dear mother, who has ever been all in all to us and who gave me Alma – from Gustav in undying gratitude, Munich, 9 September 1910', and for Alma the complete orchestral score 'with its dedicatory page'. Mahler himself, Alma noted, looked ill and run down. He had had a recurrence of his sore throat, she explained, and had 'taken to his bed'. She regretted that she had 'not been there to look after him'.[58]

The première of the Eighth Symphony generated acute interest amongst an eclectic audience: Stefan Zweig, Thomas Mann, Arnold Berliner, Paul Clemenceau and Max Reinhardt were joined by Bruno Walter, Siegfried Wagner, Alfredo Casella, Willem Mengelberg and others to swell the packed Festival Hall.

Otto Klemperer was unable to attend, but, with Arnold Schön-berg and Oskar Fried, had been to the first full rehearsals, where he had been particularly struck, not only by Mahler's ceaseless alterations to the score – 'He always wanted more clarity, more sound, more dynamic contrast' – but by his wish that if, after his death, something didn't sound right, they were to change it. 'You have not only a right', Klemperer recorded him saying, 'but a duty to do so.'[59]

The impact of the music on Klemperer was immense, his biographer Peter Heyworth stated. Its effect on all those who first heard Mahler's interpretation of his great Choral Symphony on 12 September was equally profound. 'The whole audience rose to their feet as soon as Mahler took his place at the conductor's desk,' wrote Alma, 'and the breathless silence which followed was the most impressive homage that an artist could be paid.'[60] Bruno Walter believed that 'that evening in September 1910 marked a culminating point in Mahler's life and that none of the participants or listeners [would] ever forget the occasion . . . That he was permitted to release to the world through the voices of a mighty host of singers this leitmotif of his greatly agitated soul, that he was able to pronounce the message of life and faith while the seeds of death were already in his heart, was a thrill beyond anything he had ever experienced.'[61] And Thomas Mann was so overwhelmed by the experience that, at the reception held in the hotel after the concert, he was unable to put his feelings into words. Several days later he wrote to Mahler enclosing a copy of his latest novel, *Königliche Hoheit* (*Royal Highness*) and saying:

> At the hotel after the performance . . . I am in your debt for the experience of that evening. I have a strong desire to give you at least some intimation of my feelings, and so I beg you kindly to accept the enclosed book . . . It is, to be sure, a poor exchange for what I have received from you, and must weigh light as a feather in the hand of a man who seems to me to embody the most serious and sacred artistic purpose of our age . . . [62]

Uplifted by the realization of his monumental dream, Mahler sat up with Alma, 'talking until morning, with Gucki, our dear child, sleeping beside us'. Back in Vienna he saw a doctor about his throat, who, due to his patient's low pain threshold, recommended cauterization, rather than removal, of his tonsils. This he duly endured and, Alma wrote, everyone 'believed he was now safe from further attacks and Mahler himself did not want a more radical cure'.[63]

Whilst in Munich Alma had managed to snatch a few, tantalizingly short, moments with Gropius in the entrance to the Hotel Regina whilst Mahler was rehearsing. 'When will the time ever come . . .' she had written beforehand, 'when we don't have to part from one another, and when we can sleep the whole night through together? I live only for the time when I can become yours completely.'[64] From Vienna she wrote of her longing to have his child, on which she would 'lavish care and attention until the day comes when we can sink into each other's arms – without regrets, in certainty and peace'.[65]

The opportunity to consummate at least some of these yearnings presented itself unexpectedly soon. The Mahlers were due to return to New York on 14 November, and announcing that he was fit enough to fulfil an obligation to conduct in Bremen en route to Cherbourg, Mahler agreed to Alma spending some time in Paris before joining him there. Gucki and her English nurse would travel direct from Vienna in time for the sailing.

With the physical ecstasy she had dreamed about for so long within her grasp, Alma wasted no time in alerting Gropius to her plan. He must meet her, without fail, on the platform at Munich station, so that they could travel together to Paris. 'I leave here on 14 October at 11.55 a.m. on the Orient Express. My couchette, No. 13 – is in the second sleeping car,' she wrote, adding that she advised him to book his couchette in the name of Walter Grote, as someone of that name was travelling two days later and he could, perhaps, 'satisfy the list'.[66]

Gropius obeyed her instructions to the letter. There ensued, Professor Isaacs surmised discreetly, 'enchanted hours of rapture',[67] a conjecture born out by the first letter Alma managed to send from America on her arrival. 'It made me quite dizzy to see and feel what has made me so endlessly happy,' she wrote. 'I love you! . . . so, until I can be your wife - . . . keep yourself well for me. – You know the reason why.' Mahler, unaware of his wife's activities, met her and Gucki in Cherbourg as arranged. The Atlantic crossing, Alma reported, was uneventful and the weather perfect. Both she and Mahler spent the ten days at sea having a complete rest.

Immediately they arrived, Mahler embarked on a series of concerts, both in New York and further afield. Early in December he went to Springfield, Ohio, and on the 9th Alma joined him in Buffalo for a short time. On the way back to New York she read, at Mahler's suggestion, *The Brothers Karamazov*. 'Splendid journey with Alyosha,' she cabled from the Savoy Hotel. 'Journey with Almyosha much more splendid,' was the telegram she received in reply.

Just before Christmas, Mahler developed a 'slightly septic' throat, but managed to throw it off before their celebrations, which for the first time were arranged by Mahler in unusually festive spirit. All the things that Alma complained had been missing from past Christmases – 'the Christmas feeling, the giving of presents, the thrill of expectation' – were restored to her. On a table 'smothered in roses' was a mound of presents covered in a white cloth, including scent and two promissory notes: 'Bon to the value of 40 dollars for a fine spree along Fifth Avenue. From Herr Gustav Mahler on a country ramble with his Almschili', and 'Bon for the purchase of a Solitaire worth over 1,000 dollars, Gustav Mahler New York Christmas, 1910.'[68]

The sight of these unexpected tokens of devotion cast Alma into the depths of gloom. They seemed to presage disasters as yet unformulated by them both and, although her spirits lifted temporarily, they sank again on New Year's Eve, when together with Dr Fraenkel they saw in the first hours of 1911. 'The bells of the churches united in an organ note of such awful beauty that we three who loved each other joined hands without a word and wept. Not one of us – then – knew why.'[69]

In January Alma's songs were published by Universal Edition

and soon afterwards she had a visit from the soprano Frances Alda, then wife of Gatti-Casazza, the general director of the Metropolitan Opera, who wanted to include one of them in a recital she was giving in March. True to his new-found concern for his wife's reputation, Mahler urged the singer to perform all five songs, and when she demurred on the grounds that the rest of her programme was already settled, he became 'quite angry,' Alma wrote, 'and said she ought to leave out some of her other songs'. Nevertheless, he agreed to go through the song with her – another source of embarrassment for Alma who became, by her own account, almost speechless with nervousness when Mahler appealed to her for directions from the piano. ' "Is that right?" he kept asking . . . I begged him in a low voice not to ask me any more, as he knew better than I. We were very near together in those days.'[70]

On 20 February Mahler again went down with a throat infection. Earlier in the month he had written to his mother-in-law complaining that they had had no word from her about an impending visit:

> For some time your letters have made no mention of your coming, which we are all looking forward to so much. I have the feeling that Almscherl is to blame for this, with her temperamental outpourings . . . I cannot get rid of the feeling, dear little Mama, that there is something on your mind that you are keeping to yourself. Almschi is such a one for upsetting her nearest and dearest . . . But surely I don't have to tell you how well she means?

In the same letter he was able to report favourably on both his own and Alma's health and well-being: he had, he wrote, 'kept very fit this year' and as for Alma she was 'blossoming . . . keeping to a splendid diet', and '*entirely* given up alcohol' and was hard at work on a 'few delightful songs that mark great progress . . .' All he needed to make life complete was to be reassured that she would come as planned and that they could all travel back to Europe together as arranged 'on the finest ship in the German merchant navy, the *George Washington*', on 20 March.[71]

Frau Moll's slight constraint may have been due to mixed

feelings about her participation in Alma's continuing marital deception, for, as Professor Isaacs pointed out, she was beginning to realize that Walter Gropius was more than just a pleasant friend to her daughter. 'It is very sad that one is so helpless,' she wrote to him, 'but one must leave everything to time, and I am absolutely sure that with you both, your love can survive. I have great faith in you and am convinced of it. You are so fond of my child, and I know you will do nothing to make her even more unhappy.'[72]

By the time Frau Moll arrived Mahler's health had deteriorated to such an extent that not even Alma had been able to keep up the flow of letters to Berlin. At the beginning of February she had written that, unless fate decreed otherwise, they would be returning to Vienna at the end of March. But Mahler's feverish inflammation of the throat, with which, against Dr Fraenkel's advice, he had insisted on conducting the first performance of Busoni's 'Cradlesong at the Grave of my Mother' at the Carnegie Hall on 21 February, had proved unusually persistent. Despite a few days' respite after the concert when his temperature dropped to normal and he triumphantly justified his decision to go ahead on the grounds that he had conducted countless times in the past with a fever and that this time, at least, he had 'conducted himself back to health', it returned within a week with renewed vigour. After an evening during which Mahler collapsed, having suffered days of 'zig-zagging' fever, Dr Fraenkel was in no doubt about the true nature of the disease. Subsequent blood tests confirmed his diagnosis. Already weakened by his heart defect, his patient now had streptococci in the blood, carrying with them the possibility of an onset of septicaemia. 'If it were not Mahler,' Fraenkel has been reported as saying, 'I would take all his blood out and put fresh in.'[73] As it was, all that ultimately could be done was to wait and see if nature herself would give him the strength to throw it off.

The concert at the Carnegie Hall, the forty-eighth that he had conducted that season, was Mahler's last. He stayed indoors, sometimes in bed, sometimes lying on a sofa, looked after day and night by Alma. 'I looked after him now just as if he were a little child. I put every bite into his mouth for him and slept in his room without taking off my clothes. We got so used to it that he said more than once: "When I'm well again we'll go on like this. You'll feed me – it's so nice." '[74]

There were a few respites. Friends called to take her out for drives and on 2 March she went to Frances Alda's recital and had the pleasure of hearing her song encored. (Mahler, when she told him, was 'quite beside himself with joy'.) Eventually, however, the strain took its toll. On hearing the news that her husband should be sent to Europe to consult a bacteriologist, Alma fainted at his bedside. A telegram was dispatched to Frau Moll, who came straight away. With her mother taking over part of the day-nursing Alma could, as she said, spare herself a little. On 15 March she had written to Walter Gropius that Mahler had been ill for three weeks; a fortnight later she wrote again, describing her trials and tribulations. 'Momentarily,' she concluded, 'my feelings are numb. But I know that when I see you, everything in me will live again – and bloom again! ... But you ... will it be the same for you?'[75]

There was no time for a reply. In April they arrived in Paris, where Carl Moll was there to meet them. Professor André Chantemesse, the only bacteriologist available (it was the Easter holiday), could do no more than confirm Dr Fraenkel's verdict. He did, however, arrange for Mahler to go to a sanatorium in Neuilly, where he attempted a course of treatment and made various cultures from his celebrated patient's blood – all to no avail. Terrified by the daily worsening in her husband's condition, Alma telephoned Professor Franz Chvostek in Vienna, begging him to come at once. He arrived within twenty-four hours and, before he went in to see Mahler, Alma warned him not to depress her husband, already in a state of hopeful over-excitement at his coming, with gloomy diagnoses. Should his verdict be unfavourable he must tell only herself and Frau Moll. Mahler must be calmed and reassured.

The professor complied. After examining his patient he told

him that his condition was largely the result of years of overwork and nervous strain and that complete rest for six months or a year should put him right. If Mahler agreed, they could all return to Vienna that evening. To Alma he spoke the truth: there was little chance that her husband would recover, and even if he should pull through this bout of his illness, his nervous system would progressively decline. It would be better for all concerned if the end came as quickly and peacefully as possible.

Although Alma tried not to lose heart, she too knew that the end had come. Mahler, on the other hand, overjoyed by the prospect of working again, could not wait to be on the move. He was, Alma wrote, 'dressed long before it was time to start, blissful, transfigured'.[76] Their train journey, their arrival on 12 May and his removal by ambulance to the Löw Sanatorium was, Alma recorded, like the progress of a dying king. Daily bulletins were issued to the press and flowers arrived by the hour, including a basket of white flowers from the Philharmonic. Throughout it all Mahler read continuously: right up to the end, according to Alma, he was delving into Eduard von Hartmann's *Das Problem des Lebens*, a characteristically epistemological work dealing with the nature and validity of knowledge. In between he worried about Schönberg's future, and, before finally sinking into pain and confusion, gave instructions to Frau Moll about arrangements for his funeral – he was to be buried beside Putzi in Grinzing and his headstone was to have nothing but 'Mahler' written on it. As he said, 'Anyone who comes to look for me will know who I was, and the rest do not need to know.'

In his last few days Mahler had difficulty with his breathing and was given oxygen. Alma was sent from the room during his dying hours which, like his father-in-law's, were accompanied by loud claps of thunder. His last word spoken before he died, at midnight on 18 May 1911, was 'Mozart!' His last written words to Alma are scrawled across the fragmentary sketch of the Tenth Symphony: 'To live for you, to die for you, Almschi.'

8 Consolations

'After the death of Gustav Mahler . . .' Alma recorded briefly, 'I went through a long period of mental and spiritual agony. I simply could not grasp that I was now separated from him for ever. I felt completely rootless.' Exhaustion and grief had also taken a physical toll: Dr Chvostek, examining her shortly afterwards, warned her that her lungs were affected. 'If you go on like this,' he told her, 'you'll soon be where your husband is.' According to *And the Bridge Is Love*, Alma welcomed this news (implying that had the custom of suttee been prevalent in Austria nothing would have given her more pleasure than to hurl herself onto a funeral pyre). 'Chvostek's warning had given me my first happy moments since Gustav Mahler's death. I *wanted* to follow him.'[1]

Not mentioned in her memoirs was the solace she found from writing to Walter Gropius, on whose birthday Mahler had died – a coincidence Alma felt, despite everything, to be a hopeful sign. When Gropius appeared in the flesh, however, it was not an unqualified success. Faced with Alma's need to make him understand her husband's dependence on her before he died, and the affection this had engendered between them, Gropius became unaccountably irritable. As Professor Isaacs wrote, 'Unhappily Walter Gropius was not yet the understanding and tolerant man that he became in later life – he was, after all, only twenty-eight, and he reacted with vehemence . . .'[2] In a letter written from his hotel room he reproached her bitterly for her faithlessness, and begged her to tell him honestly when she had 'returned to her G[ustav], for it was now quite obvious that her passion for him had been an aberration.' His only consolation, he concluded sadly, was the thought that he had reunited 'two such wonderful people as yourselves'. All he had left was to wait and hope. 'I realize that I may have to wait and long for you for years on end, and must always be available, if and when you need me.'³

On this unhappy note Gropius returned to Berlin where, within a few days, he received an anguished letter from Alma, begging him to excuse her behaviour. But Gropius, shaken and confused, felt he needed time for reflection and, although they continued to exchange letters, he put off a planned visit by Alma to Berlin in September 1911 on the grounds that since he had been away from her 'a great feeling of shame' had come over him, which made him want to avoid meeting her. 'I must go away for a while and find out whether or not I was blind . . . to cloak my love in such a perfect form . . . and whether it compensates for the sorrow that I . . . caused Gustav and you . . .'⁴

By the time they did meet again – briefly in Berlin at the end of the year – Alma herself had undergone an emotional metamorphosis. After weeks of lying in bed talking to a picture of her dead husband she had begun, with Anna sitting beside her on the piano-stool, to make music again. Frustratingly, in the light of her perpetual sense of creative deprivation during her marriage to Mahler, Alma did not specify if she was merely playing *Tristan and Isolde* or whether she had started to compose any of the five songs that were published after Mahler's death. All of these except one – 'Der Erkennende', a setting of a poem by Franz Werfel, which she mentions writing in the autumn of 1915 – are undated, but if they were arranged chronologically for their publication in 1924 (and 'Der Erkennende' is No. 3) it is tempting to conclude that Nos 1 and 2, both highly mystical in tone, were conceived between 1911 and 1912.

More certain is that a month or two of comparative solitude and total immersion in her musical life bridged the gap between death and life, refreshing the spirit and banishing all morbid thoughts of self-immolation. At thirty-one, Alma retained the physical attributes that had so enamoured past admirers: her face with its long, sloping nose, sensual mouth and large, slanting eyes, remained as clear-skinned as ever, her figure as voluptuously statuesque. Before he died Mahler had stipulated that she should on no account go into mourning: she should go to concerts, visit friends and go to the opera and theatre as she had always done. And, as she was by her own account more than adequately provided for materially, with her widow's pension and money accrued from Mahler's American tours, Alma began, gradually, to resume her favourite activity – that of peopling her garden with geniuses.

It was not until the spring of the following year that Alma found a wholly satisfactory addition to her collection. In the meantime she had to make do with Franz Schreker, founder in 1908 of the Vienna Philharmonic Choir, who introduced himself after one of his choir rehearsals. Schreker was a composer whose operatic style was a heady mixture of Debussy, Wagner, Strauss and Puccini ('What need have we of Wagner?' one critic wrote approvingly during the Twenties, when 'we have Schreker, whose works completely eclipse the works of Wagner?'). He enjoyed an enviably high reputation amongst his peers from 1912, when his first opera, *Der ferne Klang* – a strong influence on Berg's *Wozzeck* – was staged, until 1932. After that his work was banned by the Nazis and he himself forced to resign from the post to which he had been appointed in 1920, of director of the Berlin Hochschule für Musik – events which, combined with the failure of his last opera, *Der Schmied von Ghent* (a 'fiasco' witnessed by Alma Mahler at the Opera House in Charlottenburg in 1932), brought on a nervous breakdown and led to his premature death in 1934.

Schreker became a frequent visitor, but his appeal was shortlived. 'For a while I saw much of Franz Schreker,' Alma wrote, 'but he played no part in my life; I walked beside him for a stretch and left him at the right time.'[5]

Another suitor was Dr Fraenkel who, if not a genius, was extremely gifted. He also turned out to be in love with Alma, and on a visit to Vienna 'after a decent interval' proposed marriage. Alma refused him.* Much as she revered his intellect, she had no desire to tie herself to a man who, she remarked brutally, might have been a great name in medicine in America but in Europe was merely 'an elderly, sick little man quite unheroically nursing a fatal intestinal ailment'. [6]

Her farewell letter was couched in kindlier terms, citing differences in temperament as the main obstacle to their union:

> The fate that parts us is the divergence of our own souls. Every fibre of my heart draws me back into true life, while you are striving for consummate de-materialization.
>   What is salvation to you strikes me as madness. That's how different we are!
>   My watchword is: *Amo – ergo sum.*
>   Yours: *Cogito – ergo sum* . . . Today I know the eternal source of all strength. It is in nature, in the earth, in people who don't hesitate to cast away their existence for the sake of an idea. They are the ones who can *love*.[7]

A month or two later, on her way back from Munich, where Bruno Walter had conducted the first performance of *Das Lied von der Erde* on 20 November 1911, Alma shared a railway carriage with a man impulsive enough to cast his whole existence into jeopardy for the sake of an idea. Dr Paul Kammerer's unorthodox approach to experimental biology eventually cost him his life: he shot himself on 23 September 1926, finally putting an end to a scientific scandal still able to arouse passions amongst proponents of the theories of Darwin and Lamarck. Had he or had he not deliberately misled the scientific establishment by injecting Indian ink into the glands on the nuptial pads of the midwife toad in order to substantiate his Lamarckian claim that the toads – whose normal habitat was on land – when reared under water bequeathed these special mating characteristics to subsequent generations?

Remembered with warmth by Anna Mahler, for whom he made an aquarium, Kammerer started life as a musician, only changing to zoology after he had finished his course at the Vienna Academy. It was, his biographer Arthur Koestler wrote, 'a bad

---

* Dr Fraenkel eventually married the singer, Ganna Walska.

mark against him the Establishment never forgot. For a scientist to play the piano, as a hobby, is permissible; for a pianist to switch to science is not. It inflicts on him the stigma of dilettantism which he will never get rid of. "Ne supra crepidam", the robed Viennese academics would quote to each other with a knowing titter; the cobbler should stick to his last.'[8]

Whilst at the Academy Kammerer composed some songs and conceived a love bordering on idolatry for their main influence, Gustav Mahler. He joined the newly formed Institute for Experimental Biology at the Vivarium in 1906, at the age of twenty-three. A few years later he wrote to the object of his devotion, asking if he could see him. (According to Anna Mahler he wrote offering his services as a butler!) Mahler, attracted by his admirer's obvious originality and interested in the nature of his work, invited him to Maiernigg. But by the time he actually arrived Mahler's patience had worn thin. A daily avalanche of letters from Kammerer devoted entirely to the subject of music in general and Mahler's work in particular had not endeared him to his future host, who had been hoping to hear something about his guest's scientific discipline. 'When he finally came himself,' wrote Alma, 'this obtrusive mail campaign had put us into a rather icy mood, but Kammerer did not notice. We thought we might learn from him and raised biological questions, but he wished to discuss music only. Soon he got so much on Mahler's nerves that the visit came to a natural end.'[9]

Kammerer must have remained oblivious to Mahler's irritation, for his obsession never wavered. Indeed, it even threatened to cut short his own life. So grief-stricken was he at the death of his hero that he wanted to kill himself there and then on top of his grave, in order to be able to join him in the world beyond. Presumably his first wife, the former Baroness Felicitas Maria Theodore von Wiedersperg, whom he married in 1906, and who shared her husband's passion for music and animals – her own father, apparently, kept snakes, two monkeys, a bat, a squirrel and a stork – was able to deter him.

Under the circumstances it was only natural that Kammerer

should be stirred by the plight of his idol's widow. 'The gap left in my life by Mahler's death will scarcely have been closed for you,' he wrote to her from the Biological Institute on the morning of 31 October 1911:

> One can never make judgements about love with a member of the opposite sex; I myself have experienced the uplift and constant demands from something one believed was eternal, only to have it disappear more or less painlessly within a few years, even months. But here I *know* the loss is irreplaceable. It is inconceivable that, without sexual undercurrents, close family ties, and really, without overt pronouncements of friendship, I could have loved Mahler so much. That is not just admiration, enthusiasm for art, or for the individual, that is Love![10]
>
> Therein, for me, stood Mahler . . . amongst all those (and there have not been many) whom I have loved the most. And now I will, for as long as you will accept it, transfer this feeling to his loved ones, to his wife and daughter . . .
>   How wonderful to be able to talk everything over impartially with you, dear lady; and how far removed is your conduct from the hypocrisy of insincere sorrow! And how pure is the sorrow that springs from Love![11]

During the afternoon and evening Kammerer pursued his theme, confessing that, at first, he had sometimes been jealous, not only of Mahler's friends, but also of his wife – feeling that they might distract him from his creative life. 'Time and time again,' he told her, 'I have seen even the most hard-working and capable of men run to fat and become mentally sterile after marriage . . .', but, he continued, he soon realized that Mahler was 'not such a one. His output appeared to soar . . . also family misfortunes, such as the death of his child, were incapable of changing the course of his ever-ascending line . . .' Kammerer was determined to follow his example. 'My first thought after deciding to get married was that the wedding should not interrupt my work. On the morning after the ceremony, to everyone's astonishment, I sat in my laboratory . . .'[12]

Alma obviously replied sympathetically to these ruminations, for two days later he wrote proposing a series of biological outings 'to the zoo and plant-houses at Schönbrunn, to the Museum, to the University Institute Botanical Gardens and Glasshouses . . . etc', adding as an inducement that not only could Gucki go with them but that, with him as their guide, they would have access to the most interesting corners 'that ordinary mortals never see'. As an additional carrot he suggested visiting a little park that he had made for some of his pupils, where there was 'an aquarium, the same as I am going to give Gucki for Christmas'.[13]

The aquarium was duly delivered to Alma's new flat (she moved out of the Hohe Warte in December) and, during the same month, she took up a suggestion Kammerer had made her in the course of their train journey – to give up music for a while and work as his assistant. Her first task was to feed a box of mealworms to the reptiles. The sight of the former, she recorded, caused her to feel a 'twinge of nausea', which increased when Kammerer, surprised at her squeamishness, seized a handful and stuffed them into his mouth. 'I kept the job,' Alma wrote afterwards, ' – although for some time I could not touch noodle soup . . .'[14]

After a bit she graduated to less lowly tasks. Quite without irony Kammerer put her in charge of some experiments on the moulting habits of the praying mantis, a creature of more than usually voracious appetites, the female exceeding the male in greed and pugnaciousness with her unpleasant tendency both to fight him and, if she won, to eat him up. Alma spent long days monitoring their movements and – against their natural inclinations – trying to persuade them to eat in the dark, so that Kammerer could determine whether they lost their memories after moulting, or whether it was merely a skin reaction. The mantids, however, refused to cooperate, and Alma claimed (probably with hindsight) that her exact records of their persistent efforts to feed in the light annoyed Kammerer. He would have preferred 'slightly less exact records with positive results'.[15]

Soon, however, the daily visits to the vivarium became too time-consuming, and Alma installed a terrarium in her flat. Kammerer came round at all hours to check up the lizards and salamanders under her care, washing sand and chasing after the reptiles which frequently managed to break loose. It was not long before respectful worship of Mahler's widow was transformed into wild infatuation for his assistant. 'My beloved Alma,' he wrote in an undated letter:

> Today I am quite ill with longing for you ... pictures from yesterday chase through my mind ... Clever though you are, you don't seem to understand what I have written – no matter – I will only write, YOU! Only You, You are the only one, there is no one else but YOU! ... It is obvious that you are one of the most extraordinary beings in this world, if not in any other world. You are the sort of perfection that I could never even dream about, let alone write about. And perfection is supposed to be faultless!! How wrong! Your faults are endlessly endearing, your weaknesses are inexplicably beautiful, your longueurs incomparably sweet ... Only yesterday I was in your room in the Pokornygasse, holding your hand, half-shouting, half-crying, imploring you not to bring my visit to an end, and today I am more dependent on you than ever ... Take me, Alma, I belong only to you ... Could you not come the day after tomorrow, Thursday, as my guest to the Konstantinhugel for lunch? Why, after all, shouldn't I invite you? Can I fetch you by car? Don't let me be deprived for too long of the sight of your beloved face – Paul.[16]

In later years Alma claimed to have taken these outpourings with a pinch of salt. 'The biologist Paul Kammerer ...' she wrote underneath a typescript of the above letter, 'was a highly original being. But his world had little to do with reality. On my side our relationship was merely one of friendship, on his that of a passionate lover ... he was the clown of my whole circle, who chose to show his love for me in a most unscrupulous way ...'

Despite these protestations, Alma might have been nettled to discover that she was not the only recipient of Kammerer's attentions. He had already fallen hopelessly in love with all five sisters of the Wiesenthal family, four of whom were dancers, the fifth a violinist. First it was Bertha, for whom he wrote a dance ('The Wiesenthal Ländler'), then Erica, whom he lost to her husband, the painter Rudolph Huber. Hilda is not mentioned, but her youngest sister, Martha, was 'showered with presents' both before and after her marriage. Lastly, in the year before his death, Kammerer tried to persuade the eldest, Grete, to go with him to Moscow, where he had been invited to set up an experimental station at the Pavlov Institute. Grete, however, remained indecisive and her lack of resolution was widely held to have contributed to his suicide. 'The fatal decision to take his own life', ran the obituary in the *Neue Freie Presse*, 'seems to have been determined by the fact that a Viennese artiste who was close to his heart was unable to make up her mind to follow him to Moscow . . .'

Whether or not Kammerer threatened Grete with self-destruction before the final damning article asserting that the nuptial pads on his specimen were faked appeared in the journal *Nature* on 7 August 1926, is a matter for speculation, but Alma maintained that Kammerer made many such threats to her. The spectre of shooting himself over Mahler's grave apparently reared its ugly head every time she failed to respond with enough warmth to his overtures, but time and again he relented, only to reproach her afresh. 'My beloved Alma,' went one such letter:

> 'Already you have no more *love* for me – I beg your pardon – *liking* . . . You tell me I love without discrimination and that I am an incorrigible flirt! But I only love you: and as far as flirtation is concerned there really is only room for you in the course of one day.
> You attempt to describe what flirtation means to me. I will attempt it too. There is a little of the erotic about it, for me as well as for you. But this sort of eroticism is so inhibited, partly conscious, partly unconscious, and has been so sublimated that it is buried deep within each individual psyche.[17]

Without knowing it Kammerer had touched on a sensitive chord. Alma was no stranger to the volcanic nature of sexual attraction but, one suspects, complete fulfilment had hitherto eluded her and Kammerer, whom she announced in *And the Bridge Is Love* she found 'disgusting' as a man, was unlikely to satisfy her in this respect. Eventually she put a temporary stop to his advances by alerting his wife to the situation. 'You must thank God', she told her, 'that he ended up with me. Because of that you have not lost him.' According to Alma, Felicitas took this in good part, leaving with 'many expressions of gratitude', but it cannot have come as much of a surprise: she had already had the

Wiesenthals to contend with and must by then have been well attuned to her husband's roving eye.*

Meanwhile Alma continued to correspond sporadically with Walter Gropius. Before his death, Mahler had arranged to have another summer house built, this time on the Semmering, charging Carl Moll to draw up some plans. On the first anniversary of Mahler's death, Alma wrote to Gropius, wondering whether her late husband would have been happy to work there. Receiving no reply to this tactless letter, she wrote again: 'Why are you so silent? When are you coming to Vienna?' Gropius did not come, and in November, in response to a request from Alma to return some magazines she had lent him, wrote gloomily about unrequited feelings and whether or not they could be transformed into those of mere friendship. 'I have no notion what comes afterwards, it doesn't depend on me . . .'[18]

Had he known what was in store for him Gropius would have been even more down-hearted. Three years were to elapse before relations resumed their old intimacy for, by the time she had written to him in May, Alma had yet again been swept away on a tide of emotion. This time the merry-go-round had stopped in front of an artist. 'In the winter of 1912,'† Alma wrote, 'Carl Moll said to me: There is a young brilliant fellow, you should let him paint you. And Oskar Kokoschka came . . .'[19]

---

* So well attuned that when, a year after Alma's warning, Kammerer's infatuation for a painter, Anna Wal, drove him to ask her for a divorce, Felicitas not only agreed to release him on grounds of mutual incompatibility but when, after a few months, the marriage foundered, took him back again.
† One of Alma's many chronological errors. They met on 12 April 1912.

9 The Bride of the Wind

... *über schwarzliche Klippen*
Stürzt todestrunken
Die ergluhende Windsbraut ... *
[Georg Trakl, 1913]

In the spring of 1912, when Oskar Kokoschka was introduced to Alma Mahler, he was twenty-six years old. In a photograph taken three years before, he peers at the camera with an expression of jaundiced amusement. His long head is close-shaven, his eyebrows, nose and mouth are regular, his ears small and low set. He wears a stiff white collar, a spotted cravat and a conventional jacket. According to Kokoschka, however, it does not tell you very much about him, for in his opinion no photograph was capable of penetrating the mask of self better than a painted portrait by a sympathetic artist. Nor could it provide the sort of stimulus generated by a work of art which, if it really was a work of art, could 'create a genuine experience, a visual shock', in the consciousness of a receptive observer.

Judged by his own criteria, Kokoschka's early artistic ventures were all works of art, for the visual shock they gave their observers, receptive or otherwise, was intense. The howls of protest from critics and public alike that had greeted his début in

* Over black rocks,
  Drunk with death,
  Plunges the glowing Bride of the Wind.

1908, whilst still a student at the School of Arts and Crafts, at the first of two exhibitions organized by the Wiener Werkstätte under the title 'Kunstschau' to promote their newly conceived free association between artists and craftsmen, were proof that Kokoschka's work was capable of stirring up passions on all sides. For every one of his admirers (Gustav Klimt had called him 'the greatest talent of the younger generation', and most of his work had been sold before the exhibition opened) there were a dozen who, like the heir to the throne, Archduke Ferdinand, wanted to 'break every bone in the young man's body'. The critic Ludwig Hevesi dubbed him the 'Oberwildling' (Chief Savage). Even Richard Müther, normally receptive to all things avant-garde, described his tapestry designs as 'revolting. A mixture of fairground images, primitive Indian painting, ethnographic museum, Gauguin gone mad . . .' but was nevertheless obliged to admit that he had not witnessed such an interesting début for years: the enfant terrible was 'not an imposter at all, no, a worthy lad'.[1]

The contradictions in Kokoschka's paintings were only exceeded by those in his prose. In his plays and illustrated poems he plunged into a wrestling match between darkness and light, passion and the spirit, the tangible and the intangible, outpourings that found their expression in what he himself described as the 'bitter struggle between mind and sex, a battle won by sex', where the dichotomy between the ideal of perfect love and the physically aggressive nature of its consummation appeared to pose an insoluble problem. There was no such thing as an ordinary civilized erotic stimulus – only a heaving mass of sexual tension, pulsating under the outward formalities of social intercourse. Beneath the most innocent of encounters with the opposite sex lay the shameful knowledge that a touch of a hand, or a flirtatious look, could open up a Pandora's box of tormented longing. Out of it might burst the urge to subdue, to crush, even to kill the object of desire: as Ulrich, the hero of Robert Musil's *The Man Without Qualities*, remarked: 'There is nothing that so inflames civilized love as the flattering discovery that one has the power to drive another human being into an ecstasy in which he or she behaves so crazily that one would positively have to become a murderer in order to produce such changes by any other means.'[2]

Kokoschka explored these conflicting themes in two of his early written works: the illustrated poem *Die träumenden Knaben (The Dreaming Boys)*, printed by the Wiener Werkstätte in 1908, a fairy-tale fantasy delving into the darker side of puberty, and the play *Mörder, Hoffnung der Frauen (Murder, Hope of Women)*, first performed on 4 July 1909 in an open-air theatre at the Kunstschau, explained by Kokoschka as being a clash between the forces of procreation and destruction. In both he attempted to lift the veil of secrecy shrouding the hidden world of the self, behind which lay the irrational impulses so dear to Romantic hearts. For Kokoschka, however, the battle was not, as for Géricault or Delacroix, merely to assert the right of every artist to 'reject all fetters to the exercise of the imagination' or, as for Klimt and his fellow Secessionists, to create an artistic milieu in which purity of design reigned supreme, but to embark on a pilgrimage into the subconscious. Somewhere along the path of his journey to the inferno of self-knowledge, within the dream-ridden hinterland of the sleeping mind, lay the clues to man's inconsistencies. At the very least they should enable him, as Carl Schorske aptly put it, 'to affirm the primary reality of sex as interior personal experience'.[3]

Despite Kokoschka's affirmation that *Murder, Hope of Women* was nothing more than it seemed – a simple morality tale – neither the first-night audience, contemporary critics nor subsequent literary or art historians have seemed able to make much sense of it. Although it is by no means certain that the première aroused the unbridled passions described by Kokoschka in his memoirs,[4] it did provoke the Ministry of Culture and Education, already smarting from the outrage caused by his exhibits at the Kunstschau of 1908 (generally considered by the authorities to have been responsible for the show's disastrous financial loss) to instruct Alfred Roller, then director of the School of Arts and Crafts, to expel his recalcitrant pupil forthwith.

Kokoschka's expulsion turned out, however, to do him little, if any, harm. Adolf Loos, to whom Kokoschka had been introduced the year before, already the possessor of one of the Kunstschau's most detested exhibits – a painted clay bust by Kokoschka entitled *The Warrior* – and, together with his friend Karl Kraus present at the first performance of *Murder, Hope of Women*, offered the young artist his help and advice.

No struggling genius could have had a better stroke of fortune. In Loos, arch-priest of purity in architectural design, prophet of the modern movement, writer and aesthete, Kokoschka found the perfect complement to his artistic aims. Like his protégé, Loos had moved away from the Secessionists' conception of the decorative arts towards an uncompromisingly unadorned future. The façades of his buildings were to be uncluttered by ornament, their interiors uncontaminated by unnecessary embellishment. As early as 1899 he put these functionalist theories into practice with a design for the Café Museum which, owing to the spareness, even severity of its decoration, became famous under the sobriquet 'Café Nihilismus'. Eleven years later they reached their apogee in an apartment block and store in the Michaelerplatz opposite the gates of the Imperial Palace. The new building's studied simplicity aroused even more fury among passers-by than the cabbage dome of the Secession. 'Choose a point on the Michaelerplatz from which to observe the new building . . .' wrote the *Neue Freie Presse*, 'and immediately some passer-by will latch on to you, repeating out loud what you had been thinking to yourself, cursing the revolting edifice to its face, and pass on his way, muttering imprecations. Seldom has a work of architecture called forth such universal opposition . . . How can anyone have thought it possible to harmonize this blatantly dissonant modernism with its timeless, historic surroundings?'[5]

Kokoschka's portrait of Loos, painted in 1909, accurately reflects both the internal nature of the subject and the extent of his empathy with him. The asymmetrical planes of the face and the jagged outlines of the clasped hands stand out from the upper part of the sitter's body, which, like the blurred background, is painted in sombre blues and browns; the arms and shoulders are wide and heavy, the head disproportionately small in relation to the hands. It is to Loos's stonemason's hands that the eye is drawn, and to his eyes, behind whose hooded lids lies the soul of an aesthete.

Later, Kokoschka wrote that his meeting with Loos had been decisive not only for his career but for his life: 'It may be immodest, but I must say of Loos what Dante said of Virgil: he led me through the heaven and hell of life as a faithful companion and guide . . .'[6] It was Loos, after all, who encouraged him to paint portraits, found him commissions amongst his richer clients, and introduced him to Karl Kraus, Hans and Erica Tietze and Peter Altenberg, whom he painted and who became his friends. It was through Loos that he acquired his first decent suit (from the Emperor's tailor, whom Kokoschka repaid by painting his picture). It was Loos's generosity that enabled Kokoschka to accompany him to Switzerland in December 1909, where he painted one of his finest landscapes, *Les Dents du Midi*. And without Loos he might never have met the musician and writer Herwarth Walden, founder and editor of the Berlin magazine *Der Sturm*, for which he contributed drawings regularly from March 1910 until January 1912, and in which *Mörder Hoffnung der Frauen* was first printed. Nor, indeed, would he have been taken on by Paul Cassirer, in whose Berlin gallery he had his first exhibition, and from whom he received his first regular income.

Through *Der Sturm*, Kokoschka attracted wide interest amongst other artists struggling to set themselves free from the shackles of Post-Impressionism. Oskar Schlemmer distributed early copies of the magazine to his friends at the Stuttgart Academy, where they created something of a stir. 'To us in Stuttgart,' wrote Gustav Schleicher, 'the drawings in each eagerly awaited issue seemed to shake the edifice of modern art like earth tremors. The dramatic effect these "sensations" had on our group simply cannot be overstressed . . .'[7]

No such tremors shook the Berlin press at the sight of the twenty-seven oil paintings, eight illustrations and assorted drawings of nudes that made up the content of Kokoschka's first exhibition in June 1910 (the only reviews were written for *Der Sturm*, one by Herwarth Walden's first wife, Else Lasker-Schüler). But they did attract the attention of Karl Ernst Osthaus, the director of the Folkwang Museum in Hagen, Westphalia, who arranged for them to be shown there in August, and who subsequently bought one of the exhibits, a portrait of the Duchess of Montesquiou, for the museum. The fee, 800 marks, was more than welcome. Until Paul Cassirer's offer of a regular stipend Kokoschka and Rudolf Blummer, an actor friend of Walden's, shared an attic above the *Sturm* offices. There, too poor to afford much in the way of heat, light or regular meals, they shivered through the bitter winter of 1910, huddling under blankets, entertaining themselves in the dark evenings by exchanging stories, fuelled by a meagre diet of biscuits and tea. 'Today I remember that period as something out of Gorky's *The Lower Depths*,' wrote Kokoschka in his autobiography:

> It never stopped snowing. From the little window I saw the snow piling higher and higher in the courtyard, and wondered when it would reach the point where the doors would no longer be opened. Also, I needed light to work by in the winter afternoons, but the sun was pale, and often I didn't have a groschen to put in the gas meter. This gave only one hour's light per coin, and we were often left freezing in the dark, alone with our thoughts.[8]

After Cassirer came to the rescue things took a turn for the better. Evenings were spent in the Café des Westens; there was a ball, at which Georg Grosz remembered Kokoschka appearing 'with a real ox-bone dripping blood, which he gnawed at from time to time'; there was travel, with Walden and his wife to the Rhineland; and there was enough light to paint the portraits he did that year of Walden, Blummer, and others connected with *Der Sturm*. But by December he was hankering for the less frenetic life of Vienna. 'I long to get back to Vienna . . .' he wrote to a friend on Christmas Eve, 'my whole life is hellish . . . and I am a bad-tempered weakling desperate for any sympathy that comes my way.'[9]

There was little sympathy, however, from the Viennese press, when the fruits of the past year were displayed at an exhibition of contemporary art from Austria, Germany and Switzerland organized by the society for modern art, the Hagenbund, in February 1911. The twenty-five oils (including the portraits of Altenberg, Loos and Kraus), as well as ten nude drawings, produced hysterical cries: 'repulsive plague-sores', 'phantoms of a morbid youth'. Others were more enthusiastic. Carl Moll was so impressed that he asked Kokoschka to paint his own picture. The painter recalled:

> I painted Carl Moll in his patrician residence, with its neo-classical mid-Victorian décor, on the Hohe Warte, a district favoured by the prosperous Viennese bourgeoisie. I was often asked to stay to dinner. I liked the atmosphere of the house, although its slightly oriental magnificence was less reminiscent of Schindler's time than of the age of Ingres and Delacroix (or Makart, whose pupil Moll had also been): Japanese vases with great sprays of peacock feathers, Persian carpets on the walls. The table was elegantly laid; there were always flower arrangements, gleaming silver, sparkling glass – and good wine. The concert master of the Vienna Philharmonic, Arnold Rosé, and his family were close friends of the Molls, and there were often chamber recitals. The table talk was usually about art, specially after Moll's step-daughter, Alma Mahler, returned from abroad. She was the widow of Gustav Mahler, the director of the Opera, who had died a year before. It must have been difficult for her to take leave of the little man on his bier and to find herself suddenly removed from the atmosphere of fame and consequence that she had shared with her husband . . . Following Mahler's funeral she had cut herself off for a time from everybody; but she was young, and now she wanted company again. She was curious to meet me.[10]

Both Alma and Kokoschka claimed that the other had fallen in love at first sight. Alma saw a young man, his shoes torn, his suit frayed, 'a handsome figure, but disturbingly coarse', who stared at her so piercingly whilst he covered sheets of paper with his drawings that to avoid his gaze she asked if she could play the piano. 'We hardly spoke – and yet he seemed unable to draw. We got up. Suddenly, tempestuously, he swept me into his arms. To me it was a strange, almost shocking kind of embrace; I did not respond at all. And precisely that seemed to affect him.'[11]

Kokoschka remembered that after dinner Alma took him into the next room, where she played and sang *Liebestod*. He found her 'young and strikingly beautiful in her mourning' and was 'at once overjoyed and perturbed' when she suggested that he paint her portrait. Never before, he wrote, had he painted a woman who seemed to have fallen in love with him at first sight.[12]

How could he have resisted? Before him sat a tragic young widow singing the words of Wagner's unhappy queen. Was she not the answer to the questions that had haunted him for so long? Could she not assuage those inner voices that had tormented him like a hermit in the wilderness with imaginings about the female sex? Surely she, of all people, would be attuned to the consequences of an instantaneous passion that was 'strong enough to render passion itself speechless', leaving its victim in a state of mental paralysis, able to take any risk, shrug off any folly, for the sake of smile or of words he imagined were never heard before from mortal lips.

Alma's initial lack of response to these overtures must, therefore, have been a disappointment. 'He stormed out,' she wrote, but within hours he had relented, sending round 'the most beautiful love letter and proposal'.[13] Kokoschka mentioned none of this in his memoirs, merely remarking that he 'felt a certain shyness and apprehension: how could one man find happiness where another had so recently died?' It was the beginning of 'an exceedingly passionate relationship, which lasted three years'.[14] With this Alma agreed: 'The three years that followed were one fierce battle of love. Never before had I tasted so much tension, so much hell, so much paradise.'[15]

Never one to do things by halves, Kokoschka immersed himself from the outset in the insanity of love: 'You can feel icy cold and boiling hot at the same moment. When you timidly try to put an arm around the one with whom you are mortally in love, your heart begins to beat as if you were committing a sacrilege; only God, if he exists, could know how much you suffer . . .'[16] He would not rest until they were married. 'If you want to be as pure as you were yesterday,' he wrote after their meeting at the

Hohe Warte, 'when I knew you in a higher and better sense than all the women who could only demoralize me – then make a real sacrifice and become my wife: in secret, whilst I am poor.'[17]

Alma's reluctance to sacrifice her precious security was always a bone of contention between them. No one knew better than she the trials and tribulations of aspiring artists, and their need for a creative life free from debt and from the necessity of painting purely for money. But to give up all her hard-earned comforts and live a life of spartan aestheticism as the wife of a struggling young artist – however touched by the hand of genius – was asking too much. 'I began to curse his youthful innocence that gave him the right to sit in judgement,' she wrote. 'To justify my pleasure in my modest fortune, I explained to him that I, too, was an upstart: not' – she added unkindly – 'culturally, as he, but financially. Without a cent from home I had made myself independent, and the mountain of debts I had married along with Mahler had not been easy to clear. I begged him to let me enjoy what I had struggled so hard for; I could not learn to walk all over again.'[18]

It was as well that Mahler did not live to see this entanglement, for in this case Freud's diagnosis might not have been so reassuring. Kokoschka was twenty-six when they met, Alma thirty-three. He, by his own admission, was an 'immature youth with a tendency to run full tilt at brick walls', she a woman surrounded by ghostly and living reminders of her past. In the garden of genius Kokoschka was still a raw recruit – and at twenty-six an unlikely candidate as a father-figure. He carried with him no aura of creative sanctity, his features were not set in any recognizably Wagnerian mould, he was neither teacher, mentor nor heroic model. Yet, without any of these previously necessary psychological attributes, Alma fell instantly under his spell:

> Kokoschka was a strange mixture as a man and as a human being. He had everything a person needs to be great; I loved him for that, and I loved the ill-bred, stubborn child in him. He and I were homogeneous to the last fibre of our being. Our Catholicism came from the same sources; our delight in holidays like Christmas and Easter was not delight in gifts and glitter but in the mystic events

whose pervading radiance we would sense alike. Why, then, did it not work? Were we too similar?[19]

The answer, probably, was yes. Kokoschka's need to possess Alma body and soul, to isolate her from all vestiges of what he considered to be her shallow society life, and to forge them both into truly one flesh became an obsession that not only estranged him from his friends – Loos in particular – but eventually began to alienate him from Alma. Night after night, she recorded, he left the garden flat she had rented near the Hohe Warte, not to return to his studio on the Stubenring, but to hover in the vicinity, watching jealously for signs of any rival male caller. Only when completely satisfied did he whistle – 'the longed-for signal that he was about to depart'.[20]

To begin with, however, Alma, whirled along in a maelstrom of enjoyable emotions, abandoned herself completely to the overwhelming force of their joint destiny. The constant protestations of devotion, her daily visits to the studio, where Kokoschka drew and painted her over and over again, were intoxicating endorsements of her own view of herself as artistic muse and goddess.* All too often Mahler had detached himself from her to vanish into a creative world of his own. Walter Gropius was far away in a state of indecision in Berlin. With Kokoschka Alma had found, temporarily at least, mental and physical nirvana.

But the very intensity of their relationship bred the seeds of its destruction. 'I read in her book that she accuses me of power mania,' Kokoschka wrote, 'and complains that I treated her like a prisoner and prevented her from seeing other people. In my own defence I must say that her complaints seemed to me then utterly insignificant and trivial. And she cannot really have felt very different herself, or she would not have remained, as she did, passionate in her devotion to me until the moment when I enlisted at the outbreak of war . . .'[21]

As for Alma, she recorded that at one stage, before going to Scheveningen with Anna in the summer of 1912, 'the first great,

*Anna Mahler, then aged eight, was often taken to play in Kokoschka's studio. She once asked him: 'Can't you paint anybody but Mummy?'

unbalancing crisis occurred', when she played *Parsifal* to him and he 'switched the words he hated', whispering 'a new, eerie text' into her ears.[22] Exactly which parts of the text Kokoschka desecrated is not known: possibly he took the Nietzschean view that *Parsifal* was at best 'a morbid and unintelligible *fin de siècle* brew of religion and sex', centring upon an 'incoherent concept of redemption', and, at worst, 'a merely slow-moving, anti-dramatic product of senile prolixity' – all guaranteed to be at odds with Alma's rapturous approach to her musical hero. (More likely, Kokoschka took as his starting point the fraught relationship between the siren, Kundry, and the self-castrated magician, Klingsor, whose disability did nothing to assuage his lustful thoughts.)

Whatever the heresy, it reduced Alma to hysteria. 'I began to cry and scream,' she continued, but 'he did not stop. I fled from the piano; like Miracolo in *Tales of Hoffmann*, he kept coming after me.' The last act was played out in Alma's bedroom, where, to put an end to these loathsome impieties, she swallowed 'a large quantity' of bromide. Kokoschka, alarmed and penitent, sent for the doctor. 'Trembling, he stood before my door. I did not let him in then, nor the day after. On the third day he came, both hands full of flowers which he strewed over my bed.'[23]

Neither, when writing their autobiographies, paid much attention to chronology, but the ups and downs of the ensuing three years are reflected in the stream of letters Kokoschka wrote to Alma whenever they were apart. 'Most beloved,' he wrote on 5 May 1912:

> Had you and I trodden along life's path together, we should have come to recognize nature's mercy, just as you know it, and I foresee it . . . Alma, always be the sort of wife who never lies down under things, and who can lift herself up by contemplating the problematical, changeful elements in life, and I will be a husband whom you can never put down, so that we may become stronger, and forever united in the light of that higher nature on the other side . . . Alma, do not become weaker from tired possessions, do not become weaker from fulfilled motherhood, but above all be my second-born spiritual double . . .

And, three days later:

Alma, I now believe, stronger than anyone on earth, that you
must bind yourself to me ... Before, I put my faith in heavenly
things to come and mistrusted the present. I was cynical towards
people, and clung to a childhood vision of God that was merely a
glorification of my own self, but ... now I believe in you and am
risen from the dead ... your inner virtue, which I recognized, has
conquered my mistrust and disarmed my cruelty ... write to me
much more, dearest Alma I am so alone ... [24]

Whilst in Scheveningen Alma received a letter from Kokoschka
in Vienna, suggesting a rendezvous in Munich ('be brave, little
Napoleonic soldier, remember the way to me') with a view to
travelling on somewhere else together. They duly met and, as
Alma wrote, 'loved and quarrelled and saw a film about Christopher Columbus that ... inspired O.K. ... to give his side of
our relationship in his lithograph series, "The Fettered Columbus".'*[25] The quarrel, apparently begun beforehand, nearly
put an end to the whole project. Alma's insistence on travelling
first class, accompanied by what seemed to Kokoschka to be
an unnecessary amount of luggage, caused considerable friction.
'Don't make your old mistake of bringing every single bit of
baggage,' he instructed her on 25 July, 'and, another thing, it
upsets me very much how little you seem to realize how much
our reunion depends on the financial freedom the completion of
my work gives me.† Almi, forgive me for thinking this time about
myself, but for so long I have thought only of you, and you
really should not, however unintentionally, cause me pain by your
thoughtlessness ... I will travel alone, if you must travel like that,
for the sake of my own peace of mind ...'[26]

Their incompatibilities must to some extent have been reconciled, for when they decided to go on to Mürren in the Bernese
Oberland they took, Alma wrote, 'the most beautiful rooms in
the most beautiful hotel'.[27] There Kokoschka painted *Alpine
Landscape, Mürren*, began a portrait (finished on 6 December)

---

*Gefesselter Columbus – Columbus in Chains – twelve lithographs completed
in the summer of 1913 and first published by Fritz Gurlitt Verlag in Berlin
in September 1916.
†Kokoschka had been working on various portraits in Vienna and on
Semmering.

of Alma, and decorated in idyllic style the first of a series of seven fans, completed in 1914, charting the course of their love. Kokoschka then went on to Lauterbrunnen, but Alma, thinking herself pregnant and, once again, disliking the idea ('I was afraid of what might grow in me; I feared it might inherit Kokoschka's ferocity'[28]), hurried back to Vienna for medical advice.

That time she was mistaken, but her reluctance to bear Kokoschka's child augured badly for their future life together – a subject they discussed throughout the autumn. In October Kokoschka wrote Alma a note, telling her he had been to see Carl Moll and that Moll had given his consent to their marriage, 'without making any difficulties'. Alma, presumably, still had reservations, for whereas Kokoschka professed his undying devotion to his 'beloved wife, sister and mother', the new year came and went without any fixed promise on her side. 'Have you any idea', Kokoschka wrote sadly on 3 January, 'why we are always so unhappy?'[29] Part of the trouble, he admitted, was his jealousy of her past and the feeling he had that even her music revived memories he could not share. Mahler's death mask, recently installed in Alma's flat, and the pictures and music she kept on his desk, were a constant torment. 'One day', wrote Alma, 'Kokoschka suddenly got up, picked up Mahler's pictures one by one, and kissed Mahler's face. It was an act of "white magic" – he wanted to curb the dark jealous urges within him. But I cannot say it helped.'

To combat these destructive impulses, Kokoschka painted two double portraits of himself and Alma, one fully clothed and the other waltzing naked in a pink and green Garden of Eden, their arms round each other, their thighs touching, their physical features as alike as brother and sister. It was still not enough, however, to induce Alma to agree to a wedding date. In March they spent three weeks in Italy, visiting Venice, Naples (where Kokoschka painted the bay) and Pompeii. Soon after their return on 10 April 1913 Alma went on another cure, this time to Franzensbad in Bohemia, with the proviso that if Kokoschka painted a masterpiece whilst she was away, she would marry him.

Spurred on by this incentive Kokoschka wasted no time. 'Things are going much better for me today,' he wrote shortly after her departure. 'I am always working, only I have embarked on no easy subject . . .' Even though he had ambivalent feelings about the explicitness of the private emotions revealed on the canvas – 'it is offensive to me that so many of your and my expressions are in this work' – he had no doubts as to its worth. 'Today I spent the whole day painting your body, this is going to be my best picture . . . [it] belongs in a gallery . . .' As the painting developed he became more reconciled to its intimate nature. 'Slowly, with constant improvements – the picture advances towards completion,' he wrote in April. 'The two of us with very strong, calm expressions, clasping each other's hands, framed by a semi-circle of sea, lit up by fireworks, a water-tower, mountains, lightning, and the moon . . . despite all the turmoil in the world, to know that one person can put eternal trust in another, that two people can be committed to themselves and other people by an act of faith.'[31]

The painting, *Die Windsbraut* (*The Bride of the Wind*), was not completed until the end of the year. It was given its title by the poet Georg Trakl, who visited Kokoschka in his studio just as he was putting the finishing touches to the canvas. 'Trakl wore mourning for the death of his twin sister,' Kokoschka wrote. '. . . His grief was like the moon as it moves in front of the sun and darkens it. And then, slowly he began to say a poem to himself; word by word, rhyme by rhyme . . . With his pallid hand he motioned towards the picture; he gave it the name "Die Windsbraut".'[32]

Kokoschka was satisfied with his creation. 'The picture is an event . . . my strongest and greatest piece of work, the masterpiece of all Expressionist endeavours,' he wrote to Herwarth Walden in December. In the meantime, whilst Alma was still taking the waters, Kokoschka visited her unexpectedly and was enraged to find that the self-portrait he had asked her to hang in her room for her 'spiritual and moral protection' was nowhere to be seen. 'A storm broke, and he left unreconciled,' Alma wrote. As a result, she recorded, when she returned to Vienna at the end of the month she found the walls of his new studio (at 27 Hardt-gasse) painted black: 'Two lamps, one red and one blue, illuminating the two parts of the room, the black walls ... covered with white crayon sketches', and Kokoschka himself in a strange state of mind.[33]

In fact, it was not until September, after they had spent late August at Tre Croci in the Dolomites, that Kokoschka moved into his new studio. From there he went, in the late autumn, to Berlin, to discuss the sale and exhibition of his work with Walden, Cassirer and another Berlin art dealer, Wolfgang Gurlitt, with whom he had entered into a financial arrangement a year before. Although miserable at this exile from Alma – 'I can't bear all these voracious people ... I don't go to concerts, the cinema or the theatre, I'm so very unhappy, I must have you,' he complained in two notes sent on 15 November[34] – he wrote later that the negotiations had borne fruit. Arrangements had been made for him to supervise the hanging of four oil paintings at the 26th Exhibition of the Berlin Secession in the new year, and Cassirer had renewed his contract – worth, at the minimum, 1,500 kronen a month.

Apart from mentioning that she looked after Kokoschka in his studio 'where it mattered' (an aside open to a number of interpretations), Alma made no reference to their financial arrangements. But the difference in their incomes – Kokoschka continually living from hand to mouth, and obliged to send the bulk of what he did manage to earn to his impoverished elderly parents; Alma comfortably off with her widow's pension and money from Mahler's American contracts – suggests that on their travels together and in their daily life Alma paid many of the bills. Although they did not live under the same roof until the summer months of 1914, they spent most of their days in each other's company and, as the same letter from Berlin shows, Alma had, once at least, lent Kokoschka money to tide over his inevitable debts.

The renewal of the Cassirer contract therefore meant that at least Kokoschka felt he could compensate Alma for some of the money she had spent on them both as well as fulfilling his obligations to his own family. 'I am sad that you have not yet received your money,' he continued, 'and that I am still in your debt. . . . The money has already been earned, and . . . it would have given me so much pleasure to take care of you a little. As for my relations, I can no longer summon up the same interest in earning just for them.'[35]

These attempts to put their relationship on an equal financial footing sprang from the deep sense of depression that had settled over Kokoschka since their summer travels. No nearer to becoming Alma's husband, he was haunted by fears of a separation. 'Ever since our travels together, a melancholy feeling had taken possession of me, foreshadowing a separation. She could not forget that she had been married to a world-famous conductor and composer, while I was at best notorious – and that only in Vienna – and penniless. I hated the society gossip that made her insecure.'[36]

He put all his faith in the building of 'their' house – Alma's country villa on Semmering, completed in spring 1914 – where at last they could live alone together, away from the corrupting influences of Vienna. Over the huge fireplace, which took up the full length of the living-room, Kokoschka painted a fresco showing them both engulfed in flames – Alma rising above them 'pointing heavenward, in spectral brightness', he below in hellfire, surrounded by serpents of death. According to Alma, it was a time of perfect contentment. 'No clouds marred the beauty of our days,' she remembered:

> Work was going on in every room; curtains were sewn on the machine and hung before the windows; my mother cooked in the kitchen. In the evenings we sat around the fireplace, read aloud or made music. It was a happy, positive, forward-looking time that was cut short by the news of the assassination of the crown prince and his wife, followed by the Austrian threats against Serbia and finally by the all-destroying fact of war – a war imposed on the entire world.[37]

Kokoschka remembered things rather differently. The obscure

Serbian patriot, Gavrilo Princip, did indeed shoot dead the Archduke Franz Ferdinand and his wife in Sarajevo on 28 June, but at the time it seemed less of a trauma than his dwindling relationship with Alma. Once again, in March, she thought she had become pregnant, but this time it had been confirmed. Once again, her adherence to Mahler's memory was a thorn in his flesh:

> I had always insisted that nothing of the dead Gustav Mahler, not even his bust by Rodin, should be brought into our house. Perhaps I feared that the child she was carrying might have the features of the dead man, of whom she spoke too often for my liking. In particular I had forbidden the introduction of Mahler's death mask . . . This led to several unpleasant scenes. And then one day a box was delivered to the Semmering house, and from it she reverently took the mask, packed in wood shavings. Perhaps this finally brought the crisis; surely scandal and the advice of friends had been no more than contributory factors in the decision Alma now took, and which I never forgave. She went into a clinic in Vienna and had the child, my child, taken from her, and so, for me, our affair had already ended even before the war.[38]

Had Kokoschka known the true state of Alma's mind, he would have been even more despondent. At the heart of it lay increasing weariness: the peace and quiet of the mountains had provided the perfect antidote to the emotional buffetings of the past two years. Worn out by the exacting nature of Kokoschka's love, her thoughts had turned once again to a more soothing, less emotionally devouring companion. When, therefore, Bertha Zuckerkandl wrote in April 1914 to tell her of Walter Gropius's successful contribution to the Cologne Werkbund exhibition, she wrote to congratulate him. To his reply, asking how she was, Alma told him, in a letter written in May: 'After struggles and upsets – I am myself again. Above all, I know that I have nothing to look for – because I have found so much in life – You want my friendship – you have it – I should so love to talk to you. . . . People who have experienced something so unusual and beautiful between them should not let it slip away. Do come here, if you wish, and you have the time . . .'[39]

In the event, Gropius did not have time to visit Semmering.

But their renewed contact must have made Alma more convinced than ever that she had been right not to entangle herself further with Kokoschka by having his child. The abortion, so devastating to Kokoschka, was for her a release from bondage.

For Kokoschka, however, the bonds were not so easily severed. He wrote reproachfully on 10 May, accusing Alma of not having made allowances for his 'immature' faults of solitariness, excruciating jealousy and abject poverty: 'I saw you and believed that you were my "motherly muse". Because I had no background. And you wondered why I could find no niche in your ready-made world.' Alma had behaved like a sphinx, he said, capable of 'withdrawing from another's love, or deceiving him, for the sake of her well-being'. Yet it was not long before his letters began to resume something of their old intimacy. 'I must have you for my wife soon,' he wrote in July, 'or my great gifts will perish miserably . . . You are the woman, I am the artist . . . I can only say that if you come I can work. Today I realized from seeing what I had done to the red picture how strong you make me, and what I could do if that strength remained *steady*.'[40]

But the melancholy that had hung over him even before the abortion could not be shaken off. The last print of the lithographic series, *The Bach Cantata*, showed Kokoschka in his grave 'slain by [his] own jealousy, like Hyacinth by the discus that a treacherous fate turned back upon him', and his poem 'Wehmann und Windsbraut', begun in 1913 and published in 1915 under the anagrammatic title 'Allos Makar' (Greek for 'Happiness is otherwise'), painted a similarly bleak picture of love and death.

Occasionally he glimpsed a light at the end of the tunnel. 'My angel for you' he wrote above a short poem sent in the summer of 1914:

> WOMAN: How poor summer night vanishes
> and cries out to a falling earth
> Behind night
> long tresses spin into a web
> and heroes begin to pull themselves from danger.

MAN: From God's power sprang
creation's daughter
the tender bud burgeons in the hand
the soul, that gave birth, has become my face.

And below it: 'suddenly I was lonely, but knew what a mistake I would be making if I was not able to summon up my powers of resistance . . . My longing for your love and my obsession with your inexplicable negligence . . . must now be thrown to the four winds . . .'[41]

This inconclusive state of affairs dragged on to the end of the year. The outbreak of war had put Kokoschka in a dilemma. 'If I were able to earn enough money to keep my relatives' head above water, I would happily volunteer for the army,' he wrote to the publisher Kurt Wolff in September, 'because anyone who stays at home will never be able to live down the shame.'

The case for those who maintain (like Anna Mahler) that it was Alma who, by persistent taunts of cowardice, finally drove Kokoschka to enlist rather than to wait for his inevitable call-up is likely but not proven. It is true that Kokoschka had shown little enthusiasm for army life in the past, and had been able to stave off his military duties for legitimate reasons of health and occupation, but it was also true that, by his own admission, he was not a particularly peace-loving person, and felt the Habsburg Empire, although by no means an ideal state, had much worth preserving.

All the same, he would probably have left the empire to be defended by others more robust than himself for a little longer had it not been for the gloom cast over him by Alma's recent behaviour. The grant of 5,000 kronen he acquired in November from the Ludwig Wittgenstein Foundation was welcome, but not enough to secure his family's future. As for Alma, anything that ensured her emotional ascendancy was manna to her soul. There had never been much love lost between Alma and Kokoschka's mother who, annoyed that her son never went home, had frequently pleaded with her to give him up, appealing to her 'mature sense' and begging her to think of his career. When, inevitably, these entreaties fell on deaf ears, Frau Kokoschka threatened to shoot the Circe who had spirited her son away (threats she was unlikely to carry out since, as Kokoschka remarked, his mother had no revolver).

Ironically, it was the sale of *The Bride of the Wind* that enabled Kokoschka to buy the half-breed mare essential to his entry into the 15th Imperial Royal Regiment of Dragoons. (A Hamburg pharmacist, Otto Winter, bought the painting on 8 December for 400 kronen.) Ironical, too, that it was Adolf Loos who secured his assignment, for Loos had strongly disapproved of his protégé's entanglement with Alma Mahler, feeling that she had drawn Kokoschka away from his old friends and into the shallow world of the *haute bourgeoisie*. For her part, Alma had little time for Loos, whom she considered to wield far too much influence over her lover. As Kokoschka himself said, it must therefore have been 'a real satisfaction to [Loos], after suffering Alma's hostility, to have made it possible for me to post to one of the most prestigious regiments in the Monarchy – the one in which the upper nobility of all the Crown Lands, and members of the Imperial family itself, used to serve . . .'[42]

Before beginning his military training at Wiener Neustadt on 3 January 1915 Kokoschka asked his mother to keep a necklace of red beads, 'a memento of Alma Mahler'. Frau Kokoschka dropped it into a flowerpot 'to avoid having to look at it because it made her think of blood'.[43] From Wiener Neustadt Kokoschka wrote daily letters to Alma, to which he received sporadic and not always satisfactory replies. 'Only yesterday evening a letter came from you,' he began on 8 January, 'sadly again with a refusal and a reproach,' and (undated): 'Your letter hurt me more than anything so far. I wept, because I now realize that I have no more hope, and, in this world at least you are unable to find me pleasing . . .'[44]

In April Kokoschka was transferred to Holics to complete his training, but before the final passing-out parade he committed what he described as 'some act of insubordination', for which he was 'very nearly put in irons'. He escaped the guard-house by a characteristically flamboyant ruse. At the parade, 'when almost all the detachments that were going to the Front had been called out from the various regiments, I galloped up, planted myself in front of the astonished General Staff, and volunteered for active service.'[45] Before he went, he wrote once more to Alma – a letter providing strong evidence for those who believe in her determination to use the outbreak of war to her own advantage:

> No, my dearest Almi. I will not get away from you . . . I love you above everything . . . In a few weeks they wanted to cram me full with everything that interests me least, and I feel defiant and disheartened and this evening a little homesick, and I repeat your name as a talisman. My room is full of mortar and dust, without service and bedding, and cold! And at 6 o'clock I must get up again and be sworn at until evening, because I brought too little instruction from the regiment, because the fellows there taught us nothing, also because I had not spent enough time there, against seven months for the others, because I have not ridden from childhood, and because I am not related to any of the aristocratic officers. I should certainly not have gained my commission, except for the fact that we are sent as a team, and have to go to Russia immediately. It is dreadful to feel there is nothing ahead but useless waste and daily ignominy and deprivation. So many artists stayed where they were and I must now bear my cross, without which I could lose somebody. Almili, my dearest, I am so miserable . . . All the very best, don't write Corporal, only OK for that is who I am, the other *means nothing.*[46]

Kokoschka's cross was, indeed, to be a heavy one. During 1915 he lost Alma, and very nearly lost his life: in August, whilst serving with his regiment on the Eastern front near Luck in the Western Ukraine, Kokoschka was so severely wounded by a bullet in the head and a bayonet thrust through his lung that his death was announced in the Viennese papers. Unknown to him, Alma had married Walter Gropius in Berlin on 18 August, and the news that Kokoschka had died impelled her to recover the letters she had written to him. 'Alma did not scruple to have sackfuls of her letters carried off at once from my studio, to which she still had a key,' Kokoschka wrote in his memoirs. 'War hardens people. To me it seemed cold-blooded and out of keeping with her passionate nature. In contrast I think of the pounding heart

with which I waited every morning for the postman to bring me
the longed-for messages of love!'[47]

As he lay in the field hospital at Wladimir-Wolhynak, forty
miles north-west of Luck, to which he was taken by horse-ambu-
lance to await transport to a hospital at Brunn, near Vienna,
Kokoschka suffered from frequent blackouts and hallucinations.
Images of the moonlit forest in which he had been shot, the death
of his horse, the cries of the wounded men around him and the
ghostly figure of the young Russian whose bayonet had pierced
his jacket, flickered through his half-conscious mind. Interwoven
with these images of war were glimpses of the woman from
whom he had so painfully parted and to whom he had been so
fatally drawn.

> I felt myself succumbing to her power of attraction, as if I could
> never part from her. The head wound had impaired my power
> of locomotion and my vision, but the words of my imaginary
> conversations with her phantom impressed themselves so vividly
> on my mind that without having to write anything down I could
> progressively expand them in my imagination to create whole
> scenes.[48]

From these internal visions came his play *Orpheus and Eurydice*, which Kokoschka wrote in the hospital at Brunn. By transforming himself into the mythical being of Orpheus and Alma
into his lost love, with Anna as Psyche and Mahler (of whose
memory he had always been deeply jealous) as the dark underworld god, Pluto, he tried to contain the powerful feelings of
ecstasy, eroticism and immolation that had coursed through his
veins ever since meeting Alma three years before. Like the hero
of Robert Musil's *The Man Without Qualities*, Kokoschka's
thoughts turned to the complications that followed instantaneous
sexual attraction. 'They had certainly both felt repulsion,' Ulrich
remembered about his first call on Diotima:

> but had also been struck by the thought that they might yet inter-
> mingle to the point of dissolution. Something of this vision
> remained between them. So two heads, up in the air, turn a dread-
> ful chill upon each other, while down below the unresistant bodies
> are melting into each other at white heat. There was something

malignantly mythical about it, as about a two-headed god or the Devil's cloven hoof, something that had misled Ulrich much and often in his youth, when he had experienced it more frequently; but with the passing of the years it had turned out to be nothing but an ordinary civilized erotic stimulus, exactly the same as the substitution of the unclothed state for that of nakedness.[49]

As soon as he was able after he was returned to Vienna by hospital train in the autumn of 1915, Kokoschka visited his mother. Still on crutches, and still not fully mentally adjusted, his first question was not for news of her own health, or that of his younger brother and sister, but whether or not she had managed to keep his necklace. 'Quickly', he recorded:

> she took the flowerpot with its withered flowers from the window-ledge, shook her head as if to chase away an unpleasant thought, and dropped the pot on the floor. With her bony fingers she pulled out from the mass of potsherds and earth the necklace of red glass beads – triumphantly, as if secretly pleased that she had been proved right. There was the source of all our misfortune! Suddenly I felt cured of my tragic love, and embraced my mother. 'That's all over, I'm alive, I'm back, just as I promised you.' I told her that as far as I was concerned the war was over, too.[50]

The war was not quite over for Kokoschka. After his final discharge from hospital in February 1916 he was declared unfit for service for three months, but in July was sent to the Italian front as a liaison officer, with orders to accompany a group of journalists and war artists to the Army Command in Tolmino. A month later he was walking past a bridge over the Isonzo when it was blown up, giving him severe shell-shock. Once more he was granted convalescent leave, which he spent in Berlin at the Hotel Central, renting a studio where, among others, he painted portraits of Herwarth Walden and his second wife Nell. Had it not been for the good auspices of Albert Ehrenstein, he would probably have been returned to his regiment, but Ehrenstein, who had been worried by his friend's state of mind – 'I'm already sick to death of life and I'm waiting for the end of the world, when I hope I'll be able to find a cleft in the ground where I can rest,'[51] Kokoschka had written to him in Berlin in July – arranged for him to recuperate in a clinic in Dresden.

After six months of indifferent health he was sent by the military authorities to Stockholm, to undergo a series of tests on the consequences of his head injuries at the hands of Professor Barany, a Nobel prizewinner for research into disturbances of the sense of balance. The professor's report, doubtless benefiting numerous other similar sufferers, finally removed Kokoschka from any threat of future military service. At last the war, in which he had been such a reluctant participant ('because of a love-affair – it had, frankly been an escape from an apparently hopeless situation'), had come to an end.

Exorcising the love affair was another matter. 'Helped by a strong constitution, I recovered from my war wounds,' Kokoschka wrote in his memoirs, 'but I had lost all desire to go through the ordeal of love again. Nevertheless, for some years I derived pleasure – and this perhaps does not deserve forgiveness – from raking the ashes of a dead grief, without asking myself whether Alma's psychic wounds had healed as well as my physical ones ...' Raking the ashes took various forms. He wrote her 'hypocritical' letters, 'offering to forget the past', or sent her telegrams 'full of devotion and without a trace of reproach or recrimination'.[52]

None of these cat and mouse games could compare with his *pièce de résistance*, conceived in Dresden in the summer of 1918 and born in the spring of 1919, a few months before he was appointed to a professorship at the Dresden Academy. In collusion with the Munich dollmaker, Hermine Moos, with whom he conducted a lengthy correspondence, he conceived a life-size doll 'aged between 35 and 40, with chestnut-red hair'. The final result would be 'a project to my satisfaction, creating so convincing a magic that I shall believe when I see and touch the woman of my dreams I have made her come to life'.[53]

This effigy, when delivered, was something of a disappointment. In readiness for the doll's arrival Kokoschka had bought clothes and underwear, and secured the services of a lady's maid, 'a pretty young Saxon girl by the name of Hulda', borrowed on an hourly basis from his landlord. In a fever of anticipation 'like

Orpheus calling Eurydice back from the Underworld' he released the doll from its packing case, to find that the cloth and sawdust dummy he lifted out was a travesty of its flesh-and-blood counterpart. The colour of the skin, hair and eyes and the proportions of the body were as specified, but not even the most ardent kiss of life could breathe warmth into those lifeless limbs.

Nevertheless the figure had its uses. Kokoschka drew it time and time again and from these studies painted *The Doll*, *Self Portrait with Doll* and *The Woman in Blue*: 'the larva, after its long winter in the cocoon, had emerged as a butterfly.' Throughout their strange cohabitation, Hulda attended to her mistress's toilette and, at Kokoschka's bidding, spread 'rumours about the charms and the mysterious origins of the Silent Woman: for example, that I had hired a horse and carriage to take her out on sunny days and rented a box at the opera in order to show her off', to tantalize and shock his friends and colleagues.

But by the early summer of 1920 Kokoschka's fantastical needs had been assuaged. The prospect of a seven-month sabbatical in Vienna sounded the death-knell of the Silent Woman, who could not so easily be paraded around in the same streets as her living model. She said her goodbyes at a champagne party thrown for her by the man who had conjured up her existence. Accompanied by a chamber orchestra from the opera, she moved among the guests on Hulda's arm. During the course of the evening the strain of being passed from drunken hand to drunken hand told: her head fell off and lay, symbolically, in a pool of red wine. The next day the dustmen came 'in the grey light of dawn, and carried away the dream of Eurydice's return. The doll was an image of a spent love that no Pygmalion could bring to life.'[54] The exorcism was complete.

10 *The Green Fields*

I'm off to war in the green fields
The green fields so far away,
Where the pretty trumpets blow
I'll find my home in the earth below.
                                    Des Knaben Wunderhorn

When, following the German invasion of neutral Luxembourg and Belgium on 2 and 3 August 1914, England and France declared war, first on Germany and then on Austria-Hungary, wild scenes of jubilation broke out all over Vienna. There were a few who did not respond to the general mood of euphoria – Karl Kraus and Arthur Schnitzler among them – but in the main the call to arms after fifty years of peace aroused feelings of intense patriotic excitement and came as a shot of adrenalin to thousands of young men to whom war seemed a heroic adventure on no account to be missed. Cheered on by an admiring populace, the new recruits marched into the unknown, borne along on a tide of parades, flag-waving and band-playing.

Even Stefan Zweig, another sceptic, admitted to feelings of involuntary exultation during the early days of the war. 'To be truthful', he wrote:

> I must acknowledge there was a majestic, rapturous and even seductive something in this first outbreak of the people . . . in spite of all my hatred and aversion for war, I should not like to have missed the memory of those first days . . . A city of two million, a

country of nearly fifty million, in that hour felt that they were participating in world history . . . and that each one was called upon to cast his infinitesimal self into the glowing mass, there to be purified of all selfishness . . . [1]

The realization that war was more than a quick excursion to glorious deeds came all too soon for the newly mobilized army when, in the autumn and winter of 1914, it was required to defend its Eastern front against the Russians and in the process lost over 20,000 men before Christmas. Their struggles, however, impinged little on everyday life in Vienna. Gerhart Hauptmann, Richard Dehmel and other like-minded writers concocted stirring poems eulogizing the beauty of war and the moral benefits of sacrificing life for the common good, whilst Karl Kraus compiled his own *Götterdämmerung* in the form of *The Last Days of Mankind*, but the majority of Viennese refused to allow the outbreak of war to interfere with their pleasures. 'Life outside goes on just as usual,' Alban Berg wrote disapprovingly to his teacher, Arnold Schönberg, in Berlin, on 1 January 1915:

> I tell you . . . to watch this is as nauseating as the war is terribly painful. As if nothing had happened, people in Vienna live completely without restraint, operettas and farces 'adapted to the times' are produced, and every theatre and cinema is filled to bursting point. If the war should do what it is supposed to do – to act as a cathartic element – it is very far from achieving this. The dirt remains as before – only in a different form.[2]

Alma was no exception. Seen through her eyes Vienna changed little during the war years. There were still concerts, visits to the opera and rides in the Prater, and there was still the all-important business of tending her own emotional front whilst those unable to give it succour were away supporting a front of a different kind. Throughout the autumn of 1914 Alma waited impatiently whilst Walter Gropius fulfilled his obligations to his country by serving with the 9th Hussars in France (with distinction – he was awarded the Iron Cross, class 2, in September 1914 and the Bavarian Military Order 4th Class with bar in March 1915). Oskar Kokoschka's departure for military training in January 1915 paved the way for a reunion: on New Year's Eve Alma wrote longingly to Gropius from Semmering that she had invited some guests on New Year's Day so that she would not have to feel so alone. 'May the time come when you can be here – here, where your footsteps could make the earth move for me . . .'[3]

At last, at the end of February, Alma and Gropius were reunited. They met in Berlin, where Gropius, suffering from nervous exhaustion, was spending his convalescent leave. There ensued, Alma recorded, much mutual soul-searching, with days 'spent in tearful questions' and nights 'in tearful answers', for Gropius, whom she found as handsome as ever ('still the perfect Walther von Stolzing'), was in a mixed frame of mind. The shock of finding out the full extent of Alma's involvement with Kokoschka (which until then she had concealed from him) was great and it needed all Alma's powers of persuasion to convince him that the past three years were over and done with, and that the spark which had ignited the flame of her passion for Kokoschka had finally been extinguished.

It was no easy task, but one which Alma attacked with a will. Having removed the one impediment to their union – Kokoschka's child – Alma was determined that nothing should stand in the way of her heart's desire: to marry Gropius and start another family. Blind to the differences between them – Gropius had little musical sense and Alma neither understood nor was particularly interested in Gropius's abstract approach to the relationship between art, architecture and society – Alma concentrated on what she felt they had in common. Physical compatibility, Gropius's good and steadfast nature, combined with her own longing to lead a peaceful life free of the constraints and emotional tensions that had brought her affair with Kokoschka to its unhappy end, seemed, at the time, to be a good enough basis on which to build a second marriage. 'I have known four men extremely well in my life,' Alma wrote in her diary. 'Gustav Mahler – who struggled towards abstraction, Oskar Kokoschka, the Genius, Walter Gropius the thoughtful and cultured person – and Joseph Fraenkel, the genial improviser. I loved all of them in their way, whether they made me happy or unhappy. But from Walter I want children . . .'[4]

At the end of a fortnight she succeeded. 'At last he fell in love with me,' she wrote, 'at Borchardt's Restaurant, with wine and the atmosphere to stimulate the emotions and the farewell mood doing its share, for in an hour he had to catch a train to Hanover, to see his mother.'[5]

Her mission accomplished, Alma returned to Vienna, where in between writing daily letters to Gropius, she took up the threads of her old life. Gerhart Hauptmann and his wife called. Despite three sons at the front, he was burning with war fever: 'Nothing is more hateful than unaired rooms – people are now fresher, stronger,' he told Alma, 'in all truth.'[6] Hans Pfitzner invited himself to stay and insisted on playing his new opera, *Palestrina*, four-handed from 'little notebooks'. On the first evening Alma, who had tonsillitis, lay down on the sofa and Pfitzner stroked her feet. On the second his head 'came to rest' on her bosom and she stroked his hair. 'What else could I have done?' Alma demanded. 'He wanted to be kissed, and in the end I . . . kissed him on the forehead, loftily outlining a path of pure emotion.' On the third they sat once more on the sofa, this time in a 'cosily cool tête-à-tête, without embraces or seething passions, until the calm farewell'.[7]

Siegfried Ochs, the Berlin choral conductor, also called. He brought magnificent presents: an autograph of Goethe's, a copy of Dürer's *Christ*. In return he wanted an idyll with her on Semmering. Instead she took him for a ride in the Prater. 'Siegfried Ochs at my feet,' she wrote at the end of March, 'shaking with passion – quite mad, as only an old man in love can be . . . poor devil – but enough is enough.'[8]

Schönberg, too, was on her mind. Now married to Zemlinsky's sister Mathilde, and with a young family, Schönberg had been teaching in Berlin, but the loss of all his pupils after the outbreak of war had put him in perpetual financial straits. A year previously, when things had looked particularly bleak, Alma, in her capacity as a prominent committee member of the Gustav Mahler

Trust Fund (established after his death with 55,000 kronen, the interest to be allocated to a needy composer for a period of up to one year), had not only seen to it that the Mahler stipend of 2,000 kronen had been paid to him in full, but had materially assisted Alban Berg and Anton Webern, both trying to raise money for their old teacher from students and others, by extracting an outright gift of 500 kronen from a rich friend, Frau Lili Leiser.

The financial situation had not improved by the spring of 1915, as the bulk of the exchange of letters between Schönberg and Berg shows. Faced with the possibility that he might have to return to Vienna for military service, Schönberg worried endlessly about the attendant expenses involved in moving his family and finding somewhere reasonable to live. In a letter to Alban Berg he stated his requirements: nothing over 2,400 kronen, but it must have 'at least 6–7 rooms, as well as servants' quarters, and rooms one could turn into bathrooms or toilets. Also pantry, etc. . . . it doesn't have to be a villa . . . but gas, electric light, water, plumbing: that's necessary . . .'[9] Mentioned in the same letter was his idea, already mooted with Alma whilst she was in Berlin visiting Gropius, of conducting a classical concert in Vienna. It was this project, together with the administration of the Mahler fund, that occupied Alma during March and April.

On 25 February Alban Berg, who had appointed himself guardian of his mentor's interests, and who acted throughout as an intermediary between Schönberg and Alma in the matter of the Mahler Fund, was able to send good news to Berlin. He and his wife Helene had been invited to visit Alma, who 'in her own magnificent way' had assured them that such a concert could be arranged. Better still: at the time of writing Alma had assured Helene that a 'large-scale benefit concert (under influential patronage of some sort)' for needy musicians was indeed to take place in the near future in the Musikverein under Schönberg's direction, and would consist of two Beethoven works, the *Egmont*

Overture and the Ninth Symphony, using Mahler's retouched scores.[10]

The concert, underwritten by the generous Frau Leiser, eventually took place on 26 April, after much agonizing from Schönberg, who was in a state of acute anxiety about money, whether or not the concert would actually take place, the difficulty of getting hold of the score of the Ninth Symphony (Alma had lent it to someone else), and the problem of his military service, which he wanted to spend in an Austrian regiment.*

Neither Schönberg nor Alma were satisfied with the final performance. 'The Schönberg concert is over and was a miserable fiasco,' Alma wrote in her diary, '. . . over sticks and stones [it] lurched towards its inevitable conclusion. The concert provoked little interest in Vienna. The dress rehearsal was practically empty and the concert itself undersubscribed. Schönberg had a fixed honorarium and should still be able to keep any surplus, if there is one . . .'[11]

This episode left a bitter after-taste. Back in Berlin Schönberg continued to bombard Berg with complaints about the mismanagement of the Fund, the inadequacies of the arrangements for the concert, and the necessity of expediting the date of his military examination, whilst Berg, with commendable patience, continued to reassure him. He himself had thought the concert performance 'incomparably beautiful', and as for the Fund, he urgently recommended his friend to deal directly with Alma Mahler herself, as 'it was she who initiated the campaign, most of the results of the campaign are thanks to her efforts and influence.'[12]

This, however, was exactly what Schönberg wanted to avoid. The idea of pleading for money from the Mahler Fund when, as a needy composer himself, he regarded it as his rightful inheritance, was abhorrent to him at any time, but particularly so in the wake of recent misunderstandings with Alma. Apart from his

---

*Schönberg's father was Hungarian and his two sons both had Hungarian citizenship.

dissatisfaction over the concert arrangements, Schönberg had been incensed by her accusation that the score of *Egmont*, temporarily missing since the performance, had been mislaid by him. It eventually turned up at Frau Leiser's, but the intervening exchange of letters on the matter, riddled with accusations, hurt feelings and wounded pride, had left its mark on all concerned, and led to a temporary estrangement between Alma and Frau Leiser on one side and Schönberg on the other. 'It is out of the question that I turn directly to Frau Mahler,' Schönberg wrote to Berg on 17 May 1915. 'Apart from the fact that her extremely "peculiar" letter (as regards tone and content) has made me realize that she lacks the proper esteem for my person and achievements, after all (my reply seems to have increased the tension) – apart from that I also refuse to do it because it *has been demanded of me*.'[13]

It was left to Berg to soothe Schönberg's ruffled feathers. He begged him not to take Alma too seriously and to try and understand that, for all her intellectual attributes, Alma had the body of a woman, and that her actions were nothing but 'capriciousness, born of the moodiness of a woman used to dispensing favour and disfavour according to momentary caprice and whim'. She was, Berg continued, fully sensible to Schönberg's greatness as a composer, and wished as much as he did for their differences to be resolved. As for the missing *Egmont*, Alma was a notoriously haphazard guardian of Mahler's library of scores and manuscripts: less than two months before, an unpublished manuscript of one of Mahler's early string quartets had turned up inside the leaves of the score of Beethoven's *Coriolan*, lent by Alma to the conductor Karl Horwitz for a concert in the Musikverein.[14]

After a few more weeks of diplomatic juggling between the parties concerned, Berg's efforts were rewarded. By the end of June things had been smoothed over, Schönberg had been assured a stipend until the end of the year, and both men had been passed fit to join regiments of their choice (they had previously failed their medical examinations).* Schönberg and his wife had been Alma's guests on Semmering and they had gone on to stay at Frau Leiser's villa nearby, where they had been offered, and had accepted, the loan of an apartment in her house in Vienna for the duration of the war.

Alma, meanwhile, was in a familiar state of emotional uncertainty. May 18th, the day of Mahler's death and of Gropius's birth, brought a flurry of troubled thoughts to her diary. 'Are these things coincidences?' she asked herself. '. . . Who holds my life in his hands? I do not know. Walter Gropius, perhaps? If it were he, I would not be feeling so sad now. I would rejoice – but I cannot . . .'[15]

Part of her resentment stemmed from having received another letter from Kokoschka, full of regrets for their past life together, but it was mainly due to the dearth of letters from Walter Gropius. Then fighting on the upper Mosel, between Nancy and Epinal, Gropius had little time for correspondence of any kind. Nevertheless, Alma had become increasingly depressed by what she saw as his thoughtless lack of response to her pleas for an early marriage. 'I feel your pleasure is less than mine,' she wrote after he had failed to reply to a proposal that she and Gucki should come to nearby Moussy for a couple of days, so that they could get married, 'so – I will go quietly out of your sight – you will see no more of my misery.'[16] Within a few weeks, however, she had a change of heart, and sent another letter, signed 'AlmaMGropius AMariaGropius', again suggesting that they

---

*Although technically declared fit, neither composer saw active service. Within a few months of his assignment to the Vienna-based Hoch Deutschmeister-Regiment Berg's already indifferent constitution broke down and he was sent to the military hospital at Bruck, suffering from asthma and bronchial catarrh. When even guard duty (from which, as his biographer Mosco Garner pointed out, his rank as an officer-cadet should have exempted him) proved too strenuous, he was transferred to the War Ministry, where he remained until November 1918. Schönberg was finally called up in December 1915 and began his training with the same regiment at Bruck in March 1916, during the course of which he too suffered a physical collapse, which contributed to his early discharge in October 1916.

should marry when he next had some leave, and begging him to call her by his name.

Towards the end of May Gropius felt the time had come to alert his mother – hitherto unaware of the extent of her son's involvement – to the situation, and used a few days' leave to go to Berlin with Alma to explain matters. The visit was a strain for all of them. Wounded to the quick at not having been taken into her son's confidence, Frau Gropius found the idea of his association with a widow who had a nine-year-old child of her own as unpalatable as had Frau Kokoschka before her. 'The days that I had to experience and struggle through with you and Frau Mahler were like a whirlwind,' she wrote to Gropius after their departure, 'and left me battered and exhausted. I am in such a state of agitation I don't know if I'm coming or going . . .' But, she added, 'perhaps I will understand things more when I get to know her better . . .' Later Frau Gropius relented sufficiently to write to Alma, asking if she could call her by her second name – Maria – as 'Walter writes to me so often of his dear Maria, that it seems natural to me to address you so . . .',[17] but she remained unreconciled to the prospect of their marriage.

Frau Gropius's consent was desirable, but not essential. Eliminating the last vestiges of Gropius's jealous feelings towards Kokoschka was vital for both of them. In June, to test both him and herself, Alma sent Gropius the Munich magazine *Zeit-Echo*, which had printed Kokoschka's illustrated poem 'Allos Makar', an anagram of Alma and Oskar. In her accompanying letter she wrote:

> I have the feeling that something lies unspoken between us, so I am sending you Nr. 20 of the *Zeit-Echo* . . . I think the second and third drawings are very good – 1–4–5 dreadful. But the poem is really beautiful . . . I am so happy that there is nothing now that I cannot say to you. I will never see this person again. . . . Look at 'Allos Makar' how you will – it won't affect me – the only thing that matters to me is whether or not the thing has artistic merit . . . Isn't it marvellous, that you are so wonderfully strong and that I can say all this to you . . . [18]

Gropius's reply is unknown, but he obviously passed this test with flying colours, for on 18 August 1915 he and Alma were married secretly without his mother's knowledge in Berlin. Two days later he was back at the front, leaving his bride to muse on her fate. 'On August 18th I married Walter Gropius,' she recorded in her diary. 'Nothing shall deflect me from my course, my will is clear, I want nothing but to make this man happy. I am triumphant, calm, excited . . . God preserve my love!' And the following day: 'I sit on the Frankfurt-Vienna train. Walter Gropius is back in the field. I am now alone again.'[19]

The war, which had provided such a convenient way of parting from Kokoschka, suddenly became an irritant. Without all that upheaval there would have been no need for such secrecy, the wedding could have taken place in Vienna and they would not now be separated. 'I have been married for a month,' Alma wrote on 26 September. 'It is the most peculiar marriage imaginable. So unmarried . . . so free, and yet so bound. No one else attracts me. I almost prefer the company of women – at least they are not contentious. But in the long run I should like to be in safe harbour . . . for the time being our marriage must remain a secret.'[20]

On Semmering after their clandestine marriage Alma continued to chafe against her lot, grumbling in her letters to Gropius about the necessity for secrecy, about his family and about the cost of entertaining the stream of guests in the summer villa, whilst emphasizing in the same breath how 'indispensable such distractions were to her'. The fact that her husband was an officer in the field was an irrelevancy best forgotten: far more important was his apparent lapse in forgetting her thirty-sixth birthday on 31 August, an oversight he redeemed handsomely by sending her an onyx necklace – a present that sent her 'mad with joy', not least because it arrived whilst 'Gretel C. and Baronin von Therlitz were there. And both were eaten up with jealousy.'[21]

The veil of secrecy was lifted in February 1916 when, after an idyllic Christmas spent together in Vienna, Alma found she was pregnant. At last Walter Gropius had fulfilled his designated function, and on 5 October, 'in terrible pain', the perfect Aryan child of Alma and Walther von Stolzing was born. 'I gave birth to a sweet girl; Manon,' Alma wrote. 'I am in love with this creature.'[22] Gropius, waiting impatiently for news, responded to the telegram heralding his daughter's birth with muted pleasure. 'Now my child has really come into this world,' he wrote to his mother, 'I cannot see it, I cannot hear it, only a short telegram announcing the birth, "after difficult preliminaries". I can't rejoice until I know how they are, and I wait with chattering teeth for what fate has in store for this wretched, helpless, man . . .'[23]

These vague presentiments of doom were to be amply fulfilled. When Gropius finally managed to get leave to visit his daughter, he found Alma reluctant to allow him near her. She wrote in her memoirs:

> I stood in front of the swaddling table . . . and refused to let him approach her . . . Only after long pleading did I allow him to glance at his child from a distance.
> He told me later that I had been like a tigress, frightening in the defence of my maternal responsibilities. But the truth lay deeper. I was still unaware of it and had been acting instinctively, but there was more to it than notions of hygiene: I would not let him share possession of the child because my fears had come true – because my feelings for him had given way to a tired twilight relationship. I, for one, could not sustain a marriage at long distance.[24]

Gropius returned to the front unaware of his wife's frame of mind, and he was none the wiser when he parted from his family again after an apparently harmonious Christmas leave. Alma, however, began 1917 low in spirit. Tired from the after-effects of the birth, depressed by the seemingly endless separations and the effect they were having on her feelings towards her husband, she succumbed to ill-health. Her heart, she recorded, 'threatened to give out' and she lay indoors brooding on her fate and musing on death. 'I felt no regrets at the prospect of leaving this world that had given me so much true, genuine life,' she wrote. 'For what would come now? At best, an hourly repetition of all that had gone before.'[25]

When speculating in years to come about the reasons for the disintegration of her short marriage to Gropius, Alma asked herself why, when they had so much in common, and she had 'liked him so well, had fallen in love with him, had loved him dearly', had it not continued? Was it merely their physical separations, or had it to do with Gropius's lack of musical understanding? Or was it due to her 'indifference to his mission': her inability to show enough enthusiasm for his architectural and human goals?

Alma made no attempt to solve her own conundrum, whose solution probably lay in a combination of all three, but perhaps it was the latter – Gropius's messianic vision of an architectural Utopia – that most eluded her. His belief, before the war, that it was the accepted values in art and architecture and society which had led to the degradation of man's essential humanity and his determination after it to bridge the disastrous gulf between reality and idealism were abstract concepts unlikely to sustain his wife's voracious appetite for immediate artistic nourishment. It was some time before he was able to put his ideas fully into practice. They are summed up in a proclamation, issued soon after his appointment in 1919 as head of an amalgamation of the two existing art schools in Weimar (The School of Arts and Crafts and the Academy of Fine Arts, re-christened by Gropius 'Das Staatliche Bauhaus Weimar'), urging artists and craftsmen to unite in order to create 'the new building of the future, which will embrace architecture and sculpture and painting in one unity and which will rise one day toward heaven from the hands of a million workers like the crystal symbol of a new faith'. By then, however, their differences had become irreconcilable, and besides, in the autumn of 1917 Alma had met Franz Werfel.

Furthermore, the introduction was effected by Franz Blei. The playwright and founder-editor of the Swiss Expressionist magazine *Die weissen Blätter* had, as Alma put it, joined her circle earlier in the year. By the spring her health had picked up, Gropius was temporarily out of sight and mind in France, and Alma began to entertain her old friends again. Spurred on by the likes of Max Burckhard, Gustav Klimt, the Zuckerkandls, Bruno Walter and Alexander Zemlinsky, Blei made a brilliant début, during which he hypnotized all around him with the breadth of his knowledge and his ability to communicate it at considerable length. All too soon his star waned. 'Finally he annoyed everyone,' Alma wrote. 'Tongue-tied Gustav Klimt, in particular, was jealous of Blei's superior knowledge, and we conspired to bring up a subject of which we thought he was going to be ignorant. We agreed on botany. But lo! Blei opened the pigeonholes in his brain and buried us under an avalanche of learned words and concepts of which *we* were ignorant.'[26]

In the summer, sensing that some other attraction was needed in order to prolong his intimacy with Alma, Blei asked if he might bring the writer Franz Werfel, recently transferred from the Eastern Front to the War Archives in Vienna, to see her. At once Alma's antennae were on the alert. She remembered a day in Berlin in 1915, immediately after her marriage to Gropius, when she had bought a magazine from a book pedlar's cart and opened it to one of Werfel's poems – 'Der Erkennende' – which she had later set to music. Now she was curious to meet this most humane of all Expressionist poets.

For, in contrast to Kokoschka's dark sexual undercurrents, Franz Werfel's early poems were lyrical affirmations of the power of the human spirit. The idea that man alone can give meaning to a world whose creation is inhuman and devoid of meaning and is thus inexplicably doomed to suffer was one that permeated his work throughout his life. But, where others might preach doctrines of nihilism and despair, Werfel embodied Expressionism in its purest form. The concept of man as a creature of God, trapped in a perpetual state of unreality, provided the perfect framework for his continuous interest in the liberation of the human soul.

His work had already aroused ecstatic admiration. In 1909 Max Brod, his senior by six years and an ex-pupil of the Prague Stefansgymnasium at which Werfel was then in the eighth grade, had been shown some of the young poet's earliest efforts by Willy Haas. 'Haas showed me some poems, none of which were futile, none full of the meaningless phrases common to all the poetry beginners usually brought me,' Brod wrote later. 'Everything moved in a new light.'[27]

This optimistic verdict was transformed into hero-worship after the two poets met. Werfel, whom Brod described as being 'of medium height, blond, high forehead, rather plump, with a ravaged childlike expression, was at first very subdued and shy', but blossomed when he began to recite. 'His manner changed immediately . . .' Brod remembered:

> He knew all his poems by heart. He spoke them from memory, without falter or mistake, with fire, and a throbbing, intense or triumphant voice, whichever was appropriate – now loud, now soft but always very rich, varied modulations. And he wouldn't stop. I'd never heard anything like it. I was captivated. As always when confronted with great art, I felt an enormous gift had been bestowed on me, the kind of gift one never finds in any other sphere of life.[28]

From then on Brod made it his business to champion his new friend's cause. Some of the poems recited at their first meeting were from Werfel's recently completed but as yet unpublished collection entitled *Der Weltfreund (Friend to the World)* – already received with much enthusiasm by his contemporaries, who were circulating them amongst themselves 'after the manner of the old oral tradition'. Like Brod, they were astounded at the 'enchanting phenomenon' of a poet able to express with such deceptive innocence their common disillusionment with an age full of 'rampant materialism . . . hypocrisy, complacency and corruption'. 'They hailed Werfel's freshness and lack of sophistication, his frank outpouring of emotion and his precocious pleas for good will among men . . . wherein the theme of the conflict between the generations, so characteristic of German Expressionism, was enlarged into a polemic against all authority, whether in the private, social or religious sphere.'[29]

Aflame with excitement over the new star on his horizon, Brod sent a batch of his protégé's poems to Camill Hoffmann, literary editor of the *Wiener Zeit*, a recent daily competitor of the *Neue Freie Presse* and the fleeting repository of many a young avant-garde's dreams. 'We had great hopes for it as an organ for the modern literary movement of free speech and unchauvinistic Viennese politics,' wrote Brod. 'But it could not muster great powers of survival and in a few years it was dead . . .' Before its demise, however, Hoffmann printed what Brod described as the least characteristic poem in the whole bundle, 'The Gardens of Prague'. Nevertheless, it was a satisfactory enough début and the two young men continued their friendship 'borne along on a naïve wave of mutual admiration'.[30]

Werfel introduced Brod to his circle, which included Ernst Popper, 'bursting with ideas which at the time seemed remarkably vague', Paul Kornfeld, Hans Janowitz, who later attracted some attention by his work on the film *The Cabinet of Dr Caligari*, and Ernst Deutsch, 'famous, first and foremost, for his prowess at tennis and for his beautiful sister, and shortly afterwards as an actor in his own right'. In return Brod bestowed on Werfel the 'supreme accolade' – introductions to Franz Kafka (then aged twenty-six) and to the philosopher Felix Weltsch. Both were equally impressed by the nineteen-year-old's achievements and by his 'frank nature and powers of genius'.[31] From then until 1912, when, at his father's bidding, Werfel left Prague for Hamburg to work for an export business, in order to prepare himself for entry into the prosperous family glove factory, the four German-Jewish intellectuals were constantly in each other's company.

'We met each other either at my place or at Werfel's lovely apartment,' wrote Brod, '(we still lived with our parents and had only one room for our own use) or at the wise blind poet's Oskar Baum . . .' Apart from their indoor discussions there were outdoor excursions – long hikes through the woods on the outskirts of Prague, extended rambles 'haunted . . . by the melodies of Smetana and the inspiration of Berlioz's songs'.[32]

There were other diversions in those peaceful days before the war:

> We went by steamer to the Moldau Rapids, or by train to Senohrab, where the delightful valley opens up to the famous Karlstein Castle. We bathed in forest streams, for in those days Kafka and I shared the curious belief that possession of a landscape

is incomplete as long as contact has not been physically established by bathing in the living stream of its waters . . . One lovely summer's day we journeyed out to the silvery waters of the Sazawa, discarded our clothes in the depths of the forest by an open-air pool which we far preferred to civilized swimming pools and, naked as Naiads and Dryads, we listened to the resounding new verses of the Friend to the World and then swam for hours. In my memory this wonderful Hellenic day will last for ever.[33]

By the beginning of the war Werfel had been rescued from his brief, unhappy stint in Hamburg by Kurt Wolff, who had taken him on in Leipzig as a publisher's reader. The publication in 1911 of *Der Weltfreund*, combined with his outspoken views on the shortcomings of contemporary politics, had attracted a number of new friends, amongst them Karl Kraus, but Werfel was not destined to claim intimacy with the satirist for long. Kraus approved of his initial stance over the mobilization of the Habsburg war machine, when together with Max Brod he attempted to persuade Thomas Masaryk to 'use his good offices with Italian public figures in order to bring about a peace initiative', and registered his lack of enthusiasm in two pieces written in 1914, 'Der Krieg' and, shortly afterwards, 'Ein Ulan'. However, Werfel's timely transfer to the Kriegspressequartier* produced a series of vitriolic polemics. It was not good enough, in Kraus's opinion, for writers such as Werfel to complain that they were torn between the freedom to do their own work within the government departments in which they were employed, and the fact that they were often compelled, against their own inclination, to write propaganda for the war-effort. The more Werfel protested that the moral dilemma of writers in wartime was not easily resolved, the more Kraus railed at the dishonesty of it all.

Alma, at their first meeting, was less interested in Werfel's problems as a wartime writer than in his physical appearance and magnetic personality. 'Coming home . . .' she wrote in October 1917, 'I found Blei and a colleague he had brought along, a

---

*After training Werfel served with a regiment of heavy artillery as a gunner and a telegraph operator, but took part in little combat. In 1917, at the instigation of Count Harry Kessler, he was transferred to the War Archives in Vienna.

stocky man with sensuous lips and large, beautiful blue eyes under a Goethean forehead.' Already in love with his poems and delighted to find that Werfel had wanted to meet her because of his admiration for Mahler's music, Alma fell instantly under his spell. Neither the differences between their ages (he was twenty-seven, she was thirty-eight) nor the fact that she was still legally bound to her husband could restrain Alma from sinking once more into the arms of romantic temptation.

According to Werfel, his feelings towards Alma did not develop fully until later the following year. Alma, however, was instantly engulfed in what was to be the last grand passion of her life. Alas for poor Gropius, neither godlike good looks, sanguine tempera-ment nor architectural distinction were enough to prevent him being set aside when more exciting pastures beckoned. Even the one thing Alma had wanted so keenly from him – a child of Wagnerian purity – had failed to forge a lasting bond.

Unaware of the speculative gossip already surrounding his wife and Franz Werfel, Gropius arrived in Vienna for his Christmas leave. Still nursing jealous feelings towards Kokoschka (he had once thrown one of Kokoschka's seven painted fans on the fire in a fit of rage), he kept up his campaign to rid the flat of all memories of Alma's recent past – little imagining that it was now her present that threatened their fragile union. To placate him Alma agreed to send Kokoschka's portrait of her and all his drawings to Karl Osthaus's Museum of Modern Art in Hagen. The fans she kept: even though, as she wrote, 'the love they depicted was dead' she 'could not bear to part with them'.[34]

During Gropius's stay Werfel was a frequent visitor, together with Franz Blei, and there was much music-making and reciting. Werfel had a good singing voice and Alma played for him – Wagner, Charpentier and Verdi – but Gropius (if a letter to his mother, written after returning to his military duties, is to be taken seriously) appeared to object to Werfel's presence less for fear of any possible infidelity than on anti-Semitic grounds: 'the Jews . . . are the ruin of us. Social Democracy, Materialism, capi-tal gains, profiteering . . . everything is their doing.' It was, as

Professor Isaacs explained, an uncharacteristic outburst, springing from the constant pressures of war and the feeling that 'all the sicknesses of the world were linked in some way to Vienna and to Alma and her circle'.[35]

It also, no doubt, had something to do with a recent encounter with his wife. On the afternoon of her husband's departure to the front Alma was due to attend the first of a series of Mahler concerts conducted by Willem Mengelberg. After seeing him off, Alma went to lie down to rest before the matinée, and was disagreeably surprised when Gropius (having missed his train) came back shortly afterwards. Her mind already on other things, Alma made difficulties about including him in the concert party. 'Later, as I sat with Anna in a horse-drawn cab that slowly ploughed through the deep snow, Gropius walked beside us for a long time, pleading with me to take him along to the concert. But I had no ticket for him, and my heart was hardened by my new love, of which I was still unaware. Besides, my knowledge of the gulf between our approaches – the difference in hearing and understanding music, for instance – paralysed me.' On this painful note Gropius left. From the border he sent her a telegram quoting Werfel: 'Splinter the ice in your features'.[36]

On New Year's Day, after a concert featuring Mahler's Fourth Symphony and Richard Strauss's *Ein Heldenleben*, Alma gave a party in Mengelberg's honour. Among the seventy people crammed into her flat were Gräfin Wydenbrück, Graf Dubsky, Franz Schreker, Julius Bittner and his wife, Alban and Helene Berg, Franz Blei, Johannes Itten and Ludwig Karpath, but Alma's happiest moments were when she was able to talk 'unobserved' with Franz Werfel.

The following day Mengelberg conducted his final concert, and Alma, overcome by a combination of Mahler's music and the naked currents of electricity coursing between herself and Werfel, succumbed to the inevitable. 'In the intermission he came to my box; we went home together and our eloquent silence carried us to the brink.'[37]

She was reminded of an earlier passion when Gustav Klimt

died in February 1918, whilst Werfel was away in Switzerland on an official lecture tour initiated by the War Press Office (an opportunity he used to preach the pacifist gospel). 'How ardently I had once loved him!' she wrote. 'And I had never stopped loving him, though in a different fashion.'[38]

The following month Alma found herself pregnant again, and it was during the latter stages of her pregnancy and in the aftermath of the premature birth of her fourth child, Martin, on 2 August – 'the most fateful season of my life' – that she was not only joined 'inseparably and forever' to the man who was to be her 'lover and companion until death parted us many years later',[39] but also began the painful process of parting from Walter Gropius.

Werfel blamed himself for his son's early entrance into the world and for his short life. Had it not been for his sexual 'impetuosity' on the night of his arrival on Semmering in late July, both Alma and her child might not have had to go through the agonies they undoubtedly endured. The woman he described as 'one of the very few magical beings there are'[40] might not have suffered a severe haemorrhage and might have been spared a long, debilitating labour followed by a difficult birth, with the added complication of a threatened post-natal haemorrhage. She would certainly have been spared the near-fatal ministrations of a Viennese physician summoned by telephone – an 'unspeakably stupid man who came at last and wanted to perform one of the most complex obstetric operations by candlelight. (I looked at his butcher's hands and forbade him even to touch me.)' She might have avoided the fearful journey to the sanatorium in Vienna – carried upside-down to a cart which took her to the station and then travelling by train, 'in an army car that usually carried corpses',[41] with Gropius – who had also been summoned – by her side.

As for Walter Gropius, nothing could have prevented his eventual discovery of his wife's change of heart, but perhaps he might have found out under less humiliating circumstances. Under the impression that the baby was his, he wrote to his mother from

Vienna, telling her of Alma's trials and tribulations, and of her courage and selflessness. 'The Molls have been a wonderful help, and . . . I can see from the attentions she has had from her friends how much love she excites . . . I do believe you have not got the full picture of how much she has suffered – and what an exceptional person she is. In the midst of her great pain she always thought of others, never herself. That is the central core of her nature.'[42]

Sadly, these illusions were shattered on 25 August, when Gropius, arriving unexpectedly and carrying a huge bunch of flowers, overheard Alma talking to Franz Werfel on the telephone. The intimate 'Du', her use of his Christian name and the tone of her voice, left him in no doubt of the nature of their relationship. Alma wrote of 'the grey Sunday when Gropius – who had deserved a better fate – learned the truth and crumpled as though struck by lightning; and the agonizing weeks that followed . . . Things took their historic course.'[43]

In October Gropius was sent on leave, on doctor's orders. From Berlin he wrote to Alma asking her to give him Manon. She, after all, had Werfel, his son, and Gucki with whom to make a new life. 'I was so upset I cried all day until Gropius and Werfel came,' Alma recorded. 'Then I told them my decision: to give up both of them, to keep my children and go my way to the end, alone. Gropius fell on his knees, begging my pardon; Werfel said a few, thoughtful unpretentious words that calmed us all. But in me there was a deep loneliness.'[44]

Neither his penitent feelings at having caused Alma such distress nor his genuine sympathy for the plight of her baby – sickly from birth and, at three months, with an enlarged head and showing signs of brain damage – prevented Gropius from continuing to try and gain custody of his daughter. In the meantime, before returning to Berlin in the third week of November, he extracted an agreement from Alma to bring Manon to visit him at least twice a year.

A week before he left Gropius unwittingly found himself on the fringe of an act of political extremism. In retrospect, it was a demonstration of slight importance, an uprising put down as quickly as it had begun, but it carried the hopes of revolutionary-minded workers and disaffected soldiers recently returned from the front as well as commanding the sympathy and participation of many left-wing intellectuals, among them the Prague journalist Egon Erwin Kisch, Franz Blei and Franz Werfel.

It occurred on 12 November – the day the Habsburg Empire finally died and the new Austrian Republic was born. The death, in 1916, of Franz Josef and the accession of the Emperor Karl, followed by the collapse of the Austrian armies in the early autumn of 1918, brought to a head the desire of the satellite lands for self-determination. On 16 October the Emperor attempted to stem the tide of nationalism by issuing a manifesto that proposed the transformation of the empire into a federation (a plan swiftly vetoed by President Wilson and by Thomas Masaryk, who had spent most of the war in America, campaigning vigorously for Czech independence). They were joined by all the representatives of the non-German nations within the imperial parliament, none of whom wished to remain under Habsburg rule.

At the same time as these decisions were being made in the old city of Vienna, flames of Bolshevism were being fanned on the other side of the Danube amongst workers and soldiers exhausted and disillusioned by the confusion, food shortages, illness and poverty that hung over the city in the wake of Austria's defeat. Anarchy and revolution were in the air: Hungary had fallen under the sway of the communist Bela Kun, and Bavaria was already a Communist Workers' Republic. Austria, isolated and defenceless, looked ripe for the taking.

That the country did not fall victim to communism seemed to Stefan Zweig little short of a miracle. The failure of the Emperor Karl's plans for federation led to the dissolution of the imperial parliament and on 25 October a provisional assembly called on all the old Habsburg lands to form their own three-party assembl-ies. In Vienna things took a particularly menacing turn for the worse when on 30 October a mass rally of soldiers and workers resulted in the setting up of a Provisional Central Committee of

Soldiers – a potentially explosive situation defused by the left-wing Social Democratic party who, through their already strong organizational network inside the army and factories, managed to transform the soldiers' councils into instruments of law and order.

On 1 November a coalition government was formed, with the Social Democrats firmly resolved to work in tandem with their more conservative allies, the Christian Socialist and German Nationalist parties, in the interests of national stability. The following day the armistice was signed in Padua, and on 11 November the Emperor Karl, bowing to the will of the people, removed himself from Vienna.

The sight of a new republic coming into existence with the balance of social forces untipped towards revolution was anathema to Egon Erwin Kisch, then leader of the so-called 'Red Guard' unit in Vienna. Unlike Franz Werfel and Franz Blei, who merely dipped into the melting-pot of ideological ingredients circulating amongst the habitués of the Café Central and drew out a mixture of Catholicism and Communism, Kisch was a lifelong Communist dedicated to the overthrow of the system, and it was with this in mind that he led his band of sympathizers, including Werfel and Blei, to the Parliament Building on the night of 12 November.

Three years later Werfel began a novel, *Barbara oder Die Frömmigkeit* (*Barbara or Piety*), recreating the events of that abortive uprising, which petered out within hours. As Werfel had done himself, his hero, together with other members of the Red Guard, harangued the motley crowd of soldiers and workers surging towards the Parliament Building with revolutionary slogans. With them he fired a few putative shots into the building's entrance and was calmed down by unarmed deputies; and, as had happened in reality, one of his friends (Kisch) led a mob into the offices of the *Neue Freie Presse* where, before being ejected by the authorities, they managed to print a broadsheet outlining their intentions.

Alma, too, remembered the evening: 'On 12 November I sat

with some people in my red music room when the so-called "revolution" broke out. It was both ludicrous and gruesome. We had seen the proletarians march to the parliament building: ugly types, red flags, nasty weather, rain, slush – everything grey in grey. Then shots rang out, and now the once dull, orderly procession came streaming back as a noisy, undignified tide.' When Werfel appeared the next day Alma was revolted by his unkempt appearance – 'His eyes were red and bloodshot, his face bloated and filthy, his hands, his uniform – there was a blight on everything, and he reeked of tobacco and cheap liquor.'[45] She sent him away. For a few days he was sought by the police for questioning about his political affiliations and went into hiding. The fact that he was not found was due to an extraordinarily magnanimous gesture on the part of Walter Gropius, who made it his business to trace his rival's whereabouts and warn him of impending danger.

Before he left for Berlin Gropius made a last-ditch effort to wean Alma from her new obsession, taking her to visit Werfel in the flat he shared with Franz Blei and his mistress, in the vain hope that its seedy aspect would bring her to her senses. Alma professed herself horrified at the signs of dissolution on the part of Blei and his companion: Werfel had, apparently, to vacate the room when 'orgies' were being held and the room 'reeked of vices . . . innocent books – Swedenborg, Kierkegaard, old Fathers of the Church – had to submit to the touch of depraved fingers.' Nevertheless, she was not disgusted enough to separate herself from Werfel. Three weeks later she wrote that he was 'the resolving chord' of her life and when, at the end of January 1919, their baby son underwent his first cephalic puncture Alma wrote that Werfel was her 'sole support; his composure gave me strength to bear it. I love him devotedly and critically . . . If only the child can be saved! Then all will be well.'[46]

By mid-February, however, Alma had given up all hope of her son's life and on the 20th he went into hospital, never to return. On 15 May, whilst Alma and Manon were fulfilling their obligations by visiting Gropius in Berlin, Martin died. Before his inevitable death Alma had him baptized. 'To what end?' she wondered. 'Yet the baptism touched me strangely . . . These strong, eternal symbols!'

Throughout this ordeal Gropius was characteristically generous-hearted. 'He was touchingly kind to me,' Alma wrote, 'as always, but he could give me no help. Through no fault of his, I was lost to him forever – and this despite my own feeling that no one nobler, more generous had ever come in to my life.'[48]

In June Alma went with him from Berlin to Weimar, where Gropius was deeply involved in the early stages of realizing his revolutionary concept of uniting art and technology at the Bauhaus. His ideas had acted as a magnet to students of all ages from all over the country, many of whom had been at the front and most of whom were penniless. To satisfy their creative appetites Gropius appointed a number of new teachers, under whom they could learn typography, furniture design, rug-making, pottery, bookbinding, and how to work in glass, stone, wood and metal, alongside pure painting. The academic artists of the Weimar establishment were introduced to the unfamiliar work of Johannes Itten, Gerhard Marcks and, most controversial of all, Lyonel Feininger, whose extreme brand of Expressionism many felt to be an insult to the ideals of the former academy. Later recruits included Paul Klee, who delved into the intricacies of linear form, Wassily Kandinsky, conducting his experiments with colour, Laszlo Moholy-Nagy, in charge of the preliminary course and later director of the metal workshop, and Oskar Schlemmer, head of the department of fresco-painting.

Although Alma appreciated the courage of the enterprise and the 'soaring passionate faith' that kept it alive, it was not enough to keep her away from Vienna and Franz Werfel. She and Gropius quarrelled fiercely over Manon, culminating in a particularly heated argument during which Alma fainted away and had to be revived by a doctor, who according to Alma told Gropius he would kill her if he continued to badger her in that way. Stung, Gropius wired for Werfel to come and meet Alma in Dresden. This he did, and, having taken the precaution of engaging a nurse* for Manon, they went on to Berlin. As soon as they were apart, Alma wrote, Gropius relented. He 'suddenly became the gentleman I always knew he was. He not only agreed to the divorce, but he did everything necessary to co-operate in obtaining it.'[49]

Alma and Gropius were finally divorced on 20 October 1920, but long before then they had settled into a 'harmonious friendship', their encounters with each other untainted by bitter recriminations. At one such meeting, in Berlin in March 1920, they watched from the windows of the Hotel Elephanten whilst striking workers rioted in the streets below in protest at an attempt by a right-wing faction of the disbanded German army to install an obscure civil servant, Wolfgang Kapp, as chancellor. The putsch failed, and next day they opened their shutters to see the bodies of those killed lying where they had fallen, or being carried in endless processions to their resting places.

By the time Werfel came to claim Alma things had, superficially at least, returned to normal. Together they visited Max Reinhardt and Werfel read his Expressionist allegory *Mirrorman* to the director and some of his aides. 'They all went wild with enthusiasm . . .' Alma commented. 'Then Werfel and I went to Reinhardt's Kammerspiele theatre, to see *Dame Goblin* by Calderon, and our psychic vibrations were so intertwined that no greater intensity seemed possible. We were one soul.'[50]

---

*Sister Ida Gebauer (later, Wagner), who was to be associated with the family for many years to come.

11 *Currents of Intoxication*

In February 1918 Franz Werfel wrote from Zurich:

> Alma, I think of your music, I think of your songs, of my song
> and above all of that of Novalis... You are my wife and my
> comrade, we sleep in music – I am one with you... I long for
> you... for the red room, for your golden dress, for your powers
> of insight, for your inner delicacy and refinement... I yearn end-
> lessly for you. I am so sure you can help me, because you are
> strong, and because you want a great deal from me... with you
> I can be completely honest... Breath of my life, earthmother,
> fount of all peace, Alma... [1]

Two years later he sent her a poem, entitled 'to Alma', which
ended:

> You are the heavenly *GOLDEN* light,
> The Fruitful *GOLDEN* Light,
> Through which I must grow
> To become the purest *WHITE* light.
> Out of all the vaults of madness
> You gather me anew into your womb.
> O Golden Light! O Fecund Creature!
> Be more to me than a Mother!
> Be the instrument of my Rebirth!*

And in 1939, twenty years after they had first met, he wrote

---

*Du bist das Heilig GELBE Licht,
Das Weltfruchtbare GELBE Licht,
Durch das ich wachsen muss
Um WEISSES Licht zu werden,
Aus allen Gruften der Zerfahrenheit
Verzammelst du mich neu in deinem Schoss.
O Gelbes Licht! Gebärerin!
Sei mehr als Mutter mir!
Sei Wochnerin meiner Wiedergeburt!

again from Zurich: 'My Almschi! Your letter made me so very happy. I don't have to fall in love with you AFRESH, I have only to be away from you for a few hours to find out how eternally in love with you I am . . .'[2]

Albrecht Joseph, Franz Werfel's secretary in America during the Second World War, once observed that the well-spring of his employer's work was childhood. 'When confronted with the adult world of literature, the theatre, publishers, business, he was mature, independent, incisive. But in the hidden depth from where the power of his unique talent sprang he kept the memories of childhood alive. This, I believe, was a deliberate act, and it made him a happy creature.' It was a part of the secret of Alma's perpetual appeal that she fitted into this secret garden of infantile memory and nourished the gifts that flourished there – even if they did not take the form they might have done if untended by her ambitious hands.

> Clearly Alma represented to him a childhood figure, and from the viewpoint of his greatest need she was probably an almost ideal partner. She could give him what he wanted, what he was asking of her without having to put it into words. Alma could be hard, ruthless, even cruel – it was part of her Nietzschean credo that a superior human being had to be that way – but in contemplating her relationship to Werfel one must consider that she also was very feminine, very Viennese, and that it would have been an almost physical impossibility for her to transgress in words or acts the limits of civility . . . From personal impression I can say that I am sure Alma loved Werfel. She appreciated his uncommon gifts though for her he could never be in the same class as Mahler. It was her belief that she moulded his talent and helped it come to its fruition.[3]

Werfel himself admitted that had it not been for Alma he might never have produced such a flow of financially successful novels – he once remarked: '*Ich kann nicht sagen ob Alma mein grösstes Glück war – oder mein grösstes Unglück!*' (I cannot say whether Alma was my greatest stroke of luck or my greatest misfortune)[4] – but, as Albrecht Joseph pointed out, that did not necessarily mean the path he chose was best for him:

> Without Alma . . . his home would have been a Viennese coffee-

house. He would have worked very little – he was lazy and enjoyed being lazy – and a great deal of his time and energy would have been spent in endless arguments with his friends, grouped around a small table with a marble top, sipping coffee and smoking innumerable cigarettes . . . aside from poetry he might have written some short stories about subjects that concerned him deeply, some essays, perhaps a few plays – but certainly none of the big novels that began, under Alma's stimulus, with his Verdi-novel.

When reviewing the content of Werfel's literary output between 1922 and 1945 it is, indeed, tempting to lay at Alma's door the blame for his undoubted decline as a poet and his rise to fame as the author of a collection of worthy but mainly unsatisfactory novels and plays. Certainly, if money was the prime motivation, Werfel's contracts with Paul Zsolnay Verlag, Simon and Schuster and, from 1936, the Viking Press, indicate a steady rise in his literary income. In 1924, Simon and Schuster paid an advance of $1,250 for *Verdi, Novel of the Opera*, at a time when dollars were particularly welcome in inflation-ridden Austria, and in 1929 the same publisher paid $2,000 for *Barbara or Piety*. The switch to the Viking Press in 1936 was even more profitable: they agreed to pay him a monthly stipend of $1,000, covering royalties from *The Forty Days of Musa Dagh*, the *Collected Works of Franz Werfel* and the novella, *From the Twilight of One's Own World*, but not including an advance payment of $5,000 on receipt of the manuscript of his next novel.

None of these American earnings, of course, detracted from Werfel's German-language royalties which, by 1930, were also mounting up. All in all, including royalties on other sales, especially *Barbara or Piety*, Alma totted up their potential assets for the last half of the year as 73,932 Austrian schillings (around £2,000), indicating that Werfel's annual earned income was in the region of £5,000. Combined with their private means – despite the havoc wrought on Alma's pension by inflation – Werfel's profitable output freed Alma from haunting memories of past money worries. Although, once again, it was left to her to manage their affairs, she had solid financial ground upon which to build a secure future for herself and Manon.

Alma's hand in his affairs cannot, however, mitigate Werfel's own part in the transformation of his vision of the power of the human spirit into prosaic rather than poetic forms, any more than Mahler's ultimatum to forgo her life as a composer whilst married to him explains Alma's lack of impetus as a composer after his death. Werfel's literary odyssey charted the ups and downs of his spiritual and political beliefs. It can no more have been merely to please Alma that the epitome of neo-classical pacifist Expressionism, *Die Troerinnen*, ceded to speculations on the problems of revolution (as in *Spiegelmensch, Bocksgesang* and *Barbara oder Die Frömmigkeit*), the folly or otherwise of attempting to establish a utopian state in the real world (*Juarez und Maximilian*) and the possibility of reconciling political activism with personal integrity (*The Forty Days of Musa Dagh*), than it was deference to Mahler's memory that prevented Alma publishing only fourteen songs in her lifetime, only one of which* was certainly written after his death.

His precocity as a poet, the effect of the war and its rootless aftermath, unexpected nostalgia for the vanished certainties of empire and yearnings for moral probity in the midst of political oppression, all played their part in Werfel's development as a writer, just as Alma's precocity as a gifted seventeen-year-old contributed to her frustrated musical ambitions. The attributes which had ensnared Burckhard, Klimt, Zemlinsky and Mahler became one of the instruments of her artistic destruction. Even with his blessing, living in the shadow of Mahler's genius was bound to have an inhibiting effect on the development of her own youthful talents as a composer; without it they lay embalmed in early promise, unable to be fully resurrected after his death. Nevertheless, had Alma been less dependent on the good opinion of her mentors – all of whom were emotional substitutes for the father she had lost at thirteen – and as self-reliant a composer as she was a pianist and magnetic force, the flame might not have been so easily put out. She was eternally the pupil; it was the

*'Der Erkennende' is based on a poem by Franz Werfel written in 1915.

craving for approval from masters she admired that had kept Alma's compositional talent alight. With the transition to mother-figure came desires of a different kind.

In Franz Werfel Alma had the perfect love-child – adoring, creative, obedient, good-natured and, above all, male. His Jewish-ness, later a source of political bickering, was at first overlooked – excused, as Mahler's had been, by his creative ability. Neverthe-less, Alma's peculiarly insensitive brand of anti-Semitism, on the one hand typical of her Viennese upbringing (Karl Lueger had a lot to answer for) and on the other testament to her capacity for muddled thinking, was always a conundrum. For, whilst always having much to say on the subject of what she believed to be the physical defects inherent in the Jewish race, she still managed to rhapsodize on the beauty of Mahler's profile and the nobility of Werfel's forehead; and while she was prejudiced enough to want a pure Aryan child from Walter Gropius, she was prepared to conceive a child with Werfel within months of their meeting, regardless of miscegenation, and to bear two such children by Mahler.

During the first years of her life with Werfel, however, such distasteful subjects were left in abeyance. Their yearly routine settled into the pattern most familiar to Alma – easing Werfel's working path, making and listening to music, social life and travel. In the summer of 1919 she converted the attic in the Semmering villa into a study for him and, whilst he worked on a novel – one which he was never to finish – *The Black Mass*, 'spoiled him like a child'. In September Anna, then fifteen years old, developed an infection of the ear and Alma took her 'crying with pain with a temperature of 104 degrees' to Vienna for treatment, to be followed by disconsolate letters from Werfel. 'I shall go into a decline if I don't have you here soon,' he wrote soon after they left, 'please telegraph and tell me how things are going with you. Is Anna up at last, the heroine? Come soon, my sweet and only wife. When we two are alone together I feel liberated, contented . . . I want nothing in the world but you . . .'[5]

When Alma returned she too was convalescent, having caught tonsillitis from Anna. Before the end of October, however, she had regained her strength and, in a rare reference to post-war food shortages, recorded that she had been busy 'digging potatoes, storing apples on straw, pulling up beets – in short playing the farmer's wife . . .'

It was in October that Alma first realized that Anna had fallen in love. Alma was by no means against the idea. Although only nineteen, the object of Anna's affections, Rupert Koller, was the son of a neighbouring Breitenstein landowner and as such a far from unsuitable match. When he came to see her, therefore, Alma looked kindly on him, and gave the young lovers her blessing. Almost immediately she felt a twinge of regret – 'Suddenly I had become a sort of mother-in-law!' – but revived when the post brought her two love-letters, 'one from a musician and one from a poet'.[6]

Alma's consent to the unofficial engagement of her under-age daughter to the first man with whom she thought she had fallen in love deserves a moment's reflection. Since she disliked competition of any kind from her own sex and, with the exception of herself, had little regard for female creativity, Alma's relationship with her two daughters was a mixture of sentiment, indifference and jealousy. Anna once remarked, in old age, that jealousy was one of her mother's main characteristics – 'If you don't know that you don't know Mummy' – and it was Anna, witness to so many of the vicissitudes of Alma's emotional life, who bore the brunt of her maternal inconsistencies. Not only did she have her gender and her artistic talents to contend with – she began to draw and paint in 1919 and later went on to study sculpture, first in Rome and then in Paris, where she won the Prix de Rome in 1937 – she had the added misfortune of being, in her mother's eyes, racially tainted.

Anna's alliance with the Kollers, therefore, not only satisfied Alma's snobbish instincts, but also distanced her from a daughter who was, albeit unconsciously, becoming, with her youth, beauty and talent, a threat to her mother's supremacy. When the marriage, which took place in the summer of 1920, collapsed after a year, Alma wrote rather defensively in her diary for September 1921: 'Today my Anna left, having stayed with me for over a month. I have a strong feeling of loss; everything is empty. I love her passionately; this is why I was so disconsolate last summer. She is unhappy, suffers, is finished with her husband. He had been her choice, not mine. If she left him and came back to me, I'd be happy beyond measure.'[7]

Anna, however, did not return. She went first to live in Weimar with Walter Gropius (her favourite amongst her surrogate fathers) and then to Berlin, where she took up with Ernst Krenek, then attending Franz Schreker's composition class at the Hochschule für Musik. The brevity of their subsequent marriage, dissolved within three years, and of Anna's next ill-fated liaison with Paul Zsolnay, against whom Alma issued dire warnings for not altogether altruistic reasons, 'since Zsolnay was Werfel's publisher and this was bound to cause trouble', brought Alma to the conclusion that her daughter's doomed excursions into affairs of the heart were due to lack of judgement: 'She tends to go wrong because she does not seek – and therefore will not find – the superior type.' With typical lack of self-awareness, Alma blinded herself to the fact that Anna sought only the love, affection and artistic encouragement that she had failed to provide: competition for capturing geniuses as husbands did not come into it.

This reprehensible failure to ally herself with men of genius came to a head with Anna's fourth marriage to the Russian-Jewish violinist and conductor, Anatole Fistoulari, a misalliance which threw Alma into paroxysms of outspoken bigotry. Albrecht Joseph (later her fifth husband) commented:

> When she was angry with her daughter Anna, mainly because Anna had married a Jewish conductor whom Alma considered an inferior creature in every respect, though she had never heard him conduct, a man . . . being unworthy to inherit, though only at a great remove, the mantle of Mahler, she would shrug her shoulders and say: 'What can one expect? Miscegenation.' She used to talk of Anna, who is in fact a single-creature justification for the existence of mankind, as if she were a biological monster and referred

to her as 'the bastard'. It made no difference to her that she was
her own child and Mahler's daughter and that she had conceived,
borne and raised her, fully aware of what she now called 'misceneg-
ation'.[8]

Manon could not be accused of miscegenation, but she too
was unable to escape her mother's insecurities. No amount of
sentimental outpourings could disguise Alma's essential lack of
interest in her offspring. The need to gain custody of her three-
year-old daughter from Walter Gropius was not just maternal.
Manon was the very embodiment of Alma's procreational existence: the need to possess the perfect human being she had created
consumed her, but once Manon was within her grasp – although
she wrote frequently of her beauty and natural talent – her interest
waned. As always, Alma's energies were directed towards
smoothing the path of the masculine genius currently in need of
her attentions.

November 1919, therefore, saw Alma and Werfel back in
Vienna where Alma, her senses 'purified by the heights' of their
harmonious summer in the mountains, had some difficulty
readjusting to city life. Until her divorce from Walter Gropius in
October 1920 she and Werfel maintained separate establishments
whilst in Vienna, and Alma found their separations irksome.
'Vienna was one perpetual telephone call, a succession of visitors
opening my door to each other,' she complained, '– people I had
ceased caring for in the months of living solely for one kind,
sublime human being. Life no longer made sense to me without
Werfel, without looking after him steadily, sharing his joys,
instantly knowing each bit of work he had done.'[9]

Early in the new year they were together again, travelling with
Manon and her nurse, Sister Ida, to Rome and Naples. The trip
was only partially successful – the weather was wintry, Naples
in the grip of sleet and pouring rain, the trains dirty and overcrowded, and Manon caught a cold – but Alma managed to do
something she had been meaning to do for a long time: she
'bought a tuning fork, made a sketch of the well-tempered clavi-
chord, and with these two aids taught Werfel the musical interval

system. Soon he could read music and distinguish and sing a third, a fifth, and so on.'[10]

In May 1920 Alma went with Anna, but without Werfel (whose invitation had inexplicably not arrived), to Amsterdam for a Mahler Festival to celebrate Willem Mengelberg's twenty-five years as conductor of the Concertgebouw. Schönberg and his family, Egon Wellesz and his wife and Anton von Webern were also included in the guest list. Alma took with her the manuscript of Mahler's Seventh Symphony as a present for her host – 'a gift he had more than earned already by his efforts on behalf of Mahler's work during his lifetime'.[11]

The celebrations were lavish. On the Sunday after their arrival the entire orchestra played a serenade under the windows of Mengelberg's house. When it was over the conductor appeared on his balcony to wave to the crowd and, Alma wrote, 'the thousands waving back, the bright handkerchiefs, the bright dresses of the women, made a most colourful picture.' Schönberg and his party were particularly appreciative: the journey to Amsterdam had been undertaken in a spirit of keen anticipation. 'All were in a cheerful mood,' wrote Egon Wellesz, 'and happy to be able to escape for the time . . . from the misery of Central Europe, the shortages and bad food. Arriving at the Dutch frontier, Webern laughingly threw an empty tin out of the window and said: "No more corned beef" – it was the only meat that one was able to get in Austria.'[12]

Schönberg was feeling especially benign. Not only was he returning to Amsterdam where, through Mengelberg's good auspices, his work had already found a sympathetic audience, but he was, after the hiatus of the war years, at last beginning to find recognition at home and abroad. The Konzertverein and the Society for the Friends of Music in Vienna had decided to perform the *Gurrelieder*, Wilhelm Furtwängler had invited him to conduct *Pelleas und Melisande* in Mannheim later in the year, there were plans for performances of *Pelleas*, the *Gurrelieder* and *Pierrot Lunaire* in Berlin, of *Erwartung* and *Die glückliche Hand* in

Leipzig, and of *Pelleas*, to be conducted by Otto Klemperer, in Cologne.

Alma met the Viennese contingent at the station and found the Schönbergs in high spirits. After the concert that evening Mengelberg broached a subject near to his heart – the foundation of a Gustav Mahler Society – and the following day Alma was offered and accepted the position of the society's patroness. At her suggestion Schönberg was appointed president with power, in consultation with Mengelberg, to draw up the statutes.

The mantle of being Mahler's widow was, however, becoming increasingly irksome, yearning as she was 'for Werfel, for his total proximity and for the phraseless candour of our relationship'. Neither was she fully in accord with his music. To combat these feelings of isolation Alma attached herself to the Schönbergs with whom, for the first time, she became on intimate terms. The three of them were 'inseparable' for the remaining two weeks, and Alma had long arguments with Schönberg on the rival merits of Puccini and Verdi, the genius of Beethoven and the monotony or otherwise of Bach.

At the final dinner, attended by the Dutch Prince Consort, Alma sat, as she had requested, between Schönberg and Mengelberg. The Prince had installed himself directly opposite and they instantly struck up a rapport. 'A famed but homely music critic spoke about Mahler, stressing the element of love in Mahler's music. The prince looked at the speaker's bearded face. "The gentleman talks about love," he murmured . . . "What can he know about it?" '[13]

These promising exchanges paved the way for an unprecedented waiving of royal etiquette. Faced with the prospect of ploughing through course after course of rich food, Schönberg muttered to Alma that he could not manage without a cigarette. Prince Henry noticed his discontent and asked Alma what he wanted. When told he promptly asked Schönberg for a cigarette. Passed 'an indescribably battered tin case across the table', the Prince took one out and lit it. Had the Queen been present, Alma observed, 'no such liberties could have been taken'.

Back in Vienna, one of the highlights of the summer was the long-planned performance of the *Gurrelieder*, which took place on 12 and 13 June. Schönberg conducted the Vienna Philharmonic himself and the result was 'generally regarded on both evenings as the climax of the Vienna Festival. Schönberg was given ovations and even the critics praised the work and the performance which he gave of it.' Alma, sitting with Franz Werfel, was enchanted. 'I had long understood Schönberg the man, now I grasped the musician.'

In the interval she had the 'great good fortune' to renew her acquaintance with Giacomo Puccini, whom she had last met with Mahler in New York. She was, however, unable to persuade him to remain for the rest of the concert. Disappointed that he had not found something radical enough – or, indeed, anything at all to surprise him – Puccini left before the second half.

The following year Alma introduced various other foreign composers to Schönberg's work. Maurice Ravel, in Vienna for a concert of his own music, was exposed to the Chamber Symphony. Ravel found the experience baffling. To his mind the music bore none of the marks of human creation and showed all the signs of having been conceived in a test tube. 'That isn't music,' he said to Alma at the end, 'that comes out of a laboratory!'

Both Ravel and Alfredo Casella, who had come from Rome for the Frenchman's concert, stayed with Alma in her flat. Casella, however, left the day after the concert, leaving Alma to a three-week tête-à-tête with Ravel, which although interesting in all sorts of ways, put a strain on the laundry arrangements. Much enamoured of his own appearance, Ravel took infinite pains to look his best at all times. Rouged and perfumed, his hair and moustache fresh from their nightly douche of black dye, he appeared each morning for breakfast wrapped in bright satin robes, leaving a trail of black-stained pillow-cases in his wake.[14]

On another occasion Alma hosted two performances of *Pierrot Lunaire* in her red music room, the first conducted by Erwin Stein, with Erica Wagner, personally coached by Schönberg, speaking the vocal part, the second conducted by Darius Milhaud, with the vocal part sung by Maria Freund. The majority of the eighty-strong audience who had listened with 'more or less of an effort to the austere wonders of atonality' preferred the Milhaud interpretation, finding Schönberg's version less easy on the ear, but Alma thought that 'Schönberg's rhythmicized version of accentuated speech was unquestionably more original as well as . . . more authentic'.

Milhaud and Poulenc stayed on for a while in Vienna and Alma arranged another session, this time without an audience, to try and bridge the gulf between the two musical cultures. Eduard Steuermann, Schönberg's tireless champion and pianist for the society for Private Musical Performances, played his own piano arrangement of the Chamber Symphony in front of the Schönbergs, Alban and Helen Berg, Cyril Scott and 'other Schönberg devotees'. But, as might have been expected, the gulf remained as wide as ever. 'Each camp negated the other,' Alma wrote. 'If Schönberg was atonal Poulenc and Milhaud were polytonal . . .'[15]

Whilst Alma devoted herself to bridging musical divides Werfel watched over preparation for the première of *Mirrorman* in Leipzig in the winter of 1922 and, spurred on by Alma, conceived a novel based on his childhood hero, Giuseppe Verdi, an idea he found both exhilarating and daunting. 'I am not quite ready to assemble this massive work,' he wrote to Alma from Breitenstein in the early spring of 1923, 'and again I am afraid of being guilty of distortion and untruth when dealing with an existing character. I must just wait for the courage that I had in December . . .'[16]

That spring Alma was in Italy, supervising the modernization of a house she had bought the previous year, after a long bout of cold rainy weather on Semmering had driven her to beg Frau Moll to go with her to Venice to help find somewhere warmer to spend the summer months. The result was the Casa Mahler (San Tomà 2542), which had a garden and a 'magnificent old gate, under government protection as an historic monument'.

For all its beauty the house had one serious drawback: the

current owners had a change of heart and refused to move out and Alma was obliged to take them to an Italian court, a procedure 'as funny as a Goldoni comedy'. The lawsuit finally won, Alma set about installing two bathrooms and enlarging one of the rooms in preparation for Werfel, who had gone from Breitenstein to Vienna for the opening of *Mirrorman*. He arrived in a low state. *Mirrorman* had not only been sparsely attended but had received 'wretched' reviews, and Alma blamed herself bitterly for not having been at his side to share in this humiliation. Venice, however, had a healing effect. From their small hotel on the Grand Canal they watched the progress of their house or took excursions in a motorboat to Giudecca. And, fittingly, Werfel was able to get down to work in the house of a fellow poet. Friends, Alma wrote, 'had obtained permission for him to use the magnificent study in Gabriele d'Annunzio's house next to Santa Maria della Salute.'

No mention was made of a recent encounter in the Piazza San Marco when Kokoschka, in Venice for a showing of his paintings at the International Exposition, materialized in front of her, and they went to sit in the Café Florian. After a few recriminations (which reduced Alma to silent tears) the conversation took a more amicable turn. 'We both felt the strangeness of talking together, so near and yet so far in the city where we had once been so happy.' It was left to Frau Moll to intervene: 'we continued our "friendly chat" until Mama, as the jealous guardian of Franz Werfel's rights, came to fetch me.'[17]

The incident left Alma feeling emotionally unsettled – on 19 April she wrote in her diary that she 'continually longed for OK', even though she was 'deeply bound' to Werfel. The summer months on Semmering did much to restore her equilibrium. Throughout them Werfel continued his herculean task of weaving the threads of fact and fiction around his great theme. Alma was indulgent, but not convinced of the importance of the subject matter. Verdi, for all his versatility, could never compare with Wagner. Nevertheless when, after a protracted stay, Ernst Krenek left – having, as Alma observed, unwittingly provided Werfel with the model for Verdi's opposite in the novel, 'the modern musician who does not build on melodies but on mathematics' – she reported that the summer 'grew harmonious, gay and full of love', with Werfel 'finishing a great novel, presenting splendid perceptions in their natural and necessary form'.[18]

Towards the end of the year, however, Alma once more confided to her diary that all was not well with her emotional life. 'I am ill, miserable, worn down, wretched, alone . . . oh SO ALONE,' she wrote in December, and the new year found her equally out of sorts, both with herself and Werfel. 'I don't love him any more!' she complained on 22 January 1924. 'My life no longer hinges on being together with him. He has once again shrunk to the small, hateful, corpulent Jew – my first impression . . . I dream . . . of living in my house in Venice. But I still don't know whether I can bear it – whether I can endure the last great solitude . . .'[19]

As it turned out Alma did not have to put herself to the test. Within a few months of completing his work on Verdi, Werfel conceived an idea for another play – this time based on the ill-fated reign of the Emperor Maximilian in Mexico. In April Alma and Werfel spent a month together in the newly completed Casa Mahler which, Alma wrote, had turned out to be a paradise. 'We were happy. Nothing remained to be desired from the outside world . . .' Refreshed and rejuvenated, they moved back to Vienna and then up to Semmering, where Werfel wrote *Juarez und Maximilian* in three weeks. The spring idyll lasted into the summer: 'Werfel is enchanting – absolutely an angel,' Alma wrote approvingly in her diary in July.[20] Werfel himself was aware of her changes of mood (but hopefully unaware of her more spiteful thoughts), for he wrote to her from Breitenstein during a brief absence that he had 'dwelt the whole night on our difficult times, and thought of you, and particularly of you up here. You are deeply a part of me (far deeper than I am of you), and I embrace you . . .'[21]

Alma's restlessness was not just due to thoughts of Kokoschka or temporary upsets with Werfel: she had begun working on a memoir of her life with Mahler, which revived agonies and ecstasies long unmentioned, leading to physical traumas. 'No pulse,' ran a diary entry for August, 'and I'm in the middle of a real cramp, such as I've never known before. Both hands asleep – the right side of the face immovable . . . The doctor forbade me work of any kind, but during the night I understood the true cause of my ailments, my writing about Mahler that has agitated me so much these past weeks. I have literally been writing day and night, from fear that I could lose the memories . . .'[22]

To relax from their combined labours Alma arranged a trip in the new year of 1925 to Palestine, where Zionists had long awaited a visit from Werfel. En route they went to Egypt, explored Cairo and took a trip up the Nile to Luxor and Karnak. They were overwhelmed by 'the agelessness of civilization . . . the abundance of nature'. Palestine was equally enthralling: the old city of Jerusalem, the biblical landmarks and the strange Dead Sea landscape moved Alma to think of buying 'a remote little house' by the Sea of Galilee, where 'both men and nature were deeply romantic, utterly unawakened, and momentous . . .' Less romantic were the early kibbutzniks, whom Alma found 'unkempt and slovenly', and the food, which both of them found inedible.[23]

The remainder of the year was taken up by a lecture tour in Germany, the première of *Juarez und Maximilian* – 'a great success' – a month in Venice, where Alma continued writing about her life with Mahler: 'Difficult to be objective, when one is in such a subjective position . . . ! But my nervous condition has other causes than this work . . .',[24] and the summer on Semmering, where Werfel drafted and wrote a play inspired by his visit to the Holy Land, *Paul Among the Jews*.

But it was 14 December that constituted the highlight of the year. With financial help from Alma, the completed score of Berg's opera *Wozzeck* had been printed and accepted for performance by Erich Kleiber at the Berlin State Opera House. Berg himself had arranged the libretto from a play by Georg Büchner – a grimly symbolic work felt initially by Schönberg to be of 'such extraordinary tragic power that it seemed forbidding to music'. The musical result was an amalgam of oddly assorted technical devices: on the one hand Berg maintained a classical approach, using the suite, the rhapsody, the song, the march, the passacaglia and the rondo in the first act and a five-part symphony in the second. On the other he asked his soloists to intersperse their songs with ordinary speech and *Sprechgesang*, and his chorus to snore. All this, combined with other exigencies in a score that Kleiber pronounced to be prodigiously difficult, led to a disproportionate amount of time being set aside for rehearsals. At first it was thought that 137 full rehearsals would be required, but in the end the performance went ahead after only thirty-four orchestral and fourteen ensemble rehearsals.

Berg went to Berlin to watch over the progress of his opera and sent copious letters to Helene, alternating between extreme optimism and total despair. 'I am up sixteen to eighteen hours without a break,' he wrote a week before the opening night. 'How all of this – orchestra and stage – will be ready in eight days is beyond me, and I am comforted only by the conviction that Kleiber will not let anything unfinished out of his hands. He knows the success of the première depends on him . . .'[25]

In the end Berg need not have worried. News that the State Opera was producing a new work after so many years attracted numbers of Berlin journalists, who had been clustering outside the darkened auditorium, like buffaloes at a watering hole, wondering what was going on inside. But, unlike Alma, to whom the work was dedicated and who, with Werfel, had arrived in Berlin in time to see the final rehearsals, the critics had to wait until the opening night before satisfying their curiosity.

Both they and their first-night audience were surprisingly restrained. The audience, although divided in its reactions, was more or less in favour of the work, despite a few fist fights, angry challenges shouted across the orchestra seats and deriding boos and 'hostile whistles that threatened . . . to overpower the small, but at last vigorous group of believers'. As for the critics, apart from Paul Zschorlich of the *Deutsche Zeitung*, who felt he 'was not leaving a public place dedicated to the arts but a public insane asylum', all took the opera seriously and some allowed themselves a note of qualified approval. The Social Democratic newspaper *Vorwärts* thought 'the hard logic of this drama was ennobled, humanized, psychologized through the spirit of music . . .' and even the conservative *Kreuz-Zeitung* wrote that in this opera Alban Berg had 'revealed himself as a progressive in the "moderate" sense of the word'.*[26]

In the early autumn of 1926 Werfel, ever on the look-out for congenial places to work, found the perfect spot. On a trip to the Italian Riviera, he and Alma came across the Hotel Imperial at Santa Margherita, high in the hills above the coast. Its palatial rooms with their high painted ceilings might have been especially designed for Werfel, who had a horror of working in cramped conditions, and they immediately rented a particularly sumptuous one with an enormous terrace.

This agreeable setting became Werfel's favourite retreat. There was no shortage of company: Gerhart Hauptmann, Fritz von Unruh, the austere author of a number of pacifist tracts and plays, Max Brod and the playwright Hermann Sudermann all had houses nearby and many visits were exchanged. At the Gerhart Hauptmanns' there was much to raise Alma's spirits. 'It's a pity,' he apparently once said to her, 'that the two of us don't have a child together. That would have been something!' And on another occasion he remarked: 'In another life we two must be lovers. I make my reservation now.' Alma could only listen 'reverently, happy that my miserable self was still capable of kindling joy in features I worshipped as much as Gerhart Hauptmann's.' (Frau Hauptmann was less impressed: 'I'm sure Alma will be booked up there, too,' she remarked.)[27]

These boosts to her morale were more than welcome, for once again Alma was tortured by conflicting feelings towards Werfel. For the past eight years she had played the part of 'a recognized

*It was a different story in Prague, where the audience's first reaction to the set which, Alma recorded, consisted of 'nothing but some dirty, ragged army beds' was a roar of disapproval, causing the conductor and the members of the orchestra to flee from the pit.[28]

writer's great and in a manner of speaking happy love', yet she felt neither like his mistress nor like his wife. For eight years Werfel had pleaded with her to marry him, and since her divorce she had been free to do so, but, Alma explained, something in her was unwilling. It was not just the various disturbing sightings of Kokoschka in Venice, or her long talks in Vienna with Arthur Schnitzler (whose own marriage had long been in difficulties) on the diminution of self often suffered by married women, particularly those attached to creative artists. Neither was her reluctance entirely due to the difference in their ages, although, at forty-eight, Alma was beginning to think she was too old and tired for Werfel. 'My breath of life, Franz, is away . . .' she wrote in her diary in August 1927. 'I sent him away myself, now I am wretched. I am too old for him. And so used up! Why do I live, when he is not with me?'[29] Rather more, it was the divergence in their political opinions.

Their differences were fundamental, and were mirrored by the increasing polarization, throughout the Twenties, of the two main political parties and their leaders. Under the authoritarian Roman Catholic Ignaz Seipel, the Christian Socialist party was pushed more and more to the right, whereas the Social Democrats, under the Marxist Otto Bauer, veered to the other extreme – divisions further complicated by the emergence, in the military vacuum created by the Armistice of 1918, of the conservative, anti-socialist armed band known as the Heimwehr (Home Defence Movement) and its republican counterpart, the Schutzbund (Defence League).

For, in contrast to the Schutzbund, which had the clear-cut aim of protecting the working class from reprisals in the event of any revolutionary activity, the Heimwehr had no such positive objective. Drawn from the urban middle class, ex-servicemen, students and farmers, its creed was anti-Marxist and anti-Semitic but not, in the early years at least, especially pro-Fascist. Indeed, its anti-Semitism was profoundly Austrian: one of the movement's most strident supports was the Jewish-owned *Neues Wiener Journal*, most of its arms were supplied by the Jewish industrial and munitions king, Fritz Mandl, and much of its finance was derived from a small section of the wealthy Jewish bourgeoisie.

The dangers inherent in having two such diametrically opposed home defence forces became glaringly apparent in 1927. Since 1920 the Social Democrats had been out of power in parliament but in municipal control of Vienna. True to their principles, the Social Democrats had used their new-found powers to embark on an ambitious building programme for workers' flats, schools and other social amenities – partly financed by government funds but mainly funded by imposing heavy taxes on Vienna's wealthier inhabitants.

Impotent and indignant, middle-class Viennese could do little but dream of the demise of their political enemies. The Heimwehr, on the other hand, dreamed of liberating Vienna from its socialist stranglehold by armed confrontation with the Schutzbund. It was in this uneasy atmosphere of class divisiveness that a clash occurred, in January 1927, between the two rival armed forces in Schattendorf in Burgenland, during which two workers were killed. Seven months later, when it was discovered in Vienna that those accused of the killings had been acquitted, a mass demonstration took place outside the Palace of Justice, which was set on fire. The Schutzbund were unable to control the violence, mounted police were sent in, and by the time the fighting had been brought under control eighty-four people had died and over five hundred were injured.

The episode left a bitter after-taste. Whilst those on the left mourned the death of ideals, those on the right deplored the influence of so-called intellectuals meddling in politics, stirring up aspirations of equality amongst the working classes and threatening the established order. As for Alma and Werfel, both had come to the conclusion, by different routes, that intellectuals had no place in politics, but Werfel's concern for justice and freedom for the proletariat aroused little enthusiasm in Alma, whose sympathies were firmly on the side of those already in command. Like Permanent Secretary Tuzzi in Musil's *The Man without Qualities*, she held to the belief that 'ideals made excessive demands on human nature, such as must lead to ruin . . .'[30] Ideals and eternal verities were political luxuries that simply could not be indulged in by rulers of nations. Politics, if one thought about them at all, were best left in the hands of those members of the upper classes most able to sustain the status quo.

'Intellectuals are scholars, artists, moneymen . . . but they should keep out of politics,' Alma wrote in the first week of July 1927, in response to a letter from her friend the anatomist and later welfare minister, Julius Tandler, asserting that the forceful suppression of those involved in the recent demonstrations was the 'defenestration of all ideals'.[31] 'Why cannot he see this?' In Alma's view, the bloody quelling of these violent eruptions was essential to remind the duped members of the proletariat of the fallibility of their intellectual masters.

Two years elapsed before Alma finally gave in and agreed to marry Werfel. Why, she asked herself, did she do so? She was still not feeling any younger and increasingly conscious of recurring ailments: 'I was failing everywhere,' she wrote about her condition just before their marriage. 'My eyes would no longer keep up; my hands slowed down on the piano; food did not agree with me, standing did not, walking did not – nothing did but drinking, perhaps. It was often the only way to control the chills and shudders in my body, since I had . . . a weak heart and a slow pulse.'[32] Walter Gropius had long since re-married, she was certainly not doing it for 'the neighbours'. Perhaps she was doing it for Manon – 'to let her grow up in orderly Western circumstances'. Whatever the final catalyst, on 6 July 1929, a few weeks before Alma's fiftieth birthday, they were married.

The wedding brought a reminder of tragedy. In the same month the previous year Arthur Schnitzler's only daughter, Lilli, had shot herself at the age of nineteen in a gondola in Venice. Against her parents' will she had married a young Italian Fascist army officer, Captain Cappellini, and when the marriage had run into trouble she tried to frighten him by wounding herself. The bullet was rusty, the wound became infected and she died, tended during her last hours in the absence of her parents, who could not bring themselves to see her, by her friend Anna Mahler.

'There is no word to describe these days here,' Olga Schnitzler wrote to Alma, 'over this terrible, meaningless destruction . . . to lose a beautiful beloved child is hard enough, but to lose her in such a way goes beyond bearing . . .'[33] When Alma visited Arthur Schnitzler she found a 'faded, seemingly extinct old man'. They went into the garden and talked. 'In 1907,' said Schnitzler, 'I saw Gustav Mahler sitting alone on a bench in Schönbrunn, his head bowed in mourning. Your daughter Maria had just died, and I asked myself: How can the man survive that? If I could have looked into the future and seen his other child ease the last moments of mine!'[34]

It was as well Alma could not see into the future. The stirrings of the movement embraced by Captain Cappellini were as yet those of an unborn hydra. Within five years it would have broken from the womb and thrust its poisoned tentacles deep into the fabric of political life. And within six years Alma herself would have to face a loss as unbearable as any she had been faced with in the past.

12 *Requiem for an Angel*

It was Anna's opinion that the years between 1930 and 1938 brought out the worst in her mother. Various political friendships fuelled her already reactionary stance, and the mansion on the Hohe Warte into which she and Werfel moved in March 1931 inspired delusions of social grandeur which her daughter found both comic and distasteful. Only in 1938, when it was finally brought home to her that neither her friend Chancellor Kurt von Schuschnigg nor even her admired Mussolini was going to be able to protect Austria against the inexorable tide of German territorial ambition, did the reality of the danger to her husband sink in. Once it had, all Alma's old practical instincts came to the fore. There was no time, then, for false pride. The main thing was to put their affairs in order and leave, before Austria was finally lost to the powers of darkness.

Alma's belief that somehow Austria could be saved from annihilation was shared by many. Largely unaware of Hitler's implacable determination, spelt out in *Mein Kampf*, to 'reinstate' Austria as part of the Third Reich, the majority of the less fanatical pan-German members of Austrian society trusted their political leaders to stick to their nationalistic guns.

Neither was Alma helped by her political naïvety. Attracted like a moth to a flame by the slightest whiff of power, her judgement was inevitably clouded by her conviction that, provided they were either well-born or staunchly conservative (and preferably a combination of the two), those who held high offices of state could be relied upon to act for the public good. Marriage did not resolve the political differences between herself and Werfel. Many of what Alma referred to euphemistically as their 'little political fights' sprang from his inability to puncture his wife's reactionary élitism and to soften her social outlook. Alma still clung to the idols of her youth, Wagner and Nietzsche. (Possibly she had failed to understand much of the latter's political antipathies: messianic nationalism, particularly of the new German brand, was anathema to him.) She took a wholly different stance from Werfel on such issues as the existence of a master-race, the place of the working class in society, and the nature of heroes and heroism.

As for the latter, Werfel only partially succeeded in weaning Alma from the concept of an all-powerful superman and converting her to the idea of an involuntary hero caught up in events beyond his control. That he did so at all was due to another extended tour of the Near East they made between their marriage and moving into their new house on the Hohe Warte in the spring of 1931, during which Werfel had been shocked to discover that the 'emaciated children with El Greco faces and enormous eyes' sweeping up the debris in a carpet factory in Damascus were the offspring of Armenians massacred by the Turks during the First World War. The image of these dispossessed beings haunted him through the remainder of their travels, and on his return Werfel persuaded his friend the French ambassador to extract the complete record of the atrocities from the Ministry of War in Paris. With these in his possession he was able to map out his novel, one which Alma devoutly hoped would be 'the great work of our dreams' – *The Forty Days of Musa Dagh*.

This book, begun in July 1932 and finished in March the following year, showed a marked change in Werfel's attitude towards political activism. Written in the shadow of Hitler's rise to power, it set out to demonstrate the moral and spiritual integrity of those prepared to resist persecution by any means at their disposal. Submission – in this case by the Armenian communities in Syria – would lead not only to physical destruction, but to spiritual death. But, much as Alma appreciated her husband's courage in tackling this heroic subject under such troubled circumstances, writing in her diary: 'It is a titanic achievement for a Jew to write a work like this at such a time, exposed to such animosities,'[1] it did not stop her musing on the beneficial aspects of a world governed by a Fascist leader with the breadth of vision of Mussolini, who she firmly believed would never adopt Hitler's alien policies towards the Jews.

She was able to explore this theme more fully when, in November 1932, Werfel went on a lecture tour to Germany. In the course of two 'beautiful, richly impressive' weeks they dined at the house of the Socialist Prussian minister, Hilferding, where Alma found herself sitting next to the recently deposed chancellor of the Reich, Heinrich Brüning. Amongst other things they discussed employment, an issue waved away by Brüning as being 'actually non-existent, with a standing army of 800,000 who are fed for three years'. Alma remembered him continuing: 'And the women the war brought into all offices, where they flirt and will not make room! Mussolini realized this in time. He gave women back their womanhood. It's their most beautiful feature anyway – a bit of earth, since Heaven is beyond us and our dreams!'[2]

There was no mention, apparently, of the circumstances surrounding Brüning's departure from office. The running sores of inflation, unemployment and political instability, as rife in Germany as they were in Italy and Austria in the years following the First World War, proved, despite Brüning's denial, impossible to heal. After his appointment by President Hindenburg in 1930 Brüning embarked on a series of stringent anti-inflationary policies, designed to boost conservative morale, but devastating to the workers. Despite these conciliatory right-wing gestures he failed to win the support of the Nazi party who, in the elections of September 1930, gained over six million votes, giving them 107 seats in the Reichstag and making them the second largest party in parliament. Germany needed a saviour and unfortunately Adolf Hitler, with his extraordinary powers of oratory and capacity to generate physical excitement, had persuaded a large section of the country during his election campaign of 1930 that he was just such a deliverer.

Emboldened by their successes at the polls, the Nazis had

become increasingly vociferous and militant. Fanned by propaganda from the Nazi press, skilfully manipulated by Joseph Goebbels, party fanatics began to militate actively against Communists and Jews. 'The Jew', shouted Goebbels to ever-larger rallies, 'is the real demon of destruction. We are the enemies of Jews because we identify ourself as Germans. The Jew is our greatest curse. But this will change, as surely as we are Germans.'³

By the end of 1931 membership of the Nazi party had risen to nearly one million and it became more necessary than ever for the party in power to convert the Nazi movement into a prop for the government, rather than a persistent thorn in its side. General Kurt von Schleicher, a General Staff officer of more than usually calculating temperament, made it his task to reconcile the Nazi party to the existing regime, and persuaded first President Hindenburg and then Chancellor Brüning to meet Hitler.

Hitler's response to these overtures was tempered by an outspoken desire to get rid of Brüning – whom he blamed unequivocally for the ills of the republic. This he achieved in 1932, when he stood against President Hindenburg in the presidential elections, coming a close second. A month later, on the advice of General von Schleicher, Brüning was dismissed, to be succeeded by Franz von Papen. The road to barbarism had begun.

On their last day in Germany the Werfels caught a glimpse of Hitler in Breslau. Both were curious to see the face that had 'enthralled thirty millions' but the result was disappointing. The face they had been waiting for had, in Alma's opinion, 'clutching eyes – young, frightened features – no Duce! An adolescent, rather, who would never mature, would never achieve wisdom.'⁴ Werfel, when pressed for his opinion, did not reply.

Back in Vienna they returned to the Hohe Warte. As well as being saddened by his differences of opinion with Alma, Werfel never felt at ease in their new house. The vast marble-walled hall, lit by bronze-bracketed lights illuminating the cabinets housing Alma's collection of manuscripts and autographs (amongst them the first three movements of Bruckner's Third Symphony recovered from Mahler's dead brother Otto's effects), made an impressive if somewhat chilly entrance to the rest of the house, all of which had been furnished, decorated and arranged by Alma 'in breathless haste' after she had moved in.

Werfel was installed at the top of the house in an enormous room, sealed off from domestic noise by an iron door, containing a huge sofa and a portable piano (a present from Alma) on which he was able to pick out Verdi melodies with one finger. Downstairs was the dining-room, in which hung some 'excellent modern pictures', and Alma's library and music room, painted her favourite dark red, spacious but, in Albrecht Joseph's opinion, so awkwardly laid out that it was almost impossible to sit down and talk.

As often as possible Werfel escaped to one or other of his retreats in order to distance himself from Alma, whose concern for his daily literary output verged on the inquisitional. Lack of progress was frowned on, and any tendency to spend the day wrapped in thought or doodling on the piano was liable to bring on disapproving looks. 'While [Alma's] instinct and enthusiasm were magnetic when she felt in the presence of creativity,' wrote Joseph, 'she was irritated with the process of slow gestation . . . The slow, patient, waiting and spinning a thread, like the silk-worm, was not for her. She wanted things to happen and, mainly, she wanted to be on the scene and be part of it. Knowing that Werfel was by nature lazy and confessed it freely she was apt to mistake periods of slow incubation for indolence.'[5]

By a curious chance both Werfel and Joseph found themselves in Bad Ischl in the winter of 1936. Each was engaged on a literary activity of their own: Werfel at the start of *Hearken Unto the Voice*, a novel with the prophet Jeremiah as the central figure, and Joseph on a screenplay. Werfel confessed that he had slipped his leash: Alma was on the Semmering and wanted him with her. Grinning, as Albrecht Joseph recorded, 'like a naughty boy,' he said: 'But I got away.' He spoke too soon. That evening Joseph, eating alone in a restaurant, was an unwilling eavesdropper on a conversation from the adjoining booth. Filtering over the partition came a voice that could only belong to Alma. 'Very well, one may not be able to write down anything in one week, or even two weeks, but you have been here for three weeks, and what is the result on paper? Not one line!' Bumping into a dejected Werfel the following morning he was told: 'My good time is over. She has come here from Vienna. She is taking me back tonight.'[6]

It has to be said that Albrecht Joseph was not one of Alma's most ardent admirers. He first heard of her in Berlin in 1921 whilst acting as assistant to Heinrich George, then directing and acting in Kokoschka's *Orpheus and Eurydice*. When he was eventually introduced to her in Vienna twelve years later, by his friend Carl Zuckmayer, he found it difficult to reconcile the physical reality with the devouring maenad described by George. How, he wondered, remembering the rivulets of tears streaming down Kokoschka's face during rehearsals, could the matron in front of him ever have been cast in the role of a seductress? Whilst admitting that, although ageing, she had a 'good, even beautiful face,' and that her bearing was still 'imposing, regal, radiating authority ... her firm conviction of being a unique beauty immensely attractive,' her figure left a lot to be desired. 'From the head down she was simply a bag of potatoes, veiled in flowing robes, usually black and with many veils charitably shrouding chest and stomach.'

Veils or not, Alma had recently made another conquest: neither a musician, artist nor writer, but one, ironically, associated with her return to the Catholic Church. The encroaching tide of Nazism had, as she observed, already changed many minds. Hans Pfitzner, an early Hitler devotee, renounced his creed in 1933, and in the same year Schönberg reverted to Judaism determined, as he wrote to Anton von Webern, 'henceforth to do nothing but aid the Jewish national cause ...'[7]

Alma re-joined the Catholic Church in the summer of 1932, 'after years of feeling expelled from the communion of the saints'. Confession, she admitted, 'came hard after so long a time; I almost fainted with the excitement of it.'[8] Soon afterwards, whilst Werfel was busy working on *The Forty Days of Musa Dagh* in

Santa Margherita, Alma attended the enthronement of Cardinal Innitzer as archbishop of Vienna. Her guests for lunch that day included Father Müller, Professor Weissenböck, the cathedral organist, and Father Johannes Hollnsteiner, professor of theology.

It did not take long for Professor Hollnsteiner to form a bond with his hostess. How long had it been since he had met a woman who expressed such deep interest in religious matters? He hastened to answer her questions on the meaning of the Mass and the nature of indulgences, and, to further these fruitful discussions, called at the Hohe Warte within a few days. 'I wished to profit from him, from his intellect, his solid knowledge, his noble, unostentatious way of communicating his knowledge,' Alma wrote, preceding these high-minded sentiments with the ominous aside from her diary: 'Johannes Hollnsteiner is thirty-eight years old and thus far has not met Woman. He is the essence of a priest.'[9]

Professor Hollnsteiner soon became a frequent guest at Alma's many soirées, joining regulars such as Egon Friedell, the Zuckmayers, Franz Theodor Csokor and Ödön von Horvath in the consumption of generous amounts of food and drink. 'Alma was a pleasant relaxed hostess,' said Albrecht Joseph, who was usually brought by the Zuckmayers.

> She was not aloof but rather overdid being down-to-earth, jolly, very Viennese, enjoying food and drink and having great fun with her guests of whom there were a good many on those occasions when I was one of them ... And there was always the professor of theology, Hollnsteiner. He was rather too smartly dressed for a cleric and his face was unhealthily pale, as were his opaque, mocking eyes behind his glasses. I did not know that he had an affair with Alma and it should not have interested me. He probably was the last of her lovers. He was put into a concentration camp by the Nazis, and when he was released, left the Church and married.[10]

Albrecht Joseph's disapproval of Alma's behaviour was heightened by his growing feelings of warmth towards Anna, who, at twenty-nine, was separated from her third husband, Paul Zsolnay. Anna disliked Hollnsteiner intensely, but found her mother's flagrant desire to topple a priest from his religious perch equally shameful. Much against her will, she occasionally yielded to Alma's demands that she join the ill-assorted pair in the small flat Alma rented for their assignations, to help them consume the champagne and caviar and other delicacies the professor was unable to afford for himself. Even more distasteful than these Lucullan feasts, though, was the knowledge that Franz Werfel knew of the affair. Possibly from prudence, but probably because he was no stranger to his wife's inconsistencies and preferred a quiet life, Werfel turned a blind eye.

In the midst of this squalid interlude, which Alma forbore to mention in any of her writings, but which has been amply testified to by her daughter Anna,[11] Alma cast a thought in the direction of her husband. 'I worry for Franz...' she wrote in September 1933. 'For over forty years he was a born child of fortune... And now suddenly comes the German persecution of the Jews! His books are burned; he is not wooed any more; all at once he is a nosy little Jew with no great talent for the masses...'[12]

Werfel was in distinguished company. Stefan Zweig counted it an honour to have shared the fate of such eminent contemporaries as Thomas and Heinrich Mann, Franz Werfel, Kafka, Freud and Einstein when, in a symbolic act of vandalism against truth and logic, their work was burned on bonfires throughout the country 'for the protection of the German people'. Kokoschka suffered with them. In 1937, at the end of a major retrospective exhibition organized by Carl Moll at the Österreichisches Museum für Kunst und Industrie, he tried to warn the authorities of the possible danger to his pictures lent from German collections. In vain: the paintings were returned and, in keeping with Hitler's view that art should be uplifting rather than disturbing, were rooted out, torn from their frames and exhibited in Munich as examples of degenerate art. Four hundred Kokoschkas, 1,000 pieces by Nolde, 700 by Heckel, 600 each by Schmidt-Rottluff and Kirchner, 500 by Beckmann, 3–400 each by Feininger and Otto Müller, 2–300 by Otto Dix and George Grosz, as well as smaller numbers of Cézannes, Picassos, Matisses, Gauguins, Van Goghs, Braques, Pissarros, Dufys, Chiricos and Max Ernsts were held up to ridicule, jumbled together 'as if arranged by fools or children', many carrying offensive captions ('Jewish desert-longings find expression', 'German peasant looked at in the Yiddish manner'). In 1939 four thousand paintings were publicly burned in the courtyard of the Berlin Fire Brigade.

Hitler's rise to power in Germany had cast a dark shadow over political events in Austria. Encouraged by the success of their fellow Nazis across the border, the Austrian National Socialist party stood for and won fifteen seats on the Vienna Provincial Council in the provincial elections of 1932. Engelbert Dollfuss, installed as chancellor in the aftermath of these troubled elections with a majority of one in the National Diet over an opposition of Social Democrats and Pan-Germans, found himself politically at the mercy of the Heimwehr (now under the leadership of the crypto-Nazi Prince Starhemberg), representatives of which he had been obliged to bring into the government in order to enable him to achieve his slender victory.

Starhemberg, at first indecisive as to the relative attractions of Hitler and Mussolini, had eventually come down on the side of Il Duce. For his part, Mussolini had already decided, in conjunction with the Hungarians, that maintaining a right-wing government in Austria was essential to the stability of Europe, and from 1928 onwards he had provided a steady flow of money and arms to enable the Heimwehr to preserve the status quo.

The price that Austria had to pay for Mussolini's protection was a heavy one, and one of which Dollfuss was only too well aware. The Heimwehr, flushed with success, put constant pressure on the new chancellor to have a final showdown with their left-wing enemies, the Social Democrats, but Dollfuss, who had recently secured a twenty-year loan from Lausanne of 300 million gold schillings to fill the monetary vacuum created by the economic slump brought about by the collapse of the Boden Kredit Bank in 1929, was disinclined to meet their demands. Under the terms of the loan Austria was to give up all thought of the Anschluss, or of a customs union with Germany.

With Hitler's accession to power in Germany on 30 January

1933, cooperation between all political parties became a matter of life and death. Determined to save Austria from moral and physical destruction, Dollfuss postponed all parliamentary elections, formally dissolved the National Socialist party and expelled its members from the country. By then it was already too late. The poisonous seeds of Nazi propaganda sown with such effect over the border had taken root. Dollfuss had no option but to put his faith in Mussolini, who urged him to act quickly in three directions: constitutional reform, the building up of the patriotic Catholic movement, the Fatherland Front, and a clamp-down on Marxism. To achieve these ends his protector advised Dollfuss to make his government 'markedly dictatorial'.

With characteristic pragmatism Dollfuss managed to sidestep many of Mussolini's demands, and continued his efforts to come to some sort of agreement with his left-wing opponents. It was, therefore, not clear to either side how the events of February 1934 came about, except that the atmosphere in Vienna was far from calm. 'Two or three days in Austria were enough to see how much worse the situation had become within the few months of the new year, 1934,' wrote Stefan Zweig, returning after a stay in England. 'Coming from the serene and secure atmosphere of England into the fever-and-struggle-shaken Austria was like suddenly, on a stifling hot July day in New York, changing from an air-conditioned room to the steaming street.'[13]

The revolt, when it occurred, was short and bloody. On 12 February the Heimwehr raided the Social Democrat headquarters in Linz, allegedly the repository of a stock of arms, and were violently resisted – despite, as Kurt von Schuschnigg has pointed out, a previous direction from Otto Bauer that, should such a search be made, there was to be no retaliation. When the news reached Vienna, the left-wing leadership ordered a general strike and mobilized the Schutzbund, which had continued to flourish as an underground movement after having been made illegal the previous year.

For the next three days the Schutzbund, which had ignored an appeal from Dollfuss to lay down its arms and agree to an amnesty, held out against infantry attacks launched against the workers' flats by the regular army, only surrendering after the artillery was brought in. The dead and wounded were fairly evenly distributed: on the government side 105 dead and 319 wounded, civilians approximately 400 wounded and 137 dead. Stefan Zweig was in no doubt that 'this decisive battle ... was no less than the suicide of Austrian independence'. Certainly the uprising and its attendant causes and effects paved the way, a few months later, for Dollfuss's murder.

Whether or not it was carried out at Hitler's behest, or was masterminded by the sinister Major Fey, a confirmed Nazi and commander of the Vienna Heimwehr, or by the politically ambitious ambassador to Rome, Anton von Rinteln, is still open for debate, but it was indubitably the handiwork of a group of frustrated Austrian Nazis seething with impotent rage at the drawing of their political teeth a year before. In the event the putsch was unsuccessful, all the protagonists were arrested, and Dollfuss was succeeded by his testamentary choice, a thirty-four-year-old lawyer from Innsbruck, Kurt von Schuschnigg.

During the February uprising Alma and Manon were in Vienna whilst Werfel worked at Santa Margherita. Soon after the general strike began, Schuschnigg, then Minister of Justice, telephoned the Hohe Warte to suggest that, as they were in a 'zone of imminent danger', they should move to his family's house. 'But I could not desert my servants and Manon's French governess,' Alma wrote, 'so I declined with thanks.'[14] Far from being appalled at the sight of the upheavals around her, Alma found them positively stimulating: 'To me the firing in our immediate vicinity was terribly exciting, almost thrilling; I packed a suitcase for the eventuality of flight and sent the governess to the cellar for a bottle of champagne, which we emptied standing, constantly on the alert.'

Soon afterwards Alma became embroiled in a bizarre political *mise-en-scène* involving both Ambassador von Rinteln and Kurt von Schuschnigg that was more testing to her nerves. Rinteln, an old suitor of Alma's and a great admirer of Manon's youthful beauty, had long had his eye on the chancellorship. Alma, whose grasp of political reality was minimal but whose appetite for intrique was infinite, readily agreed to invite herself to tea with Schuschnigg in order (as she thought) somehow to enable Rinteln to stage a coup against him. Blinded by the excitement of being party to such high affairs of state, Alma duly played her part. The next day she telephoned Rinteln to find out why nothing had happened. As she did so she looked out of the window and saw two policemen at the door. Convinced that she was about to be, at the very least, imprisoned for treason, Alma prepared to meet her doom. Dressed in her best black frock and wearing her pearls she swept down the stairs, holding out her hands in a queenly gesture to be kissed. Neither of her potential jailers batted an eyelid. They merely asked if she would like to buy some tickets for the police ball. Had Alma been listening more closely to Rinteln, she would have realized that he had been making general, not specific plans to oust his rival.*[15]

In April 1934 an event occurred that overshadowed everything else: Manon became ill. By general consent Manon was beautiful, intelligent and good-natured. She was also tactful – a necessary quality, for by the time she was seventeen her beauty had attracted the attention of a number of her mother's courtiers and, at fifty-five, Alma's appearance had settled into blowsy middle-age. Her fine features – her slanting eyes and tapering nose – and clear smooth skin remained as striking as ever, but the generous supplies of alcohol she allowed herself every day had wreaked havoc with her figure, which, until the day she died, remained shrouded in a loose black dress, her only ornament a long string of false pearls.

To some extent age had mellowed Alma's more strident feminine competitiveness, for, as she later remarked, Manon's adolescence did not affect their relationship. 'She was always a miracle to me,' she wrote, 'and yet she never seemed a stranger, as Anna did at times . . . She was not yet sixteen . . . when I spent

---

*Rinteln's plotting and duplicity did, however, lead to his arrest and imprisonment. He was released after the Auschluss in 1938.

ten days with her at a hotel in Carinthia and rejoiced to see how greatly she pleased everyone.'[16]

Alma first realized that something was wrong with her daughter when she and Werfel returned to the Casa Mahler in Venice, where they were all staying, after a trip to Milan for a performance of *La Forza del Destino*. They found Manon pale, with no appetite and, it transpired later, suffering from painful headaches.

A week later the Werfels went, as planned, to Vienna, to hear Bruno Walter conduct *Das Lied von der Erde*, and Manon, at her own request, stayed behind. Alma's last glimpse of her looking well was waving from the end of the platform before the train pulled out of the station at 5 a.m. Within two days her condition had worsened. A telephone call from Venice saying that 'Miss Manon wasn't well; something in her head . . .' frightened Alma into booking two tickets for the morning plane for herself and Sister Ida. Before they took off she telephoned for news and spoke to Manon's governess, who kept shouting the same word over and over again in a tear-choked voice: 'Camphor – Camphor.'[17]

The diagnosis of poliomyelitis came as no surprise, but the speed of Manon's decline into total paralysis numbed all who saw it. Werfel, Anna, Paul Zsolnay and a Viennese specialist, Dr Friedmann, followed Alma to Venice on the afternoon flight and watched helplessly as paralysis of the legs, and then of her whole body, began. Respiratory paralysis set in after a week. 'It was only Anna's quick, energetic action', her mother wrote, 'she went, in a downpour, for an oxygen apparatus and finally located one in a outlying pharmacy – that avoided this earlier death. Dr Friedmann administered twenty-one injections.'[18]

Eventually Manon was moved back to Vienna, transported in a former imperial ambulance car put at her disposal by the Austrian government. The last year of her short life was a triumph of mind over matter. From her bed or wheelchair Manon received a steady flow of admirers. Alban Berg and Carl Zuckmayer were among the most frequent. Zuckmayer brought her a small snake which she kept on her counterpane, and spent many hours talking to the beautiful invalid, captivated by the depth and vividness of her imagination and by the stoicism with which she bore her fate. The actor Werner Krauss came every day to rehearse his parts with her and Manon, despite the lack of movement in her limbs, directed him with fierce attention to detail. 'I'm desperate,' he once told Alma, 'I've read the soliloquy four times now, and Manon still isn't satisfied!'[19]

For the first few months doctors felt there was a chance that their patient would be able to walk again. Walter Gropius came to visit his daughter in June, stayed a week and left after having been assured the disease was under control. It was to be their last meeting. To keep up her spirits Werfel coached his stepdaughter in the leading role of *La Forza del Destino*, with Alma accompanying them on the piano. 'She looked quite regal in black tights, doublet and hose,' Alma wrote in *And the Bridge Is Love*, 'and spoke from her wheel-chair like a consummate actress . . . It was a charming little performance that we put on for our friends.'[20] And, to further encourage Manon's burgeoning acting talents, Max Reinhardt's play editor, Franz Horch, came regularly to give her acting lessons.

None of these diversions, however, could conceal the fact that Manon was deteriorating and that her will to live had weakened. At the onset of her illness Manon had pleaded with those around her not to let her die, but by Easter 1935 she could stand it no more. On Easter Monday, 22 April, Alma wrote that Manon's voice was 'all but extinguished. "Let me die," she said. 'I'll never get well, and my acting, that's just what you make up for me out of pity . . . You'll get over it, Mummy, as you get over everything – I mean," she corrected herself, "as everyone gets over everything." '[21]

They were her last words. 'The worst had happened,' Alma continued, 'Today my beautiful, blessed daughter has been taken from me . . . Unfathomable are the ways of God. No one who knew her will forget her. We are all left impoverished. Hollnsteiner has been a great help to us.'[22]

In his funeral oration Professor Hollnsteiner spoke of Manon's beauty and purity. 'She bloomed like a beautiful flower. Pure as an angel she went through the world . . . She is not dead, she has gone home . . . her eyes without sadness or pain . . . no eye can see or ear hear what God has prepared for her.'[23]

Her two most faithful visitors were each deeply disturbed by Manon's death. 'Rarely has a human being's death affected me as much as this one,' Carl Zuckmayer wrote to Franz Werfel from Salzburg on 28 April.

> I only knew her for six months – and only saw her a few times, but something irreplaceable has vanished from my life. The very fact that I only got to know her during her illness and not earlier made a deep and unforgettable impression, and the thought that it might have been my privilege to bring a little joy into her life fills me with as much happiness as misery . . . I cannot see any plants or flowers growing this spring without thinking of Mutzi, and my thoughts go out to you . . .[24]

Manon's suffering and death also had a profound effect on Alban and Helene Berg. 'Always beloved Almschi!' wrote Helene. 'Mutzi was not only a singular child, she was also mine. But we must not grieve that God has seen fit to take her, for she is now an angel . . .' Although, as Berg's biographer, Mosco Garner, has remarked, it would be 'ludicrous' to suggest that without the tragedy of the early death of Manon Gropius, Berg would not have conceived the Violin Concerto, at the time of her death it was commissioned but as yet unformed and the trauma undoubtedly contributed to its final form: that of a symphonic poem with the character of a Requiem. Berg wrote to Alma, asking to be allowed to dedicate the work 'To the Memory of an Angel'.[25]

As for Alma and Werfel, they left Vienna, going first to Venice to sell the house in which they had been so happy but which now held so many painful memories of the recent past, and in November to New York, where Max Reinhardt was rehearsing Werfel's biblical cavalcade, *The Eternal Road*. The attendant problems of producing this Old Testament epic – massive even by Reinhardt's standards – kept them both fully occupied, as did the celebrations surrounding the American publication of *The Forty Days of Musa Dagh*, in the course of which they were fêted by the New York Armenian community 'with immense feasts and fiery speeches'.

Christmas was spent with Raimund von Hofmannsthal and his English wife, and it was during their stay that Alma, rising early, went downstairs and found the morning paper with a picture of Alban Berg above a description of his sudden death. Soon after completing the Violin Concerto in July 1935 he had developed an abscess on his back, which, together with boils, continued to trouble him on and off for the rest of the year, eventually leading to an infection of the blood. A few days before Christmas an operation was performed, but failed to find the source of the infection and, on 24 December, after his heart 'which has been strengthened by drugs during the previous days, gave out' he died. Alma could not bring herself to break the news to Werfel. 'Quietly, by myself, I wept for Alban, whose last work had been a requiem for my child. Now it had become his own . . .'[26]

In February the Werfels returned to Europe, travelling via Paris, where there were more festivities arranged by Armenians in honour of *Musa Dagh*, to Zurich, where they met Professor Hollnsteiner and took him on with them to Locarno. They were still there on the anniversary of Manon's death, when the professor 'read a Mass for her and suffered with us'.

Unlike the death of Maria, which had estranged Alma from Mahler for so long, the terrible loss of Manon and the sudden death of Alban Berg had brought Alma and Werfel closer together. Indeed, in the midst of the turmoil in the outside world it was the one thing they had in common, for with the outbreak of the Spanish Civil War in 1936 their old political differences again came to the fore. Werfel was reduced to impotent fury by Alma's defence of her latest Fascist hero's virtues. 'During the Spanish Civil War,' Albrecht Joseph said, 'the situation between Werfel and Alma became so strained that he seriously thought of leaving her. Alma took Franco's side and Werfel battled [with] her, using all his temperament and intelligence. But he could not win. He arranged for secret meetings with Anna, told her how miserable he felt and that he could not go on like this. He seemed ready for the final break. But he could not bring himself to really do it. He returned home, continued fighting with Alma, being miserable, eventually giving up. Anna thinks that it was the last time that he tried to assert himself against Alma and that, spiritually, he died right then.'[27] Had it not been for their shared grief, and their deep dependence on one another Werfel might, in that miserable time, have separated from Alma. But the bonds between them were by then too strong to be broken.

The following spring of 1937 Alma decided to sell the house on the Hohe Warte, where they had all been so uncomfortable. Later she wrote: 'There have been guilty and innocent houses and homes in my life: wherever a beloved died there was guilt . . . Buying the mansion on the Hohe Warte was a mistake for which I paid with Manon's death.'[28]

Before leaving they gave a party that lasted from 8 o'clock in the evening until 2 p.m. the next day. The *Neues Wiener Journal* of 11 June 1937, Alma recorded with some satisfaction, 'took a full column for the names and titles of those it did not dare omit from among those present.'

> There were three cabinet members and the wife of a fourth, three ambassadors and the wife of a fourth, two chargés, several ministers in retirement. There were princes and princesses, counts and countesses, barons and baronesses. There were a dozen Burgtheater stars, including one who was Countess Thun in private life and another who was waiting to become Princess Starhemberg. There were the Burgtheater's director and its director emeritus, the director emeritus of the Opera, the publisher of the *Journal*, the former publisher of the *Neue Freie Presse*. There were the ranking musicians, of course: 'Generalmusikdirektoren' Bruno Walter and Artur Rodzinski, Professor Dr Lothar Wallerstein, Wilhelm Kienzl, Alexander von Zemlinsky. There were the writers, from Karl Schönherr, the aged folk dramatist, whom Gerhart Hauptmann classed with himself, to young Ödön von Horvath, whose genius required another world war to be appreciated.
>
> There were incredibly comical moments, as, for example, when Frau Kienzl kept pulling her old master near the minister of education and both of them barely missed landing in the pond . . . Carl Zuckmayer bedded down in the dog basket after midnight 'to get closer to nature'.

Franz von Papen, who had ceded his position as German chancellor to Hitler, and was then ambassador to Vienna, 'chatted with an Austrian monarchist leader. "If we were living three hundred years ago," he said, "I would have Hitler and his men burned at the stake. Since that isn't done any more, we must wait for him to burn in his own fire.'[29] It was, perhaps, the last great Viennese social event of its kind.

13 *Into the New World*

This wind of a strange continent
Blows through me body and soul,
The ice cripples my frostbitten heart,
The emptiness is like a fallen woman.

This wind of a strange continent
Has the breath of another time.
Other people born into another world
Refresh me. I am lost like a wild
Beast that screams in the winter night.*

Carl Zuckmayer to Alma, undated, about 1939

By the beginning of 1938 the German-Austrian sickness, so long diagnosed as a case of political indigestion, had developed cancerous growths that showed few signs of being curable. Franz von Papen's indiscreet remark at the Werfels' party a year before was doubtless a diplomatic gesture designed to endear himself to a fellow guest. As ambassador he had been instrumental in negotiat-

*Dieser Wind der fremden Kontinente
Bläst mir noch die Seele aus dem Leib,
Nicht das Eis lähmt mir das frostgewohnte
Und die Schwüle nicht das lang entthronte
Herz, das leer ist wie ein ausgeweintes Weib.

Dieser Wind der fremden Kontinente
Hat den Atem einer andren Zeit.
Andre Menschen, einer andern Welt geboren,
Mags erfrischen. Ich bin hier verloren,
Wie ein Waldtier das in Winternächten schreit.

ing the nefarious Austro-German pact of 1936, in which both governments agreed not to interfere in the other's internal affairs, but which included a key clause stating that Austria acknowledged that 'with regard to the German Reich' she was a German state. On the surface the agreement seemed reassuringly to reinforce the status quo; in practice it was a smokescreen for the Führer's plan to deprive Austria of her sovereignty.

This became apparent all too soon, when the sting in the tail of the final document was included in a supplementary 'Gentlemen's Agreement' in which Schuschnigg, in return for promises that Berlin would keep control of Austrian Nazis, agreed to appoint two representatives of the 'National Opposition', i.e. pro-Nazis, to the government. Their appointment paved the way for further erosions of independence. Far from curbing the activities of Austrian Nazi sympathizers, Berlin merely turned a blind eye towards their increasingly overt attempts to stir up unrest, and much anti-government capital was made from Schuschnigg's countermeasures to quell them.

Further nails were hammered into the coffin of Austrian freedom when Schuschnigg, in the interests of cohabitation, allowed 'acceptable' Nazis into the hitherto patriotic Fatherland Front. Even worse, the chancellor, persuaded by von Papen to visit Hitler at Berchtesgaden in February 1938 on the understanding that the 1936 agreement was still intact, returned having signed a document giving Germany unprecedented powers of intervention in Austrian affairs – in particular the police were to come under the control of a Hitler nominee. Schuschnigg imagined that he was buying time. In fact he had sold Austria's soul to the devil.

Unlike many, Alma had been prepared for the final turning point. Christmas 1937 was spent in Vienna. She and Werfel were joined by Anna, now divorced from Paul Zsolnay, who had been working with the sculptor Maillol, in Paris. One of her works, a seven-foot female figure, had won first prize at the Paris World Fair – her first triumph as an independent artist. It was, however, a sad festival for them all. Werfel had bronchitis and Alma was consumed by memories of Manon. 'It was Manon's unfathomable faculty for love that had opened my eyes to the world's feast of joy,' she wrote, 'and without her I could no longer celebrate it. . . . I felt strangled by pain and despair.'[1]

As soon as Werfel's bronchitis allowed they left Vienna. In January, after a trip to Milan, where they stayed at the Grand Hotel in a flat which once belonged to Verdi and went nightly to La Scala, the Werfels travelled south via Naples to Capri. Once again they installed themselves in 'wonderful rooms at the best hotel, with a large corner room with balcony for Werfel', who started writing poetry 'for the first time in years'.[2]

These attempts to create order in the midst of impending chaos did not last long. Wherever they went the shadow of fear hung over them and when, in February, Werfel burst into Alma's room waving a newspaper proclaiming that Schuschnigg had gone to Berchtesgaden, they both realized that Austria was in deadly peril. Alma instantly made plans to leave for Vienna – without Werfel, whom she deemed, rightly, to be at risk. He therefore remained behind, impatient for news of Alma and of the state of affairs in Vienna. 'I am dreadfully impatient for a letter,' he wrote from Capri on the morning of 26 February. 'Please write INSTANTLY; is my gloom and sorrow to continue, shall I perhaps leave Capri? Write and tell me what to do . . . and write and tell me the truth about Vienna, as soon as you know what's happening. I am in a fever for an answer, and that's no understatement. My Almerl, I had really no idea how much love for you I have . . .'[3]

The state of affairs in Vienna was even worse than Alma had imagined. 'I had asked no one to meet me at the station.' she wrote, '–not Hollnsteiner, not the Molls, not anyone. For two days I remained incognito, looking at my Vienna, which stared back at me with utterly strange eyes.' When she finally emerged from the self-imposed isolation, Alma telephoned Hollnsteiner and told him of her fears. The professor 'radiated optimism' – in his opinion she had been 'overexcited by the foreign press'.[4]

Had she telephoned Stefan Zweig she would have found a sympathizer. In his English exile he had read of the particular points on which Lord Halifax hoped to come to an understanding with Hitler. 'One of them was a paragraph on Austria. And between the lines I read, or permitted myself to infer, the surrender of Austria, for what else could a discussion with Hitler mean?' He, like Alma, instantly returned to Vienna, to find his friends astonished at his hasty return:

> How they ridiculed me when I indicated my concern; I was still the same old 'Jeremiah', they mocked. Was I not aware that the whole population of Austria now stood one hundred per cent strong behind Schuschnigg? . . . I had learned and written too much history not to know that . . . the same voices which yelled 'Heil Schuschnigg' today would thunder 'Heil Hitler' tomorrow. But everybody I spoke to in Vienna showed an honest unconcern . . . In the last analysis it seems likely that they were wiser than I, all those friends in Vienna, because they suffered everything only when it really happened, whereas I had already suffered the disaster in advance of my fantasy and then again when it became reality . . . It is not a decorative afterthought but the sober truth when I say that in those last two days in Vienna I looked at all the familiar streets, every church, every park, every hidden corner of my native city, with a despairing silent 'nevermore'. I embraced my mother with the secret thought, 'It is the last time'.[5]

Ironically it was a visit to her own mother and stepfather that finally convinced Alma there was no longer a place for herself and Werfel in Austria. She found the Hohe Warte a hotbed of Nazi sympathizers (Carl Moll a true convert, Frau Moll remaining ideologically vague, but sure the Führer would always act for the best) all exulting over the 'capers' Schuschnigg cut in his desperation after Berchtesgaden – i.e. freeing Nazis imprisoned before the meeting, allowing the Nazi salute and repealing the ban on the swastika arm-band. This macabre gathering drove Alma to the State Bank, where she put her financial affairs in order and withdrew the balance of her account, which she was obliged to take in hundred-schilling bills, 'since the banks had orders to withhold large denominations'. The money was then sewn into 'the girdle of our good Sister Ida, who had offered to smuggle it to Zurich'.

Nevertheless, everywhere she went amongst her old friends, there was still a feeling that she was making a mountain out of a molehill. Carl Zuckmayer and his wife, celebrating their newly acquired Austrian citizenship, laughed at Alma's morbid reflection, 'What, now that Austria is lost?' Bertha Zuckerkandl, writing from Paris on 5 March, urged her to remember that, whereas her own work was concentrated in Paris, Alma's lay 'in Vienna, so that we can work together for Mahler, for Werfel. Naturally, the government would put a foundation at our disposal . . . think, Alma, of everything we suggest, and what we can eventually achieve.'[6]

All too soon, however, Alma's prophecies were fulfilled. News that the chancellor was planning to invite the Austrian people to place their confidence in their country's sovereignty by taking part in a plebiscite to be held on 13 March 1938 was leaked to Hitler on 8 March, with the result that on 11 March it was announced by radio that the plebiscite had been 'postponed'. Later the same day Schuschnigg broadcast to his people for the last time:

> Austrian men and women! This day has brought us face to face with a serious and decisive situation. The Government of the German Reich presented a time-limited ultimatum to the Federal President demanding that he appoint a candidate chosen by the Reich Government to the office of Chancellor and also follow its suggestions when selecting the ministers to serve in that cabinet. Should the Federal President not accept this ultimatum then German troops would begin to cross our frontiers this very hour. The Federal President has instructed me to inform the nation that we are giving way to brute force. Because we refuse to shed German blood even in this tragic hour, we have ordered our armed forces, should an invasion take place, to withdraw without serious resistance . . . so, in this hour I bid farewell to the people of Austria with a German word and a wish from the bottom of my heart: 'God save Austria.'

Alma did not wait for the invaders. Together with Anna (who was reluctant to leave) she packed two suitcases, said goodbye to her mother and went to her hotel, where she, Anna and Hollnsteiner sat up all night, listening to the 'drone of planes heralding Hitler's arrival'. Everything else, including the Bruckner manuscript, had to be left behind. Sister Ida and Carl Moll came to see them off. Alma was less than pleased to see her stepfather. 'He had always been my enemy, and in showing me this man now . . . Vienna bade me a fitting farewell.'[7]

In order to reach Milan, where Werfel was waiting for them, without trespassing on the new 'German soil', they had to travel via Budapest, Zagreb and Trieste. On the Czech border they were told to produce baptismal certificates and forced to submit to a thorough body search. Milan, when they finally arrived, had lost all its former savour. In low spirits they accepted an invitation to stay with Werfel's younger married sister, Marianne Speiser, in Zurich. They were all very much aware of the precarious nature of their journeyings: the sad fact was beginning to come home to them that they had now joined those tens of thousands of émigrés fleeing from Nazi tyranny and had become, ipso facto, refugees.

Alma's own account of the ensuing two years, culminating in their escape across the Pyrenees to Lisbon and America, is, as both Anna Mahler and Albrecht Joseph agree, the most authentic part of her memoirs. Her chronicle of disorientation, deprivation, fear and hope mirrors the plight of all such uprooted persons. Stefan Zweig, who had once 'imagined how beautiful it would be, how truly in accord with my inmost thoughts, to be stateless, bound to no one country and for that reason undifferentiatedly attached to all', found the reality less than edifying. From one moment to the next he had, in the eyes of the British authorities, slipped from the status of a 'gentleman who was spending his international income and paying his taxes' to that of the 'lesser if not dishonourable degree' of immigrant.[8]

Werfel and Alma were initially protected by Werfel's Czech passport. It enabled them, albeit after considerable difficulty, to cross the Swiss border into France, where Alma drew 'her first happy breath since the flight from Vienna'. Another restorative came in the form of an invitation from Willem Mengelberg to visit Amsterdam for his May Mahler Festival. In as yet uncontaminated Holland they could almost imagine themselves back to normal. Alma was once asked why she had not yet written a memoir of her life with Mahler. She replied that she had 'long since done so'. As a result of this encounter a representative of the Dutch publishing house of Albert de Lange called and, after much persuasion (Alma had not, initially, wanted the book published in her lifetime), she agreed to arrange for the manuscript to be sent to them. It might, after all, be her last chance to see the book in reputable hands.

Anna had gone on to London, where she was later joined by Alma and Werfel. For a miserable three weeks, whilst Werfel, who spoke some English, caroused with publishers, Alma endured the rigours of English life. She detested everything about it, finding London 'an absolutely frigid city. No one here comprehends the Austrian fate – it is unbearable . . . I must jettison everyone I loved in Vienna . . . I must forget. I will forget.'[9]

News of friends, when it came, was mixed. Egon Friedell was one of the hundreds of Jews who killed themselves rather than submit to the degradation and physical violence that would accompany their inevitable arrest: he threw himself from a top-floor window after seeing two paratroopers outside his front door. Kurt von Schuschnigg, whose place was briefly filled by Seyss-Inquart, was imprisoned, as was Professor Hollnsteiner.

Others were more fortunate. Theodor Csokor wrote to Alma from Poland at the end of March that he was experiencing 'the greatest kindness' from all around him, his only complaint being that he had been able to bring nothing with him – 'I only have two suits, two pairs of shoes, some washing things, and a type-writer.'[10] Carl Zuckmayer, who eventually managed to get to Switzerland, wrote cheerfully in August that he had 'completed a small novel that would appear in the autumn in book form' with the possibility of a film* to follow.[11] Unluckiest of all was Zuckmayer's friend and fellow playwright, Ödön von Horvath, who joined him in emigrating to Austria from Nazi Germany in 1933, and successfully evaded his oppressors again by fleeing to

*Probably *Ein Sommer in Österreich*, later filmed as *Francine*.

Paris in 1938, only to be killed by a falling tree while strolling down the Champs-Elysées.

As for Anna, Alma was not to see her again for over eight years. They were emotionally as well as physically estranged, for, as has already been observed, Anna's marriage, soon after he settled in London for good in 1940, to the Russian-Jewish conductor Anatole Fistoulari was anathema to her mother, who considered her new son-in-law unworthy to inherit (even at such a remove) Mahler's mantle.

Back in France, Alma tried to arrange a normal life for Werfel. She installed him in a room 'as big as a riding school' in the Hotel Henry IV in St Germain des Prés, she herself remaining in the small hotel near the Louvre in which they had first stayed. At the end of June Alma went south in search of a Riviera summer house to take the place of Breitenstein and Santa Margherita. She found what she wanted in Sanary-sur-Mer, a fishing village between Toulon and Bandol – 'an old watchtower which a painter had remodelled with good taste and few conveniences'. In the midst of arrangements for its lease she was given a message. Werfel had had a heart attack.

'After all the terrible things that have happened to me, now Franzl is seriously ill,' Alma wrote in her diary. 'I love him and feel for him. He is my last love. I am with him day and night . . . frightened of his and my fears. His blood pressure went up to 250, it is apparently the highest a man can have . . . his furious smoking has been stopped. But for how long? This man of smoke is supposed to "normalize" . . . but smoking is his element . . . I cannot contemplate his death.'[12]

It took Werfel more than a month to recover from the physical effects of the attack and from the mental anguish the spectre of death had aroused in him. When, at last, they were able to move into the watchtower, Alma was still gripped by melancholy, despite the fact that her husband was fit enough to start work on the first of his religious novels, *The Embezzled Heaven*. 'What will become of us?' she wrote on her sixtieth birthday. 'I have been through so much ... I long for a long winter's sleep, to forget all the pain ...'[13]

The winter, however, brought more sadness. 'It is a grey, unfriendly world,' Alma recorded at the beginning of October. 'For three weeks we have been hanging between war and peace. And we are here, homeless ... ignorant of the language ... the greatest barrier of all. I yearn to be at home in Vienna ...'[14] Frau Moll had become gravely ill. Six weeks later she died. 'Mami is no more,' Alma wrote in her diary on 29 November, 'and for the first time I felt flesh of her flesh, as though the cold flesh petrifying in Vienna was chilling *me* to the bone ...'[15] She wasted no sympathy on the plight of her stepfather, whose grief was such that he had to be watched day and night in case he took steps to follow his wife to the grave, merely commenting: 'Why don't they let him get on with it, he is quite right.' Alma had her revenge in 1945, when Moll, his daughter, Maria Eberstoller, and her husband committed suicide to escape retribution for their Nazi activities during the war, but for the moment the only bright spot was the reappearance of the Bruckner manuscript, smuggled out of Vienna by Sister Ida, who had parcelled it up and given it to the wife of an emigrant music critic without telling her of the contents.

Throughout all these trials and tribulations Alma displayed stoical qualities. Always an excellent traveller, she adapted easily to strange places and, although no linguist, managed by sheer force of her personality to make herself understood. Smoothing Werfel's path was, as ever, the most important thing in her life, and if to do so she had to endure bureaucratic obstinacy or personal discomfort, she endured it with commendable resignation.

During 1939 they were continually plagued by mistrustful bureaucrats. Hitler's absorption of Czechoslovakia in March forced Werfel's dying father and the rest of his family out of Prague and, after much haggling, they managed to obtain the necessary travel documents to enable them to visit him. The journey was both tiring and tinged with danger. Alma, sixty and never very strong on her legs, had, with Werfel, to stand on the train from Sanary to Lyon, and in Lyon, where they had to wait six hours for a connection, Werfel was taken away for questioning by a French plain-clothes policeman who had overheard them speaking German in a restaurant. Only his Czech passport saved him from the fate of less fortunate Austrian and German refugees – that of being consigned to a concentration camp.

Back in Sanary Alma and Werfel felt increasingly menaced by the local population, whom they suspected of harbouring both anti-Semitic and anti-Communist prejudices, suspicions reinforced by almost daily visits from the police inquiring into their papers, or searching the house for Communist propaganda. The atmosphere of reciprocal mistrust engendered by these forays into their privacy, combined with the expensive business of bribing their persecutors to stay away, took its toll on their health. Somehow, through thick and thin, Alma managed to get hold of her daily bottle of Benedictine, a habit begun as a boost to her morale, but which became a necessity for the rest of her life. (Only in her last years did her doctor insist that she reduce her alcohol intake to one bottle of sherry a day.) As for Werfel, Alma worried constantly about his powers of resistance. 'His condition is getting worse,' she wrote. 'He is completely enfeebled . . . and very hopeless. Exile is a terrible disease.'[16]

Only in Paris was there some semblance of normality: the new year of 1940 found them surrounded by old friends and fellow exiles: Bertha Zuckerkandl, Bruno Walter, Fritz von Unruh, Erwin Piscator, Franz Lehar, Otto von Habsburg, Emil Ludwig and Annette Kolb joined French friends such as Gustave Charpentier, Darius Milhaud, Paul Géraldy and Count Clauzel in Alma's small hotel room. And on their way back to Sanary they managed to have a 'relatively amusing time' in Marseille, 'going to the opera and to art exhibits, visiting a studio where a modern art magazine was turned out and making friends with the editors'.[17]

Had it been left to Alma, though, they would long since have made plans to join the swelling ranks of German immigrants in

America. But, until the very moment French troops were driven east by the advancing Germany army, Werfel clung to France as the last bastion of European civilization. Whilst Hitler marched through Luxembourg to the Low Countries Werfel continued to comfort himself with his belief in the invincibility of the Western allies. The collapse of Belgium on 28 May 1940 was, however, enough for Alma, who packed their bags and moved them both to Marseille in the hope of obtaining exit visas from France and entry visas into the United States.

For days on end they queued without success. In mid-June, in the wake of the alarming news that the German army was in Paris and that the French army was fleeing south, Marshal Pétain's government headquarters at Bordeaux seemed to hold out the only hope of escape. For 8,000 francs they hired a car and a driver, loaded up their luggage and set out. There ensued an uncomfortable, frustrating and often dangerous journey, only made bearable by thoughts of freedom from what had become yet another alien land.

Bordeaux, when they finally reached it, turned out to be no haven. Having been forced to abandon their car and driver at a roadblock outside Carcassonne, Alma and Werfel endured twelve hours on an overcrowded, insanitary train only to find the station crammed with people waiting to travel anywhere, so long as it was in the opposite direction. News of an armistice, at first greeted with emotions of relief by all refugees in the city, had turned to panic when it was rumoured that Germans had been sighted as near as Bayonne.

In the midst of these disquieting tidings the Werfels left their luggage at the Terminus hotel which, like all other hotels, was full to overflowing. They managed to hire another car and, having spent a bizarre night in a brothel (the result of a chance offer of a bed on the station platform), were driven to Biarritz. From there Werfel tried, yet again without success, to make arrangements for their visas with the consul in Bayonne, and whilst doing so heard that the Germans were indeed hard on their heels. Biarritz was likely to be occupied any minute, they were told by some Czech friends in the same predicament. It would be better for them all to move south to Hendaye on the Spanish border, where there was reputedly a kind-hearted Portuguese consul. But Hendaye, too, proved to be a red herring. Worse: after a few days of fruitless visa-hunting word came that German troops had been seen disembarking at the station. This proved too much for Werfel, who 'threw himself on the bed, sobbing convulsively'. His relief was all the more intense when, after twenty-four hours of misery at the hands of assorted taxi-drivers, without luggage and without having had any sleep or food, they arrived on 27 June in the as yet unoccupied town of Lourdes.

The physical and spiritual refreshment provided by a month spent in comparative calm in the vicinity of the grotto at Massabielle did much to restore Werfel's optimism. 'Franz Werfel's possible rescue, my rescue – everything lies in a clouded future that we know nothing about,' Alma wrote. 'The grotto of Lourdes has a healing effect on our souls while we are here; once we go away, this effect will cease, and our hearts will be burdened again . . .'[18]

Their benevolent imprisonment came to an end on 3 August, when the Lourdes police finally stamped their safe-conduct passes back to Marseille, by then the last hope of obtaining visas. Before they left Werfel made a vow. Should they ever reach America he would write a life, dedicated to Manon's memory, of Saint Bernadette.

For the first few weeks it looked as if this promise was unlikely to be fulfilled. Days of queuing in blistering heat reduced Werfel to tears of frustration, causing Alma to worry constantly about the effect the strain of waiting might have on her husband's weak heart. At last their patience was rewarded. Not only did a cable arrive from New York advising them that their American visas had come through, but one of the trunks Alma had thought lost forever in Bordeaux turned up at the station. A benign stroke of fate ensured that it was the one containing the scores of all Mahler's symphonies, together with the manuscript of Bruckner's Third.

From this time on there is a divergence of opinion as to exactly what happened next. Undoubtedly Alma and Werfel managed to obtain the necessary Spanish and Portuguese transit visas enabling them to travel through Spain to Lisbon, as a result of the intervention of a fellow Zsolnay author, Hertha Pauli; and undoubtedly they joined forces with Heinrich and Nelly Mann, together with Thomas Mann's second son, Golo (recently escaped from a Vichy internment camp), in a concerted attempt to cross the frontier. It is the *deus ex machina* of this expedition that varies according to who is telling the tale.

No history of the rescue of stranded exiles from France between 1940 and 1941 is complete without reference to the representative of the American Emergency Rescue Committee in Marseille, Varian Fry. By 1940 there were more than four million refugees trapped in France's unoccupied southern provinces, and from August of that year Fry, a thirty-two-year-old Harvard-trained classicist, together with a small band of dedicated helpers, enabled over one thousand hand-picked artists, musicians, writers, scholars, politicians and their families to leave France in safety. Among them were André Breton, Marc Chagall, Marcel Duchamp, Max Ernst, Kurt and Helen Wolff, Alfred Döblin, Hertha Pauli and Lion Feuchtwanger.

All had been selected by the committee as being persons of exceptional talent, whose lives were in danger from the Nazi regime. Visas for the United States had become increasingly difficult to obtain. Since the fall of France the issuing of visitors' visas to people who could return to their homelands, as well as transit visas to those en route to third countries, had been drastically curtailed, and they were granted only in exceptional circumstances to 'persons of exceptional merit, those of superior intellectual attainment, of indomitable spirit, experienced in vigorous support of liberal government and who [are] in danger of persecution or death at the hands of autocracy'. All applications had to be approved by the President's Advisory Committee on Political Refugees, or a related agency, cleared by the Justice and State departments and then passed on to the American consuls overseas. Each member of the escaping party was a person of outstanding talent and indomitable spirit, but, equally, each had good reason to fear the heavy hand of an alien bureaucracy. Without the direct intervention of Varian Fry they might never have made their escape.

It was Lion Feuchtwanger, according to Heinrich Mann, who masterminded the operation, which he had plotted in the same vein as one of his best-selling historical novels, weighing up the pros and cons of having themselves smuggled aboard a fishing smack to Tunisia – a likely place to find a boat to Portugal, but 'what sort of a novel would it have been if on the high seas our rented boat had been stopped by an enemy vessel and the cargo for North Africa had revealed only three mutton carcasses and six still living émigrés?'[19]

Alma does not mention Lion Feuchtwanger at all in her account, although Heinrich Mann wrote that he travelled with them. According to *And the Bridge Is Love* it was Varian Fry, albeit laconic and gruff in manner, who 'did the job'. It was he who decided that, as none of them was likely to obtain an exit visa, and as each further day in Marseille was becoming increasingly dangerous, the time had come to cross the border by illegal means.

At 3 a.m. on 12 September the party took the train from Marseille via Perpignan to Cerbère, each carrying a rucksack containing essential possessions. (Alma's included money, her jewels, the Bruckner manuscript and the Mahler scores.) Whilst Fry took the main luggage on to Port Bou by rail the rest, escorted by a young American Unitarian guide, began their ascent of the Pyrenees. 'I will not easily forget the steep road,' wrote Heinrich Mann, then in his seventy-first year, 'empty except for our rucksacks which we let dangle from our arms to look as natural as possible . . .'[20] Slithering and sliding 'with nothing but thistles to hold on to', they dragged themselves up two thousand feet to the Spanish border post. 'In a sudden burst of kindliness,' Alma wrote, 'the officer waved us through.'

There remained the dreaded moment of confrontation with the

passport authorities below at Port Bou. 'Like poor sinners we sat in a row on a narrow bench,' Alma wrote in *And the Bridge Is Love*, 'while our papers were checked against a card index.'

> Heinrich Mann, greatly endangered because of his leftist tendencies, was travelling with false papers, under the name of Heinrich Ludwig; Werfel, travelling under his own name, had heard in Marseille that Hitler himself had put a price on his head; Golo Mann was in danger as his father's son. Yet Golo sat quite calmly reading a book, as if the whole business did not concern him. Nelly Mann had half carried her aged husband over the thistly mountainside, and her stockings hung in shreds from bleeding calves.
>
> After an agonizing wait we all got our papers back, properly stamped, and were free to continue through Spain. When I think how many killed themselves up there on the hill or landed in Spanish jails, I see how lucky we were to have our American scraps of paper honoured by the officials at Port Bou.[21]

Reunited with their luggage they slept the night in Port Bou, continuing the next day to Barcelona, 'a war-devastated, starved, impoverished city that must have been beautiful once'. There followed a fifteen-hour train journey to Madrid, from where they flew to Lisbon. At the airport a passport official, noticing amongst the list of Franz Werfel's works attached to a letter of recommendation from the Duke of Württemberg *Paul among the Jews*, asked if he was of Jewish descent. Werfel said nothing. 'The official sneered,' Alma wrote, 'as if to indicate that Werfel's descent was obvious to everyone. Then he gave us the stamp that meant admission to Portugal.'[22]

No matter that they had to wait a fortnight for the Greek ship *Nea Hellas* to take them across the Atlantic. After months of persecution they were free.

14 *The Dance of Death*

Death waltzed me in a merry round
At first I did not lose my breath,
Stepped smartly in the Dance of Death
Till he changed to a faster bound.*

Franz Werfel, 1945.

Two months after the *Nea Hellas* berthed at Hoboken, New Jersey, on 13 October 1940 Alma received a letter from Georg Moenius, a friend of Johannes Hollnsteiner and a fellow professor of theology. 'Most Honoured and dear Alma Mahler,' he wrote from St James Cathedral, Seattle. 'Your letter, with the brief mention of your flight literally drove me to a handwriting expert. I felt as the poet Dante must have done when he was confronted in a dark wood by three beasts. But . . . I thank God that you are safely here in the United States'[1]

News that the party of distinguished émigrés had reached Portugal and were en route to America had filtered through to friends in New York, and they arrived to an emotional welcome from a mob of well-wishers waiting on the quayside, all of whom, Alma recorded, were 'in tears, and so were we'. The press, too, were out in full force, but Werfel spoke for all the group when he

Der Tod hat mich im Tanz geschwenkt.
Ich fiel zuerst nicht aus dem Trott
Vom Totentanz und steppte flott,
Bis er das Tempo
hochgelenkt.

refused to give any details of their escape in case of compromising those left behind. 'I can't speak', he told the *New York Herald Tribune.* 'Most of us are all still in France. My friends are all in concentration camps.'[2]

After nearly three months in New York, during which Werfel was much in demand as a speaker (one of his first public appearances was at Columbia University, where he read his lecture 'Can We Live Without Belief in God?), the Werfels removed themselves to California. Early on the morning of 30 December, having made a brief stop in Chicago, they arrived in Los Angeles. Friends were at the station to meet them and take them to the small house leased on their behalf where, Alma noted approvingly, everything had been taken care of: 'The kitchen was stocked with all necessary supplies, and they had hired a butler . . .'

The butler, August Hess, proved a considerable find. A man of tact and resource, he managed to fulfil the needs of both his employers by the simple expedient of remaining extremely reticent. When Alma, delighted to find her new butler was a purebred, non-Jewish German operetta tenor, urged him to sing, or decided to introduce him to works of Shakespeare so that he could begin writing plays (thus transforming him into that most necessary of beings in her eyes – a creative person), August maintained a pleasant but stolid front. Likewise, when Alma attempted to draw him into one of her frequent diatribes against the defects of the Jewish race, he sensibly declined to say anything at all. As a result he was able to deal very well with Werfel, to whom he became devoted.*

Other members of the émigré community had been occupying themselves that day, as every day, waiting for news of the progress of the Battle of Britain and the Blitz, which came through from London at midnight California time. Bruno Frank and his wife, Albrecht Joseph, Thomas Mann, Fritzi Massary, Bruno Walter and his daughter Lotte remained glued to the radio for hours

---

*Poor August came to a sad end. An amateur chemist, he blew himself up during one of his more elaborate experiments soon after he had left Alma's employ.

beforehand 'greedy for every bit of information', even though they all knew, that, barring some sensational development, there would be no real news during London night-time. 'To make the waiting . . . easier,' Albrecht Joseph wrote:

we met after dinner and played games. The most popular . . . was the Game, a charade. One half of the party acted out a line of poetry or a famous quotation, wordless. The other half had to guess the meaning of the pantomine. The acting was often quite funny, sometimes wild. The guessing was done aloud with vigorous shouting and laughter . . . The Game was often played at the Franks' house, and one particular evening Bruno was crawling on the floor, trying to impersonate, I think, a mouse, which, considering that he had the head and body of a Roman emperor, was a rich treat. Unexpectedly, the door from the street opened . . . and there in the open house door stood Alma and Werfel. Years later Werfel kept saying that of all the fantastic experiences in those tumultuous years his first encounter with the Los Angeles chapter of German intellectuals – Bruno Frank on all fours imitating a tiny animal, the group of guessers yelling madly at one another – remained one of his most baffling encounters.[3]

Despite Alma's language problems, neither she nor Werfel suffered the deprivations endured by many fellow exiles. If not as luxuriously accommodated as the Feuchtwangers, whose 'Spanish style home with a view of the mountains and ocean; all kinds of fruit trees; a garden filled with flowers; a park with benches and breakfast tables' in Pacific Palisades was the envy of less fortunate intellectuals, they were, thanks to Alma's foresight and Sister Ida's ingenuity, insulated from the outset by a degree of financial security. Unlike Alfred Döblin, Bertolt Brecht, Heinrich Mann or Carl Zuckmayer, Franz Werfel did not have to eke out his existence struggling to meet the demands of rapacious Hollywood studios eager to exploit the monetary frailty of the new scriptwriting talent at their disposal. Although Alma mourned the beauties of the European landscape – 'The countryside empty and monotonous', she wrote in her diary in March 1942. 'Italy is our spiritual homeland' – they were reasonably contented with their lot.[4]

Most important of all in Alma's eyes, the house found for them proved a satisfactory place for Werfel to work. Standing a thousand feet above Hollywood Boulevard, it was situated in The Outpost, an old residential district in the centre of old Hollywood, laid out 'like other similar residential areas in Los Angeles, in a maze of small streets that were supposed to give the area a quaint, cosy, old world atmosphere but merely made it impossible to find a house the first time one went there.' From the back they could look down into the Hollywood Bowl, and on concert nights the music filtered up, 'lovely and clear, much better than from any seat in the Bowl itself'.[5]

Inside, the house was small. The ground floor consisted of a living-room, entered directly from the street, which contained a grand piano for Alma, a modest dining-room and a kitchen. The bedrooms were downstairs, built into the hillside and connected to the ground floor by a narrow, winding wrought-iron staircase designed, like the rest of the house, in Spanish-colonial style. The perilous business of getting down them was a constant difficulty for Alma, always unsteady on her legs, and particularly so by the time it came to the close of the day and the end of another bottle of Benedictine. More than once she fell down the hated 'chicken ladder', suffering painful bruises and sprains.

Within a few days of their arrival Werfel began to write *The Song of Bernadette*, dictating the result of the first draft to Albrecht Joseph, who had taken leave of absence from his previous employer, Emil Ludwig, to act as his secretary. In conditions of extreme proximity they worked in Werfel's downstairs bedroom, also his study, a 'tiny, whitewashed cell, just big enough for a narrow bed, a dresser, a table, and two chairs'. Whilst Werfel consulted the pencil hieroglyphics in one of the exercise books he habitually used for literary purposes, Joseph waited to type them out. When, a few years later, Joseph asked him whether these 'schoolbooks had any connection with childhood memories', he 'smiled and said: "As a boy I was forced to write in those books what I did not want to write. It is a sweet revenge for me now to write in them as I please." '[6]

Five months later Werfel had fulfilled his vow. 'None of my books,' he wrote, 'not even *The Forty Days of Musa Dagh*, is so full of meaning as *The Song of Bernadette*. I am finally convinced that I have written a book appropriate to these times . . .' For now, instead of one community fighting for physical and spiritual survival, it was the whole world that needed to be reminded of the principles of spiritual life and spiritual death. 'No one understands this war who still believes that it is a war of nations . . .' Werfel wrote in an article on the gestation of the book in May 1942. 'No! Not a material but a spiritual principle is at stake . . . On the one side stands radical nihilism that no longer regards the human being as the image of God but as an amoral machine . . . On the other side, our side, stands the metaphysical, the religious concept of life, the conviction that the Cosmos was created by the spirit and that a spiritual meaning lives and breathes in every atom . . .'[7]

It was this attitude towards the spirituality of mankind in general that led to confusion over Werfel's particular religious affiliations. How, it was asked, could a man able to penetrate so deeply into the heart of the Catholic faith, and to correspond on equal theological terms with numbers of prominent Catholic divines, remain unaffected by the central tenet of their creed? How, in other words, could he remain a Jew?

Many views have been expressed on the subject. It was suggested, among other things, that as an artist Werfel rejected the world; that as an economic man with a living to earn he accepted it; that he never converted to Catholicism because he did not believe in the miracle of Bernadette Soubirous; that even in so 'Catholic' a novel as *The Song of Bernadette* he remained an Expressionist writer; and that the novel's religiosity was the product of simple piety.

The answer, as is sometimes the case, was the simplest one. It was supplied by Werfel himself at the end of his introduction to the novel:

> I have dared to sing the song of Bernadette, although I am not a Catholic but a Jew; and I drew courage for this undertaking from a far older and far more unconscious vow of mine. Even in the days when I wrote my first verses I vowed that I would evermore

and everywhere in all I wrote magnify the divine mystery and the holiness of man – careless of a period which has turned away with scorn and rage and indifference from these ultimate values of our mortal lot.[8]

In other words the great mysteries of divinity, redemption and spiritual growth were, to Werfel, as they were to Mahler, part of the enormity of the universal whole. They were not, and never could be, confined to followers of any one Church.

Nor, despite his wife's posthumous efforts to have her husband buried in the rites of the Catholic Church, was Werfel ever knowingly baptized. The question of whether or not he had received the sacrament was cleared up in his answer to a courteous enquiry from the archbishop of New Orleans on behalf of his parishioners, many of whom found it difficult to believe that the author of *The Song of Bernadette* was not a practising member of their Church.

In this reply, Werfel stressed that although he had always felt close to the mysteries of Christianity, and held the faith of its believers in the greatest respect, he himself could not take the decisive step for three reasons. First, having been born a Jew he felt it his duty to remain a member of that body which, together with the Christian, 'had been chosen to work out, in antiphony, the destiny of Western mankind until the coming of the Last Judgement'. Second, in times like these it might look as if he were seeking some personal advantage by denying that he belonged to 'an unfortunate, cruelly persecuted minority'. Third, 'the Catholic Church, throughout its long history but also in the present time, had played an active part in this persecution of the Jews, and had never seriously regretted and denounced such activities'.[9] Self-respect, if nothing else, would make it impossible to join an institution so blemished.

This last observation caused Alma much agitation – not, she hastened to add, for philosophical reasons, but because she feared for Werfel's popularity. She need not have worried. The archbishop did not reply, and in any case by 1943, in spite of the initial reservations of Ben Huebsch of the Viking Press, who wrote to Werfel after receiving the manuscript that he was only printing the book because he had printed all his other novels, *The Song of Bernadette* was an assured best-seller, selected by the Book of the Month Club and turned into an Academy Award winning film by Warner Brothers. At long last he had written the great work of Alma's dreams – one combining artistic integrity with financial reward. Carl Zuckmayer echoed the feelings of many of his contemporaries when he wrote to his friend from Barnard, Vermont, in March 1942 that he had read the novel through twice at a sitting and found it 'a masterpiece ... I am quite certain that it is the most beautiful and worthwhile book that has been written in our time. One can only thank God that there is someone capable of creating such a marvel.'[10]

Alma, too, had received a number of letters from readers of her account of Mahler. Stefan Zweig was particularly appreciative. 'You have no idea what your book on Mahler meant to me,' he wrote from Lyncombe Hill, Bath, in March 1940. 'May you have many such readers ... what luck that this book is, at long last, *there* – and the way it is ...'[11]

In the summer of 1942 Alma decided they were able to afford a house of their own. 'I bought a house in Beverly Hills ... the smallest I could find, knowing that servant trouble and high taxes made large houses impossible to keep.' It was in this bungalow, at 610 North Bedford Drive, that Franz Werfel spent the last three years of his life.

It is entirely in character that Alma should have omitted to mention the bombing of Pearl Harbor, or indeed much of the progress of the war, either in her memoirs or in her diary. Apart from the indubitable fact that she was in an English-speaking country, surrounded by large numbers of transplanted German-speakers, the majority of Jewish extraction, Alma could almost imagine herself back on European soil. Insulated from the inconveniences of occupation, air-raids, food shortages or threat of invasion, she was able to devote the whole of her attention to preserving the pattern of their old way of life. Whilst German tanks rolled towards Cairo and Stalingrad, Alma played Wagner and Bach* for herself and Verdi for Werfel, learned to drive (she eventually bought a Sleier car) and, assisted by her admirable butler, August, a cook and a maid, entertained her German and Austrian neighbours.

Bertha Zuckerkandl, writing from Algiers, might muse on the tragic plight of Europe in general and France in particular, and mourn the 'graveyard' that was once Vienna, but Alma, with a perverseness not easily explicable chose to lard her conversation, both in public and in private, with anti-Semitic, anti-Allied bait. If nothing else, it is a testament to Alma's ability to succeed in her self-created minefield that regular visitors, among them Schönberg, Thomas Mann, Bruno Walter, Erich Korngold, Bruno Frank and Alfred Döblin, continued to gather in her living-room in the full knowledge of some of her views. She remarked, for instance, if not actually in their presence, that 'the Allies ... were weaklings and degenerates, the Germans, including Hitler, supermen'; that 'the humanistic, liberal cause was lost and the blond beast would triumph'; that 'the Nazis, after all, had done a great many praiseworthy things' and that one should not believe all one heard about concentration camps. 'I know for a fact', she once said at a tea party for Ernst Deutsch and his wife, 'from a friend of mine, a registered nurse in a top position ... that the camps have excellent medical care and that the Red Cross is conscientiously watching over the welfare of the prisoners.'

Albrecht Joseph was present at the tea-party. He recalled:

> For a moment we all just sat there, paralysed. Then Werfel jumped up, screaming, his face a deep purple, his eyes bulging. I would have hardly have believed before that the humorous, slightly cyni-cal, wise man could ever be aroused to such a pitch of fury. I do not remember verbatim what he said but it was like the thunder of one of the Old Testament prophets. He was beside himself, had completely lost control and was dangerously close to a fit of apoplexy ... Alma appeared unmoved and retracted nothing. She

---

*Although she was once confined to bed for several days in a state of emotional upset by Anna's confession that she preferred Bach to Wagner, Alma was frequently heard playing from *The Well-Tempered Clavier*. Her prejudice against Bach, like her prejudice against Jews, was a weapon to be used at whim.

probably felt that Werfel, being childish, had childishly misbehaved . . . [12]

When asked by some of his left-wing friends how he could continue to see Alma, who represented 'the kind of German which had . . . become taboo to [him]', Thomas Mann was reported to have 'puzzled seriously for a few moments and thought the problem over, then to have smiled and said: "She gives me partridges to eat, and I like them." '[13] His answer was as good as any, for Alma's continuing anti-Semitism was an absurdity that can only be explained on her own terms. The paradox was that Alma would have been outraged if anyone else had voiced such extreme sentiments in front of Schönberg or Werfel. Only she, in her privileged position as a creature who had moved between two worlds, been married to Mahler and Werfel, had Jewish friends all her life and still claimed Anton von Rinteln, Schuschnigg and Hollnsteiner among her intimates, could be allowed to express what she felt regardless of the sensibilities of those around her. It was up to them to make of it what they could. They should realize that Alma, although never a Nazi, was always on the side of a pure-bred German against a Jew, but that the Jews among whom she moved were singled out and excused by their talents, which set them apart from less fortunate members of their race and made them worthy of her love or friendship.

However hard they were to stomach at the time, Alma's bouts of racialist fickleness did not have any lasting effect on her marriage. Even those who looked on her with a more than usually jaundiced eye were obliged to admit that she had a Viennese feminine softness which, even in her most awful moments, made it difficult to really dislike her, and Werfel's vitriol soon evaporated. He wrote from Santa Barbara in 1944: 'To the one I love the most – it is still a heavy sacrifice and a deep deprivation to be without you . . . I must keep to my work so that I won't be tempted to come back to you!'[14]

The previous year Werfel had returned to his old habit of writing away from home, one reason being the difficulties he was having with his play, *Jacobowsky and the Colonel*, another the gestation of what was to be his last novel, *The Star of the Unborn*. In *Jacobowsky and the Colonel*, two Poles, an officer and a Jewish businessman, meet in France and, in the course of their successful attempt to outwit the Nazi dragnet and escape to England, each unwittingly adopts some of the other's ways of dealing with the world. The play was not, as Alma observed, one of her husband's most profound works but the failure of *The Eternal Road* had left its author intent on a theatrical triumph to equal the success of *The Song of Bernadette*, and when the New York producers, having seen the first English translation, suggested an adaptor to make it more 'suitable for presentation', Werfel agreed. Clifford Odets was engaged for the task and proceeded, as Albrecht Joseph recorded, to make 'a thorough hash of it'. Unable to understand the point of the play, which was to poke gentle fun at the foibles of an officer and a gentleman and a moderately unscrupulous small-time operator, Odets's main contribution was to turn Jacobowsky into a 'civilized businessman, the founder of a symphony orchestra', who took a 'portable phonograph along on the flight from Paris to the French border, playing Mozart recordings with the Gestapo lurking in the bushes nearby'.[15]

Odets's successor, a Mr Jed Harris, was equally unsatisfactory. Tall and gangly 'with burning eyes, a cross between Dr Miracle out of the *Tales of Hoffman* and a hungry Jewish tailor', he forced Werfel to rewrite the play three times whilst he himself used the opportunity of being in Hollywood to find a job as a film producer. Each time, in Joseph's opinion, the play became a little worse. Finally it was put in the hands of S. N. Behrman, the author of a number of successful drawing-room comedies, to the satisfaction of the backers, if not of Joseph, who found the end product very flat compared to the original: 'He had eliminated the few amusing and fantastic episodes that could have lifted the play above a run-of-the-mill Broadway spectacle, and the director then eliminated some of the remaining humorous and significant speeches that made the whole product worthy of having been written by a man of Werfel's stature.'[16]

On top of the attendant worries of the play's reconstruction,

Werfel had to cope with squabbles over the distribution of royalties. In the end he had to submit to the profits of what became a considerable commercial success being divided up between Odets, Behrman, the Theatre Guild, his American and German publishers and Max Reinhardt's son Gottfried, who claimed to be the originator of the whole idea and threatened to go to court unless his part in the venture was financially rewarded.

In June he went to Santa Barbara to rewrite the play for the fourth time, and in August Alma joined him, reporting on her birthday that it was 'a paradise' and that Werfel, despite all his own frustrations, had been 'wonderful' to her. In September they went home to celebrate Werfel's birthday. Three nights later, on 13 September, he had a heart attack. To spare his patient worry, the doctor told Werfel that he had nicotine poisoning, and recommended complete rest and abstinence from the habit. With this in mind they returned to Santa Barbara, but within a few days Werfel took a turn for the worse and they hurried back to Bedford Drive. There his condition appeared reasonably stable until 29 September, when he suffered another, near-fatal, attack.

'Franzl has been deathly ill since yesterday,' Alma wrote, '. . . and now his heart is dreadfully weak. Without him I cannot go on living. He is the core of my existence.'[17] This time the three doctors who were summoned gave a gloomier prognosis. Their patient was too ill to be moved for an X-ray; all they could do was try to lower his mounting fever with morphine and administer oxygen in the hope that the heart would revive. For a month Werfel lay 'motionless in the bed that was wheeled out on the patio each morning into the sunny garden'. An X-ray was attempted on 23 November, but abandoned when Werfel had yet another seizure, followed three weeks later on 14 December by his fourth attack in three months. 'He was suffocating, more dead than alive, but grand as ever. "I'm so happy with you," he said.'[18]

On 17 December Werfel recovered enough to ask for pen and paper, and set down the four verses of his poem 'The Dance of Death'. Its completion temporarily cheated his hooded pursuer. Gradually, after months of what Alma described as 'permanent torture' for them both, during which she 'wept through many days and nights' whilst Werfel lay immobile – 'touchingly patient; longing to live again and doing all one asked of him' – he began to regain his strength. By July 1944 he was almost back to his old self, although both he and Alma remained conscious of the fact that one of his heart chambers was permanently defective.

Nevertheless they both cheered up. Alma had found a new friend, the humorist Ludwig Bemelmans, who became a frequent visitor to Beverly Hills, as well as entertaining them both at his converted beach hut on Malibu beach. On one such occasion in April 1945 he invited them to a party. Accompanied by their butler, August, who carried the food Bemelmans had asked them to bring, the Werfels arrived, rang the bell and, when there was no answer, sent August inside to look for their host. August returned, puzzled, to say that there was no sign of Bemelmans but that there was a strange man – possible Turkish, possibly Romanian – with a long black moustache, lying on a couch. On inspection it was found to be Bemelmans, fully masked, drunk, and suffering from a high fever. 'My temperature is one hundred and five,' he announced. 'Pneumonia . . . An ambulance will come for me at midnight, but I don't want to lie here alone and depressed . . . Make yourselves at home; there's plenty of champagne on ice. Be merry – I need it.'[19]

Also that spring Alma noted various dates in her diary. 'Our dear friend Bruno Frank died today,' she wrote on 20 May, 'a sensitive poet and a man of infinite kindness and nobility . . .' Earlier, on 28 April, she recorded Mussolini's ignominious end: shot through the head, his body dumped in the Piazza Loretto in the centre of Milan together with that of his twenty-five-year-old mistress, Clara Petacci, and twelve other Fascists caught by the partisans. 'It was not a hero's death;' she wrote of her old idol, 'he first promised the killers a kingdom if they would let him go . . .'[20]

Ignoring Hitler's death on 1 May, Alma concentrated on the first good news from Vienna. 'On June 3rd Gustav Mahler's First Symphony will be performed again . . . after seven years. Before the start, a memorial tablet will be unveiled in the Konzerthaus, with the following inscription: IN MEMORY OF THE HISTORIC DATE OF GUSTAV MAHLER'S RESURRECTION IN VIENNA.'[21]

Also in June Werfel was able to hear at first hand news of his homeland, when Jan Masaryk, in San Francisco for a conference, paid them a visit. Having served Czechoslovakia first as its ambassador to Britain before the war, when his father, Thomas, was president, and until the Soviet 'liberation' of Prague on 9 May, as foreign secretary in exile in London under President Beneš, Masaryk was well placed to offer an opinion as to its future. He was cautiously optimistic. It was true that the Czechs had been shocked by the behaviour of Soviet troops, but the tumultuous welcome given to Beneš when he entered Prague on 16 May was testament enough to the feelings of the majority. However, he added, should the worst happen and Czechoslovakia fall into Communist hands, he would resign as foreign minister and live in America.*

July found Werfel busy putting the finishing touches to the first draft of *The Star of the Unborn* in Santa Barbara, looking 'splendid', Alma wrote after a brief visit in August. Confident of his improving health and mindful of her own – she had recently been in the grip of a tenacious fever brought on by the worry of the past two years – Alma left her husband in the care of one of his doctors and went back to Beverly Hills. On 12 August, the date after she arrived, she received a poem by special delivery:

An Alma	To Alma
(Nach dem Abschied)	(after saying goodbye)
Wie ich dich liebe, hab ich nicht gewusst,	How much I love you was not known to me,
Bevor mich überfiel dies rasche Scheiden,	Before the onset of these quick goodbyes.
Ich bin ganz blutarm von soviel	I'm drained of blood by all the

---

* Three years later the worst did happen. Masaryk was denied the opportunity of emigrating and was found dead underneath a bathroom window outside the Czernin Palace at 6 a.m. on 10 March 1948. The verdict remains open, but many believe that he was murdered.

Erleiden.
Warum wird man bewusst erst
durch Verlust?

agony.
Why must we lose so as to realize?

Was gestern du berührt hast, starrt
nun leer.
Die Dinge sind wie tief gekränkte
Tiere.
Mein Leben nicht, das deine *war*
das ihre.
Und darum haben sie kein Leben
mehr.

What yesterday you touched stares
empty now.
Things are like animals, aggrieved
and sore.
Your life, not mine, was theirs – and
that is how
They're only things today, alive no
more.

Ich geh herum, zuzammgelasst und
scheu
Aus Angst von meines Herzens
überschwellen.
Im Haus versuche ich mich blind
zustellen
Denn Zeit ist trettlos, aber Raum
ist treu.

I wander to and fro, lost and shy,
My heart swelling with fear.
At home I delude myself, and try
To believe that time is fickle, but
space endures.

Im Raum hier nebenan dein Leben
schwang.
Hier atmetest du rufend, lachend,
sprechend;
Und ich, und ich – wie ist das Herz
zerbrechend –
Nahms an, nahm ihn und fühlste
mich nicht lang.

In the room next to me, your life
went on,
You breathed, called out,
laughed and spoke;
And I, and I – whose heart is
broken –
Accept it, for my time is not long.

Five days later Werfel telephoned in high spirits to announce
the completion of his novel. 'The ending, he said, was quite unlike
his original idea; he had found an altogether different solution.
Now he wanted to get home as fast as possible.' When he arrived
Alma was worried to find him looking tired and grey and moving
slowly – worries that intensified the next day when he broke out
into a sweat and seemed on the point of total collapse. Alma
'massaged him and warmed his hands and feet with hot towels'
and sent for medical help, but by the time the doctors arrived he
had rallied. He did, however, take their advice to spend three
days in bed, during which he improved enough to revise one or
two poems, and was well enough on 25 August to go out to

dinner with Bruno Walter – a near neighbour – and his daughter Lotte.

The following afternoon, after a short rest, Werfel went to his desk in the small semi-detached studio that he had built onto the back of the house to do some more work on his poems. It was there that Alma, looking in on him as she 'used to do from time to time', found him lying on the floor, 'a smile on his face, his hands limp, unclenched'. At first Alma refused to believe her husband was dead. Her screams brought August to her aid, she put an oxygen mask over his mouth and 'massaged his heart, hands, and feet', and together they carried him to his bed. She then telephoned some friends, Professor and Mrs Arlt, who were there within minutes. August telephoned Albrecht Joseph, who arrived ten minutes later. But by then Alma knew there was nothing anyone could do. 'Slowly turning to stone,' she wrote, 'his beautiful face grew more and more sublime, more and more monumental.'[22]

Franz Werfel was buried in the chapel of the Pierce Brothers Mortuary in Beverly Hills on 29 August 1945. According to his instructions he wore full evening dress to which was pinned the Bundesverdienstkreuz awarded him by Chancellor Schuschnigg for services to literature, and beside him lay a spare silk shirt and a second pair of glasses.

Alma did not attend the funeral. Albrecht Joseph, asked to act as an usher to help deal with the large numbers of expected mourners, called at North Bedford Drive on the day of the internment and found her seated at Werfel's desk 'in a house dress . . . writing'. When told it was time to leave she informed the astonished Joseph that she had no intention of going. 'She looked at me reprovingly and said "I never go." ' It sounded, he added, as 'if she had been asked to break with a hallowed tradition, as if burying her husbands were a regular occurrence . . .'[23]

She did, however, have a hand in the funeral oration. Monsignor Georg Moenius, with whom she had struck up a close friendship in the intervening years, had been entrusted to write the eulogy, and duly presented his script for inspection shortly before he was due to deliver it. It did not meet with her entire approval. Whilst the assembled mourners waited in the chapel of rest and the mortuary attendants became increasingly restive, Alma pencilled in her alterations. After more than an hour, during which Bruno Walter calmed the tense and oppressive atmosphere by playing Schubert on the mortuary piano, the Monsignor appeared 'in clerical garb, his revised script in hand, and took his post behind the lectern'.

It soon became apparent which part Alma had doctored. 'The Church', he intoned in the course of his peroration, 'recognizes three kinds of baptism: baptism by water, baptism in an emergency which can be performed by any practising Catholic when there is not time to call a priest, and finally baptism by desire [*Begierdetaufe*], which means that someone who in his last moments on this earth earnestly desires to be received into the Church can become a Christian by the mere force of his desire although no visible or audible rites are performed . . .'[24]

Nothing was going to persuade Alma that it was not better to die a Catholic than a Jew.

15 *And the Bridge Is Love*

'There is a land of living and a land of the dead, and the bridge is love.'
Thornton Wilder.

Alma made one final attempt to ensure her husband's entry into the Christian afterlife. The day after the funeral she drove to the cemetery with Father Moenius, and with special permission from the archbishop a blessing was bestowed on the 'remains of Franz Werfel, an unbaptized Jew'. Only then did she succumb to the enormity of her loss. 'Why am I still alive?' she wrote on 2 September 1945. 'A week ago I lost my sweet man-child. I still can't grasp it. I keep thinking that he must come home from Santa Barbara. But he will never come home . . .'[1]

Werfel's death left a chasm that could never be filled. To try and postpone the moment when the permanence of his absence would become a painful reality, Alma spent days and nights in her lost husband's room dictating *The Star of the Unborn* to Albrecht Joseph's successor and sleeping fitfully in his hospital bed. Late in October, when it was done, she went to New York, but found it a lonely, heartless place without her companion of the past thirty years. 'New York is changed without Franz,' she wrote. 'I must reconstruct my whole being, to be again what I was before his time.'[2]

A reminder of her more recent past came in the form of a letter of condolence from Kurt von Schuschnigg. 'I don't know what to say to you,' he wrote on 10 September, 'and it is better that I do not try and search too long for the right words, as I shall never be able to find them . . . I was absolutely shattered to hear the news of Franz Werfel's death . . . and had no idea that he was so seriously ill . . . How much he was able to give! Despite everything – wonderful, fortunate man!'[3]

Another moving revival of past times was provided by Josef Szigeti, who wrote on 28 October:

> We need not assure you how intensely we feel with you in your recent irreparable loss. Although I know that in these times you probably do not feel up to listening to music, in a crowd, still I want you to know that I will be playing the Alban Berg Concerto with Klemperer on December 13th and 14th and it would mean a great deal to me and also to Klemperer, to have you present at least at one of the final rehearsals.[4]

It was in December that Alma, lying ill in bed in her New York hotel room, heard on the radio that she was about to marry again – an announcement that caused a flurry of press speculation the following day. 'Two weeks before Franz Werfel died,' Hedda Hopper wrote in her Hollywood gossip column on 6 December, 'his great friend, Dr Bruno Walter, bought a house next door to him. Now Werfel's widow and Dr Walter will wed and occupy the house themselves.'

Jolted out of her mourning, Alma was enraged, though less at the tasteless insinuation that whilst she 'lay heartbroken over the death of Franz Werfel' she was already planning her fourth trip to the altar, then at the subject of the innuendo. Good friend and distinguished interpreter of Mahler's music he might be, but Alma's private view was that, as a mere conductor of other people's works, Walter was not qualified to tread in the footsteps of the creative men of genius with whom she had walked in the past. Nevertheless, the episode did much to boost her morale, and publicly she did no more than state that her friendship with Bruno Walter had been a 'purely intellectual one for over four decades'.

As for Walter, the episode did nothing to impair his sympathetic friendship. 'Who can understand better than I', he wrote at the end of April 1946, 'what a tragic change you have had to bear in your life? I can see you in front of me now, alone in the evenings in your room, bowed down by the weight of it all . . . only the knowledge that . . . Franz's lifegiving spirit is there and will always remain with you . . . can and must give you consolation.'[5]

Somewhat restored in mind and body, Alma decided she was able to face North Bedford Drive. Despite the ghostly presence of Werfel that haunted her day and night she remained in California until the autumn, whiling away the empty hours by starting to write her autobiography and, with the help of a secretary, putting her husband's papers into some sort of order. She began to feel her age. 'I'm getting old,' she grumbled later in the year:

> I'm to take it easy, not to walk too much, not to play the piano too long at a time . . . The job of arranging Werfel's writings . . . gives me a great deal of satisfaction. Of his manuscripts many are scribbled in pencil, some all but illegible. It is hard work, but it keeps me near him. Some day, unfortunately, even this fount will run dry . . . [6]

Another less rewarding activity, but one which occupied her until the day she died, was the matter of reclaiming money and property left behind in 1938. In the autumn of 1947, armed with a certificate of American citizenship awarded by a Los Angeles court on 14 June 1946, Alma returned to Vienna in an attempt to unravel her affairs. During the past two years she had besieged the authorities with impassioned pleas as to the justice of her case, which consisted in the main of accusations of fraud and deception against Carl Moll, his daughter and her husband. Moll in particular was charged with defrauding her of her paternal inheritance (50,000 Swiss francs) during Frau Moll's lifetime, and after her death taking it upon himself to sell *Sommernacht am Strand* by Edvard Munch for the paltry sum of 7,000 schillings to pay for the roof repairs at the Hohe Warte. On top of this he had, without permission, 'willed' three Schindler landscapes, loaned by Alma to the Modern Gallery for two years in 1937, to the same gallery for an indefinite period, and the Gallery now flatly refused to hand them over to their rightful owner.

As all three of the accused were unable to give an account of themselves – they had committed suicide two years before – it was left to Alma to try and convince the trio's many remaining friends in the Justice Department that she had a case to answer. She found it a wearing and depressing task. After an emergency landing in Newfoundland and a twenty-four-hour wait for another aeroplane, Alma broke her journey in London, where she saw Anna again, looking tired and drawn after the rigours of the war years. And, when she finally arrived in Vienna, 'worn out, with swollen feet', the sight of the ruins of the Opera, the Burgtheater and St Stephen's prepared her for the fate of the Hohe Warte: 'uninhabitable – the roof gone, the top floor collapsed, the interior in ashes, heating plant, water and electricity ruined, the marble panelling torn out, used for officers' bathrooms in the neighbouring villas . . .'[7] Both Mahler's and Werfel's desks had been burned to cinders, as had the manuscripts of all her songs. All that she managed to retrieve were two of Mahler's notebooks, and at the end of a fruitless month which had achieved nothing more than a promise from American Army headquarters to reimburse her for the price of her marble, Alma flew back to New York adamant that the matter was not yet at an end.

The spring of 1948 provided some welcome light relief with the publication in February of Thomas Mann's novel, *Doctor Faustus*. Criticism of the book had been by no means favourable – a long tract set in Germany between 1939 and 1945 taking as its theme the discord between genius and sanity was not quite, perhaps, what the general public wanted to read so soon after the war – and Mann was in a nettled frame of mind when Alma suggested that the central character, a musician who invented a twelve-tone theory and sold his soul to the devil to ensure its success, was obviously based on Schönberg. Alma described how:

> When I saw him again, I praised the beauty of the novel and discreetly remarked that it had surprised me to find Schönberg's theory so popularly and yet recognizably presented.

'So you recognized it?' Mann was slightly put out.
I said no musician could fail to recognize it.
'Do you think Schönberg will mind?' Mann asked, and I shrugged, not wanting to set off a general discussion.[8]

Schönberg, who suffered from a nervous eye complaint, had not read *Doctor Faustus*, but Alma hastened to alert him to the ambivalence of his position. Was it not possible, she asked, that the invention of the twelve-tone system might be attributed to Mann and not to himself? The very thought was enough to give Schönberg palpitations. To nip such a heresy once and for all in the bud he composed a mythical contribution to the *Encyclopaedia Americana* of 1988, supposedly written by an historian in the third millennium, confirming that 'the German writer Thomas Mann', who 'in his youth . . . urgently wanted to become a musician', was the inventor of the method of composing with twelve tones but, as he had given up composing himself, 'allowed Schönberg to use it and publish it under his own name'.

The whole affair was meat and drink to Alma, to whom it gave a fresh interest, as well as an opportunity to feel that, once again, she was influencing the decisions of great men. She was therefore delighted when, before sending his contribution to the *Encyclopaedia* to Mann, Schönberg read it aloud to her first. Shortly afterwards she went to see Mann and 'let it be known that Schönberg was furious'. Mann, however, professed himself baffled. Replying on 17 February he said that 'the curious document, a sign of the zealousness of Schönberg's followers, was gripping and comic at the same time. Anybody who had merely taken his book in his hand knew who had invented the twelve-tone technique, and Schönberg's historical importance would not be lessened by the novel. What was this document indeed, a letter or an article?'[9]

The business rumbled along for the next two years. Neither the insertion of a dedication 'to Arnold Schönberg, the real owner' nor an additional explanation in which Mann referred to 'a contemporary composer and theoretician' – both, Alma claimed, the result of her many telephone conversations with Mann's wife,

Katia – were enough to soothe Schönberg's ruffled feelings. In January 1949 he raised the matter again through the columns of the *Saturday Review of Literature*, reiterating his complaint that his 'cultural property had been purloined', that the central character in the novel was a portrait of himself and that the fictional composer's paralysis and mental instability was an insult to his factual counterpart, who had never suffered any form of mental disturbance.

Mann's reply, published in the same issue, pointed out that the central character could as well be modelled on Nietzsche as Schönberg, since Nietzsche had suffered from the same mental illness, or indeed upon Mann himself, as he had given his hero many of his own characteristics. 'Instead of accepting my book with a satisfied smile as a piece of contemporary literature that testifies to his tremendous influence upon the musical culture of the era,' he concluded, 'Schönberg regards it as an act of rape and insult. It is a sad spectacle to see a man of great worth . . . almost wilfully yield to delusions of persecution and of being robbed, and involve himself in rancorous bickering. It is my sincere hope that he may rise above bitterness and suspicion and that he may find peace in the assurance of his greatness and glory!'[10]

Part of Schönberg's sense of pique stemmed, as his biographer Harold Stuckenschmidt has pointed out, from Mann's having sought advice from his arch-enemy Dr Theodor Wiesengrund-Adorno, a self-professed expert on his own work whose elaborately structured formulations Schönberg felt obscured rather than threw light on his musical intentions. 'If Mann had only asked me,' he remarked to his pupil Dika Newlin, 'I'd have invented a special system for him to use!'[11]

The hatchet was finally buried in the new year of 1950. Yet another outburst from Schönberg (this time in the London magazine *New Survey*) drew a conciliatory response. 'You are attacking a bugbear of your imagination,' Mann wrote, 'so there is no desire for revenge . . . you will not succeed in making me your enemy.' Illness prevented Schönberg from replying at once to this olive branch, but as soon as he was able he wrote welcoming 'the hand that I believe . . . is the hand of peace'.[12]

Alma had long regretted her part in the affair. 'What I had wanted at all costs to prevent', she once wrote, 'was a complaint by Schönberg against Mann. Sadly Arnold Schönberg did not ask me whether he would be doing right by me when he mentioned my name in a newspaper polemic – just what I have always tried to avoid in life. I wanted nothing that was not for the best . . . and justice. That things now seem unfair and unjust is not my fault.'[13]

Ripples of the estrangement had penetrated deep into the far corners of the émigré world. 'What do you say about *Doctor Faustus?*' the painter W. E. Wiedermann wrote to Alma from Colombia. 'I'm longing to have some fun with you about it all. In any case, it's a most interesting book, although I found much of it superfluous and boring, and only the masterly linguistic control helped it over many unmemorable passages. Is that music or science? . . . What do you think? Naturally I can't speak for the musical side. – Here in Bogota everyone is arguing over this book.'[14]

Friendships with Wiedermann – whose talents Alma congratulated herself on spotting before anyone else, comparing him to Gauguin – with Erich Maria Remarque and Benjamin Britten helped fill the gap left by friends of longer standing. Alexander von Zemlinsky had died in New York in 1942, Gerhart Hauptmann, from whom she had been estranged since 1937 on account of his pro-Nazi sympathies, in 1946, and in May 1949 her 'beloved, admired, dreaded friend', Hans Pfitzner, died in Salzburg. 'Gradually, inexorably, my loves turn into grey shadows,'[15] she wrote in her diary. Walter Gropius had turned into an old friend – they still corresponded and met occasionally in New York – but her dead husbands reached out from the grave to haunt her, their shadows looming larger and larger as time passed. 'By now, Gustav Mahler's shadow has completely devoured his small human form, and it is growing still. Franz

Werfel's shadow has not yet reached such dimensions; but his is also growing fast. Their stately advance is an epic . . .'[16]

The advance of old age continued to give Alma little pleasure. She found some consolation in the celebrations for her sixty-ninth birthday, when, after receiving some 'thirty well-wishers before noon' and spending the afternoon drinking Benedictine with the Arlts, she returned home to find Bedford Drive lit up and sixty people gathered inside.

> A chamber orchestra played a birthday fugue composed of Mahler themes, followed by the Adagietto from his Fifth Symphony. Erich Korngold brought me the proofs of a violin sonata he had dedicated to me, and Thomas Mann brought his latest book, inscribed 'To Alma the personality, on her birthday, August 31, 1948, from her old friend and admirer'. It was an odd feeling, to be fêted on my own account after a lifetime of hiding behind my distinguished husbands![17]

On her seventieth birthday the following year she received a letter from Kokoschka:

> My dear Alma, You're still a wild thing, just as when you were first carried away by *Tristan and Isolde* and used a quill to scrawl your comments on Nietzsche in your diary, in the same flying, illegible hand that I can make out only because I know your rhythm. . . . We'll always be on the stage of life, we two, when disgusting banality, the trivial visage of the contemporary world, will yield to a passion-born splendour. . . . Take care of yourself, and spend your birthday without a hangover.[18]

A month later, in September 1949, Alma finished making fair copies of all Werfel's letters to her – a task she had begun five months before – and returned to her autobiography. In 1950 Anna, whose marriage to Anatole Fistoulari had broken up the year before, came to California to live, accompanied by their daughter Marina.

Although Alma wrote warmly in her memoirs of Anna's sculptural 'works of strength and beauty' and welcomed the new-found harmony between them, in reality she showed a minimal amount of interest. On her first visit to California after the war (she came for a month at the beginning of 1948) Anna was surprised to find that none of her mother's friends had any idea that her daughter was a sculptor, still less that she had won the coveted Prix de Rome at the World Exhibition in Paris in 1937 (an attitude reinforced by letter after letter Alma received from old friends during the war, asking repeatedly what had become of Anna).

Nevertheless it was with Anna that Alma drove to Schönberg's death-bed in July 1951 (he died on Friday the 13th), where Anna sculpted his death mask, and photographs of Anna's heads of Werfel and Schönberg were kept in her sitting-room. It was Anna, too, who persuaded her to play a few bars of 'Der Erkennende' for the short film Albrecht Joseph made of her in 1956, and to Anna that she turned in the last years of her life for reassurance and support.

Alma never lost her craving for love and attention. 'She wanted to be adored, she expected to be loved by everyone and to give nothing but her smile or kisses which she distributed lavishly,' Albrecht Joseph commented. 'Love was due her as a natural tribute and when it was not forthcoming she got angry, spiteful, depressed.'[19] Joseph and Alma, however, had always regarded each other with a certain amount of mutual suspicion. In Alma's eyes not only was Joseph not creative enough to warrant much interest, he was also Jewish, and she strongly disapproved of his burgeoning friendship with Anna on both counts.

Despite these misgivings Alma's more endearing qualities were not lost on her future son-in-law. Like many of her more devoted admirers Joseph appreciated her vitality, her 'strong but quirky mind', her generosity with food and drink: 'Although she ate very little herself she appreciated good food, and she fed me royally in times when I could not have dreamed of going at my own expense to the luxurious restaurants where she was a well known, welcome, guest.' He respected her gifts as a pianist and what he could only describe as the 'infectious, corybantic, tornado-like force of her spiritual excitation' when whirled onto a higher plane by an exceptional musical performance.

One such performance had been in July 1948, when Eugene Ormandy conducted Mahler's Eighth Symphony in the Hollywood Bowl in front of an audience of twenty thousand. Alma went to every rehearsal and 'frankly gave my opinion whenever Ormandy asked for it'. The result convinced her, if she had ever needed convincing, how right she had been to throw in her lot with Mahler 'at a time when people thought of him as just a conductor and opera director and would not believe in his creative genius'.[20]

Her appearance altered little. Well into her seventies her skin remained clear and smooth, her shape concealed behind the fold of her habitual black dress, a string of pearls round her neck, her hair piled on top of her head. Dika Newlin's first impression, on meeting her with Franz Werfel at a performance of her own setting of some of Werfel's poems for voice and piano at UCLA in 1941, was that she was 'very different from what you might expect to see; quite excessively plump, with frizzly [sic] hair whose blondness seems to owe quite a bit to the beauty-shop. In fact, when she first came into the concert-room to sit down beside me, I thought, "Why, she looks like an ex-Follies queen!" But a few minutes of conversation with her utterly destroyed that impression; she is a charming person, and must have been lovely to look at in earlier years . . .'[21]

In 1952 Alma sold her house on North Bedford Drive and moved to New York, and for the first time since Franz Werfel's death, entered into a 'new, rich life'. Her book-lined rooms on the third floor of her old house on East 73rd Street were crammed with mementoes of the past: Kokoschka's portrait, his six remaining fans, The Colts of Tre Croci and, in response to a press campaign calling for 'an end to judicial scandal', her father's landscapes.

When the condition of her heart allowed – her regular consumption of Benedictine had led to an inevitable deterioration of her arteries – she travelled, to Paris once and to Rome twice. She never returned to Vienna. 'My beloved Almschi!' Helene Berg wrote in the summer of 1956:

> Is there something wrong with your heart again? I am so very sorry that your European journey is not to be and I worry about

your health. Did the doctor forbid you to come? Or were you anxious about the long flight? I had been so looking forward to seeing you again! I am as lonely as you are, in spite of the people who come to see me – it is now another world from the days when I was 'at home'; I live as you do, with my loves, that I can only carry in my heart.[22]

The flames of conquest had not yet, however, been quite extinguished. On her seventy-fifth birthday Alma received a tribute from Franz Csokor: 'The number of this birthday is unimportant, for the lady who celebrates it has long ago conquered time through her unquenchable appetite for life. . . . Peter Altenberg, the Verlaine of Vienna, once wrote of a feminine type which he called the 'Hero's Muse'; meaning the kind of woman who, through her camaraderie, understands and demands from her chosen man the ultimate in artistic performance. That was and is *Alma Maria Mahler-Werfel* . . .'[23] And, on her last return voyage from Rome, Alma was sitting alone on deck, reading, when 'a tall, Apollonian figure of a man' stood before her and introduced himself as Thornton Wilder. 'Great men somehow continued to cross my path,' wrote Alma with some satisfaction.[24]

The publication of *And the Bridge Is Love* in the summer of 1958 turned Alma into a figure of legend. Speculation as to the number of her extramarital affairs and the extent of her influence on the artistic development of her husbands occupied the minds of all who read it. Unacquainted with Peter Altenberg and the myth of the Hero's Muse, the general public latched eagerly onto a good story. 'To be sure,' wrote *Le Soir*, which had acquired the rights to the German edition that enjoyed a furtive success under brown covers, 'we have lacked information about what goes on, from an intellectual point of view, in German-speaking countries . . . therefore it comes as no surprise that *My Life*, by Alma Mahler-Werfel, has been one of the best-sellers of the winter season.'

Walter Gropius was less enthusiastic, distressed at Alma's descriptions of their battle for custody of Manon. 'Dear Alma,' he wrote on 17 August 1958. 'The love-story that you attribute to my name is not ours. You should have been prevented from revealing the content of our experiences with Mutzi, and this literary exposure has harmed the flowering of my own memories. The rest is silence.'[25]

Alma replied on 20 August that she had been very ill for a year and could, unfortunately, not supervise the final version of the book as thoroughly as she had wished. 'So the adaptor, Ashton, had a free hand!' But, she added, she had expressed the wish that the publisher should check *everything* before publication. After all, the book was not a novel.[26]

The book needed a considerable amount of pruning. The original manuscript, copies of which Alma circulated amongst her friends, was too outspoken for many of them and she was advised, particularly by Professor Arlt of UCLA, to tone it down. It would have taken a daring publisher to unleash the unadulterated script, for Alma, who merely believed that she was telling the truth, had not watered down her views on Jews and Jewishness, neither had she spared her husbands or lovers from caustic references to their sexual habits. But, for all that, the final version remains very much a part of Alma. Its very inconsistencies have the ring of truth, its evasions and omissions tell one as much about its author as the actual content. It is, after all, an autobiography, not a biography, and its author is entitled to present herself as she wishes you to see her – not, perhaps, as she really was, but as she would like to have been. In this, she succeeded. From it Alma emerges, in her own eyes, as a figure of power and allure, with tenacity and a big heart. She portrayed herself as a devoted wife and mother, who put aside her own talents in the interests of others. She was friend and mentor to many great men. In her own words: 'My life was beautiful. God gave me to know the works of genius in our time before they left the hands of their creators. And if for a while I was able to hold the stirrups of these horsemen of light, my being has been justified and blessed.'

On 31 August 1958 Alma celebrated her eightieth birthday with Anna over lunch at the Hotel St Moritz. Anna found her confused (who, Alma asked her, had won the war?), although she had managed to correspond with Benjamin Britten a few months before, accepting with pleasure his offer to dedicate to her his 'new Nocturne for Tenor and small orchestra. . . . a setting of eight songs about sleep and dreams . . . one, I really think, of my best and most personal works'.

It was an apposite dedication, for, gradually, Alma's sense of reality began to fade and she slipped into the arms of the past. Looked after by Sister Ida, who had come from Vienna to be with her old mistress, she battled with her heart and her lungs. Day after day she telephoned Anna in Los Angeles: 'Now I am here again where my lovely father painted his pictures.'[27]

The prospect of death worried her. A month before she died she was visited by an American friend of long standing, Suma Morgenstern.

> The shadow of death was already upon her. As she seemed to be easily exhausted, I rose to take my leave. She begged me to stay. After a short time she said: 'I want to ask you something. You must answer me. Without evasion. You are younger than I am, but you are a man, and you have been in a war . . . Did you ever, when you were a soldier, have a fear of death?' I told her, 'As a soldier one has the fear of any creature faced with the prospect of dying. One must just overcome it. But when one is young, when one does not know what one is losing, it is not the same.' 'But now,' she insisted. 'How is it now? Do you think often about death? Are you afraid?' 'Yes,' I said, 'I think often about death, and have done for some time. And I can remember very well when it began. I once read a little story that I found particularly shocking on the subject of death.
>
> 'A mystical thinker, his name was Sussja von Anopol . . . his great friend Martin Buber compared him with St Francis of Assisi – said shortly before his death to his disciples . . . 'When I arrive in the next world, will someone there ask: Sussja, why have you not become Moses? . . .' No one will ever ask you such a thing. You, Alma, are what you have always been, Alma Mahler.'
>
> After a short silence . . . came the reply. 'You call that a little story? I call that a great story. Come again soon. The story has done me the world of good. Come soon and tell me the story once again.' Having restored her peace of mind, I left, feeling wretched. I had a premonition it would be the last parting. The time for grief was very near.[28]

Alma Mahler died on Friday, 11 December 1964, in her eighty-sixth year. The funeral service was held at five o'clock in the afternoon on Sunday, 13 December, in the Frank E. Campbell Funeral Church, 81st Street and Madison Avenue. At her own request, she was later buried beside Manon at Grinzing. 'Only five years ago,' wrote the *New York Journal*, 'Mrs Werfel lamented the lack of contemporary genius: "It is not as it used to be." '

Afterword

Alma would have approved of her obituaries. The *New York Times* wrote that she was once described as the most beautiful girl in Vienna; the London *Times* that she had been at the centre of a 'peculiarly rich cultural epoch which, with her death, may be thought to be virtually closed'; and Willy Haas, in *Die Welt*, wrote that she was an 'inspirational woman, who felt deeply for the friends within her circle, and this had nothing to do with eroticism in its literal sense. Her intimate knowledge of so many distinguished men enhanced her in stature and self-knowledge to an extent beyond our understanding.'

Willy Haas touched on an important point. Alma was fond of the words 'erotic' and 'unerotic', which she used frequently to describe men she found worthy or unworthy of her attentions. No man, in Alma's eyes, could be 'erotic' without outstanding creative talent. To be dubbed 'unerotic', therefore, did not mean that the man in question was passionless, merely that he belonged to another caste of human being. He was, quite simply, of no interest at all.

One of the questions most raised in any discussion of Alma Mahler has been whether or not sex was important to her. Another was how she managed to reconcile her (albeit patchy) adherence to the Catholic Church with her patent disregard for its teachings.

The answers to both are inextricably entwined. Alma despised conventional morality: her early introduction to Nietzsche had fuelled her belief in herself as a creature set apart from the common run by birth and talent. All that she did, therefore, was justifiable on those grounds. She needed to conquer earthly gods to establish her *raison d'être*: the heavenly one could wait. In any case, as Friedrich Torberg once observed, Alma's Catholicism was more for show than anything else, and Alma herself admitted to him that she was something of a heathen.[2]

Albrecht Joseph also spoke of Alma's 'heathenish innocence: whatever she did, said, wrote, was alright because it was she who did it. Ordinary mortals have no such licence.'[3] Judged by today's moral standards, however, Alma had comparatively few sexual liaisons – and modern methods of birth control would doubtless have prevented her need for abortion. And, except for Walter Gropius, to whom she was drawn at a time when she felt particularly neglected by Mahler, none of Alma's affairs of the heart were motivated by purely physical attraction. She once told Mahler that all she loved in a man was his achievement, and if she should meet a man with a greater talent than his own she would 'have to love him'.[4]

It was this passion for intellectual communion with creative supermen that was Alma's ultimate aphrodisiac. To be loved by such men, and to have them in her emotional thrall, was a stimulant without compare. As for her own compositional talents, left undirected they withered. During Mahler's lifetime Alma constantly railed against the loss of her freedom to compose, but his death did not release her. Alma lost her youth with her first husband, and with it her craving for approval from a father-figure. Her burgeoning talent could only flourish with the help and encouragement of a male mentor: when these were withdrawn Alma's will to create weakened and died.

There is one other puzzling question. How, particularly during the Second World War when her provocative brand of anti-Semitism was at its most trying, did Alma manage to stay on good terms with her Jewish friends? The explanation is a simple one. Alma had been at the heart of Viennese social life for over forty years. Those who could not stomach her tactlessness (she once told Franz Werfel, whom she adored, that he could never write pure German because he was a Jew!)[5] had long since distanced themselves. Those who continued to be fond of her – and there were very many – tolerated her barbed remarks as familiar aberrations. There was, after all, some justice in Alma's own views on the matter. She had been married to Mahler, she was married to Franz Werfel and she had expressed disgust and contempt for her stepfather's Nazi sympathies. She was, she felt, entitled to her prejudices.

After Alma and Werfel had arrived in America Friedrich Torberg, a fellow exile, sent Alma a list of her 'inconsistent qualities', addressed to 'His New Friend, to be taken with a grain of salt'. On the positive side he found her 'Pretty; Clever; Lively and temperamental; Extremely observant; Naturally witty; Astonishingly instinctive; Interested in everybody; Bohemian and Eternally Young.'

On the negative side he listed: 'Affected; Critical; Unbearable jokes at the expense of the Jews; Arrogance; Over-hasty judgement; Inability to adapt to circumstances.'[6]

The very last word, therefore, can be left to Torberg. 'Alma Mahler-Werfel was a great personality and a great woman. Alma Mahler-Werfel was the last of her kind.'[7]

Source Notes

For the sake of convenience I have shortened the titles of Alma Mahler-Werfel's published works to the following: *And the Bridge Is Love* (Hutchinson, 1959) to *Bridge; Gustav Mahler, Memories and Letters* (3rd ed., John Murray, 1973) to *Memories*. Alma's handwritten diary is cited as *MS diary*; her typewritten entries as *MS typescript*; the typescript memoir of Alma Mahler by Albrecht Joseph (in possession of the author) as *Joseph Memoir*. Unless otherwise stated, all translations from German into English are by the author.

Introduction

1 Diary of Franz Werfel, quoted in *Bridge*, p. 102.
2 Franz Theodor Csokor, 'Die Heldenreizerin', an eulogy in honour of Alma's seventy-fifth birthday, Van Pelt Library.
3 Graphologist's report in possession of the author.
4 Friedrich Torberg, 'Ein Denkmal ihrer selbst', article in *Die Münchner Zeitung*, December 1964.

Chapter 1

1 *Bridge*, p. 12.
2 Heinrich Fuchs, *Emil Jakob Schindler* (Vienna, Selbst Verlag, 1970), p. 16.
3 ibid., p. 17.
4 *Bridge*, p. 12.
5 Fuchs, p. 15.
6 ibid., p. 19.
7 ibid.

8 ibid., p. 20.
9 ibid., p. 22.
10 ibid., p. 23.
11 Carl Moll, *Memory of Plankenberg*, Van Pelt Library.
12 Fuchs, p. 34.
13 *Bridge*, p. 12.
14 ibid., p. 13.
15 ibid.
16 ibid., p. 14.

Chapter 2

1 Robert Musil, *The Man Without Qualities* (Picador, 1979), vol. I, p. 3.
2 Frank Field, *The Last Days of Mankind, Karl Kraus and His Vienna* (London and Mystic, Conn., 1967), p. 24.
3 C. E. Williams, *The Broken Eagle* (Paul Elek, 1974), p. 157.
4 Franz Werfel, 'Glosse zu einer Wedekind-Feier', *Prager Tagblatt*, 18 April 1914, quoted in Williams p. 65.
5 Ilsa Barea, *Vienna, Legend and Reality* (London and New York, 1966), p. 165.
6 *Bridge*, p. 12.
7 ibid., p. 15.
8 ibid.
9 Bertha Zuckerkandl, *Österreich intim* (Frankfurt/M, 1970), p. 45.
10 *Bridge*, p. 16.
11 ibid.
12 ibid.
13 Stefan Zweig, *The World of Yesterday* (Cassell, 1943), p. 64.
14 Allan Janik and Stephen Toulmin (ed.), *Wittgenstein's Vienna* (Simon & Schuster, 1973), p. 64.
15 H. G. Schenk, *The Mind of the European Romantics* (OUP, 1979), p. 154.
16 *Bridge*, p. 17.

Chapter 3

1 *MS diary* 1898, Van Pelt Library.
2 Carl Schorske, *Fin-de-Siècle Vienna* (Weidenfeld & Nicolson, 1980, p. 212.
3 Robert Musil, *The Man Without Qualities* (Picador, 1979, vol. I, p. 58.
4 *Bridge*, p. 17.
5 Schorske, p. 209.

6 H. G. Schenk, *The Mind of the European Romantics* (OUP, 1943), p. 61.
7–14 *MS diary.*
15 *Neue Wiener Tagblatt*, 24 January, 1943.
16–20 *MS diary.*
21 Typescript letter from Klimt to Carl Moll in possession of the author.
22–25 *MS diary.*

Chapter 4

1–4 *MS diary.*
5 Quoted in Henri Louis de la Grange, *Mahler*, vol. I. (Gollancz, 1974), p. 550.
6 Zemlinsky to Alma Schindler, undated, Van Pelt Library.
7–9 *MS diary.*
10 Zemlinsky to Alma Schindler, undated, Van Pelt Library.
11–14 *MS diary.*
14 Zemlinksy to Alma Schindler, undated, Van Pelt Library.
15 Horst Weber, *Alexander Zemlinksy* (Vienna, Verlag Elisabeth Lafite, 1977), p. 13.
16 Quoted in H. H. Stuckenschmidt, *Arnold Schoenberg, His Life, World and Work* (Calder, 1977), p. 38.
17 *Bridge*, p. 18.
18 *MS diary.*
19–25 Zemlinsky to Alma Schindler, undated, Van Pelt Library.
26 *MS diary.*
27 ibid.
28 This version of the first meeting between Alma Schindler and Gustav Mahler is taken from Bertha Zuckerkandl, *Österreich intim* (Frankfurt/M, Verlag Ullstein, 1970), pp. 42–3.
29 ibid., p. 43.
30 *Memories*, pp. 4–5.
31 ibid., p. 5.
32 *MS diary.*
33 ibid.

Chapter 5

1 Natalie Bauer-Lechner, *Recollections of Gustav Mahler* (Faber & Faber, 1980), pp. 83–4.
2 Kurt Blaukopf, *Gustav Mahler* (Allen Lane, 1973), p. 129.
3 ibid., p. 17.
4 Bauer-Lechner, p. 38.
5 *Memories*, p. 7.

6 Blaukopf, p. 220.
7 Deryck Cooke, *Gustav Mahler, An Introduction to His Music* (Faber & Faber, 1980), p. 9.
8 Blaukopf, p. 32.
9 Bauer-Lechner, p. 23.
10 Part of a letter from Mahler to Josef Steiner, dated 17 June 1879, printed in Knud Martner (ed.), *Selected Letters of Gustav Mahler* (Faber & Faber, 1979), p. 54.
11 *Programme of the Second Symphony*, by Gustav Mahler, reproduced in *Memories*, p. 213.
12 *Memories*, p. 3.
13 Blaukopf, p. 54.
14 Edward R. Reilly, *Gustav Mahler and Guido Adler: Records of a Friendship* (Cambridge University Press, 1982), p. 20.
15 Blaukopf, p. 82.
16 ibid., p. 83.
17 Reilly, p. 23.
18 Bruno Walter, *Theme and Variations* (Hamish Hamilton, 1947), p. 173.
19 Bertha Zuckerkandl, *Österreich intim* (Frankfurt/M, Verlag Ullstein, 1970), p. 40.
20 *Memories*, p. 15.
21 ibid., p. 16.
22 *MS diary*, quoted word for word in *Memories*, p. 18, except that there the words 'elderly degenerate' are used in place of 'dirty Jew'.
23 Martner (ed.), p. 81.
24 Blaukopf, p. 74.
25 ibid., p. 74.
26 ibid., pp. 117–18.
27 Martner (ed.), p. 191.
28–31 *Memories*, pp. 18–20.
32–40 *MS diary* 1901.
41 *Memories*, p. 208.
42 Part of a letter reproduced in Henri Louis de la Grange, *Mahler*, vol. I (Gollancz, 1974), pp. 684–90.
43–47 *MS diary*.

Chapter 6

1 *Memories*, p. 23.
2 ibid.
3 Henri Louis de la Grange, *Mahler*, vol. I. (Gollancz, 1974), p. 697.
4 *Memories*, p. 27.
5 ibid., p. 43.
6 *Memories*, p. 29.
7 *MS diary* 1902.

8 *Memories*, p. 43.

9 ibid., pp. 27–8.

10 ibid., p. 221.

11 ibid., p. 33.

12 ibid., p. 34.

13 ibid., p. 36.

14 Natalie Bauer-Lechner, *Recollections of Gustav Mahler* (Faber & Faber, 1980), p. 63.

15–16 *Memories*, pp. 41–2.

17 Bauer-Lechner, p. 56.

18 ibid., p. 152.

19–20 La Grange, pp. 625–6.

21 *Memories*, p. 47.

22 ibid., p. 46.

23–24 *MS typescript* 1902.

25 *Memories*, p. 25.

26–27 *MS typescript* 1902.

28 *Memories*, p. 229.

29 ibid., p. 61.

30 ibid., p. 58.

31 *MS typescript* 1903.

32 Letter from Pfitzner to Alma, 12 March 1903, Van Pelt Library.

33 Pfitzner to Alma, June 1903, Van Pelt Library.

34 *Memories*, p. 60.

35 Berndt W. Wessling, *Ein prophetisches Leben* (Hamburg, Hoffman & Campe, 1974), pp. 292–3.

36 *Memories*, p. 62.

37 *MS typescript* 1904.

38 *Memories*, p. 68.

39 Knud Martner (ed.), *Selected Letters of Gustav Mahler* (Faber & Faber, 1979), p. 278.

40–43 *Memories*, p. 236.

44 ibid., p. 240.

45 ibid., p. 70.

46 Translation taken from Deryck Cooke, *Gustav Mahler, An Introduction to His Music* (Faber & Faber, 1980), p. 79.

47 *Memories*, p. 70.

48 ibid., p. 53.

49 Alfred Roller, 'Theater und Kunst', *Neues Wiener Tagblatt*, 5 October 1934, quoted in Peter Vergo, *Art in Vienna* (Phaidon, 1975), p. 158.

50 Alfred Roller, *Max Mell* (Vienna, 1922), quoted in Vergo, p. 156.

51 Kurt Blaukopf, *Gustav Mahler* (Allen Lane, 1973), p. 170.

52 *Memories*, p. 72.

53 ibid., p. 244.

54 ibid., p. 252.

55 H. H. Stuckenschmidt, *Arnold Schoenberg, His Life, World and Work* (Calder, 1977), p. 103.

56 Bruno Walter, *Theme and Variations* (Hamish Hamilton, 1947), p.186.
57 Bruno Walter, *Gustav Mahler* (Kegan Paul, Trench, Trubner, 1937), p. 50.
58 *Memories*, p. 81.
59 ibid., p. 261.
60 Letter from Erica Conrat-Tietze to her mother, Ilsa Conrat, August 1904, Van Pelt Library.
61 ibid.
62 *Memories*, p. 102.
63 ibid., p. 306.
64 Translation taken from Cooke, p. 102.
65 *Memories*, p. 103.
66 Edward R. Reilly, *Gustav Mahler and Guido Adler* (Cambridge University Press, 1982), p. 29.
67 *Memories*, p. 64.
68 ibid., p. 119.
69 Reilly, p. 35.
70 *Memories*, pp. 289–90.
71 Blaukopf, p. 215.
72 Walter, *Theme and Variations*, p. 194.
73 Martner (ed.), p. 31.
74–76 *Memories*, pp. 121–2.

Chapter 7

1 *Memories*, p. 123.
2 Kurt Blaukopf, *Gustav Mahler* (Allen Lane, 1973), p. 218.
3 Bruno Walter, *Theme and Variations* (Hamish Hamilton, 1947), p. 195.
4 *Bridge*, p. 38.
5 Blaukopf, p. 220.
6 *Memories*, p. 127.
7 *MS typescript*.
8 *Memories*, p. 130.
9 Knud Martner (ed.), *Selected Letters of Gustav Mahler* (Faber & Faber, 1979), p. 316.
10 *Memories*, p. 134.
11 Martner (ed.), p. 318.
12 ibid., p. 316.
13 ibid., p. 319.
14 ibid., p. 321.
15 *Memories*, p. 142.
16 The last lines of *Das Lied von der Erde*, translated by Deryck Cooke in *Gustav Mahler, An Introduction to His Music* (Faber & Faber, 1980), p. 113.

17 Martner (ed.), p. 326.
18 Quoted in *Memories*, p. 142.
19 *Memories*, p. 143.
20 ibid., p. 306.
21 Blaukopf, p. 225.
22 Martner (ed.), p. 346.
23 *Memories*, p. 148.
24 See chapter 9, p. 193.
25 Martner (ed.), p. 333.
26 ibid., p. 339.
27–32 *Memories*, pp. 332, 154, 323, 169–170, 171.
33 *Bridge*, p. 52.
34 Reproduced in Reginald Isaacs, *Walter Gropius, Der Mensch und sein Werk*, vol. I (Berlin, Gebr. Mann Verlag, 1983), p. 97.
35 *Bridge*, p. 52.
36 *Memories*, p. 330.
37 ibid.
38 Martner (ed.), p. 359.
39 *MS typescript*.
40 *Memories*, p. 173.
41–42 *Bridge*, p. 53.
43 Alma to Gropius, quoted in Isaacs, p. 99.
44 Gropius to Alma, ibid., p. 99.
45–48 *Bridge*, pp. 53–4.
49 Isaacs, p. 100.
50 *Bridge*, p. 54.
51 Freud to Theodor Reik, quoted in Ronald W. Clark, *Freud, the Man and the Cause* (Jonathan Cape and Weidenfeld & Nicolson, 1980), p. 194.
52 *Bridge*, p. 54.
53 *Memories*, p. 176.
54 ibid., p. 178.
55 Isaacs, p. 102.
56 *Memories*, p. 335.
57 ibid., p. 338.
58 ibid., p. 178.
59 Peter Heyworth, *Otto Klemperer, His Life and Times*, vol. I, *1885–1933* (Cambridge University Press, 1983), 48.
60 *Memories*, p. 181.
61 Bruno Walter, *Theme and Variations* (Hamish Hamilton, 1947), p. 206.
62 Blaukopf, p. 232.
63 *Memories*, p. 182.
64–67 Isaacs, pp. 103–4.
68–70 *Memories*, pp. 186–8.
71 Martner (ed.), p. 370.
72 Isaacs, p. 105.

73 Told to Anna Mahler by her mother.
74 *Memories*, p. 191.
75 Isaacs, p. 110.
76 *Memories*, p. 199.

Chapter 8

1 *Bridge*, p. 66.
2–4 Reginald Isaacs, *Walter Gropius*, vol. I (Berlin, Gebr. Mann Verlag, 1983), pp. 112–113.
5–7 *Bridge*, pp. 67–8.
8 Arthur Koestler, *The Case of the Midwife Toad* (Hutchinson, 1971), p. 19.
9 *Bridge*, p. 70.
10–12 Paul Kammerer to Alma, 31 October 1911, Van Pelt Library.
13 Kammerer to Alma, 2 November 1911, Van Pelt Library.
14 *Bridge*, p. 70.
15 ibid.
16 Kammerer to Alma, undated, Van Pelt Library.
17 Kammerer to Alma, undated (Vienna, Friday), Van Pelt Library.
18 Isaacs, pp. 114–15.
19 *Bridge*, p. 71.

Chapter 9

1 Peter Vergo, *Art in Vienna* (Phaidon, 1975), p. 199.
2 Robert Musil, *The Man Without Qualities* (Picador, 1979), vol. I, p. 338.
3 Carl Schorske, *Fin-de-Siècle Vienna* (Weidenfeld & Nicolson, 1980), p. 334.
4 Oskar Kokoschka, *My Life*, trans. David Britt (Thames & Hudson, 1974), p. 29. (Henceforward *My Life*.)
5 Vergo, p. 172.
6 *My Life*, p. 35.
7 Paul Raabe (ed.) *The Era of German Expressionism*, trans. J. M. Ritchie (Calder & Boyars, 1974), p. 357.
8 *My Life*, p. 60.
9 Kokoschka to Frau Lotte Franzos, 24 December 1910.
10 *My Life*, p. 72.
11 *Bridge*, p. 71.
12 *My Life*, p. 73.
13 *Bridge*, p. 71.
14 *My Life*, p. 73.
15 *Bridge*, p. 72.

16 *My Life*, p. 27.
17 Kokoschka to Alma, 15 April 1912, Van Pelt Library.
18–20 *Bridge*, pp. 73–4.
21 *My Life*, p. 73.
22 *Bridge*, p. 74.
23 ibid.
24 Letters dated 5 May and 8 May 1912, Van Pelt Library.
25 *Bridge*, p. 73.
26 Letter dated 25 July 1912, Van Pelt Library.
27 *Bridge*, p. 75.
28 ibid.
29 Letter dated 3 January 1913, Van Pelt Library.
30 *Bridge*, p. 75.
31 Letters dated April, Van Pelt Library.
32 *My Life*, p. 79.
33 *Bridge*, pp. 76–7.
34 Kokoschka to Alma, 13 November 1913, Van Pelt Library.
35 Kokoschka to Alma, November, 1913, Van Pelt Library.
36 *My Life*, p. 76.
37 *Bridge*, p. 77.
38 *My Life*, p. 77.
39 Reginald Isaacs, *Walter Gropius*, vol. I (Berlin, Gebr, Mann Verlag, 1983), p. 115.
40 Kokoschka to Alma, July 1914, Van Pelt Library.
41 Kokoschka to Alma, undated, Van Pelt Library.
42 *My Life*, p. 84.
43 ibid., p. 85.
44 Kokoschka to Alma, 8 January 1915, Van Pelt Library.
45 *My Life*, p. 85.
46 Kokoschka to Alma, January 1915, Van Pelt Library.
47 *My Life*, p. 74.
48 ibid., p. 96.
49 Musil, p. 338.
50 *My Life*, p. 97.
51 Kokoschka to Ehrenstein, quoted in *Oskar Kokoschka 1886–1980* (Tate Gallery, 1986), p. 304.
52 *My Life*, p. 74.
53 Kokoschka to Hermine Moos, quoted in *Oskar Kokoschka 1886–1980*, p. 304.
54 *My Life*, p. 118.

Chapter 10

1 Stefan Zweig, *The World of Yesterday* (Cassell, 1943), p. 173.
2 Quoted in Mosco Garner, *Alban Berg* (Duckworth, 1975), p. 40.

3 Reginald Isaacs, *Walter Gropius*, vol. I (Berlin, Gebr. Mann Verlag, 1983), p. 140.
4 *MS typescript.*
5 *Bridge*, p. 83.
6 *MS typescript.*
7 *Bridge*, p. 80.
8 *MS typescript.*
9 Juliane Brand, Christopher Hailey and Donald Harris (ed.), *The Berg-Schoenberg Correspondence* (Macmillan, 1987), p. 228.
10 ibid., p. 230.
11 *MS typescript.*
12 Brand, Hailey, Harris (ed.), p. 238.
13 ibid., p. 241.
14 ibid., 243.
15 *MS typescript.*
16 Isaacs, p. 142.
17 ibid., p. 143.
18 ibid., p. 146.
19 *MS typescript.*
20 *Bridge*, p. 85.
21 Isaacs, p. 157.
22 *MS typescript.*
23 Isaacs, p. 168.
24 *Bridge*, p. 87.
25 *MS typescript.*
26 *Bridge*, p. 89.
27 Max Brod, 'The Young Werfel and the Prague Writers', in Paul Raabe (ed.), *The Era of German Expressionism*, trans. J. M. Ritchie (Calder & Boyars, 1974), p. 53.
28 ibid., p. 54.
29 C. E. Williams, *The Broken Eagle* (Paul Elek, 1974), p. 60.
30 Raabe (ed.), p. 56.
31 ibid., p. 57.
32 ibid.
33 ibid., p. 58.
34 *Bridge*, p. 92.
35 Isaacs, p. 176.
36 *Bridge*, p. 93.
37 ibid., p. 94.
38 ibid., p. 95.
39 ibid., p. 98.
40 Diary of Franz Werfel, quoted in *Bridge*, p. 102.
41 *Bridge*, p. 118.
42 Isaacs, p. 182.
43 *Bridge*, p. 115.
44 ibid., p. 119.
45 ibid.

46 ibid., p. 121.
47 ibid., p. 124.
48 ibid., p. 126.
49 ibid. p. 127.
50 ibid., p.136.

Chapter 11

1 Werfel to Alma, February 1918, Van Pelt Library.
2 Werfel to Alma, Zurich, 1939, Van Pelt Library.
3 *Joseph Memoir*.
4 ibid.
5 Werfel to Alma, September 1919, Van Pelt Library.
6 *Bridge*, p. 131.
7 ibid., p. 146.
8 *Joseph Memoir*; reiterated to author.
9 *Bridge*, p. 131.
10 ibid., p. 133.
11 ibid., p. 138.
12 H. H. Stuckenschmidt, *Arnold Schoenberg, His Life, World and Work* (Calder, 1977), p. 265.
13 *Bridge*, p. 141.
14 *Bridge*, p. 147. (Anna Mahler added the story about Ravel's dyed moustache.)
15 *Bridge*, pp. 148–9.
16 Werfel to Alma, undated, Van Pelt Library.
17 *Bridge*, p. 152.
18 *Bridge*, p. 154.
19 *MS typscript*.
20 ibid.
21 Werfel to Alma, 19 July 1924, Van Pelt Library.
22 *MS typescript*.
23 *Bridge*, p. 157.
24 *MS typescript*.
25 Mosco Garner, *Alban Berg* (Duckworth, 1975), p. 35.
26 Susanne Everett, *Lost Berlin* (Bison Books, 1979), p. 123.
27 *Bridge*, p. 170.
28 ibid., p. 64.
29 *MS typescript*.
30 Robert Musil, *The Man Without Qualities* (Picador, 1979), vol. I, p. 119.
31 *Bridge*, pp. 194–5.
32 ibid., p. 183.
33 Olga Schnitzler to Alma, July 1928, Van Pelt Library.
34 *Bridge*, p. 180.

Chapter 12

1 *MS typescript.*
2 *Bridge*, pp. 196–7.
3 Susanne Everett, *Lost Berlin* (Bison Books, 1979), p. 133.
4 *Bridge*, p. 197.
5 *Joseph Memoir.*
6 ibid.
7 *Bridge*, p. 199.
8 ibid.
9 *MS typescript.*
10 *Joseph Memoir.*
11 In conversation with the author.
12 *Bridge*, p. 201.
13 Stefan Zweig, *The World of Yesterday* (Cassell, 1943), p. 288.
14 *Bridge*, p. 203.
15 Anecdote told to the author by Anna Mahler and Albrecht Joseph.
16–22 *Bridge*, pp. 204–10.
23 Hollnsteiner Funeral Oration, Van Pelt Library.
24 Carl Zuckmayer to Franz Werfel, 28 April 1935, Van Pelt Library.
25 Garner, p. 136.
26 *Bridge*, p. 212.
27 *Joseph Memoir.*
28 *Bridge*, p. 213.
29 ibid., p. 214.

Chapter 13

1 *Bridge*, p. 217.
2 ibid., p. 218.
3 Werfel to Alma, 26 February 1938, Van Pelt Library.
4 *Bridge*, p. 219.
5 Stefan Zweig, *The World of Yesterday* (Cassell, 1943), p. 303.
6 Bertha Zuckerkandl to Alma, 5 March 1938, Van Pelt Library.
7 *Bridge*, p. 222.
8 Zweig, p. 307.
9 *MS typescript.*
10 Theodor Csokor to Alma, March 1938, Van Pelt Library.
11 Carl Zuckmayer to Alma, August 1938, Van Pelt Library.
12–16 *MS typescript.*
17 *Bridge*, p. 233.
18 ibid., p. 240.
19 Nigel Hamilton, *The Brothers Mann* (Secker & Warburg, 1978), p. 313.
20 ibid., p. 314.
21 *Bridge*, p. 246.

22 ibid., p. 247.

Chapter 14

1 Georg Moenius to Alma, 17 December 1940, Van Pelt Library.
2 Jarrell C. Jackman and Carla M. Borden (ed.), *The Muses Flee Hitler* (Washington, DC, Smithsonian Institute Press, 1938), p. 86.
3 *Joseph Memoir*.
4 *MS typescript*.
5 *Joseph Memoir*.
6 ibid.
7 Franz Werfel, 'The Writing of *The Song of Bernadette*', typescript, Van Pelt Library.
8 Franz Werfel, 'A Personal Preface', *The Song of Bernadette* (Hamish Hamilton, 1942), p. 5.
9 Franz Werfel, 'The Writing of *The Song of Bernadette*'.
10 Carl Zuckmayer to Franz Werfel, March 1942, Van Pelt Library.
11 Stefan Zweig to Alma, March 1940, Van Pelt Library.
12 *Joseph Memoir*.
13 ibid.
14 Franz Werfel to Alma, 1944, Van Pelt Library.
15 *Joseph Memoir*.
16 ibid.
17 *MS typescript*.
18 *Bridge*, p. 260.
19 ibid., p. 262.
20 ibid., p. 263.
21 ibid.
22 ibid., p. 268.
23 *Joseph Memoir*.
24 Funeral Oration by Monsignor Georg Moenius, Van Pelt Library.

Chapter 15

1 *Bridge*, p. 269.
2 ibid., p. 270.
3 Kurt von Schuschnigg to Alma, 10 September 1945, Van Pelt Library.
4 Josef Szigetti to Alma, 28 October 1945, Van Pelt Library.
5 Bruno Walter to Alma, 29 April, 1946, Van Pelt Library.
6 *MS typescript*.
7 *Bridge*, p. 273.
8 ibid., p. 275.
9 Thomas Mann to Alma, 17 February 1948, Van Pelt Library.

10 Nigel Hamilton, *The Brothers Mann* (Secker & Warburg, 1978), p. 351.
11 Dika Newlin, *Schoenberg Remembered* (New York, Pendragon Press, 1980), p. 337.
12 H. H. Stuckenschmidt, *Arnold Schoenberg, His Life, World and Work* (Calder, 1977), p. 495.
13 Alma Mahler, typescript on *Doctor Faustus*, Van Pelt Library.
14 W. E. Wiedermann to Alma, undated, Van Pelt Library.
15 *Bridge*, p. 278.
16 ibid.
17 ibid., p. 277.
18 ibid., p. 278.
19 *Joseph Memoir*.
20 *Bridge*, p. 276.
21 Newlin, p. 296.
22 Helene Berg to Alma, 10 June 1956, Van Pelt Library.
23 Franz Theodor Csokor, eulogy in honour of Alma Mahler-Werfel's seventy-fifth birthday, Van Pelt Library.
24 *Bridge*, p. 280.
25 Walter Gropius to Alma, 17 August 1958, Van Pelt Library.
26 Alma to Walter Gropius, 20 August 1958, Van Pelt Library.
27 Told to the author by Anna Mahler.
28 Suma Morgenstern, 'Nachruf an Alma Mahler 13.XII.64', typescript in author's possession.

Afterword

1 *MS typescript.*
2 Friedrich Torberg, 'Ein Denkmal ihrer selbst', *Die Münchner Zeitung*, December 1964.
3 *Joseph Memoir.*
4 *Memories*, p. 71.
5 *Joseph Memoir.*
6 Friedrich Torberg, 'WERTUNGS-TABELLE', undated, Van Pelt Library.
7 Torberg, 'Ein Denkmal ihrer selbst'.

Select Bibliography

Antcliffe, Herbert, *Short Studies in the Nature of Music*, Kegan Paul, Trench, Trubner, 1929.

Barea, Ilsa, *Vienna, Legend and Reality*, London & New York, 1966.

Bauer-Lechner, Natalie, *Recollections of Gustav Mahler*, trans. Dika Newlin, Faber Music/Faber & Faber, 1980.

Bentwich, Norman, *Refugees from Germany, April 1933 to December 1935*, George Allen & Unwin, 1936.

Blaukopf, Kurt, *Gustav Mahler*, Allen Lane, 1973.

Brand, Juliane, Hailey, Christopher, and Harris, Donald (ed.) *The Berg-Schoenberg Correspondence*, Macmillan, 1987.

Brook-Shepherd, Gordon, *Anschluss, The Rape of Austria*, Macmillan, 1963.

Burbridge, Peter, and Sutton, Richard (ed.), *The Wagner Companion*, Faber & Faber, 1979.

Canetti, Elias, *The Tongue Set Free*, Picador, 1979. *The Torch in My Ear*, Picador, 1982.

Clark, Ronald W., *Freud, The Man and the Cause*, Jonathan Cape and Weidenfeld & Nicolson, 1980.

Cooke, Deryck, *Gustav Mahler, An Introduction to His Music*, Faber Music/Faber & Faber, 1980.

Craig, Gordon, *Germany 1866–1945*, OUP, 1981.

Crankshaw, Edward, *The Fall of the House of Habsburg*, London, 1963; New York, 1966.

Everett, Susanne, *Lost Berlin*, Bison Books, 1979.

Field, Frank, *The Last Days of Mankind, Karl Kraus and His Vienna*, London and Mystic, Conn., 1967.

Fischer, Wolfgang Georg, *Interiors, A Novel Set in Vienna 1910–1938*, Peter Owen, 1971.

Fuchs, Heinrich, *Emil Jakob Schindler*, Vienna, Selbst Verlag, 1970.

Gainham, Sarah, *The Habsburg Twilight, Tales from Vienna*, Weidenfeld & Nicolson, 1979.

Garner, Mosco, *Alban Berg, The Man and the Work*, Duckworth, 1975.

Gehl, Jurgen, *Austria, Germany and the Anschluss 1931–1938*, OUP, 1963.

Grange, Henri Louis de la, *Mahler*, vol. I, Victor Gollancz, 1974.

Heyworth, Peter, *Otto Klemperer, His Life and Times*, vol. I, *1885–1933*, Cambridge University Press, 1983.

Hodin, J. P., *Oskar Kokoschka, The Artist and His Time*, Cory, Adams & Mackay, 1966.

Hoffmann, Edith, *Kokoschka, Life and Work*, Faber & Faber, 1947.

Hubman, Franz, *The Habsburg Empire*, Routledge & Kegan Paul, 1972.

Isaacs, Reginald, *Walter Gropius, Der Mensch und sein Werk*, 2 vols, Berlin, Gebr. Mann Verlag, 1983.

Jackman, Jarrell C., and Borden, Carla M. (ed.), *The Muses Flee Hitler, Cultural Transfer and Adaptation 1930–1945*, Washington, DC, Smithsonian Institute Press, 1983.

Janik, Allan, and Toulmin, Stephen, *Wittgenstein's Vienna*, Simon & Schuster, 1973.

Kann, Robert A., *A History of the Habsburg Empire 1562–1918*, University of California Press, 1974.

Koestler, Arthur, *The Case of the Midwife Toad*, Hutchinson, 1971.

Kokoschka, Oskar, *My Life*, Thames & Hudson, 1974.

Mahler, Alma, *And the Bridge Is Love*, Hutchinson, 1959. *Mein Leben*, Fischer Bücherei, 1960. *Gustav Mahler, Memories and Letters*, ed. Donald Mitchell, Faber & Faber, 1973.

Mann, Thomas, *Diaries 1918–1939*, selection and foreword by Hermann Kesten, Robin Clark, 1982.

Martner, Knud (ed.), *Selected Letters of Gustav Mahler*, Faber & Faber, 1979.

Musil, Robert, *The Man Without Qualities*, 3 vols, Picador, 1979.

Naylor, Gillian, *The Bauhaus*, Studio Vista/Dutton Pictureback, 1968.

Nebehay, Christian M., *Dokumentation am Klimt*, Vienna, 1969.

Newlin, Dika, *Schoenberg Remembered, Diaries and Recollections (1938–76)*. Pendragon Press, 1980.

Opel, Adolf (ed.), *Anthology of Modern Austrian Literature*, Oswald & Wolff, 1981.

Oskar Kokoschka 1886–1980, commemorative volume published by United Technologies Corporation in collaboration with the Tate Gallery, 1986.

Pehnt, Wolfgang, *Expressionist Architecture*, Thames & Hudson, 1973.

Raabe, Paul (ed.), *The Era of Expressionism*, Calder & Boyars, 1974.

Reilly, Edward R., *Gustav Mahler and Guido Adler, Records of a Friendship*, Cambridge University Press, 1982.

Samuel, Richard, and Hinton Thomas, R., *Expressionism in German Life, Literature and the Theatre (1910–1924)*, W. Heffer & Sons, 1939.

Schenk, H. G., *The Mind of the European Romantics*, OUP, 1979.

Schopenhauer, Arthur, *Essays and Aphorisms*, Penguin Books, 1970.

Schorske, Carl E., *Fin-de-Siècle Vienna, Politics and Culture*, Weidenfeld & Nicolson, 1979.

Stewart, Desmond, *Theodor Herzl, Artist and Politician*, Quartet Books, 1974.

Stone, Norman, *Europe Transformed 1878–1919*, Fontana Paperbacks, 1983.

Stuckenschmidt, H. H., *Arnold Schoenberg, His Life, World and Work*, Calder, 1977.

Vergo, Peter, *Art in Vienna, 1898–1918*, Phaidon, 1981.

Wade, Graham, *The Shape of Music*, Allison & Busby, 1981.

Walter, Bruno, *Gustav Mahler*, Kegan Paul, Trench, Trubner, 1937. *Theme and Variations*, Hamish Hamilton, 1947.

Weber, Horst, *Alexander Zemlinsky*, Vienna, Verlag Elisabeth Lafite, 1977.

Wessling, Berndt W., *Gustav Mahler, Ein prophetisches Leben*, Hoffmann und Campe, 1974.

Williams, C. E., *The Broken Eagle, The Politics of Austrian Literature from Empire to Anschluss*, Elek, 1974.

Wollheim, Richard, *Freud*, Fontana, 1979.

Zuckerkandl, Bertha, *Österreich intim*, Frankfurt/M – Berlin – Vienna, Verlag Ullstein, 1970.

Zweig, Stefan, *The World of Yesterday*, Cassell, 1943.

Index